Eldridge Cleaver

Twayne's United States Authors Series

Frank Day, Editor

Clemson University

TUSAS 583

Eldridge Cleaver in 1968
Courtesy of AP/WIDEWORLD PHOTOS

Eldridge Cleaver

Kathleen Rout

Michigan State University

Twayne Publishers
A Division of G. K. Hall & Co. • *Boston*

Eldridge Cleaver
Kathleen Rout

Copyright 1991 by G. K. Hall & Co.
All rights reserved.
Published by Twayne Publishers
A division of G. K. Hall & Co.
70 Lincoln Street
Boston, Massachusetts 02111

Copyediting supervised by Barbara Sutton.
Book production by Gabrielle B. McDonald.
Book design by Barbara Anderson.
Typeset in Garamond by Huron Valley Graphics, Inc., Ann Arbor, MI.

10 9 8 7 6 5 4 3 2

The paper used in this publication meets the minimum requirements
of American National Standard for Information Sciences—Permanence
of Paper for Printed Library Materials, ANSI Z39.48-1984. $\otimes^{TM}$

Printed and bound in the United States of America.

Library of Congress Cataloging-in-Publication Data

Rout, Kathleen.
    Eldridge Cleaver / Kathleen Rout.
        p.   cm. — (Twayne's United States authors series ; TUSAS 583)
    Includes bibliographical references and index.
    ISBN 0-8057-7620-6
    1. Cleaver, Eldridge, 1935– . 2. Afro-Americans—Biography.
I. Title.   II. Series.
E185.97.C6R68   1991
323'.092—dc20
    [B]   91-6688
                                                                  CIP

Contents

Preface

When he was in prison in 1966, Eldridge Cleaver wrote an autobiographical narrative entitled *The Black Moochie,* an account of his early years as a gang member in the Los Angeles area. Even then, his anger and his sense of dispossession were clear. As he described the fear and confusion of his young friends and as he hinted at their awareness of the hopelessness of their futures, he also made it clear that he knew, at least as an adult, why their lives were so circumscribed. "When I write," he declared, "I want to drive a spear into the heart of America."

The man who wrote those words was the author of *Soul on Ice,* 1968's Book of the Year, according to the *New York Times,* and a text that was soon to be regarded as the "Red Book" of the second American revolution. *Soul on Ice* would sell 1 million copies rather quickly, and 2 million copies over the next decade. It plunged the recently paroled author into immediate fame, making him an object of adoration for thousands of rebellious students and liberal adults even as it earned him the hatred of racists and political conservatives all over America. When the book appeared, Cleaver had already joined the Black Panther party of Oakland, California, which had been in existence since October of 1966, as its Minister of Information. Although he was the celebrity, he deferred to the courage and judgment of Panther founder Huey Newton, declaring that he, along with co-founder Bobby Seale, would place his life in Newton's hands.

Cleaver's life after the February publication of *Soul on Ice* seemed almost out of his control. His sudden celebrity created a demand for his appearance as a speaker all around the country, while his membership in the newly notorious Panthers drew antagonism from the police. On 6 April, two days after the assassination of Martin Luther King had stunned most of America, a number of Panthers were involved in a shoot-out with the Oakland police. After most of them had been taken into custody, the battle narrowed down to a basement in which Cleaver was huddled with Bobby Hutton, the youngest Panther recruit. After a 45-minute gun fight, Cleaver and Hutton surrendered, and Hutton was shot to death in the street by the police. Cleaver was arrested, his parole was revoked, and he was back in prison. From then until his exile in November of the same year, he was first freed, then ordered back to prison; in between, he was nominated for the presidency by the Peace and Freedom party and ranked among the nation's foremost internal enemies by J. Edgar Hoover.

With Newton in prison after an October 1967 shoot-out that left a police officer dead, Cleaver was easily the Panther with the highest profile. He spoke at a number of college campuses and in major urban centers; he even taught a class at Berkeley. With King also dead, Cleaver became the focus of much of the attention of those Americans, white and black, who were looking to black leaders for a guide to action. Notwithstanding a defense committee and an appeal to Thurgood Marshall, Cleaver was forced to choose between jail and exile. Many felt that he made the wrong choice in leaving the country, that he should have let himself be vindicated in the courts. Cleaver believed, however, that he would be murdered in prison, and so he left, committing instead what author Don Schanche would call a political and social "suicide." Distance gradually made Cleaver irrelevant; only readers of the *Black Panther* and other underground publications remained aware of him. A flurry of activity in 1971 in Algiers, where he was in exile, led to his alienation from the white Left over his conflict with Timothy Leary and the black Left over his split with Huey Newton. By March he was alone.

When Cleaver surfaced again in 1975, he was almost a stereotypical flag-waver. Declaring America the "freest country in the world," insisting he was willing to return to prison to await trial on the shoot-out charges because he'd rather be in prison in America than free anywhere else, he infuriated those who had forgotten about him. During his prison stay in the winter of 1976, he announced that he had established a personal relationship with Jesus and that he was a born-again Christian. His news was met with derision and disgust on the part of those who had known him before, and with credulous joy on the part of true believers who had not. A complicating factor was his new pants design for men; intended to free men from the restrictions of an antisexual culture, the codpiece was met with shock and dismay by people from the full breadth of the political and religious spectrums.

After an attempt at a career in evangelical circles that included the incorporation of the Eldridge Cleaver Crusades, Cleaver abandoned mainstream Christianity for his own variation on religion, a short-lived synthesis of Christianity and Islam called Christlam; when that failed to appeal to the audience of black ex-prisoners he had hoped for, he became a Mormon and ran for office as a conservative Republican. Now out of politics, at least for the time being, and divorced from the wife who stood by him for almost 20 years, from 1967 until their separation in 1986, Cleaver still has hopes for a career in the limelight.

Midlife changes in politics are commonplace. In Cleaver's heyday, the calming effect of age was paid tribute to with the phrase "You can't trust anybody over 30." Former hellions like Bobby Seale, Huey Newton, Jane Fonda, Tom Hayden, Jerry Rubin, and Abbie Hoffman all settled into liberal activism or straightforward entrepreneurship with few hard feelings directed toward them from an American public accustomed to their previous radicalism. Cleaver's case, though, is different, partly because of his unpredictability and partly because of his claim to a religious conversion that also conveniently provided him with a means of income. The enigma of Cleaver as a personality remains intriguing; he does not communicate on the subject of his personal feelings, and he never did. Each phase is treated as "true," as if it were the only phase there has ever been; he has always resisted introspection and rejected psychiatric interpretations of his behavior or his belief systems. His latest work, the 1978 *Soul on Fire*, speaks of the past as past. It offers no self-analysis, and it makes no attempt to assess what Cleaver was then or now.

This study is an attempt to understand Cleaver by reading between the lines; even a militantly secretive and unanalytical person, if he publishes enough material, reveals things he would rather not. Often contradictions and inconsistencies, never double-checked at the time, come out under careful examination of texts and events, manifesting covert motives or self-serving rationalizations that provide valuable clues to the internal makeup of the subject. And so it is with Cleaver. Although our knowledge is incomplete, we can piece together from his own words a reasonable explanation for his varying creeds that can help us to understand this unusual and complex personality. Cleaver's position, even if only briefly, as arguably the most charismatic black figure of the late sixties, warrants this attention. To understand Cleaver is not only to understand one man, but also to gain a hint of the compound influences of childhood and family, socioeconomic status, current events, and peer personalities that condition all our decisions and beliefs, even at times of greatest stress. How much sixties' radicalism was merely trendy? How much of the anger of white and black youth was directed against the political system and how much against hated authority figures? Would Cleaver have had the white support he did without the war in Vietnam? Was Cleaver's cell-block conversion in 1976 sincere to any degree, or merely an opportunistic hoax designed to get rich conservatives to pay his legal expenses? Do his arrests for drug possession and burglary in 1987 and 1988 prove that his religiosity was fraudulent all along, although it took 11 years for him to "slip up"? This book does not answer all these questions with absolute authority, but it does attempt to provide some insight into the intricacies of motivation and belief.

Acknowledgments

Excerpts from *Soul on Ice* by Eldridge Cleaver © 1968 by McGraw-Hill Publishing Company. Reprinted by permission of the publisher.

Excerpts from *To Die for the People: The Writings of Huey P. Newton* © 1972 by Stronghold Consolidated Productions. Reprinted by permission of Random House, Inc.

Excerpts from *Soul on Fire* by Eldridge Cleaver © 1978 by WORD Inc., Dallas, Texas. Reprinted by permission of the publisher.

Chronology

1935   Eldridge Cleaver is born on 31 August in Wabbaseka, Arkansas, near Little Rock.

1946   Family moves to Los Angeles area, settling in largely Chicano district called Rose Hill.

1949   Cleaver is first sent to reform school, where he converts to Roman Catholicism.

1954   Is first sent to prison, on a felony charge for selling marijuana.

1958   Is arrested when he attempts an armed rape of a nurse in a parking lot; is charged with attempted rape and assault with intent to kill. Is sent to prison again for assault with intent to kill.

1966   Is paroled in November.

1967   Marries Kathleen Neal on 27 December.

1968   *Soul on Ice* published in February. Bobby Hutton is killed and Cleaver is wounded in a shoot-out in Oakland on 6 April; Cleaver's parole is revoked. Is released by Judge Sherwin on 12 June. Is nominated by the white radical Peace and Freedom party for the presidency of the United States. Release is canceled and Cleaver is ordered back to prison on 27 November. Leaves the country for Cuba by way of Montreal on 26 November, arriving in Cuba on 25 December.

1969   Lives in Havana under guard for seven months, and is abruptly sent to Algiers in July. Son, Antonio Maceo, born on 29 July. Cleaver publishes "Three Notes from Exile" and *The Black Moochie* in *Ramparts* and "The Flashlight" in *Playboy*.

1970   Daughter, Joju, born in North Korea.

1972   Two groups of black Americans hijack planes to Algiers, bringing $1.5 million in ransom money with them. Algeria returns the money, precipitating a conflict with Cleaver.

1973   The Cleavers set up residence in Paris.

1974   Cleaver obtains legal residency in France through the help of Giscard d'Estaing; legal matters and the production of a manuscript for Viking fill Cleaver's time. In Paris, Curtice Taylor interviews Cleaver, whose views begin to turn conservative.

1975   Sometime in the early fall, while at his apartment in the south of France, has what seems to be a vision of Christ in the moon. Decides to return to the United States on FBI terms—as a prisoner.

1976   Is released on $100,000 bail.

1977   Preaches on his own and in concert with other evangelists. Founds Eldridge Cleaver Crusades.

1978   *Soul on Fire* published.

1980   Is placed on probation for the events of the night of 6 April 1968. Creates a new church, a synthesis of Christianity and Islam, called Christlam.

1984   Runs for Ron Dellums's seat in the House.

1986   Runs in the primary for Senator Alan Cranston's seat as a conservative Republican.

1987   Is arrested for cocaine possession in October.

1988   Is arrested in February for theft from a residence; is ordered to make restitution and placed on parole for three years. The Cleavers divorce.

Chapter One
Childhood to Prison: "The Foundation Years of My Life"

The keynotes of Eldridge Cleaver's life have been change, with all its broadening influences and its attendant insecurity, and contradiction, with its connotations of ambivalence and confusion. The themes that are apparent in Cleaver's accounts of his early life are traceable, in ways that are sometimes painfully ironic, through the years as he moved from radical to conservative, from atheist to born-again Christian, from leader to follower.

The stories about Cleaver's early family life mostly stem from his years in exile, when he began to examine his past and to evaluate how he, an anonymous black boy from Wabbeseka, Arkansas, near Little Rock, had come to be where he was: a best-selling author, a one-time candidate for president, and an exile—living first in Cuba and then in Algeria as a revolutionary expatriate. We have three separate works that illuminate his early years: *The Black Moochie,* parts 1 and 2, a loosely knit autobiographical novella begun in prison in 1966 and completed in Algiers, published by *Ramparts* magazine in the fall of 1969; "The Flashlight," an autobiographical short story published in *Playboy* in 1969 and later chosen for the O. Henry anthology of prize stories for 1971; and his autobiography, *Soul on Fire* (1978), an account of Cleaver's life from his early childhood in Alabama and his reckless young adulthood in Los Angeles, through his Panther years and his seven-year exile, to his decision to return to the United States for trial and resume his life as Christian and patriot.

Childhood

Eldridge Cleaver, the third child of six and the eldest son of three, was born in the red clay country of the Deep South on 31 August 1935 and named Leroy Eldridge Cleaver, after his father. The family moved three times before Eldridge was 12, leaping first from little Wabbaseka

to Phoenix and from there to East Side Los Angeles, ending in subur-
ban Rose Hill, an old Chicano community near South Pasadena.

In the short chapter entitled "Childhood Lessons" in *Soul on Fire,*
Cleaver demonstrates his ambivalence toward both parents. In addition
to his obvious attachment to home and mother there is his terror of the
all-engulfing female in his description of the ubiquitous clay "out of
which mother said we had been formed."[1] He loved the "cool texture,"
the "pungent odor of the soft clay." He squeezed it in his hands and
through his toes, he ate it, he played with it, and he suffered for years
from recurrent nightmares about "great tidal waves of red gooey muck"
that threatened to swallow him up. "In the dream I was always fleeing
or flopping about, always on the verge of being overwhelmed" (36).

This early portrait of the devouring mother figure appears only
briefly; the major emphasis in all of Cleaver's early writing is upon his
mother as victim. Later, however, a stronger and more hostile view
forms, one that dominates the young Cleaver's ambivalent attitude
toward women. In *The Black Moochie,* part 2, first written in 1966
when Cleaver was serving time for assault linked with an attempted
rape, he recounts a traumatic episode of public humiliation that occurred at the beginning of his adolescent interest in female love objects.

Soon after the Cleaver family's removal to Rose Hill, Eldridge developed a crush on Michele Ortega, a girl in his class. "Her skin was white
as milk and she had long black hair. She was very delicate, very
feminine—even at that titless shapeless age."[2] The teacher that year
was Miss Brick, a blond woman who resembled Betty Grable. "All the
cats were in love with her. . . . We'd dream about her at night" (1:22).

One day, while the class was changing rooms for music period, he
told Michele he loved her. But her response was vehement: "I hate
you!" In the otherwise-unreported exchange of insults that followed,
Cleaver says he told Michele her mother was an elephant. When she
burst into tears, the beautiful Miss Brick turned on Eldridge: " 'You
black nigger!' she snarled, and slapped my face . . . ! Her words
brought tears to my eyes" (1:22).

This twofold rejection, public and outspoken, hardened Cleaver toward both of them. The teacher, he says, still looked beautiful, "but
my feeling for her was no longer the warm desire of the lover. What I
felt for her was the lust/hatred of the rapist. I felt about the same for
Michele. . . . [B]etween us there was a deep abyss into which something of us that was bathed in sunlight had fallen forever" (1:22). A
meditative passage follows (whether written in 1966 or in exile in 1969

we cannot be sure), in which Cleaver forgives Michele. He places what happened between them in the context of a "land of blood," implying that interpersonal suffering is inflicted for racist reasons. There seems to be no awareness on Cleaver's part that he may have nursed a hatred toward all women as a result of that experience; nor does he evidence having any idea that this hostility, combined with his mixed attitude toward his mother, has been a major theme of his life.

Cleaver says that when he was about 13, he "distinguished himself" among the other children by attempting to help his mother, who was working as a custodian, "clean up those schoolrooms" (in Arkansas she'd been the teacher in the little segregated school), but there are hints that Thelma needed far more help than any child could give. Though Cleaver is taciturn about his mother's circumstances, in *The Black Moochie* he refers obliquely to her apparent absence: "Richard and Rudy used to taunt me: 'At least I got a mother!' My most beautiful cap could be crumbled by that one all-purpose retort: that was the ace up their sleeve" (1:27). A few lines later, part 1 ends with Cleaver's memory of his "embarrassed mother. No father" (1:27). The term *embarrassed* might refer to her being without a husband; it may be the closest that Cleaver is willing to come to saying that his mother seemed strange in her ways.

These two passages help to explain much of Cleaver's rage toward women and his sexual confusion that carried over well into adulthood. The dichotomy between the mother as a battered woman and the mother as an earthmother—a destructive, overwhelming, and suffocating tide of red clay who failed to engulf her son only by virtue of her abandoning him, at least emotionally—is more extreme than any with which most males are ever expected to cope. It is not surprising that Cleaver omitted overt complaints about her from his account of his youth, for he may have refused a conscious acknowledgment of his anger.

His attitude toward his father was equally ambivalent. The first information he offers about him in *Soul on Fire* concerns the antagonism between his father's side of the family and his mother's, the Robinsons, a situation that represented the "classic dichotomy" in the black race. While the Robinsons were "part of a great tribe of mulattoes" and Grandfather Robinson was an African Methodist Episcopal preacher with his own church in Little Rock, the Cleavers were darker and poorer. Grandpa Cleaver was "tall and black-skinned," also a minister, but a "CC rider, a circuit riding preacher," one who had settled in Wabbaseka to farm and raise hogs and chickens. Adopting the nomenclature of Malcolm X, Cleaver explains that "Grandpa Robinson was a House Nigger and Grandpa Cleaver was a Field Nigger" (*Fire*, 37).

In identifying his father as a Cleaver "Field Nigger," Cleaver bonds himself to his father as a fellow troublemaker. His admiration for his father's aggressiveness emerges in the description of how the father dealt with the black preacher next door. Leroy hated "chicken-eating preachers," who reminded him of his own father, and refused to attend the Baptist church in Rose Hill, even though the preacher owned the house they were renting. When the minister, possibly in retaliation for this indifference, destroyed some wooden stairs Leroy had built into the hill leading up to his home, the following Sunday Leroy took a hammer, attacked the drummer outside the church, and then destroyed the drums. Inside the church he advanced upon Elder Richardson. As Eldridge recalls the episode, "Daddy walked up and hit that old man on the head with the hammer, and then started smashing up everything in sight. The people ran outside, Elder Richardson foremost among them. There was blood pouring from an ugly cut in his skull. I remember watching Daddy very deliberately take Elder Richardson's false teeth, which had fallen out of his mouth, and smash them to bits with the hammer" (*Fire*, 60). Leroy Cleaver was arrested briefly, but he returned to rebuild the stairway. Elder Richardson, we are told, "never held services in that church again." Eldridge and his friends turned it into a clubhouse and slowly destroyed it over the years.

It isn't hard to trace Leroy's function as a role model—as a radical who defied authority, who saw violence as the only means by which one could deal with people who could not be appealed to through reason—in his son's later life. But Eldridge's attitude toward his father was far more complex than that, for the violence with which Leroy commonly made his point was in the home too.

Loss of Innocence

"One day" back in Arkansas, when Eldridge was no more than six, "a dark shadow fell across [the family's] home" (*Fire*, 40), he reports. First his father took an ax and chopped up the previously sacrosanct piano, followed by the dishes, the glass on the pictures, and even the little family "shrine" in the corner that highlighted his and Thelma's wedding photo. From then on, "every Saturday night, without fail, Daddy started beating Mother. . . . It was everybody against Daddy, and we'd all hit him as hard as we could, trying to get him to stop hurting our mother. That was the beginning of my driving ambition to grow up tall and strong, like my daddy, but bigger and stronger than he, so I could beat him down to the ground the way he beat my mother" (*Fire,* 41). The children were never told what precipitated the violence, but one may theorize that it stemmed from a major disappointment for the senior Cleaver, who was both a railroad dining car waiter and a weekend piano player who had accompanied Dick Powell[3] in a club in Little Rock before Powell's Hollywood success.

One day Leroy announced that the family was to move. He preceded them to Phoenix, a stopping-off point on his railroad job, in the fall of 1943 and later sent for them. The move to Phoenix in the late spring of 1945 put the Cleaver children into culture shock. The Cleavers endured the common trauma of black displacement from "home" to urban center that befell thousands of the migrants who left the South looking for greater freedom and economic advancement. Once poor and oppressed but also outside in the fresh air, with a few animals and a small garden full of greens and sweet potatoes and corn, the Cleavers and others were now just as poor and just as despised but also locked in a small, underheated apartment in the filthiest, most crime-ridden section of town.

Leroy's violence did not abate with the move. When he was home from his railroad job, he continued beating his wife, Thelma, now pregnant with the sixth child. To young Eldridge, "it was as though Buckeye Road walked across the vacant space and entered our house" (*Fire,* 44). After the baby girl, Claudette, was born in December 1945, the fights continued. "It was war as usual." One humiliating event that Cleaver recounts was the interruption of a game of marbles when his mother ran by screaming, with his father in pursuit. Furious, 10-year-old Eldridge chased after them, "already tensing up to hit my father with all my might" (49).

The move to Los Angeles in 1946 hardly decreased the level of noise and violence to which the children were exposed, but when the family finally moved to Rose Hill, they regained privacy in a calmer, more established neighborhood. The domestic violence didn't end, however, until Eldridge grew big enough to do Leroy real harm. His father was beating him nightly while still abusing his wife every Saturday night. Mother and son were equally victims, and the rebellious Eldridge thus took the point of view of both combatant and avenger as he "slowly

began to conceive the idea of killing [his] father," in a literal reenact-
ment of the oedipal struggle.

One night when Eldridge came home past his 8:00 P.M. deadline,
his father was waiting for him with the usual stick, which Eldridge
seized and took from him. Previously, he had hit his father only when
the father was beating Thelma and had received his own blows passively. But "this night I let go with my right hand and hit Daddy a
staggering blow in his chest" (*Fire*, 63). As soon as Leroy recovered, he
beat Eldridge into unconsciousness with the stick—but he never dared
beat him again. "Nor did he hit my mother again. Instead he disappeared, went away. It was five years before I saw him again" (64).

Eldridge is quite vague about the years on Rose Hill, and so it is not
certain just when he drove his father from the house. There is, in *Soul on
Fire*, however, a reunion photograph of himself and his father sitting
together in a restaurant in 1953, the year Eldridge turned 18, indicating that the decisive confrontation took place in 1948, when Eldridge
was 12 or 13. By the time he was an adult, Eldridge was six-foot-two
and weighed about 200 pounds. In the photo, Leroy appears less heavily built.

A Criminal Career

Eldridge Cleaver was first arrested at age 12, for bicycle theft, and
thus began a long career in penal institutions. He spent time at three
reform schools before the long, almost-unbroken stretch from 1954 to
1966 in adult prisons: Soledad, San Quentin, and Folsom.

Ironically, Cleaver's trouble began because of his love for the freedom
of running with a gang. From his glorious days in the streets and parks
of Phoenix, through his less and less innocent escapades with the
Chicanos in Rose Hill, through his "solidarity and brotherhood" with
fellow Black Muslims in prison, to his days in the Black Panther
uniform, Cleaver has most preferred a male-bonded group, and within
such groups he has often been a leader, though not as a rule *the* leader.
Until he was past 40, Cleaver seems always to have sought someone else
to follow and obey. In prison he was a loyal Muslim, and chose to
follow Malcolm X when he split with Elijah Muhammad in 1963. It
was Malcolm's 1965 assassination, reportedly at the hands of Elijah's
followers, that first led the floundering Cleaver to write, to "save"
himself from chaos and inarticulate suffering, and it was only a short
time after his 1966 release that he devoted himself wholly to Huey

Newton. This decisive union of Cleaver and the Panthers would ultimately put Cleaver in more legal trouble than he had ever imagined, and curtail his freedom altogether.

Pre-Panther Religion

Until his break with the Muslims, Cleaver had always looked to religion for the leader and the worldview that would organize his life and let it make sense. At the Whittier Reform School in 1950, he was baptized and confirmed in the Roman Catholic faith. He recalls, "The reason I became Catholic was that the rule of the institution held that every Sunday each inmate had to attend the church of his choice. I chose the Catholic Church because all the Negroes and Mexicans went there. The whites went to the Protestant chapel. Had I been a fool enough to go to the Protestant Chapel, one black face in a sea of white, and with guerrilla war going on between us, I might have ended up a Christian martyr—St. Eldridge the Stupe."[4] Such a motivation would not be likely to lead to a profound commitment in any case, but for Cleaver only one setback was enough to end the affiliation before his stay at Whittier was even over. One day a priest asked the catechism class whether anyone "understood" the Mystery of the Holy Trinity. Cleaver thought he did, and not realizing the question was really just a nasty trap to help the priest make a point, he volunteered. Immediately he was told he had to be lying, that not even the pope really understands the Trinity—that's why it's called a *Mystery*: "I saw in a flash, stung to the quick by the jeers of my fellow catechumens, that I had been used, that the Father had been lying in wait for the chance to drop that thunderbolt, in order to drive home the point that the Holy Trinity was not to be taken lightly. I had intended to explain the Trinity with an analogy to 3-in-1 oil, so it was probably just as well" (*Ice*, 31). Cleaver's relationship with institutional religion ended at that point and did not resume until 10 years later, when his newly radical ideas, fostered by Thomas Paine and Frederick Douglass as well as by the Russian theorists, led him to Malcolm X, Elijah Muhammad, and the Nation of Islam, or Black Muslims.

While his later politics remained far to the left, his affiliation with the Nation of Islam eventually dissolved under the stresses of conflict and betrayal. During the sixties Cleaver, like many in the Black Panther party, revealed the influence of Black Muslimism, and especially of Malcolm X, in his acquired beliefs, but revolutionary politics from a

black perspective, not religion, gave purpose to his life. Cleaver did not
mention religious belief again until 1975.

The Black Moochie

While there is little in these early years that passes for political
awareness, Cleaver has taken care to note the fear and resentment
among his contemporaries in Los Angeles, along with a generalized
sense of their irrelevance and dispossession. In their favorite public
park, he writes, "we felt like aliens, expecting someone to run us away.
We had no idea that we had a perfect right to use this city property, to
be in the park, to stay as long as we liked. We had no sense of a 'right'
to use the park, or anything else—not even a right to life" (1:22). And
in school, they secretly expressed their cynicism by making a mockery
of the Pledge of Allegiance: "I hedge all-allegiance to the flag of the
Disunited States of America and to the republic for which it falls, many
nations, divisible, with liberty and justice for some" (1:23). (In those
days, the phrase "under God" had not yet been added, and so the boys
were unable to corrupt those two words.) In spite of poverty and an
outlaw status, the gang provided the identity and feeling of belonging
that the larger society withheld. The camaraderie with other young
people from the school and the neighborhood created a basis for
Cleaver's later commitment to the party and to the poor: "Huntington
Drive Street School, the core of our relationship, brought us together. I
feel that I knew and loved people then as I have never done since. . . .
Those were the beautiful days of my youth. Those are the days to which
I flee for refuge. . . . The beauty of our lives then—we were all fresh
and could have been saved" (1:24).

Cleaver's nostalgia is so strong in the first part of The Black Moochie
that he becomes poetic in a Whitmanesque litany 73 lines long that
evokes the mood and locale of "my youth, the foundation years of my
life":

> Far from the industrial heart of Los Angeles
> A forgotten hamlet
> A peaceful spot
> We knew Rose Hill as our own.
> We'd bow down on hands and knees to kiss our dirt.
>
> The mail man delivering the mail was ours
> The Good Humor Ice Cream man with his musical wagon was ours
> The Helms Bakery Man with his musical wagon was ours.

And he concludes: "We had a sense of ourselves / We said Rose Hill and we meant all things in it" (1:26).

Part 2 of *The Black Moochie* is bleaker, angrier, and more aggressive than part 1, and it establishes even more emphatically the political alienation and class resentment of the future revolutionary. Cleaver begins with the image of himself in solitude, without the emotional reinforcement of the group, lying in the grass and trying to figure out how to master the "huge, swiftly spinning merry-go-round" of "the world," that is, the social system. "I was drunk with a loathing for my own impotence," he says, and describes a surrealistic vision of how church and state, represented by a cardinal, the mayor, and other officials (including the corrupt police chief), cut up the great cake that was Los Angeles County, while a smaller group of six Negroes shoot pool. "A Negro in Khaki uniform" waits to catch the crumbs from the cake and bring them home to his huge family.

The segment that immediately follows re-creates the boys' fear of the police: "We did not do these things; rather, they were done to us. But we felt guilty. Our terror was knee deep. We walked in a fog. Nowhere was there a way out. We grew up, grew older, and kept a keen eye out for a chance to move toward the future. . . . So we bored into the mud of North America and waited for something unique to come along" (2:14).

Almost a Man: The Marijuano

"The Flashlight" is a story of coming-of-age. Here, a young boy named Stacy, who lives in a Rose Hill–like project named Crescent Heights, experiences a poorly understood impulse to make something of his life. Like Cleaver himself, Stacy appears to be the only non-Hispanic in the area, and like Cleaver he is the leader of a gang of young boys who raid the white neighborhoods of nearby El Serrano regularly, stealing anything they find and deciding later whether it has any value. In contrast with the darkness of the Crescent Heights neighborhood, the lights of El Serrano beckon with money and its attendant power. "Where there is light," the boys' maxim goes, "there is wealth."[5] More and more, Stacy has begun to feel the frustration of a life with no future to it. Although he never puts a name to this dissatisfaction, it is surely the "impotence" that Cleaver spoke of in *The Black Moochie*. There is no outlet for a young man who wants to make a mark, break the mold of his life; the petty theft doesn't really hurt the white world, and the goods stolen are barely worth the risk.

One evening Stacy lifts a large four-battery flashlight from the seat of a car. This oversized phallic symbol, representing wealth and power, entrances Stacy, but he doesn't understand how to use it to his advantage. There is a gang of older males, all Chicano, who sell marijuana to customers from all over the area. The kids refer to them as the Marijuanos: "They were the alienated sons, in their 20's, of the people of the hills, those sons whom the metropolis had found indigestible. They had criminal records or had dropped out of high school without acquiring any skills to fit into the economy. And they were either unfit or disinclined to enter the Armed Forces. They had fallen back on the skill of the hills, the knack of eluding the police while trafficking in contraband" (240). Stacy surprises the Marijuanos when they are dealing. He sneaks up on the group and shines the light on them; they scatter in panic, and he feels the satisfaction of the destroyer. Briefly, he has these drug dealers at his mercy. Even though they soon try to catch him and beat him, they always fail. Now his life is filled with drama. He expects the older gang members to accost him even in his classroom. The flashlight has made him a power to be reckoned with, someone who cannot be ignored.

But this form of self-assertion is negative from the beginning; it has no future in itself. The breaking point comes when Chico, the leader of the Marijuanos, offers Stacy protection in exchange for the flashlight: the chance to surrender his tie with the powerful white neighborhood and to accept his fate as a gang member in the "marijuana capital of Los Angeles." Neither he nor Stacy is aware of the irony or the fatalism of his words: "It goes around and it comes around; you take it a little way and then pass it on. Pretty soon the little kids will be calling you Marijuano and someday kids that are not even born yet will be calling them Marijuanos. It will never end. . . . I'm not giving you the money to buy you off. I'm giving it to you to wake you up" (256). To become one with the group that had inspired Stacy's gang with "a romantic apprehension just short of fear" (240) is an honor in Crescent Heights. It replaces Stacy's confused drive for independent action and power with an ersatz manhood based on criminal behavior and adhesion to the gang and its code. As soon as Chico walks away, one of Stacy's younger friends suggests a raid on El Serrano again. " 'Count me out,' Stacy said with mock astonishment, 'I might find another flashlight' " (257).

Stacy's initiation into manhood consists of getting stoned on too much "weed"; becoming a man in this environment means finding a way to dull one's aspirations and surrender one's need for independent action. As Stacy turns to go home, carefully guided by his new leader, Chico, he feels "serene, lucid, triumphant, peculiarly masterful and at peace" (260). For a moment he stops, missing something; then he recalls that it was only his flashlight, and he laughs. "He did not know yet whether a Marijuano had any use for a flashlight. As he walked dreamily home, he had no doubt that he would soon find out." But we already know the answer.

It seems, from the references to merry-go-rounds, that part 2 of *The Black Moochie* and "The Flashlight" concern approximately the same period of time. What Cleaver sees as the "merry-go-round" of society is a hard and competitive world in which one grabs onto anything one can that represents security. It is for the sake of this sure thing, the drug dealing, that Stacy gives up the high-risk opportunity to become something on his own. A firmer link between *The Black Moochie* and "The Flashlight" is found in the conclusion of *Moochie,* part 2.

Once "Chico"—the same elder leader, one presumes, as in "The Flashlight"—includes Cleaver/Stacy in the group that "blows weed" and sells it, his life is devoted to drug dealing and his potential wasted. It was for the crime of dealing marijuana, back when it was a felony in California, that Cleaver was sent to prison at eighteen: "The easy dollars. Easy Money, good name for a book, Easy Come, Easy Go. One must tell a great deal about reality in order to justify writing a book, yet so many of these fools who tell nothing at all come off the presses again and again. When I write, I want to drive a spear into the heart of America" (2:15).

Chapter Two
Soul on Ice

Cleaver's stretch in adult prison was an extension of his earlier life in reform school. In 1947, when he was 12, a bicycle theft sent him to Juvenile Hall for several months; he spent a term at the Fred C. Nelles school for boys in Whittier in 1949–50 and completed his eighth-grade education at Lincoln Junior High in Rose Hill. A 1952 stint in the Preston School of Industry, for selling marijuana, interrupted his freshman year at Belmont High School. After being freed from Preston in 1953, he was soon arrested on a felony charge of possession of marijuana, and since Cleaver was then 18, he went not to another reform school but to Soledad for two and a half years.

This period in Cleaver's life marked his first awakening to the depth and extent of racism in the United States. From prison, he and the other inmates watched in "horror, disgust and outrage" as politicians and other assorted Americans argued over the implementation of the 1954 Supreme Court decision outlawing segregation, *Brown* v. *Board of Education of Topeka, Kansas.* "We knew that in the end what they were clashing over was us, what to do with the blacks, and whether or not to start treating us as human beings. I despised all of them" (*Ice,* 4).

Simultaneous with the discussions about white racism and segregation was the sexual frustration of imprisonment, and even this turned out to be under the control of the white supremacist enemy. In his cell Cleaver had a photo of a "voluptuous" white pinup girl that was removed and torn to pieces by a white guard—only pictures of "colored girls" would be permitted, Cleaver was told. This embarrassing event made Cleaver as mad at himself for his vulnerability as at the guard for his meddling; he determined to discover why he and all the other black males with whom he spoke had an obsession with white women. He felt intensely frustrated to realize how unfree he was. "In Richard Wright's *Native Son,* I found Bigger Thomas and a keen insight into the problem" (*Ice,* 10).

"The Ogre"

Cleaver leaves unspoken the exact nature of his "keen insight," but the remarks of the other black prisoners about white women and the subject matter of the first three essays in the "White Woman/Black Man" section that concludes *Soul on Ice* make the picture quite clear. An ambivalent worship of the white female, coupled with an abhorrence of the black, was the inheritance of every generation of poor and powerless black males in our European-dominated society in which the hated and envied blond Protestant female constituted the ideal of beauty. There was never any question of free choice, and little possibility, short of rape, of gratifying the drive to possess the ideal. Rape, of course—and rape followed by murder—was the crime with which the hapless Bigger Thomas was charged.

According to Cleaver, it was around this time, in 1955, that Emmett Till, a young black male from Chicago visiting in Mississippi, was lynched, "allegedly for flirting with a white woman" (10). This development enraged Cleaver, especially when he was attracted to the woman's picture in the paper "in spite of everything and against my will and the hate I felt for the woman" (11). Two days after seeing the picture, he tells us, he had "a nervous breakdown" and raved for days. He calmed down, only to find himself in a padded cell and at the beginning of "several sessions" with a psychiatrist who had no interest in Cleaver's theories about sex:

I had several sessions with a psychiatrist. His conclusion was that I hated my mother. How he arrived at this conclusion I'll never know, because he knew nothing about my mother; and when he'd ask me questions I would answer him with absurd lies. What revolted me about him was that he had heard me denouncing the whites, yet each time he interviewed me he deliberately guided the conversation back to my family life, to my childhood. That in itself was all right, but he deliberately blocked all my attempts to bring out the racial question, and he made it clear that he was not interested in my attitude toward whites. This was a Pandora's box he did not care to open. (*Ice*, 11)

A psychiatrist would certainly have treated as an evasive move Cleaver's "attempts to bring out" racism as the main issue; to Cleaver and to some other radical blacks, however, all mental and emotional problems are seen as social in origin, the normal response of a black person to white oppression. This entanglement of group psychology with individual psychology not only functionally destroys the concept of individuality but often renders analysis almost impossible, so dominant are the defenses and rationalizations of the patient. Cleaver's lifelong avoidance of introspection fits into this pattern.

An insight into Cleaver's unwittingly negative attitude toward his mother may be found in *Black Rage,* by William H. Grier and Price M. Cobbs.[1] In their chapter "Acquiring Manhood," they offer a compelling argument about the role a black woman plays in the emasculation of her sons. Speaking of patients of theirs who commonly cry "without feeling" when they see another man, black or white, succeed against the odds and stand "supreme in a moment of personal glory," they comment that the tears are for the weeper himself, "for what he might have achieved if he had not been held back" (Grier and Cobbs, 73). What held the person back was "some inner command not to excel," stemming ultimately from a hostile white society but directly from his mother, and when he perceives her role in his failure and anonymity, "he becomes enraged with her" (73). Such rage is unacceptable, and so all feeling has to be suppressed on the subject of the tears or of the individual's failure to achieve, because such feeling leads "too directly" to his mother.

The authors state that some patients, perceiving this much, immediately place the blame on white society. Others need an intermediate step: "Finally, there comes later a deeper understanding of the mother as a concerned mediator between society and the child. The patient comes to recognize that, while the larger society imposes a harsh inhibition on his development and a threat to any aggressivity, this hostility of society is communicated to him by his mother, whose primary concern is that he survive. For if he does not realize that his aggressiveness puts him in grave danger from society generally, he may not survive. With this recognition his hostility toward his mother lessens and is directed toward white society" (74). No one, of course, actually knows what the psychiatrist assumed about Cleaver's home life, but it is likely that Cleaver's rejection of black females included his mother. This factor, combined with Cleaver's early fears of the red clay "mother earth" swallowing him up and the complete absence of maternal warmth in any of his early accounts of her, could have led his doctor to conclude that Cleaver hated all women, beginning in childhood with his mother. If, after all, a black male is a victim of the white racist culture such that his preference for white females is total ("I don't want nothin' black but a Cadillac" [*Ice,* 9]), and he despises black women because they aren't white and white women because he *has* to want them, then he hates all women.

Moreover, although Cleaver says that he resented white males for their historical abuse of black women, he himself raped an uncounted number of black women as "practice" for his official assault on white society in the form of interracial rape. He was proud to have "defiled" white women, but he fails to place his molestation of black females in any such objectionable category. Actually, his indifference to black women is at least as chilling as his hatred for white women, for his assaults on the former are actually nonevents, preseason games as it were; only white women really *counted*. His crimes against the black female are made possible by his racist and sexist dismissal of their importance and also by official police indifference to their fate.

Cleaver's misogyny was given reinforcement in his early reading of such revolutionaries as Marx, Lenin, Bakunin, and Nechayev, as well as the principles of Machiavelli. These doctrines turned his sexual obsession into a political one; an "antagonistic, ruthless attitude toward white women" seemed like an apt way of demonstrating his revolt, his outlaw status. When he was paroled in 1957, he became a revolutionary rapist, so to speak. He chose to regard rape as "an insurrectionary act" simply because at that stage in his life, of all that the white world had, he wanted women more than money or political power.

Two additional passages throw light on this phase of Cleaver's life, though they were not to be printed for 10 more years. In 1978, in *Soul on Fire,* Cleaver again mentions having sessions with a prison psychiatrist who told him that he hated his mother. The circumstances, however, are so radically different that one can only conclude that either Cleaver left out one episode in writing *Soul on Ice* (both episodes had to have happened before his 1966 parole, because he clearly refers to the past, and not to the time he spent in jail in 1975–76) or he distorted the one episode two different ways to serve his purposes. In *Soul on Fire* he recounts a time when he took some of the spice called mace, began raving, found himself in a padded cell, and had sessions with a psychiatrist:

There followed months and months . . . of psychiatric questioning and counsel, during which I found myself in the clutches of some dangerous doctors. I even had group therapy, but the main round was between the shrink and myself. He eventually concluded that I hated my mother. I think, after I got to talking to him, I did express my true feelings; but I never understood why he said I hated my mother, because it wasn't true. Father hate, yes: I wanted to get him for years for what he did to me, my mother, and my family. But not my mother. This same physician, many years later, was sent to prison himself for declaring a man insane (in collusion with the man's wife) and then proceeding to take over his property. (*Fire*, 72–73)

Cleaver's attempt, in the final sentence, to discredit the psychiatrist indicates that he was still not ready to accept in 1978 what the doctor had told him more than 20 years before, although his tone has become appropriately placid. Evidently, the same event is referred to in each case.

It seems apparent that some combination of the Black Muslim religion and psychiatry caused Cleaver to renounce his career as a rapist and perhaps even to accept his mother. His readings from 1958 to 1966, and especially his authorship of *Soul on Ice*, mark this period of imprisonment as critical for Cleaver's development. It appears that everything he read was selected to give him a way of understanding the complexities of society, and thus everything he wrote was essentially autobiographical and therefore personal. Because his thoughts and opinions coincided with those of so many black and white youths, not to mention adult radicals and liberals, *Soul on Ice* was received as an authoritative comment by a leader who rose up from "the people."

Cleaver says in his essay "Becoming" that he first began to write after his return to prison in 1958. But most of the writing in *Soul on Ice* comes from the period 1965–66, after several years of reading, some of it under the tutelage of a lecturer at San Quentin named Chris Lovdjieff, and after Cleaver had taken "a long look" at himself and rejected his old Machiavellian approach. "My pride as a man dissolved and my whole fragile moral structure seemed to collapse, completely shattered" (*Ice*, 15). This does not sound like the militant Black Muslim minister who spent numerous periods in solitary confinement and who was transferred to a different prison twice—all for agitating. It sounds like a man who lost both Malcolm X and the Muslims when he left the Nation of Islam to follow the leader in 1963 and then lost the leader to assassination. Up until that point, many had hoped that the schism could be mended, and unity restored to the Nation of Islam. "But death made the split final and sealed it for history. These events caused a profound personal crisis in my life and beliefs, as it did for other Muslims" (54). Thus, the personal crisis that led Cleaver to begin to write in order to "save" himself (*Ice*, 54) may be dated by Malcolm's assassination in February of 1965. Not surprisingly, the earliest dated essay in *Soul on Ice* is "Initial Reactions on the Assassination of Malcolm X," written 19 June 1965.

To Malcolm

One reason for Cleaver's reverence for Malcolm was that through Malcolm he could combine his own fervid Muslimism with the interracial male bonding of his early and well-loved years on Rose Hill, when he ran with a largely Chicano crowd. Malcolm's "retreat from the precipice of madness," Cleaver thought, gave others permission to be both militant and nonracist, for Malcolm's credentials as an uncompromising black spokesman could not be questioned. He could be challenged on the basis of his loyalty to Elijah Muhammad, but not on the basis of his critique of white society. For him to move away from the concept of the "white devil" meant that a purely sociocultural analysis of American racism was possible for a committed black. What moved in to fill the void was a blend of Fanon and Marx (or more accurately, Stalin) that was to become a uniquely Black Panther belief system, including the Panthers' willingness to cooperate with white radicals on a basis of equality, this latter move apparently owed entirely to Cleaver's initiative.

It was the sociopolitical side of Malcolm, not his religion, that made him so powerful a spokesman. For some, the framework of Black Muslimism was an important adjunct to Malcolm's aggressive demands for fairness and equality, and the concept of the powerful but hated white man as a "devil" gave a measure of satisfaction to resentful but powerless blacks in and out of prison. That anger, however, could be expressed without the ideological confines of Elijah Muhammad's "racist strait-jacket demonology" (*Ice,* 60): "Malcolm X articulated their aspirations better than any other man of our time. When he spoke under the banner of Elijah Muhammad he was irresistible. If he had become a Quaker, a Catholic, or a Seventh-Day Adventist, or a Sammy Davis–style Jew, and if he had continued to give voice to the mute ambitions in the black man's soul, his message would still have been triumphant: because what was great was not Malcolm X but the truth he uttered" (*Ice,* 59). In this essay one can hear echoes of Cleaver's anger as voiced in *The Black Moochie.* The waste of his own potential, the surrender of his chance for individual achievement when he devoted his talents to drug dealing and suffered its penalties, his bitter awareness that he and his young friends could have been "saved" from oblivion but were instead regarded only as police problems—all stem from the undeniable fact of white racism and society's scorn for the poor. This reality informs Cleaver's observations on prisoners like himself:

Negro convicts, basically, rather than see themselves as criminals and perpetrators of misdeeds, look upon themselves as prisoners of war, the victims of a vicious, dog-eat-dog social system that is so heinous as to cancel out their own malefactions: in the jungle there is no right or wrong.

Rather than owing and paying a debt to society, Negro prisoners feel that they are being abused, that their imprisonment is simply another form of the oppression which they have known all their lives. Negro inmates feel that they are being robbed, that it is "society" that owes them, that should be paying them, a debt. (*Ice*, 58)

Cleaver's anger toward those who wanted Malcolm dead encompasses not only Malcolm's actual murderers, the Fruit of Islam, the Black Muslim guard, but whites who preferred that so forceful a figure *not* be able to reach out to disillusioned white youth and create a viable antiestablishment movement. Toward that end, Malcolm had to be destroyed; "our manhood, our living black manhood," as Ossie Davis called him, "our own black shining Prince," had to be "tarnish[ed]" and "denigrat[ed]" by those who sold out to the "white power structure" (quoted in *Ice*). The most forceful current embodiment of black manhood was murdered, but, says Cleaver, "We shall have our manhood. We shall have it or the earth will be leveled by our attempts to gain it" (*Ice*, 61).

Victims of the White Power Structure

Cleaver's title essay, "Soul on Ice," takes the "prisoner of war" argument even further. In the first paragraph, he admits to having been a rapist (he was actually in prison for assault with intent to kill, the rape charge in his final arrest having been dropped) but dismisses with the following any charges that he "owes a debt to society":

My answer to all such thoughts lurking in their split-level heads, crouching behind their squinting bombardier eyes, is that the blood of Vietnamese peasants has paid off all my debts; that the Vietnamese people, afflicted with a rampant disease called Yankees, through their sufferings—as opposed to the "frustration" of fat-assed American geeks safe at home worrying over whether to have bacon, ham, or sausage with their grade-A eggs in the morning, while

Vietnamese worry each morning whether the Yankees will gas them, burn them up, or blow away their humble pads in a hail of bombs—have canceled all my IOUs. (*Ice*, 18)

It is hard to imagine that either the white women whom Cleaver raped or the black women whom he "practiced on" beforehand would be sympathetic to this line of argument.

Cleaver's remarks about poor and Third World prisoners feeling justified in drug dealing, theft, and even homicide because they have been the victims of society's neglect have a certain truth to them, for if anyone is to be held responsible for whatever forces turn an innocent preschooler into "the scum of the earth" only 10 years later, it is surely not the child him- or herself. But the concept of excusing criminal behavior on the grounds that the society, and more specifically the government of that society, has been imperialistic toward another nation begins to move out of the arena of human relations and into solipsism. The message actually is, "I am a law unto myself (and this is my latest justification)." What has to precede such a moral position is the complete rejection of any claims on the prisoner by society or any agency or perhaps even any *person* in it, a rejection that in turn is precipitated by that society's repugnance toward the future prisoner from birth. The speciousness of the argument from international hegemony is apparent to almost every reader, even while its emotional validity for the speaker and his compatriots is undeniable.

One can see in this essay, dated 9 October 1965, and in the two undated essays in part 2 entitled "The Black Man's Stake in Vietnam" and "Domestic Law and International Order" the seeds of Cleaver's conviction that black Americans and Third World countries have strong common interests. Cleaver believed that the war in Vietnam, as a national liberation movement, posed a serious threat to "the system" of white dominance at home and in the world. Because only one area at a time can receive the full attention of the power structure, any "wars of suppression" fought abroad weaken the ability of that structure to control blacks and other minorities within the United States. But blacks, with their recent demands and their assured hostility toward the white government, function within the walls, so to speak, of the continental United States as "a Black Trojan Horse that has become aware of itself and is now struggling to get on its feet. It, too, demands liberation" (*Ice*, 121).

The only way that the white power structure can be prevented from

lynching those in this Trojan horse, Cleaver is certain, is through a
"guarantee" of safety created by "organizational unity and communion
with their brothers and allies around the world, on an international
basis." Thus, black men are "fools to go to another country to fight for
something they don't have for themselves" (*Ice*, 127). Cleaver slips up
on that line, incidentally. He appears so eager to use Paul Robeson's
argument against black troops in World War II (an argument that
would be echoed by Martin Luther King in his remarks about the
Vietnam War in 1967) that he neglects to notice that, according to the
ideology he espouses in this essay, black men in Vietnam are fighting
not for freedom but for its suppression. He does make it clear elsewhere, however, that the black man's stake in Vietnam demands "a free
and independent Vietnam, a strong Vietnam which is not the puppet of
international white supremacy" (*Ice*, 125).

One would expect that the next step in the argument would state that
blacks should refuse to serve in the armed forces, not only because of their
interest in a "free" Vietnam, indeed a "free" Third World, but also
because the United States sends a large percentage of blacks to Vietnam
for even more sinister reasons: "Some people think that America's point
in sending 16 percent black troops to Vietnam is to kill off the cream of
black youth. But it has another important result. By turning her black
troops into butchers of the Vietnamese people, America is spreading hate
against the black race throughout Asia" (*Ice*, 127). The solution offered,
instead, is black unity. "*The need for one organization that will give one voice to
the black man's common interest* is felt in every bone and fiber of black
America," says Cleaver, and his organization of preference is Malcolm
X's "dying legacy to his people" (*Ice*, 126), the Organization of Afro-
American Unity, as well as Malcolm's concept of raising the black American's "narrow plea for 'civil rights' to the universal demand for human
rights" and of pleading the cause of American blacks before the United
Nations (128). Malcolm's organization, or a similar one with a different
name, would fulfill the need for unity, in Cleaver's eyes. He does not take
into account here the problem of the types of blacks who repudiated
Malcolm and who have never agreed on any one program or means to the
end of full equality at any time since Reconstruction. The "classic dichotomy" of which Cleaver spoke when he described the two opposed camps
in black America, the "house niggers" and the "field niggers," to use
Malcolm's terms, or the middle class and the poor, operates against the
likelihood of a single organization coming into being that could actually
represent all black Americans.

Cleaver is here working toward the concept of world revolution that he would espouse in exile, but he still looks very much toward a new leader to follow. His imminent future as a Black Panther and devoted lieutenant to Huey Newton is almost foretold in the second paragraph of "Soul on Ice," in which he speaks of the things he would prefer to prison:

I'd like to . . . grow a beard and don whatever threads the local nationalism might require and comrade with Che Guevara, and share his fate, blazing a new pathfinder's trails through the stymied upbeat brain of the New Left, or how I'd just love to be in Berkeley right now, to roll in that mud, frolic in that sty of funky revolution, to breathe in its heady fumes, and look with roving eyes for a new John Brown, Eugene Debs, a blacker-meaner-keener Malcolm X, a Robert Franklin Williams with less rabbit in his hot blood, an American Lenin, Fidel, a Mao-Mao, A MAO MAO, A MAO MAO, A MAO MAO, A MAO MAO, A MAO MAO, A MAO MAO. (*Ice,* 19)

The next essay, "Domestic Law and International Order," connects the black movement with Vietnam somewhat differently. Cleaver here assumes a black awareness that police repression of the Watts riot is alike in both kind and degree to U.S. Army action against the Vietnamese. "Too many people saw that those who turned the other cheek in Watts got their whole head blown off. At the same time, heads were being blown off in Vietnam" (132). The impression created, he says, is that the United States has two powerful arms: one is the military and one is the police. These serve a system that is based on private property and controlled entirely by whites; the black middle class doesn't even count in these calculations. The masses of blacks, potentially powerful but completely deprived ("all private and no property"), are kept away from white property by the police assigned to their areas just as the Vietnamese peasants are kept from freedom by some soldier with a gun who "hardly knows what it is all about" (*Ice,* 133). Everyone serves the power structure.

The perception of this interrelationship and this hierarchy creates a kinship between the Vietcong and the black ghetto dweller, who Cleaver says begins to ask "tactical questions": "Now—NOW!—they are asking each other in dead earnest: Why not die right here in Babylon fighting for a better life, like the Viet Cong? If those little cats can do it, what's wrong with big studs like us? A mood sets in, spreads across America, across the face of Babylon, jells in black heads everywhere" (*Ice*, 137). The term *Babylon*, which was to become more and more common in Cleaver's writing after 1968, was borrowed from *Revelations* by way of Elijah Muhammad, who used it as a synonym for wealthy and decadent modern America (*Fire*, 92), although the earliest such use of the term was probably in Frederick Douglass's 1852 Fourth of July speech. Cleaver found the term attractive and functional, both in its setting up of an analogy between Babylon and the United States and in its suggestion that the person or group to condemn another in biblical terms is holier than the condemned.

First Love

Another significant effect of Cleaver's respect for and adherence to Malcolm was his newfound ability to love. In his earlier stages, Cleaver's attitude toward whites and especially toward "the Ogre," the white woman, was personal; it may have had its foundation in social problems, but Cleaver's solution—a relentless attitude toward women and the practice and endorsement of rape as "an insurrectionary act"—was useless as a means of creating black equality, unity, or wealth.

The Ogre was to come insidiously, one could almost say, into Cleaver's life by the unlikely way of a new lawyer, Beverly Axelrod. "My lawyer is a rebel," he proudly announced, "a revolutionary who is alienated fundamentally from the *status quo*, probably with as great an intensity, conviction, and irretrievability as I am alienated from it—and probably with more intelligence, compassion, and humanity." But further, and more important in this instance, is that the lawyer was "a woman . . . a very excellent, unusual, and beautiful woman" (*Ice*, 21).

The very nature of their association, throughout the months that Beverly worked for Cleaver's freedom in 1965 and 1966, tended to create a psychological and emotional bond without the possibility of sexual exploitation. He met her because of her professional identity, not only as a lawyer but as a radical whose ideals he could respect. She, in turn, respected him as an outspoken author and, no doubt even more significant to Cleaver, as a man. "I accept you," she wrote to him, "Your manhood comes through in a thousand ways, rare and wonderful. . . . I accept you" (*Ice*, 145).

It is fittingly ironic that the great love of his life, up to that point, would be a platonic one, after the ruthlessly hard attitude he had displayed toward all females in the past. Cleaver's relationship with Beverly Axelrod was one of the most decisive of his life, not because of the romantic involvement, which lasted only a short time after his release in November 1966, but because it was the means by which he was both paroled and put into touch with the local white radicals in San Francisco and with *Ramparts* magazine. It was she who contacted the editor-founder of *Ramparts,* Edward Keating, and through him managed to get Cleaver's writing read and praised by such diverse individuals as Norman Mailer, Leslie Fiedler, Norman Podhoretz, Paul Jacobs, and Maxwell Geismar, who ended up writing the introduction to *Soul on Ice.*[2] The possibility that his writing, which he had undertaken initially to "free" himself from his inner conflicts, would actually free him from prison as well inspired Cleaver to write incessantly in the hope of producing a book-length manuscript.

Babbitt's Grandchildren

One of the most significant essays to come out of this period is "The White Race and Its Heroes," Cleaver's account of the alteration in the attitudes of youthful whites toward their country's founders and fathers and of his reaction to that alteration. The change began, he says, with the example of young black demonstrators "sitting in" at lunch counters, scandalizing whites and conservative black parents while inspiring white students and galvanizing them into similar and even more extreme activities. But beyond that, the rebellion of the students implied a value system that rejected not only segregation but the full panoply of values that was once epitomized by George F. Babbitt and the epithet Babbittry: the middle- to upper-class assumptions about human worth that revered only white Anglo-Saxon Protestant, or WASP, traits but also based human worth on wealth, however gained, and respectability in the form of surface morality and personal cleanliness.

In Sinclair Lewis's *Babbitt* (1922), the central character thrusts himself into local fame by going before the Zenith Real Estate Board to make a speech in which the tribal values are solidly explicated and the type of "the Real American," the true "He-man," set forth. Self-criticism is rejected, introversion or depression feared like the Devil himself:

And when it comes to these blab-mouth, fault-finding, pessimistic, cynical University teachers, let me tell you that during this golden coming year it's just as much our duty to bring influence to have those cusses fired as it is to sell all the real estate and gather in all the good shekels we can.

Not til that is done will our sons and daughters see that the ideal of American manhood and culture isn't a lot of cranks sitting around chewing the rag about their Rights and their Wrongs, but a God-fearing, hustling, successful, two-fisted Regular Guy, who belongs to some church with pep and piety to it, who belongs to the Boosters or the Rotarians or the Kiwanis, to the Elks or Moose or Redmen or Knights of Columbus or any one of a score of organizations of good, jolly, kidding, laughing, sweating, upstanding, lend-a-handing Royal Good Fellows, who plays hard and works hard, and whose answer to his critics is a square-toed boot that'll teach the grouches and smart alecks to respect the He-man and get out and root for Uncle Samuel, U.S.A.![3]

Activist students were both depressed and outraged that so little seemed to have changed in the mentality of the Republican small-business leader in the 40-plus years since 1922. Their rejection of whatever smacked of middle-class, middle-aged square capitalism included everything from the "tradition" of racism and segregation to materialistic career goals and sometimes even respectability in speech and dress. In taking the point of view of the oppressed and the dispossessed, many counterculture youths regarded themselves as members of a great tribe that stood for the destruction of everything old, paunchy, and narrow-minded: in other words, parental.

Their bitterness stemmed from their discovery that the founding fathers were not so much idealistic as pragmatic, that the final forms of the Declaration of Independence and the Constitution itself were the result of deals made with slaveholders to water down the ideals contained therein by accommodating involuntary servitude and the extradition of runaway slaves. In fact, the students found, some of the heroes, notably Thomas Jefferson himself, author of the Declaration of Independence, were those very slaveholding hypocrites who fought for freedom from England on the grounds that all men are created equal. It was only a step from there to seeing the opening of the West as a criminal act of invasion and conquest of the Indians, who were viewed as technologically inferior but morally superior because of their lack of interest in material goods and their perceived concern for the environment.

Most white Americans knew these facts but remained indifferent to their implications. Cleaver writes, "Even when confronted with overwhelming evidence to the contrary, most white Americans have found it possible, after steadying their rattled nerves, to settle comfortably back into their vaunted belief that America is dedicated to the proposition that all men are created equal and endowed by their Creator with certain inalienable rights—life, liberty, and the pursuit of happiness.

With the Constitution for a rudder and the Declaration of Independence as its guiding star, the ship of state is sailing always toward a brighter vision of freedom and justice for all" (*Ice,* 76–77). But for the "disaffected youth," the scale finally tipped the other way. Their awareness of the "schizophrenic" nature of American assumptions about equality caused them to reject the saints of our country's past, to experience "the great psychic pain" (*Ice,* 69) of regarding the America of the past and present as an evil empire, and of seeing the entire white race, in fact, as consumed by a "Master Race psychology developed over centuries of imperial hegemony." The example set by black students served as "a catalyst for their own brewing revolt" (69). As a result, says Cleaver,

What has suddenly happened is that the white race has lost its heroes. Worse, its heroes have been revealed as villains and its greatest heroes as the arch-villains. The new generations of whites, appalled by the sanguine and despicable record carved over the face of the globe by their race in the last five hundred years, are rejecting the panoply of white heroes, whose heroism consisted in erecting the inglorious edifice of colonialism and imperialism; heroes whose careers rested on a system of foreign and domestic exploitation, rooted in the myth of white supremacy and the manifest destiny of the white race. The emerging shape of a new world order, and the requisites for survival in such a world, are fostering in young whites a new outlook. (68)

It is this new generation of whites, the first "truly worthy of a black man's respect" (82), with whom Cleaver (and later, through him, the Black Panther party) felt he could cooperate on a basis of equality and mutual respect. Old negative ideas and suspicions had to be dropped on both sides, and then the vision of equality W. E. B. Du Bois had hoped for, the world of perfect color-blind equality with advancement based solely on merit, could come to be:

If a man like Malcolm X could change and repudiate racism, if I myself and other former Muslims can change, if young whites can change, then there is hope for America. It was certainly strange to find myself, while steeped in the doctrine that all whites were devils by nature, commanded by the heart to applaud and acknowledge respect for these young whites—despite the fact that they are descendants of the masters and I the descendant of slaves. The sins of the fathers are visited upon the heads of the children—but only if the children continue in the evil deeds of the fathers. (83)

This essay was easily one of the most politically significant of its day, for it spoke to an entire generation of white youth who knew that they sympathized with the black movement from King leftward to Malcolm but who were unable to articulate their ideas as well as Cleaver could. The fact that a black man spoke for them only heightened the effect of their alienation and their sense of righteousness.

Cleaver and Baldwin

Cleaver's essay on James Baldwin, "Notes on a Native Son," melds easily with his political essays, for the piece is not so much a literary discussion as an attack on Baldwin for daring to attack Norman Mailer in his essay "The Black Boy Looks at the White Boy" (1961) in his collection *Nobody Knows My Name*.[4] In turn, Cleaver's essay provoked shocked and even outraged responses from a variety of critics.

It all begins with Mailer's "The White Negro,"[5] a 1957 essay on "the American existentialist—the Hipster," a white dropout type whom Mailer perceives as brother to the blacks who are out of the mainstream whether they want to be or not. His lengthy, often-abstract essay, which Baldwin categorized as "downright impenetrable" (180), praises the "unstated essence of Hip, its psychopathic brilliance," for its devotion to the now and its consequent rejection of not only forward-looking ambition but also "every social restraint and category" (354). Specifically, Mailer attributes every quality of hip to the Negro, the "source of Hip," who, living on the edge of society, has not been able to "afford the sophisticated inhibitions of civilization" (341) and so has cultivated the "art of the primitive," which includes not only living in the present but "relinquishing the pleasures of the mind for the more obligatory pleasures of the body" and expressing it all in jazz. Through jazz ("Jazz is orgasm," says Mailer) and marijuana ("the wedding ring"), the Negro became one with *both* the white juvenile delinquent and the white bohemian, the resultant ménage à trois creating the hipster. "The Hipster had absorbed the existentialist synapses of the Negro, and for practical purposes could be considered a White Negro" (341).

Baldwin's assessment of "The White Negro," on the other hand, was condescending. As a reformist, Baldwin wanted acceptance as a writer in a color-free society. His goals were to change society, and especially its white racist aspects, to permit himself and all other black people freedom from social and economic oppression and the resultant life of crime and futility. He never glamorizes the world of poverty and lost potential; he hated being a kid, "for children do not like ghettos. It takes them nearly no time to discover exactly why they are there" (60).

The life of the mind is exactly what he does not wish to "relinquish"; nor does he enjoy being thought of by whites as "a walking phallic symbol" (172), having to pay, as he puts it, "in one's own personality, for the sexual insecurity of others" (172). His denunciations of white America inform nearly everything he wrote.

Essentially, Baldwin regards Mailer's long-winded encomium to the hipster's blackness of spirit ("synapses") as spurious, and all the more frustrating and infuriating because Mailer "knew better." Baldwin fails to understand *why* Mailer had to "borrow the Depression language of deprived Negroes . . . to justify such a grim system of delusions," to try to re-create, if only in fantasy, "a weird nostalgia . . . a vanished state of security and order" (172). These, Baldwin asserts, are the conclusions he has come to after spending most of his life "watching white people" (172). Cleaver, the "Ofay Watcher" of "The White Race and Its Heroes," saw another reality, and he had to defend it. In his anti-Baldwin essay, then, Cleaver revealed that he was "personally insulted" by Baldwin's "flippant, school marmish dismissal of the White Negro" (*Ice,* 98). The reason behind that dismissal, he insists, is Baldwin's "grueling, agonizing, total hatred" of his own race and his "shameful, fanatical, fawning, sycophantic love" of whites (99). It is Mailer's rejection of white culture that Baldwin in truth despises; that is what is at "the root" of his "violent repudiation" of Mailer's essay (99).

Cleaver's standards permit human change in only one direction, for white culture is to him (and in this essay, at least, to Mailer also) purely white supremacist culture; the life of the mind belongs to the sexually repressed white "Omnipotent Administrator" and his lady and is therefore both racist and abnormal. For Mailer and the hipsters (and later the hippies and the entire radical youth movement), to want to become black is a sign of "convalescence" on every level, not merely the political. For Baldwin and other black intellectuals, however, to wish to join white artists as equals shows their urge to "become their own opposites, taking on all of the behavior patterns of their enemy, vices and virtues, in an effort to aspire to alien standards in all respects" (102). For Baldwin, it is to "redefine himself in the image of his white idols," to become "a white man in a black body" (103).

In the black intellectual, regardless of his actual religion, we see, Cleaver says, the "racial deathwish" (101) that is inversely typified by the Black Muslim story of Yacub, the evil scientist who created the white man devil through the careful breeding of successive generations of progressively lighter-skinned black people. In Baldwin's case, the death wish is even more extreme, says Cleaver, because of his homosexuality, for not only do black homosexuals reject the masculinity of blackness but they are "outraged and frustrated because in their sickness they are unable to have a baby by a white man" (102). Cleaver adds, "I, for one, do not think homosexuality is the latest advance over heterosexuality on the scale of human evolution. Homosexuality is a sickness, just as are baby-rape or wanting to become the head of General Motors" (*Ice,* 110). The political consequences go beyond a love of the life of the mind and an acceptance of white culture and art, for Cleaver's praise of the instinctual and sexually superior life of the black male requires that a heterosexual male be aggressive and even violent, as befits Mailer's hipster. It follows, then, that Wright's Bigger Thomas of *Native Son* and not Baldwin's "craven-hearted ghost," Rufus Scott of *Another Country,* is the hope of the future. "Yes," says Cleaver, "Rufus was a psychological freedom rider, turning the ultimate cheek" (107), transmuting what should have been manly rebellion into "lamblike submission" (108).

Cleaver's position is that Baldwin was overstepping his legitimate boundaries in criticizing Mailer, because the "kernel of truth" about a leftist shift in the orientation of youth is what should be valued, not Mailer's less-than-perfect assessment of black culture. Similarly, Baldwin's criticism of Wright for relying on "gratuitous and compulsive" violence is illegitimate, because Wright's is the masculine way, the way to create cathartic change à la Mailer. Thus, far from being an expression of masculinity, says Baldwin, Wright's drive to use violence in his work has its root in impotent rage: "It is the rage, almost literally the howl, of a man who is being castrated" (Baldwin, 151).

When we look forward in Cleaver's life, toward the Panthers and Cleaver's adulation of Huey Newton and toward his uncritical acceptance of white help wherever it appeared, we can see the direct outgrowth of his essay on Baldwin. It is apparent that in Wright and even in Bigger, Cleaver saw a bit of himself, and in Mailer and the hipster (or white radical college youth, or the Leonard Bernsteins as sponsors of a Panther benefit in their New York apartment), he saw white people who were, to paraphrase Malcolm X, part of the solution, not part of the problem.

Even critics who were otherwise delighted with *Soul on Ice* called Cleaver's attack on Baldwin "brilliant, but mean and unfair," an example of "sustained nastiness,"[6] and "ruthless."[7] A reviewer in the *Negro Digest* was furious with Cleaver for rejecting Baldwin, for severing the "information-packed lifeline" between any older black writer and his modern black readers, functioning thereby as a "tool" for the enemy. "We are a desperate people, looking for a way out of this prison-place, and nobody knows this better than brother Cleaver, himself. We need our black artists to help us see ourselves, see where we're headed. Baldwin, no less than Cleaver, can show us this. We need *both*, and then some."[8]

Some critics state that by attacking Baldwin, "his natural target" (Mayfield, 640), Cleaver was merely announcing his own arrival on the scene. But there may also be in Cleaver an underlying resentment toward Baldwin for his painfully accurate comments on subjects close to Cleaver's heart. Cleaver's statement that he was "personally insulted" by Baldwin's essay on Mailer is inexplicable if we assume that his only concern is Baldwin's fear and distrust of the masculinity in Mailer and Richard Wright. A clue to the source of the affront Cleaver felt in the Baldwin essay is found not in "Notes on a Native Son" but in "The White Race and Its Heroes." There, in the course of establishing early beatnik roots for the antiestablishment, antiracist white student movement of the sixties, Cleaver referred to Jack Kerouac's *On the Road:*[9] "The elders had eyes but couldn't see, ears but couldn't hear—not even when the message came through as clearly as in this remarkable passage from Jack Kerouac's *On the Road:* 'At lilac evening I walked with every muscle aching among the lights of 27th and Welton in the Denver colored section, wishing I were a Negro, feeling that the best the white world had offered was not enough ecstasy for me, not enough life, joy, kicks, darkness, music, not enough night' " (*Ice,* 73). Cleaver offers this excerpt as evidence of a white man's yearning for the soulful ("happy, true-hearted, ecstatic" [Kerouac, 180]) life-style of blacks as opposed to the sterile Babbittry of majority white Protestantism. It seems incredible that Cleaver could read Kerouac's statement that the "air" in the ghetto was "filled with the vibration of really joyous life that knows nothing of disappointment and 'white sorrows' and all that" (181) and accept it without irony or criticism. Indeed, Cleaver's first line echoes the anger of St. Paul over the refusal of his listeners to accept the Christian message (Acts 28: 23–27).

In Baldwin's essay, however, written five years earlier (but probably not read by Cleaver then), Baldwin had selected the first of the passages just quoted to highlight the white male's (a) sick obsession with black sexuality and (b) yearning for a share in that mellowness and lack of restraint as a way of returning to a mythical Eden, "a vanished state of security and order" (172), when everything was wonderful. Baldwin's tone toward what he considers a pretentious and condescending praise of desperately poor black people is pure derision: "Now, this is absolute nonsense, of course, objectively considered, and offensive nonsense at that; I would hate to be in Kerouac's shoes if he should ever be mad enough to read this aloud from the stage of Harlem's Apollo Theater" (182). Further, Baldwin's assessment of Wright and Bigger Thomas relegates their violence to the pointless screaming of a man in a cage. The violence in *Native Son* does not change society; the gesture is both random and futile, the hopeless lashing out of a eunuch. Could Cleaver, who had himself similarly struck out, rationalizing rape as "an insurrectionary act," miss the implication that in his identification with Bigger Thomas he was really revealing himself to be one of the black eunuchs? It was Cleaver, not Baldwin, who spoke for "all black men" when he offered himself to his queen after 400 years "minus my Balls." He needs to believe that self-assertion, including violence, creates remasculinization.

But Baldwin says in "Alas, Poor Richard" that violence is exactly what one would expect from frustrated, powerless men who could do nothing to alter their fates in any substantial way. Rioting and burning such as Cleaver and other prisoners praised in Watts in 1965 are the result of frustration, the explosion of a dream too long deferred, but are not productive of a new political and financial empowerment for the underprivileged black masses. In the sixties, such a statement was unfashionable; the message of the riots, of the Panthers and the white radicals, was to be taken seriously, as it was in the Kerner Commission report, and was supposed to lead to the victory of the Left and its humanitarian, antimaterialistic ways. No one, especially not an intelligent black male for whom established routes to self-realization appeared forever closed, wanted to hear that the other route to change, "revolutionary violence," was doomed. Cleaver's only recourse was to attack Baldwin as cowardly and lacking in masculine self-assertiveness, to attribute Baldwin's every argument to a despicable self-hatred, and to insist that all "real" black men not just stand up to trouble but go out and look for it.

The Wretched of the Earth

Cleaver's enthusiasm for "The White Negro" may have been further reinforced by his reading of "the Black Bible," as he was to call Frantz

Fanon's *The Wretched of the Earth*[10] in a 1967 *Ramparts* review. In a chapter entitled "Spontaneity: Its Strength and Weakness," Fanon warns against a "primitive Manicheeism" that sees only two opposed groups, "Blacks and Whites, Arabs and Christians," because "it sometimes happens that you get Blacks who are whiter than the Whites" (Fanon, 144) and because some white settlers "go over to the enemy, become Negroes and Arabs, and accept suffering, torture and death" (145).

Fanon, of course, refers not to the adoption of black "synapses" or the hip outlook on life from the fringes but to a serious revolutionary commitment such as Cleaver hoped the white Negro would have. He was less interested in precisely how white sympathizers thought of black people than in the ability of those sympathizers to become black enough to join the vanguard. Given the conviction that such a thing could indeed happen, it could only follow that in Baldwin, Cleaver would see a black man whose soul was white.

Is it Cleaver or Baldwin, then, who appears most eager for acceptance from whites? Which one better served the black race? It seems clear that the rivalry, couched by Cleaver in sexual terms as much as in political ones, is unresolvable on its merits. The rivalry does, however, reveal two things that would remain significant in future years: Cleaver is clearly anxious on the subject of sexuality and is, as a result, homophobic; and Cleaver tends to equate social violence with respectable masculinity and passive nonviolence with emasculation, if not the effeminacy of actual homosexual preference. His consequent scorn for the "self-flagellating" (*Ice,* 108) Christianity of King would contribute to his guilt over King's assassination and deepen his resolve to advocate revolutionary violence as a means of protection for blacks.

Cleaver understood the youth, and they him, as his popularity on various campuses was to attest in 1968. At the same time, many in the elder generation rejected the youth movement, the black movement, and Cleaver himself with "unmitigated hostility" (*Ice,* 77). Cleaver's words were too outspoken to be rationalized away, and the public actions of black and white youth, from sit-ins to riots, were too blatant an indictment of the American system to ignore. As a result, while *Soul on Ice* was on the one hand extremely successful (over its publishing lifetime, it sold 2 million copies), it was on the other hand condemned by some as a purely negative manifesto by an avowed enemy of the state.

Soul on Ice and the Critics

Most critics chose to focus on the sociopolitical essays that form the first half of the book. William Buckley dismissed *Soul on Ice* as "a searing book of hatred,"[11] but the more typical conservative, middle-aged response was the anger of a Babbitt charged with unpalatable faults. Robert Coles, for example, complained, "I don't like the way [Cleaver] lumps white men, all of them, indiscriminately together, and I'm sick and tired of a rhetoric that takes three hundred years of complicated, tortured American history and throws it in the face of every white man alive today. . . . [I]t is really stupid to tell today's white people that they caused what in fact gradually and terribly happened."[12] Coles omits any reference to Cleaver's qualifying "but only if" in the final line of "The White Race and Its Heroes" (quoted earlier) and yet inexplicably goes on to say many lines later, "He is full of Christian care, Christian grief and disappointment, Christian resignation, Christian messianic toughness, and hope" (107). Coles ends by saying that Cleaver has "begun (and only begun) to master the writer's craft" even with his reliance on "the handy political and sociological clichés that have blinded black and white men everywhere in every century" (107). Thus is the minority/New Left indictment of America's record dismissed.

Even more extreme a reaction was that of Richard Gilman in the *New Republic*. So alien does the condemnation of America and its centuries of racism ring to Gilman, so hard is it for him to relate to persons who feel themselves to be blamelessly outside the educational and economic systems, that he declares the book "was written for Negroes: it is not talking about the human condition . . . but about the condition of Negroes."[13]

Gilman went so far as to dismiss all the "new Negro writing," the product of authors denied "membership in the community of men," as therefore outside the "white, normative Western consciousness and spirit." Thus, Malcolm X's *Autobiography* and Cleaver's book (the only two mentioned by name) are not encompassed "under the great flawless arc of the Graeco-Roman and Judeo-Christian traditions." By this statement Gilman seems to mean that acceptable books like *The Education of Henry Adams* and *Apologia pro vita sua* (the only two he mentions positively) are works that trace a young man's maturation within, acceptance of, and acceptance by an established social order, whereas the black American subgenre of the bildungsroman of necessity presents a youth's developing alienation from a society that will never fully accept him. To classify these works as non-Western simply because they cannot *"take for granted* the worth, dignity and substantial being of the individual" (Gilman, 25) and to claim that one cannot therefore even evaluate them is to numb oneself to their pain and to deny it reality. In a follow-up article Gilman insisted that he *could* evaluate the writing of someone far removed from his own experience (homosexual, female), if that person put his or her perspective in fictional form. When "one's condition" is not the "raw material for art" but "the very subject of the work" (in other words, when there is no critical rubric to fall back on to objectify the material) then he cannot assess it.[14] "We can no longer talk to black people, or they to us, in the traditional humanistic ways," Gilman declared, and concluded that "something has happened to our means of gaining access to human truth, of which the Black revolution is only one sign and factor."

This "stunning misinterpretation" bothered Cleaver, who had assumed he *was* within the Western tradition, and was assuming Western values, specifically those of the sanctity of the individual soul, brotherhood, and community. "That's exactly what I was trying to write about," he told an interviewer,[15] but he wrote about their *absence* in American society as a direct result of racism, and created such defensiveness in his white reviewer that Gilman was unable to perceive what positive values were implied in Cleaver's criticism. Gilman's is the type of evasion condemned by even so moderate a soul as Martin Luther King. In the chapter "The Dilemma of Negro Americans" in his *Where Do We Go from Here?* King says uncompromisingly, "Over and over again it is said in the black ghettos of America that 'no white person can ever understand what it means to be a Negro.' There is good reason for this assumption, for there is very little in the life and experience of white America that can compare to the curse this society has put on color. And yet, if the present chasm of hostility, fear and distrust is to be bridged, the white man must begin to walk in the pathways of his black brothers and feel some of the pain and hurt that throb without letup in their daily lives."[16] Not every critic was defensive, however. While maintaining reservations about Cleaver's "dazzling and ingratiating oversimplifications" (Anderson, 64) about nearly everything, Jervis Anderson took up Gilman's question about whether black writers really communicate according to the "broad principles of humanism" (68) when they root "all their judgments about this country, the world, human beings and the universe itself" in their skin color. Whites, he implies, are obsessed not with their whiteness but with authentic personalities and sweeping general truths. Yes, he concludes, blacks living in this country *have* been exposed to and formed by Western ideals and concepts, and anyone, white or black, ought to be able to read of their bitterness and anger at being deprived of a share in this culture and understand exactly what is being said, as personally disturbing as it may be. Any "reasonably intelligent white" (69) ought to find Negro writing accessible, he argues, and not *only* black writing, for that matter, but the writing of many others who have been undereducated and more or less outside the intellectual shelter of that "flawless arc": "Why not the poor, the sick, the imprisoned, the Okies, the hippies, the Indians, and even the soldiers in Vietnam" (68)?

Blacks are obsessed with color because it is the single most determining fact about themselves, the reason they are on the far outside edge of civilizations that stand under Gilman's "flawless arc." But they don't understand *why* it matters so much, *why* it draws hatred and contempt like a lightning rod. If a person's skin color alone excludes him from "membership in the community of men," he will quite naturally become absorbed with its reality, and his usually impotent rage will consume his consciousness. This is the message of every militant black writer since David Walker wrote his *Appeal* in 1829. Cleaver is solidly within his tradition; unfortunately, many white readers and critics were solidly within theirs, too, "imprisoned," as critic Raymond Schroth put it in *America,* "in myth and illusions of their own."[17]

Sex and Racism

Soul on Ice concludes with an allegorical section of four essays entitled "White Woman/Black Man" that focus on the question of sex and racism in an abstract or general manner. Ostensibly no longer autobiographical, this section of the book, with its sociological essays, grows directly from the psychological and political materials set forth earlier in the collection. The same themes are clearly present as Cleaver works his way through a process of psychosexual development that he projects onto the entire black race, especially the black male. The first essay, "The Allegory of the Black Eunuchs," presents a discussion between a group of powerless young would-be revolutionaries and an obese elderly black man who, representing the past, articulates his obsession for white women and the "terrible horrible pain which [he] had learned to live with" (*Ice,* 166). This old man, referred to as "the Infidel" presumably because he does not believe in the Black Muslim religion, is called Lazarus, which in Black Muslim parlance refers to a still-dead Negro who has not awakened from the spiritual death white men inflicted on him with his capture from Africa to become "born again," as it were, into Black Muslimism and a consequent rejection of white values. The analogy with the Lazarus Christ raised from the dead is a deliberate ploy to attract converts who had been raised Christian. As Cleaver explains in "Lazarus, Come Forth," a "brainwashed" black male like Floyd Patterson is a Lazarus, as opposed to an awakened black man like Cassius Clay, reborn into a new black consciousness as Muhammad Ali. This Lazarus articulates the younger Cleaver's fascination with the Ogre, a fascination that once led him to become a rapist in order to strike a blow at the true target, the white male. The Infidel's thoughts and values are abhorrent to the younger Black Muslim males; the narrator, "repulsed by his monologue," rejects the old man much as Richard Gilman would Cleaver's entire book: "My dreams lay elsewhere and I could not begin to evaluate the things he had been talking about" (*Ice*, 171).

The second essay, "The Primeval Mitosis," attempts to explain the origin of the racial/sexual/class split in American society that has divided the original "Primeval Sphere" into male and female and then into classes based on power and race. The goal of all humankind, Cleaver says, is to return to the original oneness "and achieve supreme identity in the Apocalyptic Fusion" (*Ice*, 177). All this Lawrentian devotion to the mysticism of sex is actually a subtext to the economic theme, for the final fusion may take place, as it turns out, "only in a Classless Society, the absence of classes being the *sine qua non* for the existence of a Unitary Society in which the Unitary Sexual Image can be achieved" (178).

Cleaver divides society into exactly four groups, of which white men are the sexless Omnipotent Administrators, or Mind; black men the Supermasculine Menials, or Body; white women the repressed Ultrafeminine; and black women the hardworking Amazon, or Subfeminine. The struggle that matters most is that between the men for "sexual sovereignty" (190), or rule of the society. Possession of the female follows from that, for "When the Primeval Sphere split into the male and female hemispheres, the attribute of sovereignty was reposited in the male hemisphere and this attribute exercises a magnetic attraction upon the female hemisphere" (188). If there were no "racial caste system" (189), says Cleaver, dropping all pretensions to Marxism at last, there would be one united male "image" of power combining both Mind and Body and one female "image" blending femininity and self-reliance. As long as "race fears" persist, however, such unity can never occur; but in the future, "through the implacable march of history to an ever broader base of democracy and equality, the society will renew and transform itself" (190). For some reason, this transformation will be entirely due, it seems, to the Supermasculine Menial and the Amazon, who, though "in a general state of undevelopment," constitute the still-sexual "unde-essenced human raw material" needed for viable change.

The sexual confusion of whites as described herein more than balances the obsessions of a Lazarus. Because of his alienation from his body, Cleaver explains, the Omnipotent Administrator will "envy the bodies and strength" of the Body males, the Supermasculine Menials (who are, however, castrated by their powerlessness). This sexual envy is "precisely the root, the fountainhead, of the homosexuality that is perennially associated with the Omnipotent Administrator," Cleaver assures us (182).

Because of her man's effeminacy and her own quest for "frailty, weakness, helplessness, delicacy, daintiness," the Ultrafeminine lives in fear of "the Ogre of Frigidity." Her "psychic core" moves beyond the reach of "the effeminate clitoris of her man"; she runs into a "skyhigh wall of ice (If a lesbian is anything she is a frigid woman, a frozen cunt, with a warp and a crack in the wall of her ice)" (184). Her "psychic bridegroom," as it turns out, is the Body, who can "handle those Amazons down there with him," establishing in her mind the certain "intuitive knowledge" that he "can blaze through the wall of her ice, plumb her psychic depths, test the oil of her soul, melt the iceberg in her brain, touch her inner sanctum, detonate the bomb of her orgasm, and bring her sweet release" (185–86). Not surprisingly, the Body also craves the Ultrafeminine: "lust for her burns in his brain" (187). The only comment Cleaver makes about the Amazon's interests is that she "finds it difficult to respect the Supermasculine Menial" because of his powerlessness and lack of "sovereignty" (188). Thus, power is ironically the opposite of potency; true sexuality lies only in a denial of the Mind. In the unitary society of the future, though, classlessness will create sexual healing.

In "Convalescence" Cleaver describes the current society and the slow steps that have begun toward curing the four-way sociosexual split outlined earlier. The first step in cutting out the "racial Maginot Line" (192) that is "imbedded . . . in the schismatic American psyche" was the 1954 *Brown* v. [Topeka] *Board of Education* Supreme Court decision, outlawing the segregation that had been public policy since the *Plessy* v. *Ferguson* decision of 1896 sanctified the concept of separate but equal. Almost simultaneously, the Montgomery bus boycott, inaugurating Martin Luther King's career, showed us "that with this initiative, this first affirmative step, somewhere in the universe a gear in the machinery had shifted." In other words, the self-assertion of the previously passive blacks was met by an attempt on the part of the Omnipotent Administrators and Ultrafeminines to "shake the ice and cancer out of their alienated white asses" (199) by dancing the twist and twirling a Hula-Hoop. They were "storming the Maginot Line!" (198). The irrevocable switch from a "stiff, mechanical" yesterday to the funkier new "rhythm and style" of the fifties is symbolized for Cleaver by Elvis Presley's "Blue Suede Shoes" displacing the "antiseptic white shoes and whiter songs of Pat Boone" (194).

The essay that logically should follow "Convalescence" is "The White Race and Its Heroes," continuing the theme of healing the old wounds and attacking the divisions of race, sex, and class in America, but for editorial reasons that essay opens section 2 on the status quo, "Blood of the Beast," and the current section drops politics and revolt altogether in favor of an "open letter," "To All Black Women, from All Black Men," in which Cleaver, speaking as the representative black man, returns intact "from the dead" (*Ice*, 205), no longer Supermasculine Menial, and greets his Queen, no longer Amazon or the "domestic component" of womanhood but now the "Flower of Africa" (207). After "four hundred years of negated masculinity" (206), during which he could not look her in the eye for fear of her "merciless indictment of [his] impotence," he has gathered the courage to fight for his manhood and recover it: "I have died the ninth death of the cat, have seen Satan face to face and turned my back on God, have dined in the Swine's Trough, and descended to the uttermost echelon of the Pit, have entered the Den and seized my Balls from the teeth of a roaring lion!" (207). White men are referred to only in the past, in their usual role of the slave master/rapist, the conqueror of both male and female blacks, the violator of "the sacred womb that cradled primal man, the womb that incubated Ethiopia and populated Nubia and gave forth Pharaohs unto Egypt, . . . [t]he Holy Womb, the womb that knew the future form of Jomo Kenyatta" and other black militants listed in the passage. The white woman is not referred to at all, an absence symbolizing the shift in the black male's focus of attention.

The means by which this psychosexual revolution took place without a corresponding change in society is unclear, unless we are to assume that the obsession with the Ogre can be shaken by an act of will, whereas the socioeconomic situation remains essentially as it was before the spirit of revolt began to move across America. From the point of view of revolutionary ideology all things are possible; the newly militant, remasculinized black male, finally freed of his overwhelming desire for the Ultrafeminine blond ideal, confronts the (middle-aged) Omnipotent Administrator with his black Queen on one side of him and, presumably, "the vanguard of the white youth" (195) on the other, marching into the "wild and savage wilderness that's overrun with ruins" to "build a New City" that will be, perhaps, much like the "new heaven and new earth" of equality envisioned by Booker T. Washington and the "beloved community" longed for by Martin Luther King, not to mention the Garden of Eden derided by James Baldwin.

Sexual Roles and the Critics

Some critics, in evaluating *Soul on Ice,* chose to focus on the sexual material rather than the political, although sometimes they did so primarily to complain about how much space Cleaver himself devoted to it. Many white critics were as impatient with "The Primeval Mitosis" as others were with the revolutionary dissent of "The White Race and Its Heroes."

Richard Gilman spoke for many in 1968 when he proclaimed what may have been the true source of his alienation from Cleaver and the new black writing: "I find it unsatisfying intellectually, schematic and unsubtle most of the time. I don't want to hear again that the white man has been cut off from his body or that the Negro male has been forced back into his, that the Negro penis is more alive or the white woman's sexuality is artificial and contrived. Yet I don't want to condemn it and I am not sure I know how to acknowledge it without seeming patronizing . . . a myth, moreover, is not really analyzable and certainly not something which one can call untrue" (Gilman, 28). The literary critic in Gilman, however, finally came up with a rational standard in his contemplation of Cleaver's final essay. Gratefully, he acknowledged that Cleaver got him "off the hook" by writing a "beautiful section" for him to comment on, one in which "the myth's unassailable usefulness is there to see." Gilman praises the conclusion of the essay (and therefore of the collection) because it makes up "an enormously impressive fusion of Cleaver's various revolutionary strands, his assertion of a Negro reality, his hunger for sexual fullness and the reintegration of the self, his political critique and program and sense of a devastated society in need of resurrection" (28).

As quickly as he has lauded Cleaver's final effort, however, Gilman concludes by restating his conviction that this is not art, so to speak, but "writing," and therefore, as an "act of creation of the self" rather than of a literary artifact, "beyond my right to intrude on" (30). Stanley Pacion, though, was more willing to assess Cleaver's development along psychosexual lines. Pacion faults Cleaver for proclaiming the sexual superiority of blacks in the name of freedom: "Rather than breaking through the reader's conditioned thought-patterns and responses, it plays on them. Its doctrines of racial and biological superiority, though novel because Cleaver reverses them, have a long history of acceptance in the West. . . . Cleaver's scorn for the impotent, weak, degenerate intellectual and his praise of black virility have an all-too familiar ring."[18]

Even further, Pacion sees in the concluding essay not beauty but doubt, covered by too loud and too long a protestation of love:

No longer will he accept white standards that cast him as a "Menial" and force him to see his woman as an "Amazon." . . . To him this is an irrevocable liberation, and he celebrates it. For the first time—he seems to say—a black man openly declares his psychological emancipation from white society.

The crucial question, of course, is not whether Cleaver revels in his liberation, but whether he has actually achieved it. . . . If Cleaver were indeed as secure in his blackness as he claims, what inner need would drive him to write his heated panegyrics to the humanity of black people? The driven rhetoric of his last essay suggests anxiety; it bears the stamp of trauma. (312)

Indeed, the most perplexing thing about Cleaver's attitudes toward women in *Soul on Ice* is the difficulty one has in reconciling his personal love for Beverly Axelrod and his ideologically motivated love for "all black women" as an abstraction. Certainly they have in common Cleaver's renunciation of his racist obsession with the Ultrafeminine, for neither of these loves would be possible for a black man dominated by a culturally programmed preference for the dominant Anglo-Saxon blond. And perhaps that initial step, having been either created or accompanied by his growing respect for his lawyer, made it possible to "move on," as it were, to seeing women in general as real people, with a new, natural, and ideologically correct preference for his "own kind." The fact that these essays seem to have been written concurrently, however, complicates matters. We know that Cleaver was in love with Beverly Axelrod from the time of the dated letters printed here as "Prelude to Love" (September 1965) until a short time after his release in November 1966. We know that the Panthers used her apartment as a base for the printing of early pressruns of the *Black Panther* as well, which takes us into mid-1967. By Easter of 1967 Cleaver had met his future wife, Kathleen Neal, a Student Nonviolent Coordinating Committee (SNCC) volunteer, and had begun his campaign to get her to marry him; the wedding took place in December 1967. It appears, then, that we may assume that throughout 1966, at least, Cleaver was interested in only one white female for personal and professional reasons, and had perhaps successfully won his fight to be free of the Ogre and of his early resentment toward his mother, creating for himself the possibility of a love match that was, at least theoretically, unadulterated by negative psychological motives from the past.

The American "Red Book"

In its day, *Soul on Ice* was considered the "Red Book" of the new American revolution, as Chairman Mao's was for China. The major essays of *Soul on Ice* pursue the themes that were to dominate black activism in the sixties: the drive to power, the willingness to accept violence as a means to that end, the rejection of white standards of beauty, and the righteous self-assertion of black men. Under these themes, however, and simultaneously with them, we can perceive, more than 20 years later, the contradictions and self-doubt that time inevitably betrays.

Soul on Ice served more than one purpose: not only did it proclaim the New Left ideology and present the worldview of black and white radical youth more articulately than any other work did, but it released Cleaver from prison. Ed Keating's influence was extensive enough so that he could persuade famous literary figures to read and endorse Cleaver's essays and thereby prove to the parole board that Eldridge Cleaver could be an intelligent and productive citizen. The back of the jacket of the first edition is covered with excerpts from advance readings as if they were reviews: Norman Mailer predicted that Cleaver "might . . . emerge as one of the more important writers in America," which is only fair, since Cleaver had returned Mailer to a pre-Baldwin level of acceptability among the young. Liberal irony was served by Kenneth B. Clark, who first considered the contribution Cleaver would have made had he been given more opportunities, but then took it back: "On the other hand, it is quite possible that [Cleaver] could have been transformed . . . into still another inhibited apologist, disciplined and afraid to speak out against flagrant injustices because of the proverbial 'wife and two children.' " Neither Clark nor Cleaver would have guessed in 1966 that Cleaver, less than 10 years later, would return from France considerably subdued, though never "inhibited," with a wife and two children born in exile to worry about.

Chapter Three
Post-Prison Writings and Speeches: Meeting the Panthers

The two public years of Cleaver's life on parole, 1967 and 1968, have been well documented. From 2 May 1967, when members of the Black Panther party made the front pages by presenting themselves fully armed at the California assembly in Sacramento in protest of a gun control law, to Cleaver's disappearance in late November 1968 to avoid a return to prison, Cleaver and the party were the subjects of much fear and speculation, and the objects of intense interest on the parts of both media and police. These years, and the two following, were traumatic for much of the United States; they included not only innumerable riots and demonstrations but, most traumatic of all, the assassinations of two popular liberal leaders, Martin Luther King and the best-liked of the antiwar candidates, Robert Kennedy, only two months apart. The fear and sense of persecution felt by blacks and radicals over police brutality toward youthful demonstrators and especially the willingness of what were seen as repressive forces to murder respected and honored public figures were matched by the paranoia of the conservatives, epitomized by J. Edgar Hoover of the FBI, who saw in those black and white radicals a new movement to destroy the United States and substitute Communist rule.

The press was enchanted by the Panthers, perhaps most of all by Cleaver, who was photogenic, tall, handsome, charismatic, and articulate. Cleaver, in what he called his "outlaw period"—a time when he was "free, uncontrolled and anti-establishment" (*Fire*, 69)—undoubtedly appealed to black and white youth. During this period, Cleaver's life, which heretofore had been marked by isolation, reading, and writing, became increasingly filled with stress; the combination of fame and police harassment literally reduced his life to chaos. He recalls, "When I stepped out of Soledad State Prison into San Francisco in 1966 I sat my feet down in the center of the Haight/Ashbury. I embraced it, wallowed in it. For years, in prison, I had watched this scene develop, watched it grow deeper, and had come to certain conclusions about it. I saw in this ferment, this turning away in alienation and rebellion, this total disgust with the old and avid hunger for life, a new reality—I saw in this the readiness of a quorum of the people to shatter the existing structure of oppression and repression that I had come to call, with loathing, Babylon" (*Fire,* 80). Cleaver was 32, a free adult for the first time in his life. Having spent 11 of the preceding 12 years in prison, he badly needed to establish an entirely new set of acquaintances and to adopt a life-style and a career outside the criminal world. He was determined, after having begun to "free" himself through writing, to preserve the ground he had gained and to move, as he perceived Malcolm X had done, from convict to respected member of the black community. His concepts and plans were still vaguely socialistic, with no concrete program; the idea was simply that "everything" would be owned and perhaps even operated by all "the people," who would somehow know how to run things and who would do it so well that all inequity, and therefore all criminal behavior, which was motivated purely by want, would end.

The Fateful Meeting

For the first three months of his parole, Cleaver's life was without a focus. With a black poet and playwright named Marvin Jackmon, he founded Black House in San Francisco, a cultural center that quickly caught on. He spoke on the radio from time to time, and he wrote articles for *Ramparts.* But he still lacked a definite program, and most important of all, he lacked a leader. He was, in the words of Bobby Seale, "wired up behind Malcolm X,"[1] but Malcolm had been dead for nearly two years, and Cleaver's dream of rejuvenating Malcolm's Organization of Afro-American Unity was not warmly received in the Bay Area. What he did manage to gain support for was a memorial to Malcolm on the second anniversary of his death, 21 February 1965.[2] It was at a meeting to plan this memorial that Cleaver first met the Panthers, and especially their minister of defense, Huey P. Newton.

One of Cleaver's major concerns at this time in his life was black manhood; as we have seen, several of the essays included in *Soul on Ice* (as yet unpublished) lauded Malcolm as the embodiment of that lost manhood because of his courage and "the truth" he uttered. Physical courage and a willingness to use violence were the identifying marks of the kind of hero and role model Cleaver wanted and insisted, by extension, *all* black people needed. Cleaver himself was articulate but never took an unnecessary risk; he had been in trouble with the police for specific criminal offenses, but he never defied an officer on principle, risking arrest simply to show that such defiance could be done.

Huey Newton, in contrast, openly defied police harassment even before it occurred. That he and the rest of the Panthers carried guns everywhere impressed Cleaver and others deeply. In "The Courage to Kill: Meeting the Panthers," Cleaver writes,

Suddenly the room fell silent. The crackling undercurrent that for weeks had made it impossible to get one's point across when one had the floor was gone; there was only the sound of the lock clicking as the front door opened, and then the soft shuffle of feet moving quietly toward the circle. . . . I spun round in my seat and saw the most beautiful sight I had ever seen: four black men wearing black berets, powder blue shirts, black leather jackets, black trousers, shiny black shoes—and each with a gun! In front was Huey P. Newton with a riot pump shot gun in his right hand, barrel pointed down to the floor. Beside him was Bobby Seale, the handle of a .45 caliber automatic showing from its holster on his right hip, just below the hem of his jacket. A few steps behind Seale was Bobby Hutton, the barrel of his shotgun at his feet. Next to him was Sherwin Forte, an M1 carbine with a banana clip cradled in his arms.

Roy Ballard jumped to his feet. Licking his lips, he said, "For those of you who've never met the brothers, these are the Oakland Panthers."

"You're wrong," said Huey P. Newton. "We're not the Oakland Panthers. We happen to live in Oakland. Our name is the Black Panther Party."[3]

When Betty Shabazz, Malcolm's widow, arrived, the Panthers provided "protection" for her and her escort, Malcolm's cousin, Hakim Jamal. The armed Panther presence guarding her during her visit to the *Ramparts* office drew the attention of police and created near-hysteria in some of the white staff; Cleaver loved it. He described the scene excitedly: "The lobby resembled certain photographs coming out of Cuba the day Castro took Havana. There were guns everywhere" (*Post,* 32).

When the visit ended, Betty and Hakim, surrounded by Panthers, got into a car and left. The day threatened to end without incident, it seems, and so Huey Newton chose to cover a TV camera lens with an envelope. When the cameraman knocked his hand away, Huey demanded that the man be arrested for assault; when the officer said he'd rather arrest Huey himself, Huey threw the cameraman against the wall and then down the sidewalk. Even then, no fight broke out and no arrests were made, and so Huey chose to yell to Seale and the three remaining Panther guards, "Don't turn your backs on these back-shooting dogs!" Finally, one officer was provoked enough to threaten to draw his weapon on Huey, while saying, "Don't point that gun at me! Stop pointing that gun at me!" (35). Now Huey made as much as possible out of his defiance, calling the officer a "big fat racist pig" and a "cowardly dog," pumping a round into the chamber of his shotgun, and looking the officer in the eye. But the other police officers kept urging Newton's antagonist "to cool it, to take it easy" and ultimately won. According to Cleaver, "then the cop facing Huey gave it up. He heaved a heavy sigh and lowered his head. Huey literally laughed in his face and then went off up the street at a jaunty pace, disappearing in a blaze of dazzling sunlight" (36).

Cleaver was full of admiration for this pointless provocation and display of bravado. He assumed it was terror and not wisdom on the part of the police officer that ended the confrontation, and so he remarked that Newton had won through the quality of his courage. "I speak of that revolutionary courage it takes to pick up a gun with which to oppose the oppressor of one's people" (36). Cleaver insisted on seeing in Huey not a foolhardy militant who sought trouble but a dedicated guerrilla who would die for his people.

Toward the end of his essay, Cleaver elaborated on the significance of Huey as the successor to the heroic Malcolm: "Malcolm talked shit, and talking shit is the iron in a young nigger's blood. . . . Huey P. Newton is the ideological descendant, heir and successor of Malcolm X. Malcolm prophesied the coming of the gun to the black liberation struggle. Huey P. Newton picked up the gun and pulled the trigger, freeing the genie of black revolutionary violence in Babylon" (*Post,* 38). "The Courage to Kill" was written in June 1968; Bobby Seale reports that soon after that date Cleaver convinced him that since he, Bobby, knew Newton best, he should tape his recollections of him and their early days together and publish the result as *The Biography of Huey P. Newton,* with an introduction by Cleaver. Seale comments, "Eldridge said that Huey P. Newton followed Malcolm X like Jesus Christ followed John the Baptist. That made a heck of a lot of sense to me. So Eldridge got some tapes and a recorder and a typewriter, and took me down to Carmel to a little cabin to work on the book" (*Seize,* 264).

Huey as Shield and Sacrifice

When he wrote the introduction to the biography of Huey Newton, Cleaver explicitly disavowed a belief in Huey's divinity but did so in such quasi-religious language that the effect is almost the same as if he hadn't. At the time Cleaver wrote the piece, in 1968, Huey was in prison because of his role in a shoot-out that left one policeman dead. The introduction begins: "I remember once during the trial of Huey P. Newton, a lawyer stopped me in the hall of the Alameda County Courthouse. He was very nervous, and he said, 'They are crucifying Huey in there—they are turning him into another Jesus.' And I remember almost instinctively replying, 'Yes, Huey is our Jesus, but we want him down from the cross' " (*Post*, 40). Devotional language is sprinkled throughout the piece, nearly obliterating any metaphorical meaning in the first paragraph. Cleaver speaks of Huey as "above and beyond others . . . different from anybody else. You cannot help but be amazed and fascinated by his seriousness, by his willingness and readiness to lay down his life in defense of the rights of his people, his own rights, his human rights and his Constitutional rights" (*Post*, 40–41).

An additional chapter in the gospel-like recording of Huey's deeds and his meaning to "his people" is found in an essay Cleaver sent from exile to the *Black Panther* paper much later. "Huey's Standard" (*Black Panther*, 15 March 1970, 3) describes a March 1967 encounter between Huey Newton and an Oakland police officer in which Newton was at his bold and shieldlike best. This episode, which occurred soon after the incident at the *Ramparts* office, made such an indelible impression on Cleaver that he still wrote with awe three years later. He begins by asserting that the founding of the Black Panther party was so important that "you almost have to start dealing in religious categories" to talk about it, and especially about Huey, "the dynamo, the source, the prime mover" who could "infuse" his followers "with an enthusiasm that was miraculous" (3). The essay presents "Huey in action on the scene of oppression" one night in Oakland following the police killing of a young black male named Denzil Dowell.

An officer, seeing a crowd of black people gathered on the corner to protest the slaying, pulled to the curb and jumped out. Some ran; others looked at one another in panic.

Huey had his jaw set, and his eyes narrowed, and he stepped forward, and he jacked off a round in the shotgun. He pumped a round into the chamber. And he just stepped up to the curb in front of Denzil Dowell's mother and this cop. And this cop, almost without breaking his motion, looked at Huey, he looked at the other Panthers, he looked at the crowd of people there and he got back into that car and he got out of there. He split. . . . The moment Huey stepped forward, the moment that Huey jacked off that round into the chamber of that shotgun, you could see the people snap behind Huey. And it was like a rock and . . . that crowd became a crowd of Panthers. (16)

By his actions, then, Cleaver declares Huey to have "set a standard that inspires other Black men to want to emulate that standard" (16).

In Seale's account of the Denzil Dowell affair, which was printed in the *Ramparts* issue of 17 November 1968, just a week before Cleaver went into exile, he describes two related events in Richmond. His story of the first, concerning the initial Panther investigation of the incident, roughly parallels Cleaver's, but he specifically mentions Cleaver's presence only at the second event, the "official" public rally the following Saturday, when a number of "brothers" with guns reportedly scared off several cars full of "pigs" who were too frightened to leave their vehicles. In Seale's account of Huey's confrontation there is far less melodrama, and Seale himself receives honorable mention for courage: "We . . . stood tall, ready to defend ourselves. We were educating the people that we would die here for them. This was the position we always took with brother Huey P. Newton."[4]

In his introduction to a pamphlet of Newton's writings entitled "The Genius of Huey P. Newton," Cleaver had praised Huey for taking up "where brother Malcolm left off when he was assassinated."[5] As much as reporters and fans attempted to push Cleaver himself into that role, he maintained the supremacy of Huey as the man who displayed the assertiveness of a Richard Wright character, who "delivered his message to the people through his actions, down on the street with a gun in his hands" ("Genius," 2). Cleaver, who was Newton's devoted follower and recorder of thoughts and deeds, certainly saw Newton as a symbolic figure, and his narration of events concerning Huey P. Newton and what he meant to his people is colored by that devotion. Cleaver, it must be remembered, never made a practice of confronting the "pigs" when he was younger, and, by Newton's orders, was officially kept disarmed when he was with the Panthers because he was out on parole. Thus, Cleaver could not be a man of action, whatever his desires, and he could only follow the "uncommon man," Huey P. Newton, who "made no distinctions between theory and practice" ("Genius," 3).

To Newton and Seale, however, Cleaver was the man of action, the "brother" who had experience with criminal activity and prison life and who'd been through long toughening years neither of them had ever endured. And he was willing to take orders from Huey. To Cleaver, the new embodiment of black manhood lived and breathed, and stood off "pigs" on real street corners. When Huey went to prison, Eldridge not only did everything imaginable to get him out but spoke about him constantly within the group. Remarks ex-Panther Earl Anthony, "I had always had respect for Huey, but now I saw Eldridge elevate him to a level where mere respect would be inappropriate. He made Huey, and what he stood for, something that should be thought of in sacred terms."[6] Anthony thought of Eldridge as "a prophet," but *apostle* would have been more fitting, for Cleaver was not the forerunner but a follower and interpreter. He put more energy into freeing Huey than into anything else he did, even at a time when he was working at *Ramparts* and getting himself married.

The emotional intensity of this period in Cleaver's life can hardly be exaggerated. After so many years "on ice," he had thrown himself into life with full enthusiasm and within a few months had made the two major commitments of his life—to Huey and to Kathleen. The decision to join the Panthers led directly to his involvement in the police shoot-out on 6 April 1968, which in turn led to seven years of exile. The marriage to Kathleen lasted until 1988, although the relationship itself was several years shorter-lived.

Cleaver was surprised when his leftist activities drew negative criticism from his parole officer. As far as Cleaver was concerned, he was busy and useful, absorbed in noncriminal activity, his life a constant series of meetings and speeches. He had even spoken before an antiwar audience of 65,000 at Kezar Stadium in San Francisco on 15 April 1967, on the same bill with Coretta Scott King (*Post,* 5). "I thought that the parole authorities would be pleased with my new life because in terms of complying with the rules governing conduct on parole, I was a model parolee. But such was not the case" (*Post,* 4). Cleaver was ordered, he said, to "play dead" or lose parole.

From October 1967 until November 1968, life took on what must have been an occasionally nightmarish quality. One night in January, the police raided Eldridge and Kathleen's apartment at 3:30 A.M., supposedly looking for weapons, and the next month invaded Bobby Seale's home on the pretense that someone inside had been overheard plotting a murder. After *Soul on Ice* was finally published in February,

Cleaver was too constantly busy to sit down and write. The assassination of Martin Luther King on 4 April 1968 added to the other stresses Cleaver had to cope with and followed by the pressures of both the state of California's campaign to reimprison and possibly murder him and the Peace and Freedom party's campaign to elect him president, seems to have pushed Cleaver to the breaking point.

The carefully composed essay "The Land Question and Black Liberation" was published in April and May 1968 in *Ramparts;* "Revolution in the White Mother Country and National Liberation in the Black Colony," a speech originally presented to the White Peace and Freedom Foundation Convention in March, was printed in the *North American Review*'s July–August issue. The speech is actually little more than an abstract of the *Ramparts* essay, with emphasis on the role the Peace and Freedom party is to play in white America as an ally of the Black Panthers. The other pre–King assassination essays are related to one another and to "The Land Question" through the unifying theme of black power, and they look back to the political concerns of the essays in *Soul on Ice,* particularly in their emphasis on a Malcolm X–like assertiveness.

The preassassination group of essays begins not with the first essay found in the *Post-Prison Writings,* "Affidavit #1: I Am 33 Years Old," which was written in prison two days after King was shot, but with the second and third essays, "The Decline of the Black Muslims" and "Psychology: The Black Bible," a review of Frantz Fanon's *The Wretched of the Earth.* The pair offer a rationale and a reading list to underpin the theoretical arguments about American society and social change that began with Cleaver's prison essays and that would continue to inform his writings through freedom and exile.

A Reading List for Radicals

"The Decline of the Muslims" merely makes the point that the Black Muslims became a minor force in prisons following the Muhammad– Malcolm X split and the realization of Muslim prisoners that the Nation of Islam would provide them with no legal assistance whatever. These developments, on top of the failure of Allah to appear and destroy North America on cue, led to great skepticism and renunciation of the faith. Cleaver concludes: "What black inmates now look to with rising hopes is the cry for Black Power and an elaboration of its details in the name of Malcolm X. In this connection, the most popular books being read by black inmates in prisons today, Black Muslims and just plain old fed-up Negroes, are: *The Autobiography of Malcolm X, Malcolm X Speaks, Home, Call the Keeper, The Wretched of the Earth, Negroes with Guns,* and *Che Guevara on Guerrilla Warfare*—none of which lead to Mecca" (*Post,* 17). The seven books listed—which include none of the theoretical Marxist works Cleaver once pored over—constitute a short course in black militancy up to and including armed revolt. Cleaver spoke of change, especially among the young, but recommended guns for self-defense and read books on open war. His love of excitement and drama left him addicted to the idea of confrontation and the concept of revolution.

Robert F. Williams

Negroes with Guns (1962), by Robert F. Williams, is a militant text written by a man who actually took up arms against the Ku Klux Klan and its white racist followers. As a Marine Corps veteran, he organized a chapter of the National Rifle Association and enrolled 60 members who were willing to stand up to white intimidation. As NAACP branch president in Monroe, North Carolina (then the only integrated chapter in the South), he first organized a sit-in to protest whites-only use of the sole municipal swimming pool in town in 1957 and then, when attacks on demonstrators became more overtly violent, met "violence with violence."[7] Williams declared:

We are oppressed . . . , and the mind and personality of the racist doing the oppressing have been warped for so long that he is a mental case. Even if the economic situation is changed it will take quite a while, and it will require quite a shock, to cure this mental disease. . . . And the shock treatment must come primarily from the Afro-American people themselves in conjunction with their white allies; in conjunction with the white youth.

What happened in Monroe, North Carolina, had better become a lesson to the oppressors and the racists of America. Because it is symbolic of a new attitude, symbolic of a new era. It means that the Negro people are becoming restless. It means that there will be many more racial explosions in the days to come. Monroe was just the beginning. I dare predict that Monroe will become the symbol of the new Afro-American determined to rid himself of the stigma of race prejudice and the pain and torture of race hate and oppression at any cost. (Williams, 119)

Although Monroe, North Carolina, never became the symbol Williams predicted it would, he was right about the change in society. During the sixties, there would be no shortage of volunteers to administer the "shock treatment" Williams had in mind, and Cleaver was undoubtedly quick to note the presence of a kindred soul in Williams's emphasis on the involvement of radical whites. Williams, like Cleaver after him, fled first to Canada and then to Cuba for refuge from the law. Presumably (and ironically, considering Cleaver's future), it was Williams's disappearing act that had led Cleaver, in his essay "Soul on Ice," to wish for a Williams less like a "rabbit" (*Ice,* 19).

Frantz Fanon

The Wretched of the Earth is a black psychiatrist's justification of the act of revolt. Fanon, "born in Martinique and educated in Paris, . . . reached the apex of his genius in the crucible of the Algerian Revolution" (*Post,* 18). His book is in part a study of how the various segments of society, both within cities and in the countryside, usually react during the crisis of revolution, and in part an analysis of the way in which violence acts as therapy for the oppressed, who feel "an impulse to violence" in their "collective unconscious." Jung aside, what Fanon wishes to establish is that oppressed people experience serious "distortions in the personality" that can be cured only by giving vent to the "revolutionary impulse to violence" (*Post,* 20). His dispute with Baldwin comes to mind as Cleaver explains, "This book teaches colonial subjects that it is perfectly normal for them to want to rise up and cut off the heads of the slavemasters, that it is a way to achieve their manhood, and that they must oppose the oppressor in order to experience themselves as men" (*Post,* 20). Because the book was written by a non-American about Algeria and yet sounded so much like an expression of his own concerns, it helped to cement Cleaver's feeling of unity with Third World people fighting "wars of national liberation," as evinced, for example, in "The Black Man's Stake in Vietnam." Further, the amoral justification of violence, as opposite as possible from King's pacifism, blends not only with Cleaver's own preferences, but also with Williams's explicit comments about the inutility of nonviolent means of protest when violence is brought into play by the enemy. Finally, Jean-Paul Sartre's introduction establishes the black-white radical bond Cleaver had always preferred.

Che Guevara

Che Guevara's book, *On Guerrilla Warfare*, was primarily used to make radicals feel powerful and intransigent. Occasionally someone spoke seriously, as Cleaver would in exile, about using the mountains as a retreat and attacking the cities from rebel enclaves therein, but the inappropriate placement of the mountains relative to the major power centers of the United States made such plans quixotic at best. Those who hoped to use the ghettos as such enclaves usually came to see that encirclement and siegelike control of water, electricity, food, and medical supplies would be almost ridiculously easy for the "white majority government" to bring about, to the desolation of the revolutionaries. But Che's righteousness and inspirational prose served to keep the spirit of militancy high nonetheless.

Even though no Panthers fulfilled Che's definition of a guerrilla as "an agrarian revolutionary,"[8] the idea of romantic self-sacrifice for the cause of the oppressed—as exemplified in the title of Newton's collected writings, *To Die for the People* (1972)—combined with Che's emphasis on physical toughness, "force of arms and spiritual dedication" (Guevara, 31), made *On Guerrilla Warfare* irresistible reading for the quasi-military Panthers. The need for local origins, which would provide "terrain knowledge, local acclimatization, and a sense of fighting for [the guerrilla's] own area" (32), can easily be adapted to urban neighborhoods, just as the street ideals of courage and endurance can be recognized in Che's dictum that "all these conditions presuppose an iron constitution, the strength to survive illness and adversity, the ability to live like a harassed animal" (33). The final note of encouragement might have been found in Che's comment on the value of patience and confidence in victory: "The struggle will be hard, long, and will meet with reverses; only high morale, strict discipline, and deep faith in the ultimate victory will sustain the forces. In Cuba, a nucleus of twelve dedicated men—plus a Fidel Castro—were able to succeed" (68).

LeRoi Jones

Home, by LeRoi Jones (Amiri Baraka), is a collection of essays, dated from 1960 to 1965, that document the author's increasingly radical attitudes toward society. Among the essays that most obviously reveal an influence on Cleaver's own developing ideas are a lengthy description of a visit to Cuba in a group that included Robert F. Williams ("Cuba Libre," 1960); an essay on "The Dempsey-Liston Fight" that anticipated Cleaver's own discussion of the Muhammad Ali–Patterson fight in "Lazarus, Come Forth"; yet another discussion of the racial/ sexual images of black males versus white, entitled "american sexual reference: black male" (1965), which praises both Kerouac and Mailer as " 'liberated' white men"; and two radical political essays, "the last days of the american empire (including some instructions for black people)" (1964) and "the legacy of malcolm x, and the coming of the black nation" (1965).

Both of these last two essays, and especially the second one, indulge in hyperbolic intensity, and both employ the rhetoric of confrontation, black self-assertion, and social violence. "Last Days," for example, concludes: "I say if your hope is for the survival of this society, this filthy order, no good. You lose. The hope is that young blacks will remember all of their lives what they are seeing, what they are witness to just by being alive and black in America, and that eventually they will use this knowledge scientifically, and erupt like Mt. Vesuvius to crush in hot lava these willful maniacs who call themselves white Americans."[9] The Malcolm X essay, however, written, like Cleaver's, within months of the assassination, includes a call to nationhood and a "nationalization," Third World style, "of all properties and resources belonging to white people, within the boundaries of the Black Nation" (Jones, 249). There is no question of white retaliation for the takeover of valuable urban properties, for the essay operates on the level of fantasy. It concludes with a vision of Armageddon: "Only a united Black Consciousness can save Black People from annihilation at the white man's hands. And no other nation on earth is safe, unless the Black Man in America is safe. Not even the Chinese can be absolutely certain of their continued sovereignty as long as the white man is alive. And there is only one people on the planet who can slay the white man. The people who know him best. His ex-slaves" (250). Cleaver was not to become so strong an open advocate of violence until he went into exile, but the concept of a united black nation moving toward selfhood in a national liberation movement became his from the first.

Nat Hentoff

Nat Hentoff's *Call the Keeper* (1966) is a short novel set in New York City. A major character, Septimus Williams, a psychopathic black mur-

derer, bears a resemblance to a number of violent convicts. While out of
prison on parole, Septimus assaults first Horowitz, a tough little Jewish
cop who "put him away" the first time, and then Dianne Burnett, a black
woman lusted after by three other men, two of them white, but able to be
sexually fulfilled only by Septimus. Williams's planned murder of Horowitz is halted in seconds by the wiry cop's knowledge of judo, and
Septimus is slated to be incarcerated indefinitely.

The radical black survivor is John the Avenger, a worshiper of "the
Cuban Experience." Viera, at the Cuban mission in New York, offers a
little concrete advice: "If a revolutionary cadre is itself well organized—
and spread out in a number of strategic places—it can create wave upon
wave of chaos. . . . There is a direct relationship between how tightly
organized a society is and the amount of disruption that can be caused
by small but crucial breaks in that system of organization."[10] The novel
ends with the assumption that nothing will change. Its appeal seems to
lie solely in the articulation of black radical ideas on the parts of
Septimus and John, as well as in the lines of a LeRoi Jones–like play
produced on Second Avenue and attended by all the major characters.
The ironic tone of the book must have been less important to Cleaver
and his fellow inmates than the sense the novel creates of real social
issues in the lives of characters they could identify with.

Tell It Like It Is

The two remaining 1967 essays include a brief item on Bobby Kennedy entitled "Robert Kennedy's Prison," which reveals Cleaver's revulsion for Kennedy's combination of cynicism and privilege, and "My
Father and Stokely Carmichael," a pro-Carmichael essay in which Leroy
Cleaver plays only a peripheral, symbolic role. Taken together, the items
reinforce Eldridge's rejection of elder and/or establishment figures.

In the Kennedy essay, Cleaver comments that under the image of the
"fair-haired Knight of the Liberal Round Table," Kennedy's true being
can be detected: "I sat up close and got a good look at his mug. I had
seen that face so many times before—hard, bitter, scurvy—all those
things. I had seen his face on the bodies of night-time burglars who had
been in prison for at least ten years. Robert Kennedy has been in some
prison of his character for a long time. He's a convict, possibly a lifer,
and I got the impression that he lives, like convicts, by one law and one
law alone: I shall do only that which is expedient for survival so that I
will have one more chance outside of these chains" (*Post*, 21–22).

Kennedy and the other two members of the (unnamed) committee listening to the testimony of social workers at Nourse Auditorium exuded "a foul odor reminiscent of the stench of the blind, complacent rich in the hour before their doom" (22). "As I left the auditorium," Cleaver fumed, "I said to myself: We don't need a War on Poverty. What we need is a war on the rich" (22).

The same single-minded devotion to radical principles leads Cleaver to reject his father in the Carmichael essay. At some point, the elder Cleaver had moved to Chicago, where he was to live until his death in 1975. In early 1967, Eldridge arrived in town in order to interview Carmichael preparatory to accompanying him on a speaking tour. Eldridge stayed with Leroy, who on the following day went with his son to the SNCC office, where the interview was to take place; the two arrived about noon. Leroy Cleaver's negative reaction to the area was seen as symbolic by his son: " 'Jesus,' he said, 'this is really rock bottom. This is the poorest section of the Negro part of town. Why would anyone want to set up an office down here?' My father is not too hep to the action these days. He's like many old Negroes: they woke up on the white man late in their lives and are very bitter to learn that they have been tricked" (*Post,* 43). Carmichael's being detained until 1:00 P.M. gave Eldridge time to reconsider his wisdom in allowing his father to share the experience of meeting the coauthor (with Charles V. Hamilton) of *Black Power* (1967): "I didn't want to hang around that office with my father until one o'clock, mainly because he had begun asking a barrage of questions: Who's Nkrumah? Who wrote that book? So I told them that I would go pick up my luggage and hustle right back. Pa and I had lunch together. Then he ran and got his camera and started snapping pictures of me. I explained to him that this was a very important assignment for me and I had better go back alone because these people might not like it if I brought anyone else along" (*Post,* 44). Leroy Cleaver is never mentioned again; the bulk of the *Ramparts* article describes Eldridge's day with Carmichael and presents a brief discussion of Stokely's views. The sole function of Leroy Cleaver is to serve as a Lazarus figure, one of those old not-yet-born-again-into-the-truth-of-blackness Negroes whose values are still hopelessly bourgeois and whose reading is embarrassingly out of date. He is dismissed as readily as the past itself. His pride in his son, the successful reporter, as shown in the picture taking, is an irritation more than anything else, especially when displayed by a man to whom the son feels he owes so little.

The remainder of the essay is split approximately in half. In part 1,

Cleaver recounts what the day in Chicago was like, and in part 2, he encapsulates a typical speech on the tour. Part 1 is structured around the rejection of the older generation that was introduced with Cleaver's dismissal of his father. First, a confrontation—on Irv Kupcinet's TV talk show—between Carmichael and such establishment figures as Congressman Roman Pucinski and a State Department representative—left black judge and preacher Archibald Carey confused and unable to comprehend the terms of the argument. The discussion focused on Vietnam, and Carmichael's position had been that killing in war is murder, even if approved by the state. Like white radicals, Carmichael rejected the concept that killing to defend one's society is categorically different from killing a compatriot in time of peace; "If I ever reach the point where I want to kill someone," he declared, "I'm going to be the one who makes that decision" (*Post,* 47).

Neither Carey nor the other two men could understand Carmichael's position, because they accepted the traditional idea that one kills in war when there is a threat to one's society, regardless of whom one may kill, whereas Carmichael failed to identify with the society and its version of reality because he was modern, radical, and alienated. Ironically, Cleaver's later position was to advocate the same impersonal violence as did the state in war, only in the name of black and Third World liberation.

The dismissal of Leroy Cleaver and Archibald Carey is followed by an even more cavalier disregard for contemporary black moderates: "As we drove away from the studio, the radio was blowing black music. It was during this drive that I began to form my picture of Carmichael. The record 'Tell It Like It Is' began playing. This is a soulful song, the blues, of the people. When it first came on, Carmichael gave a loud whoop, clapped his hands and began singing along with the radio. I wondered how Martin Luther King or Whitney Young or Roy Wilkins would have reacted to the same music" (*Post,* 47–48). The irrelevance of the older generation is made completely clear: they didn't know who the radical heroes are, they didn't understand the moral and ideological stances of the militant young on current issues, and they were presumed to be too "uncool" to understand contemporary soul music, an indisputable sign of political and social irrelevance; incredibly, they were thought not to be "soulful . . . of the people."

Carmichael's own understanding of his culture and his constituency was revealed immediately thereafter, when he arrived—again late, as he had been all day—for a meeting with ACT for Freedom (the acronym is never explained). The ACT people concentrated on giving Stokely Carmichael a hard time for having been detained by speaking to whites. "I'm going to tell you cats just like it is," he declared, echoing the song without apparent self-consciousness, and proceeded to explain that they gave him less support than he received from blacks in the South and offered him no money for speaking, unlike Kupcinet or the whites of the University of Chicago, whom he would soon join that evening. Mollified, they abruptly asked, "Why don't you move to Chicago and help us get rid of Martin Luther King?" (50) Neither he nor Cleaver was scandalized by such a request; the seemingly "older man" (King, born in January 1929, was six and a half years older than Cleaver) was undeniably an obstructionist influence. The bond re-created, ACT members "guarded" Stokely (apparently without arms) at his speaking engagement that evening at the university, where he introduced them to the white students as "a beautiful bunch of brothers" (51).

On the remainder of the tour, Cleaver presents Carmichael as the leading example of "a new cycle" in black nationalist leaders—those who have a college education. An example of how education is put to use for "the people" consumes the remainder of the essay. Ironically— for it was Carmichael who was to balk at an alliance with the Peace and Freedom party radicals—Carmichael is praised as being unlike many black nationalists "who have been overly influenced by the Black Muslims" (53), in that he held as a policy the shopworn concept "My enemy's enemy is my friend" (53). This elementary Machiavellianism became, awkwardly, "We've got to learn who to coalition with and who not to coalition with."

Further evidence of Carmichael's high level of intelligence was apparently revealed by his ability to quote *Alice in Wonderland*—specifically, Humpty Dumpty's declaration that a word means "just what I choose it to mean, neither more nor less." In Stokely Carmichael's speeches, there was neither irony nor nonsense in the line. When he said "integration," it meant jobs and better schools, even if white people thought it meant intermarriage; when he said "black power," he was vaguer but still sure: "When I say Black Power, I know exactly what I'm talking about. But the white man runs up to me and says, 'Black Power: that means violence, doesn't it?' I refuse to react to that. I know what I'm talking about. If the white man doesn't know what I'm talking about, that's his problem, because black people understand me and that is who I'm talking to anyway" (*Post,* 56). Cleaver never defines black power or analyzes it; the picture of Stokely Carmichael as contrasted with the image of the older, "white controlled" blacks is what matters. This lack of precision had always been a fault of the movement, as James Forman admitted: "The most radical definition of Black Power that we could give at the time was 'power for black people.' Thus the door was left open for opportunists to define the term in any manner they chose. . . . We were caught by not having our own revolutionary ideology together."[11]

On 17 February 1968, Huey Newton's birthday, Cleaver organized a large "Free Huey" rally at the Oakland Auditorium, very near the Alameda County Jail, where Huey was being held. Eldridge and Bobby Seale demanded and got $600 from the Peace and Freedom party for airfare and expenses, and flew to Washington, D.C., to persuade Stokely Carmichael to speak (*Seize,* 217). H. Rap Brown and James Forman, also of SNCC, were invited as well. The intent was to extend the SNCC liaison beyond the rally into a permanent alliance. Seale writes, "So we decided that if they all accepted the ten-point platform and program, we'd make Stokely Carmichael the Honorary Prime Minister, James Forman the Minister of Foreign Affairs, and brother Rap Brown the Minister of Justice of the Black Panther Party. We thought that would give us a good group of black revolutionary leaders to unify the black liberation struggle across the country" (*Seize,* 221). Seale uses the term *alliance,* but Forman noted that Cleaver had referred to the *merger* of the two organizations, to Forman's surprise and dismay, when he introduced Forman at the Free Huey rally and again at a meeting of the leadership of both groups in July 1968 (Forman, 531, 534). This confusion and the crossed lines of communication were to remain. After only a few months, these factors, as well as "deep-seated, neurotic, egotistical power drives on the part of many people," destroyed "the working alliance" between the two groups (Forman, 537).

Blacks and the Land

The early 1968 essay, "The Land Question and Black Liberation," provides an introduction to the concept of black Americans as a colonized people within the "mother country," the United States. While the idea was attacked at the time as being an inappropriate and false analogy, in fact it was very appealing to many young black and white radicals. Its primary value lay in the emphasis it placed on America as an imperialistic power not only in its desire to establish hegemony abroad but in its control of Third World colonies along European lines.

That America's African "colonists" were imported into the United States and subsequently granted citizenship was seen by Cleaver and his sympathizers as far less important than the exploitation and oppression of an easily identifiable racial group that was locked into the lowest caste. Further, the analogy allowed radical blacks to see themselves as Third World revolutionaries like Fanon's Algerians, whose dominant psychological need was for violent self-assertion, or even Che's underclass Cubans and Bolivians, seizing the land from the upper-class oppressor.

The powerful concept, then, of blacks as a separate, non-American nation within the United States makes black power "a projection of sovereignty. . . . Black Power says to black people that it is possible for them to build a national organization on somebody else's land" (*Post,* 67). This "government in exile," founded antecedent to the obtaining of land somewhere else, wherein the nation would then "set the government and the people down on the land" (68), is seen as analogous to Theodore Herzl's National Jewish Congress, as unlike any urban guerrilla movement as one can imagine an organization to be. The Jewish analogy was later dropped when Panthers realized that Zionist sympathies were inherently anti-Arab, hence antirevolutionary (especially, anti-Algerian) and anti–Third World, or procolonialist, according to leftist teaching. It was the Muslim world with which the Panthers had to align themselves, as Cleaver later understood perfectly, writing in Algiers.

Cleaver's juxtaposition of leaders like Herzl, Robert Williams, and Che Guevara reveals an eclectic approach to nationhood based on a hodgepodge plan in which a different behavioral model is offered for each facet of the black experience. In essence, it is suggested that blacks overcome oppression by "picking up the gun" in a generally antiestablishment and antigovernment movement that will include urban guerrilla warfare as well as battling the Klan in more rural settings. When enough power has been asserted, the Afro-American nation must then take part in "a U.N. supervised plebiscite in the ghettos" (70), which will determine whether or not they want membership in the United Nations. Presumably they will, but at what point the "government in exile" will be selected and how is not specified; nor does Cleaver deal with the all-important question of racial unity, an issue he had previously ranked as vital.

The essay, which has begun with a discussion of the importance of land, ends merely with a discussion of conflict. Finally, the central

point is to express the anger and resentment of Cleaver and his radical
followers toward the United States:

So we are now engaged openly in a war for the national liberation of Afro-
America from colonial bondage to the white mother country. In our epoch,
guerrilla warfare is the vehicle for national liberation all around the world.
That it would soon come to America could have been predicted. The spirit has
always been there. Only the racist under-estimation of the humanity of black
people has blinded America to the potential for revolutionary violence of Afro-
America. Nat Turner, Gabriel Prosser and Denmark Vesey, black men who led
the most successful slave rebellions in North America, are the spiritual fathers
of today's urban guerrillas. (*Post*, 70)

In order to bring this situation about, black men know that they must pick
up the gun, they must arm black people to the teeth, they must organize an
army and confront the mother country with a most drastic consequence if she
attempts to assert police power over the colony. If the white mother country is
to have victory over the black colony, it is the duty of black revolutionaries to
insure that the Imperialists receive no more than a Pyrrhic victory, written in
the blood of what America might have become. (*Post*, 72)

"Revolution in the White Mother Country and National Liberation in
the Black Colony" is a shortened version of "The Land Question" tail-
ored to a white radical audience—specifically, the Peace and Freedom
Party Foundation Convention in Richmond, California, on 16 March
1968. Here, Cleaver melds elements of the ideas just quoted with the
basic concept of "The White Race and Its Heroes," the radicalization of
young white Americans. He writes, "Ideally, we need a revolutionary
organization that is able, guided by a revolutionary ideology and comprehending the necessity involved, to move in two directions at the
same time. We are here tonight because we believe that the Peace and
Freedom Party is the beginning of the answer to one half of this
equation and that the Black Panther Party is the beginning of the
answer to the other half."[12] Interestingly, the Panther association with
the Peace and Freedom party came about quite by chance, as a part of
Cleaver's effort to free Huey Newton from prison, and not out of a
desire by Cleaver to create a broader political base for himself (Art
Kunkin, "Peace and Freedom Chooses Candidates," *Los Angeles Free
Press*, 2 August 1968, 1). According to Earl Anthony, it was Eldridge's
idea to use the Peace and Freedom party sound truck that first brought
about contact between the two groups in December 1967 (Anthony,

58). Soon, he had convinced the white radicals to donate both the truck and $3,000 to the Free Huey movement in exchange for Black Panther help in encouraging ghetto blacks to register to vote as Peace and Freedom party members, guaranteeing the party a place on the ballot in the fall 1968 general elections. At the time, the Panthers demanded further concessions: that the local Peace and Freedom party candidates would include Kathleen Cleaver, Bobby Seale, and Huey Newton; that the Peace and Freedom party would support the Panther demand for a United Nations plebiscite; and that the party would support the Panther request for U.N. observers to come into the ghetto and oversee the actions of police. [13]

In a separate speech delivered at that conference and published by the Black Panther Party Ministry of Information as a "Black Paper," Cleaver offered his arguments as to why the Peace and Freedom party should run Huey in particular. In his usual hyberbolic manner, Cleaver presented the alternatives as Huey or obliteration even unto symbolic death: "If the candidacy of Huey P. Newton becomes a stumbling block to the Peace and Freedom Party, then its attempts to radicalize the political arena will clearly become a failure—and its attempt to practice its principles will fall flat on its face, leaving the Peace and Freedom Party to fall into the same pit of cynicism, hypocrisy, and decadence of the Democratic and Republican Parties. It would be an admission of the inability of whites to change their pattern of oppression and exploitation and an invitation to certain destruction"[14]. With Newton's congressional candidacy, as well as the lesser assembly candidacies of Kathleen Cleaver and Seale, secure before the primary in June, Cleaver could approve of the coalition that would form the one vital revolutionary organization he wanted to see: "We believe that henceforth the form of cooperation between revolutionary forces in the mother country and those in the colony must be on a coalition basis. We believe that all black colonial subjects should be members of the Black Panther Party, and that all American citizens should be members of the Peace and Freedom Party. We invite other oppressed and colonized people in America to organize themselves and to join our coalition as equal partners" ("Revolution," 13–14). The remainder of the short speech explains that while the Panthers intend to use their feeble "papier-mâché right to vote" to help the Peace and Freedom party, which will one day "argue for our position within the Senate and House of Representatives, the State Legislatures, and the city councils" (15), their "primary task" remains "to organize black people for national liberation" (14). In that work, the black plebiscite is currently the

"major political objective," in consideration of which fact the "land
question" will be held "in abeyance" (15). Paraphrasing Kwame Nkrumah of Ghana, Cleaver declared, "Seek ye first the political kingdom,
and all other things shall be added unto you" (15). To run Huey Newton
is to seek that kingdom, and by seeking it to "obliterate the difference"
between politics and the revolution. Perhaps Cleaver hoped an inatten-
tive enemy wouldn't notice, and would vote Newton into office.

A Short-lived Fame

On 28 February 1968, only 11 days after the Newton rally, *Soul on Ice*
appeared, and Cleaver immediately became a celebrity. The book was
soon to sell more than a million copies and be named Book of the Year
by the *New York Times*. Its success made manifest the possibility of
Cleaver's becoming a leading black spokesman of the day, one who
could have been as controversial as he wished, so long as he avoided
overt political activity, and never have been in legal difficulty. As
Robert Scheer points out in his introduction to *Post-Prison Writing and
Speeches*, "Had Cleaver not joined the Panthers, he would have had it
made. In America it is possible to be angry and remain safe—in fact,
anger is even desirable in a writer so long as it is diffuse and inactive; it
can make him entertaining and therefore marketable" (*Post,* xiii). In
becoming an active and committed revolutionary when he joined the
Panthers one year before *Soul on Ice* was published, Cleaver unwittingly
gave up all future security. Of course, he had no idea how important
and popular he would become, and so his forsaking of the talk-show/
cocktail-circuit fame of the best-selling author was not a conscious one.
When he first met Newton and the Panthers, they filled a need in him
that nothing else could have done—certainly not a bland career as a
Ramparts contributing editor. Unlike some other decisions, this one
was irrevocable, leading as it did to inevitable confrontations with
police, the California Adult Authority, and even then-governor Ronald
Reagan. Cleaver was already caught up in the events that would lead to
even greater political involvement, and thence forward, or at least so it
seemed, to either exile or death.

Panther speakers besides Eldridge were in heavy demand after February, too. It was, as Cleaver had declared, "The Year of the Panther"
(*Post,* 78). The popularity of the party led to the hasty formation of
chapters in major cities. And with the blossoming of Panther influence
grew the intensity of police anger and fear.

The Cleaver apartment had been raided in January (*Seize*, 227); the Seales had been arrested in their apartment by police early one morning in February. In addition, around the middle of March, when the Peace and Freedom party held its foundation convention, Seale received a call from Cleaver to meet him at his office. Seale recalls,

I went over to Ramparts, and they took me into a room. There was a white girl standing there. Eldridge said, "Tell Bobby what you told me." She ran down to me that she had been sitting in a bar and heard two cops talking about the Black Panther Party. One was saying that on April 2 they would have something for us. They said they were going to get rid of all the Panthers. I asked her if that was all she heard. She ran down some other things they had talked about, mostly negative things about the Panther Party. She said they went over April 2 again, and talked about doing the Panther Party in. I looked at Eldridge and we walked out of the office.

"What do you think, man?" he asked me.

"Man, they're going to try and attack us," I said. I asked him if this chick was reliable. Eldridge thought she was pretty reliable, so we knew we'd have to check it out. (*Seize*, 228)

The increasing paranoia was fed by (a) a black ex-policeman who also assured Seale that the police were planning to dispose of the Panther problem and (b) notes to Seale that purported to be from someone in the sheriff's department and that insisted, "You're going to get it" (*Seize*, 228).

Perhaps in an effort to seem more formidable than he felt, Cleaver insisted to a reporter with whom he was listening to a Huey Newton radio interview on 21 March that the Free Huey movement was gathering strength. He appeared to credit Carmichael's presence in Africa with what he claimed was a Free Huey rally in Tanzania, as well as the issuance of "public statements" from both Kwame Nkrumah and Sekou Toure "to the effect that Huey should be set free." These events, Cleaver said, indicated a world awareness of "the pivotal nature of the case" ("Huey from Jail," *Los Angeles Free Press*, 22 March 1968, 6).

Expecting a mass attack of some sort, perhaps on the headquarters and the apartments of individuals simultaneously, the Panthers amassed guns. Following the raids on the Cleaver and Seale apartments, Newton issued "Executive Mandate 3" on 1 March, ordering all members "to acquire guns" to be able to defend their homes, or face expulsion if they failed. Seale recommended that each home have "a shotgun, a .357 magnum, and a .38 pistol" (*Seize*, 236).

At the end of March, actor Marlon Brando reportedly visited the Cleavers in their apartment so that he could find out for himself what the Panthers and the Free Huey movement were all about. His contact with the party was Hakim Jamal, who had escorted Betty Shabazz to San Francisco in February. According to Cleaver, "We [the Panthers and Marlon Brando] had to wade through the history of the world before everything was placed in proper perspective and Brando could see where the Black Panther Party was coming from." Brando left on 1 April, after accompanying Seale to court (*Post,* 11).

When Brando saw the Panthers again, it was at Bobby Hutton's memorial tribute on Good Friday, 19 April (Anthony, 112). Martin Luther King had been assassinated on 4 April, and two days later Hutton and Cleaver had been involved in a shoot-out with the Oakland police that left Hutton dead and Cleaver wounded, traumatized, and imprisoned.

Chapter Four
Post-Prison Writings and Speeches:
The Year of the Panther

Although the assassination of Martin Luther King stunned all of America, the reaction in the black ghettos was both more extreme and more complex. Whereas to the older and more pacifist Christian blacks, King's death was a severe blow, to the younger, more militant, pro-Panther blacks, it was a guilt-producing experience as well. King had represented to them the father figure against whom they had to rebel and at whom they had to rage; they needed to mock and even scorn him for his nonviolent tactics and to blame him for the slow pace at which the black condition improved. They spoke of "getting rid" of him even before Cleaver reported remarks to that effect in Chicago more than a year before King's death. But they knew King had courage, and they saw him go to prison more than a dozen times while they sat on the sidelines and criticized. They didn't really want their "wish" to come true, and when King died, they felt guilt and sorrow for having denied him, as much as they felt grief over his death and anger at the entire white world because some white man (there was never any suggestion that the killer could be black) had killed what they knew was one of the best the race had to offer.

Cleaver's reaction, dictated two days later, on 6 April 1968, into the machine at his *Ramparts* office, was characteristically outspoken. "The Death of Martin Luther King: Requiem for Nonviolence" declares "that Doctor King would have to die was a certainty," because he had alienated both radicals and conservatives. Even so, King's death signaled the end of "a period of history . . . a hope, and . . . a dream. That white America could produce the assassin of Dr. Martin Luther King is looked upon by black people—and not just those identified as black militants—as a final repudiation by white America of any hope of reconciliation, of any hope of change by peaceful and non-violent means. So that it becomes clear that the only way for black people in this country to get the things that they want—and the things that they have a right to and that they deserve—is to meet fire with fire" (*Post,* 74). The fire will also bring in "a new and bloody chapter" in the nation's history, "a holocaust" in which America "will be painted red."

A second section contemplates placing the blame for the "gun against gun" situation that has brought "the dreadful days that we all somehow knew were coming . . . cascad[ing] down on us immediately, and the dreadful hours that we thought were years away . . . immediately upon us. And all eternity is gone, blown away, washed away in the blood of martyrs" (*Post,* 75–76). Both blacks and "millions of white people" repudiate the "political gangsters" that could have made things right and made King's death unnecessary. Then "nonviolence would prevail and the terror would not be upon us" (*Post,* 76). While "the Establishment or the power structure" represented by police, both political parties, and the government may be the "symbols of blame," in reality "Babylon" itself has allowed injustice to exist. "The blame is everywhere and nowhere" (*Post,* 77). Because every black person is now a Black Panther in spirit, this will be "The Year of the Black Panther . . . no doubt of that" (*Post,* 78).

Section 3 is brief because Cleaver broke off in the first paragraph. Words, he had been saying, are irrelevant; "action is all that counts now" (78). He ended, "I think that America is incapable of understanding anything relevant to human rights. I think that America has already committed suicide and we who now thrash within its dead body are also dead in part and parcel of the corpse. America is truly a disgusting burden upon this planet. A burden upon all humanity. And if we here in America . . ." (78–79). The phone rang, calling Cleaver away to a Panther emergency from which he almost failed to return.

In his "Affidavit #1: I Am 33 Years Old," written on 19 April in Vacaville Prison, about 50 miles from Oakland, Cleaver said, "I am convinced I was marked for death that night" (*Post,* 12). The first affidavit, however, only concludes with a mention of the incident with the police; it is in essence a brief autobiographical summary of how Cleaver became a Panther as a result of his desire to go straight, to leave the life of crime that characterized his youth and dedicate himself first to working for his race through the Black Panther party and then to getting Huey Newton out of jail, all much to the dissatisfaction of the police and his parole board. His actual account of the events of 6 April is found in "Affidavit #2: Shootout in Oakland."

Even here, Cleaver does not explain who called him with a message of such urgency that he abandoned his King article and went to Oakland; much later, *Rolling Stone* revealed that the call had come from Panther Warren Wells, warning of a police raid. The Panthers had been expecting an attack on 2 April, in line with the warnings received from the two unnamed informants. Now a black male, perhaps an FBI agent who was part of the Counterintelligence program directed against black activists (COINTELPRO), showing the badge of a San Francisco police officer, had walked into headquarters on Grove Street and told the Panthers present that "the Oakland and Emeryville [an Oakland suburb] police are gonna hit you. There's gonna be a raid on your office— soon."[1]

Cleaver reportedly decided to disperse all arms to Panther residences around the city and, accordingly, loaded the weapons into the trunks of three cars, along with food and other supplies for the fund-raiser barbecue the next day. Later, while the police claimed that the Panthers' purpose had been to shoot and kill cops, the Panthers would insist they were only transporting picnic supplies to the home of David Hilliard, a leading Black Panther (45).

The Shoot-out

When we come to the events of the night of 6 April, Cleaver is already in a car and driving to the home of David Hilliard, who chaired the party when Cleaver was in exile and Newton and Seale both in jail. Cleaver mentions that his passengers were Hilliard and two other Panthers, John Scott of San Francisco and Wendell Wade. But Wade specifies that Bobby Hutton rode in "the middle front seat" between Cleaver and himself.[2] Two other Panther cars, carrying 10 more Panthers, including Warren Wells, were following in a caravan, all heavily armed.

Accounts of the evening vary widely, and those of the Panthers, uniformly assigning to Cleaver the responsibility for their being armed and cruising around looking to get into trouble with the "pigs," were all repudiated once they were out on bail. Wendell Wade, in fact, who had declared Cleaver and Hilliard's destination to be a Panther house at 3421 Chestnut in Oakland, a place apparently used as an arms stash, said he was there waiting at the appointed hour, 8:00 P.M., and met up with the Panther caravan. Panther Terry Coton places Cleaver and Hilliard at another Panther rented house at 1478 Adeline Street, near Thirty-fourth Street, at 8:00, saying it was Cleaver's idea that they all arm themselves with any of a selection of available guns and go on

patrol. Cleaver claims that he was not armed, since he was on parole
and Newton had forbidden him to carry any guns for that reason.

According to Cleaver, he had halted his car in order to relieve himself
in the street, and had ducked to the curb when he saw the headlights of
the approaching police car. According to the police, they saw a "figure
crouching down behind a parked automobile with Florida plates"[3] and
got out to investigate. Actually, Cleaver contends, the car, a 1961
white Ford that was a gift from a white sympathizer, was well known to
the Oakland police, who constantly used the out-of-state plates "as a
pretext for stopping the car" (*Post,* 85). For that reason, Cleaver usually
drove the car, because he had "good" identification: in addition to a
valid driver's license, he possessed a "draft card, social security card,
and a variety of press cards from [his] job at *Ramparts* magazine" (85).
He contends that the police knew whose car it was and that they had
followed the caravan in order to harass the Panthers, who were still
waiting for the threatened onslaught of 2 April.

Cleaver says he hurried to finish urinating before returning to the
middle of the street from curbside:

Common sense told me that I'd best have my hands up by the time I cleared
the front of my car. But before I cleared, the cop on the passenger side of his
car started shouting and firing his gun, and then the other cop started shooting. I am not sure they were shooting at me because the lights from their car
were shining brightly at me, blocking my vision. But the explosions from
their guns sounded right in my face and so, startled, I dove for cover in front of
my car. The Panthers in the other two cars started yelling at the cops and
honking their horns and getting out of their cars, and the brothers who were in
my car scrambled out of the passenger side.

Above my head, the windshield of my car shattered and I looked behind
me. There was another cop car at the other end of the street, from which shots
were also being fired at us. In fact, shots seemed to be coming from everywhere; it sounded like the entire block had erupted with gunfire. It took only
a split second to see that they had us in a cross fire, so I shouted to the
brothers, "Scatter! Let's get out of here!" (87–88)

The police insisted that they were fired on first and that they had no
idea who was in any of the cars (they list four cars, as opposed to
Cleaver's three: besides the 1961 Ford, a 1951 Ford [some say this was
a 1954 Ford, actually], an Austin Healey, and a Toyota [Otis, 29]). But
in Wendell Wade's affidavit he specifies, "We left the Toyota up in
Berkeley" (Otis, 34). This discrepancy indicates that the police knew

which cars ought to have been on the scene, and Officers Darnell and Jensen didn't check very carefully when they wrote their report. It is certain that many rounds were fired and that within moments, Cleaver and Bobby Hutton (called Little Bobby, to distinguish him from Bobby Seale) were holed up in a walk-in basement under a frame house at 1218 Twenty-eighth Street, just off the corner of Union.

Thus began a siege that Cleaver says can be called a shoot-out only because Bobby Hutton was armed. Later, an AR-15, an M-14, and a 9-mm Browning were found in the basement, according to police. The siege began at 9:07 and lasted until 10:30. The other Panthers were quickly rounded up as they scattered; Hilliard made it as far as a bedroom of the house next door, but the residents turned him in.

During the next hour and a half, the walls of the basement above the 18-inch foundation were riddled with bullet holes, some reportedly an inch wide. Cleaver says, "It was like being the Indians in all the cowboy movies I had ever seen" (*Post,* 89). After a half-hour, the tear gas began, and Cleaver, starting to move a board over against the wall, was struck in the chest by a tear gas canister. Hutton removed all his clothes, Cleaver says, so that he could feel for blood in the dark and know where Cleaver was wounded. Then the bullets began again. "The material we had stacked along the wall was blown away by what sounded like machine gun fire" (90). When he was wounded in the leg and foot, Cleaver began to say good-bye to his new life, first to his wife Kathleen and then to the cheering crowds in the auditoriums all over the Bay Area. When Little Bobby broke in, asking, "What are we going to do?" Cleaver reports,

I felt an impotent rage at myself because all I could tell him was to keep his head down, that head with its beautiful black face which I would watch a little later, again powerless, as the mad dogs outside blasted him into eternity. Was it in cold blood? It was in the coldest of blood. It was murder. MUR-DER! . . . All [Little Bobby] asks, all Huey asks, all I ask, is what Che Guevara asked:

> Wherever Death may surprise us
> It will be welcome, provided that
> This, our battle cry, reach some
> Receptive ear; that another hand
> Reach out to pick up the gun, that
> Other fighting men come forward
> To intone our funeral dirge

> To the staccato of machine gun fire
> And new cries of battle and victory.
> (91–92)

The police firebombs ended the siege. Cleaver and Hutton threw out "the rifle" and left the cellar, hands raised, as "an army of pigs" ran to them. In the final paragraph of his affidavit, Cleaver writes, "Having been spared my life, I don't want it. I give it back to our struggle. Eldridge Cleaver died in that house on 28th Street, with Little Bobby, and what's left is force: fuel for the fire that will rage across the face of this racist country and either purge it of its evil or turn it into ashes" (94).

Both Gene Marine (*The Black Panthers,* 1969) and Don A. Schanche (*The Panther Paradox,* 1970) feel certain that the Panthers were not looking for a fight on 6 April, although they may well have been on one of their customary patrols. Marine points out that with Seale and Newton both in jail (Seale on the conspiracy-to-commit-murder charge stemming from the 25 February raid on his apartment) and with the two most important free Panthers, Cleaver and Hilliard, along for the ride, the Panthers could not risk a violent confrontation. He believes, however, that a black officer who may have been a double agent and who was perhaps the original informer, could have been at the 8:00 P.M. meeting, which Marine places at 3421 Chestnut, not Adeline Street. Panthers, some armed, did leave that meeting, but it is doubtful, Marine feels, that there were fantastic plans for them to provoke an incident in the ghetto near Berkeley and then activate a "telephone chain" that would bring white radicals pouring into the ghetto to start a riot, as the police claimed (Marine, 139). The absurdity of the "riot" story is underlined by Schanche, who emphasizes the peacekeeping role the Panthers had played since King's assassination on the fourth (*Paradox,* 59). Other major cities, notably Chicago and Washington, D.C., had burned, but San Francisco, Oakland, and Los Angeles had not, and the Panthers took full credit for that. It was Huey Newton's contention that such action was prompted by emotion and would lead not to the revolution but only to the deaths of hundreds of ghetto residents (Anthony, 104).

Robert Scheer saw Cleaver not long after his arrest: "Cleaver, who was wounded in the leg, was first taken to Oakland's Highland Hospital; then to the Alameda County Courthouse where the police made him lie on the floor while he was being booked; and finally, that same night, to San Quentin Hospital where a guard pushed him down a flight of stairs. He was brought to the State Medical Facility at Vacaville and confined in the 'hole' " (*Post,* xviii–xix). There were still five years left on his old sentence when Cleaver's parole was revoked by the California Adult Authority as a result of the events of 6 April. Listed as parole violations were possession of firearms, associating with individuals of bad reputation, and failing to cooperate with the parole officer.

Lawyer Charles Garry, arguing before the Solano County judge, Raymond J. Sherwin, managed to free Cleaver after two long months, during which Cleaver was certain he would never be a free man again. Garry persuaded Sherwin that Cleaver had handled a gun only once, in obedience to a police command, when he threw Hutton's gun out of the cellar; that Cleaver had no way of knowing whether all the people he was with had arrest records or convictions; and that he had not failed to report to his parole officer at any time, for he said he did telephone when he returned from taping "The David Susskind Show" in New York (*Post,* xix–xx). Although Cleaver was charged with three counts of attempted murder of a police officer and three counts of assault on a police officer, he was presumed innocent of these charges until proved guilty. Sherwin saw no valid reason to revoke his parole, and the writ of habeas corpus was granted.

Cleaver was released on 12 June 1968, six days after the assassination of Robert Kennedy. He was out on $50,000 bail, raised by friends and sympathizers. *Ramparts* editor Ed Keating, who picked him up at Vacaville, put up his house as part of the collateral for the bail bond. But the respite was brief. The appellate court moved to reverse Judge Sherwin's decision, and the state supreme court upheld. On 27 September, the same day that Huey Newton was sentenced to 2 to 15 years for his role in the death of Officer Frey on 27 October 1967, Cleaver was ordered to return to jail, his parole re-revoked, in 60 days.

Open Letter to Ronald Reagan

While at Vacaville, Cleaver kept writing, notably, on 13 May, his "Open Letter to Ronald Reagan." The letter commences with a tone of irony and sarcasm, with a barely restrained bitterness beneath, and maintains that voice until the final paragraph, with the exception of a few lapses into street language that allow the author's anger to flash through.

Cleaver opens by noting that he writes neither to seek mercy nor to complain but only to "call to [Reagan's] attention" the fact that "certain persons . . . have conspired to violate [Cleaver's] rights" and are holding him as "a political prisoner." He comments, "As the Chief Executive of the State of California, I thought you might want to know what the people whom you have appointed to the California Adult Authority have done" (*Post,* 95). It is to be hoped that Reagan will recognize his responsibility to ensure that his agencies not violate citizens' rights, and will "look into the matter" concerning Cleaver.

There follows a summary of Cleaver's postprison activities that emphasizes his desire to do something to help black people: "While in prison I decided that, upon my release, I would find a way to relate to the struggle of my people for a better life, to plunge myself into that struggle and contribute of myself what I possessed that could be used, without reservation: my life, my fortune, and my sacred honor which, through my struggles to survive the soul-murder of my stay in prison, I found" (97). It was the Black Panther party that offered the clearest opportunity for Cleaver to "pledge" himself, with them, like the first American revolutionaries, to the cause of freedom. His conscious echo of Jefferson's famous conclusion to the Declaration of Independence (memorized by all Panthers) was intended to underscore their image of themselves as true revolutionaries. He "quickly joined," only to be warned by his parole agent that certain politicians in Sacramento disapproved: "It was his advice that if I wanted to be successful on parole, I be cool. Be cool? For nine long years I had been on ice. Shit. I was being cool. In fact I was still thawing out, trying to warm up, so that I could really do my thing. Besides, legality was on my side. As for politicians, I was one myself" (98). Cleaver's job as minister of information of the Black Panther party was to spread the word about many problems in society, the most immediate and pressing of them being the freedom of Huey Newton.

Cleaver mentions the Peace and Freedom party coalition (but omits SNCC) and condemns the "notorious, oppressive, racist and brutal Oakland Police Department" (101), a "gestapo force" that is like "a sword buried in the heart of the people. The Black Panther Party intended to remove that sword" (102). He blames the "paranoid, fantastic notion" of the Oakland Police Department that "the Black Panther Party *might* try to invade the jail and rescue Cleaver" for having created a sense of "panic" in the California Adult Authority, leading to the decision, at 4:00 A.M. the morning after the shoot-out, to revoke his parole. He lists and refutes each parole violation claimed and concludes with a familiar prophecy of destruction:

The bottom of the world is in motion, Governor, and Bobby Dylan's "empty handed beggar" is at the door, except that his hand is not empty any more. He's got a gun in that hand. And he's stopped begging. In fact, he's nearly stopped talking, because it's becoming clear to him that hardly anybody is listening. When he finally stops talking altogether, he is going to start shooting. This brings to a conclusion what I wanted to talk to you about, and I have nothing else to say, except one question: Have you been listening to me, Governor?

Respectfully submitted,
Eldridge Cleaver
Minister of Information
Black Panther Party
(106–7)

"The Fire Now"

At Vacaville Cleaver also wrote an essay published in *Commonweal* in June 1968 (not included in *Eldridge Cleaver: Post-Prison Writings and Speeches*). The title, "The Fire Now," is an allusion to Baldwin's 1963 title, *The Fire Next Time,* which in turn refers to a black gospel tune with the words "God sent Noah a rainbow sign; no more water, the fire next time." The subtitle of Cleaver's essay, "Field Nigger Power Takes Over the Black Movement," provides the thesis: that the death of Martin Luther King has signaled the end of middle-class black control of the movement and that the street blacks, the masses, are now ready to assume control. This "new Black leadership," which is not identified until the last page of the three-page essay, is now on "center stage," and it would be useless for white America to ignore it, Cleaver says.

It is futile and suicidal for white America to greet this new leadership with a political ostrich response. What white America had better do is find out what these leaders want for black people and then set out to discover the quickest possible way to fulfill their demands. The alternative is war, pure and simple, and not just a race war, which in itself would destroy this country, but a guerrilla war which will amount to a second civil war, with thousands of white new-John-Browns fighting on the side of the blacks, plunging America into the depths of its most desperate nightmare, on the way to realizing the American Dream.[4]

Cleaver's version of the previous 63 years of black struggle sees the current leadership as the culmination and end product of an evolutionary development that began with Booker T. Washington's "genuflecting leadership," epitomized by his "notorious sell-out speech at the Atlantic [sic] Exposition in 1896" (375).

Actually, Washington spoke at the Atlanta Exposition in Georgia in 1895, not quite but almost in the "same historic breath" with which the Supreme Court made the concept of separate but equal "the law of the land" in 1896. Du Bois and the organization he helped to found, the NAACP, says Cleaver, dissented from the status quo and initiated protest "as the new posture of blacks toward white America," a policy that "held sway until 1954," when the concept of separate but equal was declared unconstitutional. At this point, says Cleaver, protest became "outmoded," but since "a new prevailing leadership had not yet defined itself," a "transitional leadership" was supplied, incredibly, by both Martin Luther King and Malcolm X, with only the latter laying "the foundation of the new leadership that would succeed him and King" (375). Cleaver's thoroughly contemporary conviction that 1968 revolutionary activism was the zenith of black social development led to an arrogant and condescending dismissal of King's life: "As far as the willingness of the white power structure to deal with black leadership goes, Martin Luther King, and the type of leadership he personified, held sway from the launching of the Montgomery Bus Boycott in 1956 down to our own day, when the vestigial remains of leadership from King's transitional era are still frantically trying to cling to power. In reality their leadership is just as dead as that of the lieutenants of Booker T. Washington at the end of their era" (375–76). As in *Soul on Ice,* Cleaver uses Malcolm's distinction between the "house nigger" and the "field nigger" to explain varied black viewpoints: "In the vernacular of the ghetto, King had House Nigger Power and Malcolm had Field Nigger Power. What we have now entered, then, is an era in which Field Nigger Power and the grievances and goals of the Field Nigger— and the leadership of Field Niggers—will dominate the black movement for justice in America" (376). The assumptions here are manifold, and all of them operate to flatter the more radical of black activists, making their "day" seem inevitable and right, while discounting the influence of King and other less aggressive blacks.

First, as Cleaver explains in the next paragraph, King's constituency, like King himself, was seen as "close to the slavemaster" and living better than other blacks, who were on a "subsistence diet" and had to work hard all day. The assumption that the black clergy did not genuinely represent or care for the black masses is difficult to accept when one recalls King's long list of arrests and his stoning in Cicero, Illinois. If any group or individual could be regarded as out of touch with the black masses, it would be Du Bois, a radical college professor who earned his Ph.D. from Harvard in the same year that Booker T. Washington accepted civic inferiority for blacks in Atlanta. Unlike Washington, who devoted his life to helping "field niggers" become tradesmen rather than sharecroppers, Du Bois was interested above all in the "Talented Tenth," the top 10 percent of black youth who belonged in college so that they could form the leadership of the next generation. Cleaver knew the NAACP was essentially a conservative, proestablishment organization from the first, but his primary concern here is the communication of his emotions and biases.

The assassination of King meant to him, as his "Requiem for Nonviolence" indicates, a final rejection among all black people of the nonviolent road to equality. It follows that Cleaver does not assess the actual relevance of Washington or King to the black masses; he wishes only to reject their reformist, procapitalist positions in favor of those articulated by Du Bois and Malcolm X, which are more militant and anticapitalist. It is only with that intent that Cleaver could embrace such a non sequitur as the belief that Malcolm's followers should now have their day because of King's death, when in fact Malcolm had been dead three years ahead of King. Yet Cleaver says, "What we have entered, *then* [my italics]," as if a logical consequence were involved.

Similarly, he defines the Black Muslims as a "transitional organization," not because they are the heirs of Malcolm X, having not only expelled him but killed him, too, but on the grounds that they represented the "black masses" and began to speak with "the brothers on the block" when the "protest leaders" were still "chatting with Charlie [the white man]" (376). Again, assumptions are made, and the wished-for unity among blacks taken for granted, in Cleaver's description of the next step in the development of black thought. Omitting all mention of SNCC, he states that when black leaders began to address street blacks, "a decisive juncture had been reached, and blacks had seized control of their own destiny. A full ideological debate ensued." It is possible that "chatting with Charlie" is meant to refer to SNCC's reliance on the support of white students and faculty as well as the establishment-oriented politics of groups like the NAACP and the Urban League, in which case the ouster of whites from SNCC (an event in which Kathleen Neal reportedly had a role) was a significant part of the "full ideological debate," the "consensus" of which was "given to the world" when "young Stokely Carmichael leaped from obscure anonymity and shouted, with a roar of thunder, WE WANT BLACK POWER!" (376).

The "only question" black people have about black power, says Cleaver, is "how to get it." He points out what needs to be dealt with in society, from "massive" bad housing and "massive" unemployment to "injustices suffered by blacks in the courts," and proposes the preferred solution. "If the experience of other colonized people is relevant," he says, then it follows that Huey P. Newton's answers "must be dealt with." The "answer" is that "we must organize [the] destructive potential" of the black people in America and "inflict a political [i.e., violent] consequence upon the system" if demands are not met. A "frontal attack upon the system" must be launched so that the present "non-functional" system can be replaced by a "functional humanistic system that can guarantee a good life for everybody" (377).

Cleaver's position here, aside from the characteristically dramatic rhetoric, goes beyond a rejection of racism and oppression and rejects equal opportunity as well, in favor of a high minimum level of support from, presumably, a revolutionary socialist government. On the one hand, Cleaver argues that anyone "capable of working is entitled to a job," but on the other, he insists that if businesspeople can't fulfill "the needs of society" then "the economic system must be taken out of their hands and rearranged." Such, he declares, is the "eternal right of a free people," an apparent allusion to the Preamble of the Declaration of Independence, wherein is asserted the right of the governed to alter governments. In this case, national economies are identified with governments as part of the establishment from which blacks are excluded.

Is this solution workable? Cleaver imagines such a question to be dismissed by the next step in his argument: the Black Panther party can deal with problems effectively. "The viability of the Black Panther Party approach to solving problems is testified to by the fact that it has engineered two remarkable feats which constitute the foundation for a revolutionary movement that overlooks nothing, is afraid of nothing and is able to resolve the major contradiction of our time" (377). The exaggeration of Cleaver's remarks becomes clear when we see that the "two remarkable feats" are in fact the alliances with the Peace and Freedom party and SNCC, the latter effective only as of February 1968 and very precarious. Nonetheless, the resulting radical union has become "the key center of the eye of the storm," the most central of all positions, with the Black Panther party as the central organization among the three, allowing for communication between the other two parts of "the machinery" (377). Again Cleaver employs the "merger" terminology that so enraged James Forman in February: "The Black Panther Party, through its coalition with the Peace and Freedom Party and its merger with SNCC, has been the vector of communication between the most important vortexes of black and white radicalism in America." Such a "functional flexibility" is, of course, vital to any black leadership "in our era with national ambitions." The desirability of the image of a conduit between two whirlwinds is questionable; aside from the oddity of it, the result is that the Black Panther party attains a passive role. Further, the common secondary meaning of *vector* as a disease-carrying organism would seem to be unattractive and even counterrevolutionary in its connotations.

The relative casualness of the three-way alliance, which was in fact questioned by members of all three organizations, is not the greatest irony in the passage just quoted; rather, it is that Cleaver ridiculed and derided blacks who had joined the Peace and Freedom party on their own, insisting that they join only the Black Panther party, and further, that SNCC had only recently become an all-black organization, proud of its independence from white students. The Peace and Freedom party comprised those students who were arguably more radical than SNCC whites had been, but it is certain that many SNCC members did not see a union with them as a step forward. Finally, while Cleaver insisted that the Black Panther party alliance with the Peace and Freedom party was only "a working coalition," with each organization retaining its autonomy, he repeatedly referred to the alliance with SNCC as a "merger," arousing fears that the Black Panther party intended to usurp the leadership of SNCC. There was already a serious conflict between Carmichael and the Brown-Forman majority in SNCC, and there would eventually be a split between Carmichael and Cleaver.

None of this underlying conflict is relevant, though, to Cleaver. He concludes his essay by listing the SNCC officers who are now Panthers (Carmichael, Forman, and H. Rap Brown) and pointing out that Newton (only) is running for office on the Peace and Freedom party ticket. He recommends militant Robert F. Williams for the Peace and Free-

dom party presidential candidate, with a later footnote: "Since this was
written, the author has been selected for this office." (The issue is dated
14 June 1968; the Peace and Freedom Party National Convention in
Ann Arbor, Michigan, did not select Cleaver until 18 August, but
Cleaver had agreed in advance to run on the Peace and Freedom party
ticket in California.) What will happen, he declares, with the Black
Panther party in control, is nothing less than a new world, economically and socially, brought about, in the last analysis, by popularity:
"And America will be astounded by this fact: not only will this leadership bear a charismatic relationship to the black masses, but it also will
exercise charismatic leadership upon the white masses as well, and it
will reach down into the bowels of this nation, amongst its poor,
dispossessed and alienated, and it will set aflame a revolutionary wave
of change that will give America a birth of freedom that it has known
hitherto only in the dreams of its boldest dreamers. And it will kill,
once and for all, all the killers of the dream" (377). Just as Cleaver had
borrowed the concept of the American dream becoming an American
nightmare from Malcolm X, so he adapted the idea of the "killers" of
the dream of equality from a 1949 book entitled *Killers of the Dream,* by
Lillian Smith, a white southerner opposed to segregation.

The Liberal Response

We are fortunate to be able to gauge precisely the white liberal
response to Cleaver's threats and overstatements, for the same issue of
Commonweal included an excerpt from Father Philip Berrigan's statement in U.S. District Court in Baltimore "before his sentence to six
years in federal prison on charges of mutilating Selective Service files."[5]
Father Berrigan declared all of us (and especially his judges) to be
"judged" not only by God but by such heroes as "Jefferson, Washington, Madison, Thoreau, Emerson, Whitman and Twain. . . . I do not
hesitate to say," he declared, "that were these men alive today they
would disobey as I have disobeyed, and be convicted as I am convicted." Berrigan's list of radicals contains as many surprises as does
Cleaver's version of the history of black protest. While Thoreau and
even Twain might be considered active protesters by 1968 standards,
the degree to which revolutionaries like Jefferson and Washington
would be shocked by "our inhuman use of human beings, our racism,
our neglect of the poor, our courts in servitude to the war" is surely
questionable. In the sixties it was popular when discussing Jefferson,

for example, to emphasize his attempt to include a condemnation of slavery in the Declaration of Independence and to disregard his owner-ship of slaves, including several he had fathered, as well as his negative remarks about black people. And the full support of all the revolutionar-ies in 1776 was surely behind, not against, the "war machine." Their inclusion in a list of radicals who would be willing to face imprison-ment on a charge similar to Berrigan's is overreaching, involving as it does the obliteration of a number of distinctions between the issues of 1776 and 1968, for example. Reportedly, Emerson even found Tho-reau's short stay in jail incomprehensible!

Berrigan's list is based on a version of the American Revolution shared by liberal historians like Staughton Lynd of Yale, who was called to testify at the 1970 Chicago Seven trial but not permitted to do so. Tom Hayden, in his account of the trial, says Lynd noted a "peculiar resemblance" between Chicago 1968 and aspects of the Boston Massa-cre of March 1770.[6] One night "a group of townspeople surrounded a particular British sentry; according to Staughton, 'They called him 'lobsterback,' because of his red coat, a kind of eighteenth-century equivalent of 'pig.' They threw oyster shells and hunks of ice at him, and at a certain point, he called out the Guard.' Staughton continued: 'It seems to me that the jury might wish to consider the entire process of the [1968] demonstration as a kind of petitioning process in which people who felt that their elected government was no longer responsible to them, who felt themselves to be in the same position as the colonists before the American Revolution, came to Chicago to make one last direct appeal to the men of power who were assembled in the Demo-cratic convention' " (Hayden, 382–83). Such historical perspective made even riots seem less threatening and more traditionally American; a number of college and high school faculty drew similar analogies.

The *Commonweal* editors, having received both Cleaver's and Berri-gan's items, thought they "required quick publication" and, in an editorial entitled "Cleaver and Berrigan," evaluated the pieces. Neither writer is faulted on any point of fact, although Cleaver's "naked uncom-promising demand" for a revolution and the fulfillment of all black needs under a new order did give the editors pause: "Mr. Cleaver breaks the rules" (372). In the end, however, after pointing out that "the same tradition out of which Father Berrigan speaks has always made room for the legitimate, violent protest," they admit, "We have no good argu-ments for refuting Mr. Cleaver's reasoning; he has us, and every other white middle-class liberal who prefers the way of patience and nonviolent protest. We had better take up the peaceful option which he advances" (373).

These exhibits afford us an excellent picture of the states of mind of some of the most committed groups in American society at that time, others being the police, the FBI, and assorted conservatives who were appalled and terrified by the activists and dismayed and angered by the liberals. It was a time of polarization, to say the least. While the leftists were willing to face prison and even death for their convictions, J. Edgar Hoover and, it would seem, all major urban law enforcement agencies were willing to oblige them. The early years of the next decade were to be clear evidence of right-wing desire to destroy the leftist movement.

The New Black Prince

Cleaver's release on 12 June 1968 freed him for an intense summer and fall. He was traveling between the two coasts much of the time, even before the Peace and Freedom party officially nominated him for president in August, and was harassed continually by various members of the police. In *Soul on Fire* he reports, "I ended up one evening at a friend's house, and I wasn't there twenty minutes when the telephone rang. We looked at each other—this was a private, confidential meeting, we thought. The voice on the other end said, 'Hi Eldridge, just didn't want you to think that we had forgotten you.' Click. I was never forgotten" (99). Don F. Schanche spent some time on the road with Cleaver that summer, accompanying him on assignment much as Cleaver once did Stokely Carmichael. Dubbing Cleaver the "Tom Paine of the New Left,"[7] Schanche presented an essentially sympathetic portrait to *Saturday Evening Post* readers that fall. In his 1970 book, *The Panther Paradox,* he described his early attraction to Cleaver in terms that may help to explain some of Cleaver's appeal to guilt-ridden whites like himself in the "Year of the Panther": "While I was reading *Soul on Ice,* Dr. Martin Luther King was assassinated—I broke off reading the book to watch on television the mournful procession behind his mule-hauled death wagon. We desperately needed a new black prince" (*Paradox,* 6). Cleaver's prominence as an author, his angry and prophetic tone, and his personal charisma all made him the leading candidate for *the* black leader now that nonviolence appeared to be passé. King's death left a leadership void that could have been filled only by someone who could articulate the fury of black and white radicals, harangue the liberals, and look good on camera while doing so. It was undoubtedly this perception that had led Cleaver to announce the "field nigger" takeover of the black movement upon King's death.

Although Schanche felt ambivalent about meeting Cleaver because of the various encounters Cleaver had had with the police since the publication of *Soul on Ice,* not to mention his previous criminal record, most leftists found him credible precisely because of that reputation; Cleaver's outlaw status gave him legitimacy second only to that of Huey Newton.

Schanche's reaction to a Cleaver "campaign" speech is as intriguing as it was probably typical, for it helps to explain Cleaver's popularity on those campuses at which the Panther point of view was alien to the white middle-class students and in fact even called for the annihilation of such students. Schanche commented on Cleaver's build, "finely muscled and tapered like a funnel," and especially his green eyes, "as cool and impervious . . . as the steel bars of a prison," in an attempt to analyze the secret of Cleaver's charisma (9–10). About Cleaver he writes:

His platform presence was so much a matter of physical and oral style that it is literally impossible to convey the truth of it by recounting his speeches, because the verbal content of much of his "political" campaigning was so appalling that no person can read the words in cold print and believe that the man who uttered them did so in such an inoffensive way that they seemed not only believable but unprovocative. I know that many others reacted to this curious conflict of style and rhetoric as I did, finding the former endearing and dismissing the latter as so much tactical talk, not to be taken seriously. (67)

The content of the harangue, recounted by Schanche complete with the reactions of the crowd, is identical to every other known speech Cleaver made that fall, with local alterations excluded:

They told me it's against the law to curse in Omaha. I'm a Presidential candidate. I'm not going to bullshit and lie.
[appreciative applause]
My parole officer must have someone here listening to me. Well, . . . fuck my parole officer. Fuck the chief of police. Fuck the mayor. Fuck the governor. Fuck L.B.J. Fuck Hubert Humphrey. To all pigs of the power structure, I say, "Fuck you!"
[loud laughter and applause]
Do you know about the Kerner Commission Report? Somebody called it the white man's confession. It's not your confession, it's your indictment. And

we're going to prosecute you. For the murder of the people, you will receive
the death sentence . . . death!

[soft applause]

Someone asked me what my first act will be if I'm elected President and move
into the White House . . .

[laughter]

I'll burn the motherfucker down.

[loud laughter and heavy clapping] . . .

Now, all of you! You have to get into the political arena to articulate what's
going on here. Power to the people! Pick up the gun. Don't stand in the
middle wondering what to do. Be part of the solution!

[boisterous applause]

If the pig has his foot on my neck and you're standing there not sure whether
you're for him or for me, fuck you and fuck him. You're not doing me any
good. You're as bad as he is!

All I ask is what Che asked when he wrote:

> Wherever Death may surprise us
> It will be welcome, provided that
> This, our battle cry, reach some
> Receptive ear; that another hand
> Reach out to pick up the gun, that
> Other fighting men come forward
> To intone our funeral dirge
> To the staccato of machine gun fire
> And new cries of battle and victory.
> (68–70)

When he spoke at Stanford on 1 October, Cleaver added "Fuck Ronald
Reagan" several times in order to emphasize his revulsion for the governor who was determined not only to keep Cleaver from teaching a course
at Berkeley that fall, but also to get him back into prison. Cleaver's
parole had just been revoked again on 27 September, and the Panther
headquarters had been shot up by two drunken off-duty Oakland police
officers two weeks before that; his anger was thus understandable.

Cleaver spoke at Berkeley a week later, before beginning another
East Coast swing; he had made a few speeches in the East after the
abortive attempt by the Panthers to present their case to representatives
of Third World states at the United Nations. Most notably, he had
spoken at Syracuse University on 27 July, and the speech he made that
day was recorded and sold under the title "Dig" by the More Record

Company. Advertisements for the recording appeared frequently in the *Black Panther* throughout 1969 and 1970.

New York Area

Cleaver first arrived in the New York City area on 11 October 1968, and he gave two speeches on the same day. In the afternoon, he was driven with a Panther escort to a little Christian Brothers men's liberal arts school in New Rochelle called Iona College. While he was there, his speech was attended by local police, a state police investigator, and an FBI agent, James Gordan, all of whom later described the events to the Internal Security Subcommittee of the Senate Judiciary Committee, headed, as was the committee itself, by conservative Senator James O. Eastland of Mississippi. The hearings at which the various law enforcement officials testified were the subject of "The Extent of Subversion in Campus Disorders," the full text of which was published in June 1969. Cleaver's talk that afternoon, which was preceded by a shorter one given by Abbie Hoffman, was recounted as only one of a number of different surveillance operations. What Cleaver had to say was taped but barely mentioned in the testimony itself, since the important part was the identification of all those present who heard his and Hoffman's questionable remarks. Only one paragraph of Cleaver's is quoted in the report: "We say to Brother Mao Tse-Tung that we recognize what you've done, that you've liberated your people from imperialism and from colonialism. And we recognize you, Brother Ho Chi Minh, what you're doing. That you're trying to liberate your country from the imperialists and we want to bring the boys home."[8] A great deal more space is taken up in the report by the list of the 22 vehicles (and their descriptions and registrations) parked in the immediate area of Spellman Hall, the steps of which served as the podium for both talks to the spare audience of some 175 students. Also of importance to the officers and the senators were the names of all the members of the black organization UHURU (the Swahili word for "freedom") that was sponsoring Cleaver, as well as of the Students for a Democratic Society (SDS), the white cosponsor. Most radicals took it for granted that they were being watched at all times. As these hearings and their accompanying photographs indicate, Big Brother was indeed watching—and filming and taping.

Cleaver's evening speech, given to striking students at New York

University, was positively reviewed in the *Guardian* by a student reporter identified only by the initial M, who declared, "The totality of his presence is overwhelming. . . . Cleaver doesn't have a speech, and he doesn't know what he'll say until it's out. He just knows he's going back to jail in 44 days and there's nothing that can stop this. He's mad and has a lot of talking to do before it's over and he needs people; got to make it grow, be real, or he won't be able to take it" ("Cleaver Speaks at NYU Strike Rally," 19 October 1968, 6).

The next day, 12 October, Cleaver and Abbie Hoffman held a joint news conference at New York's Algonquin Hotel, where the free-spirited Hoffman "amazed" the intense Panthers by playing with a yo-yo while the reporters were busy with Cleaver. Liberation News Service reporter Mark Kramer questioned a "strident and smiling" Cleaver about James Farmer. Cleaver seized the opportunity to display his snide wit: "I call upon all the Toms to get off their knees, wipe the shoe polish off their mouths, and join the fight." Had his campaign illicitly received poverty funds? "I hope so. I hope Mao sends a box of money. I hope Ho sends money. I hope your mama sends a big box of money. [George] Wallace uses public money in his campaign. Only if we do it, it'll be like Robin Hood" ("Cleaver at the Algonquin Hotel," *Liberation News Service,* 12 October 1968, 8).

On 15 October, Cleaver spoke at Columbia, where the student newspaper, the *Daily Spectator,* had endorsed him for president. A radical reporter noted that "many students could hardly stop laughing" as Cleaver again offered to whip Reagan "with a marshmallow" and led the audience in a chorus of "Fuck [Dean Andrew] Cordier" (Morris Grossner, "Cleaver at Columbia," 16 October 1968, 13). Cleaver's popularity with the students was so well remembered that when *Esquire* magazine printed a special issue entitled "Shaping the Seventies" in December 1969, it featured Cleaver on the cover in a cap and gown and identified as president of Columbia University. In a mock *New York Times* article dated 3 November 1976, Cleaver, it was noted, "has declared amnesty for all white students." Cordier, dean of foreign studies in "1976," was the "last remaining white administrator" on a campus that included LeRoi Jones as chairman of drama, "Dr." H. Rap Brown as "Visiting Professor of African Culture," and Bobby Seale as dean of the Che Guevara School of Counter-Counter-Insurgency. The occasion was the occupation of Malcolm X Hall by "armed white students" demanding White Studies and open admission for non–

Third World students, a satirical warning of the shape of things that yet could (almost) be.

The only student problems Cleaver ever had with his speeches involved his use of the phrase "Pussy Power." When he urged movement women to use their influence politically at Columbia and Stanford, he felt a feminist backlash, although Schanche noted none in Omaha (*Paradox,* 69). Not only was the language itself objectionable, but the concept appeared to assume that men would make the revolution while women encouraged or even coerced them to do so, more or less like a reversal of Aristotle's *Lysistrata,* in which the women strike for peace. Cleaver had some trouble understanding the feminist stance on this issue and attributed dissatisfaction in his audiences to prudery. At Stanford he said, "I'm sorry for all the Victorians who have had their morals ruffled, but just sit still a minute and you'll come back to earth." Tell the "males," he said, not to write love letters or call until they have become "part of the solution." Threaten to "cut off their sugar. . . . And you can have them all running around here acting like Lenin, Mao Tse-Tung and Jerry Rubin" (*Post,* 143).

Berkeley

The Berkeley experience stood out from any other because of the total incompatibility of what was easily the most radical student body in the United States in 1968 and the man who was arguably one of the least liberal and reflective of governors. In September, Cleaver was invited to team-teach a one-semester course on racism in which Oakland police chief Charles Gain had also agreed to participate. The course, "Social Analysis 139X: Dehumanization and Regeneration in the American Social Order," was to have been worth five units of credit. Cleaver told Liberation News Service reporter Marlene Charyn that one lecture would "deal with the negative influences of grade B movies on the American mentality, using Mickey Mouse Reagan's career as a text" ("Cleaver Controversy at Berkeley," *Liberation News Service,* 24 September 1968, 7).

Ronald Reagan, an ex officio member of the university's board of regents, pressured the board to bar Cleaver. He compared Cleaver's appointment as a commentator on society with "asking that famous Bluebeard of Paris, the wife murderer, to be a marriage counselor."[9] Max Rafferty, the state superintendent of public instruction, went so far as to threaten the school principals of California with loss of state aid and revocation of their credentials if they let Cleaver inside their schools. The regents voted 10 to 8 to bar Cleaver; however, because they were afraid they would be charged with denying his constitutional rights if they mentioned him by name, they dealt with him as a nonperson by passing a ruling that stated categorically that "no person" would be permitted to offer more than a single lecture on campus unless that person held an academic appointment. Thus, they limited Cleaver to 1 talk of the original 10 he was to deliver but did not bar him. The challenge aroused student militants, who demanded their right to hear any speaker they chose, as well as members of the faculty, who were accustomed to settling such matters without outside interference. The ruling was seen as a direct blow at academic freedom. Even ordinarily conservative groups like the Business School and the School of Criminology, both of which regularly relied on such nonfaculty speakers as business leaders, police officers, and even criminals, had to back Cleaver against the regents (*Paradox,* 156). Following a large student protest, the academic senate on 3 October voted 668 to 114 to defy the regents.[10] The conservative *National Review* met the vote with derision, saying, "There is as much chance of persuading the Regents to rescind their ruling as there is of converting Max Rafferty to Buddhism"—a remark meant as a critique of not the regents but the faculty, whose "view of the real world" was thought to be faulty.[11] The course was finally offered for credit, to 300 students.

Although no student evaluation forms for the course are available, Phineas Israeli, a student contributor to the *Berkeley Barb,* assessed the class for the paper right after Cleaver fled into exile. A question had once arisen as to the ethnic acceptability of two expressions attributed to Cleaver: "Fuck the white people" and "Fuck the pigs." Cleaver denied that he had ever used the former phrase, and the latter was dismissed as evidence when another student pointed out that "pigs do not constitute an ethnic group." Cleaver illustrated his analysis of ethnic conflicts through reference to an Irish archetype, as seen through activist eyes. First, the Irish gained their "piece of the money and power action" through gangsterism (Machine Gun Kelly) and then raised their sons to become police officers in order to "neutralize the power which was brutalizing their community." A skeptical student was silenced with "How do you think all the police chiefs became Irish?" Whether or not the 300 students in SA 139X acquired an impressive amount of new information, the final evaluation of the speaker was glowing: "There's an honest man in Babylon, a beautiful human being in Babylon, and his name is Eldridge Cleaver" ("He Laid It on the Line," *Berkeley Barb,* 29 November 1968, 3).

On 26 October, Cleaver published "An Aside to Ronald Reagan," in which he only briefly addressed Reagan directly but spoke of him with disrespect as "Mickey Mouse," an actor who was "a sickening mixed bag of humorless laughter and perfect Colgate teeth, with never a hint of the real funk of life" (*Post,* 108). Cleaver covered the topic of Berkeley very quickly and bluntly: "Who in the fuck do you think you are, telling me I can't talk, telling the students and faculty members of University of California Berkeley that they cannot have me deliver ten lectures? I'm going to do it whether you like it or not. In fact, my desire now is to deliver *twenty* lectures" (*Post,* 111). Since Reagan had insulted him, he insisted on a chance to "balance the books" and avenge his honor: "Therefore, Mickey Mouse, I challenge you to a duel to the death, and you can choose the weapons. And if you can't relate to that, right on. Walk, chicken, with your ass picked clean" (112).

The Garden of Eden

On the same day, 26 October 1968, Cleaver had written his introduction to the *Biography of Huey Newton,* by Bobby Seale, a project conceived and pushed by Cleaver even in the midst of all his problems in the summer of that year. A cottage at Carmel was rented in order to ensure peaceful working conditions, and Seale taped his remembrances, parts of which were subsequently published in *Ramparts* and in Seale's *Seize the Time.*

Seale recounts "a very creative moment" there in Carmel that reveals much about Cleaver's attitude toward Huey Newton and the mission of the Panthers. It seems that behind the cabin there was an apple tree, and on one occasion Robert Scheer was there with a "young white girl" whom he asked to hand him an apple from the tree. Cleaver immediately began "signifying" to Scheer, much to the latter's confusion, about the apple and the Garden of Eden. "Hey man, you better watch it," Cleaver cautioned (*Seize,* 264). Scheer did not at first understand Cleaver's allusion; nor did he connect the remark to his taking of an apple from a woman. Seale says he had to explain about the tree and the garden: "Scheer's a white cat, and he's supposed to be a liberal. He still didn't know what Eldridge was talking about" (265).

Eldridge said, "What you did is, you let the omnipotent administrator send down a pig angel. His name was Chief Gain or any chief of police in the country. You let him come down with a flaming sword. With a weapon, you let him drive you out of the Garden of Eden. And you didn't defend it, you and your woman. . . . But if it had been Huey Newton in the middle of the Garden of Eden," said Eldridge, "and the pig angel came down after the omnipotent administrator had told Huey to go forth and exercise his constitutional rights and replenish the earth—it if had been Huey P. Newton and this pig had been swinging the flaming sword at him, Huey would have jumped back and said, "No, I'm defending myself. If you swing that sword at me, I'm shooting back." (265)

Newton's role as the "shield" of his people is even clearer here than in the Christ analogy, although the two concepts seem to exist without contradiction, depending on what facet of his identity is prominent at the moment. The Garden of Eden reference, which recurs in Cleaver's writing in various contexts, is ironic in view of James Baldwin's contention that only self-pitying "white boys" hark back to a Garden of Eden to which they long to return (see Chapter Two). That September, in an interview with several journalists published in the *Los Angeles Free Press,* Cleaver had responded to a question about the fate of white allies of the Panthers: "If we are successful, they will enjoy peace and freedom with us, and will enjoy life in the Garden of Eden with us. If we are unsuccessful, then they will die with us" (Paul Eberle, "Cleaver Raps with National Press," 27 September 1968, 8).

Cleaver's introduction to the biography is brief and replete with religious imagery. He begins with the reporter's remark about Huey's trial, quoted earlier: "They are crucifying Huey in there—they are turning him into another Jesus" (*Post,* 40). It is Cleaver's aim to present Huey "along with his followers, out on the streets of Oakland at night," willing and ready, "to lay down his life" in defense of black people's rights (40), to present him "in motion" as "the baddest motherfucker ever to set foot inside of history," "a classic revolutionary figure" who literally inspires others to place their lives "in Huey's hands" (41).

The *Playboy* Interview

Sometime in October 1968 Cleaver was interviewed by Nat Hentoff for *Playboy;* the result was published in the December issue and reprinted as the appendix to *Post-Prison Writings and Speeches*. This wide-ranging and lengthy discussion reveals a fairly calm, rational Cleaver, one who exhibits the most respectable of vocabularies. Much of what he speaks of refers to and recapitulates earlier material; when asked for the "specific" program of the "new black leadership" he had referred to in "The Fire Now," for example, Cleaver offered the Panther Ten Point Program, written in October 1966 by Seale and Newton. He refers repeatedly to the "deep" radicalization of young whites, his experience with the Peace and Freedom party having served to reinforce the impression he had had in prison as articulated in "The White Race and Its Heroes," and adds the observation that these new "John Browns" will form a "coalition" with the Panthers, "*the* black-national movement" (*Post*, 172). It is precisely to "pull a lot of people together" that he chose to run on the Peace and Freedom party ticket, Cleaver says, not because he actually "dreamed of waking up in the White House" (201).

Cleaver continues to advocate the granting of "rights and opportunities for a decent life" for blacks "peacefully—before I take them forcefully. . . . This isn't a request but a *demand,* and the ten points of that demand are set down with crystal clarity in the Black Panther Party platform" (*Post*, 178). Unlike the *Commonweal* editors, though, Hentoff parried, "Many would doubt that you're serious about some of them," and proceeded to question Cleaver on such points as black exemption from military service and especially the release of all prisoners.

The threat of violence and the insistence that "civil and guerrilla war" is imminent but still avoidable (by an immediate end to oppression) run throughout the interview. Black capitalism is rejected here as elsewhere on the grounds that it affects far too few people; militarism is seen as a misuse of funds that should be "redirected to build more houses and better schools" without sacrifice by middle-class whites; and finally, President Lyndon Johnson is regarded as a "mass murderer" for his role in waging the war in Vietnam. No killer in prison, said Cleaver, "comes anywhere close to the thousands and thousands of deaths for which Johnson is responsible" (180). On many of these points, Cleaver's position is identical to that held by white radicals.

Hentoff points out, however, that whites are likely to "sell out" and lose interest in working with white organizations or in forming coalitions with black ones, a fear Cleaver could counter only by insisting, "I don't think this generation will become as rigid as the ones before"

(189). Not only is white support important to encourage the hope that black demands will be met, but as Cleaver hints here (and in his March speech to the California Peace and Freedom party), there is a strong fear among blacks that the power structure will open up "concentration camps" for them in the event that extreme repressive measures are required to suppress urban unrest. In such a case, Cleaver warned, "We won't play Jews," going quietly to the prison camps and gas chambers, but will fight back. It was believed by some at the time that a sufficient degree of white sympathy could prevent such a policy from being put into effect; there would be racists, but no "good Germans." The fear existed that the camps used to relocate Japanese-Americans during World War II would be renovated for blacks or at least for radical black leaders (there had been only 110,000 Japanese-Americans in the camps, compared with some 25 million blacks in 1968). This paranoia was fed primarily by a 1967 novel by black author John A. Williams, *The Man Who Cried I Am*, in which the central character uncovers the "King Alfred Plan," named for the English king (849–99) who ordered *The Domesday Book*, a complete census of all persons and property under his rule. [12]

Presumably, it was the authoritarianism of Alfred, an emphatically Caucasian ruler whose reign is recorded in *The Anglo-Saxon Chronicles*, that underlined the fears of Williams's readers. The title *Domesday Book* could not fail to awaken an association in their minds with doom, judgment, and last things. "The King Alfred Plan" offered a format for a "final solution" to the black problem. It allowed for the detention of minority leaders (who might be few enough to fit into the old prison camps) only when they clearly could not prevent an unspecified "emergency," presumably a state of general insurrection; minority members of Congress were to be "unseated at once." The timetable provides for only eight hours from the time local police are called in until "all units" are under "regional commands," with minority troops having been "divided and detained, along with white sympathizers, under guard" (Williams, 311).

Copies of "The King Alfred Plan" were distributed nationally without any indication that it came from a novel, and some believed that war-related items, reportedly poison gas among them, were being moved to strategic places around the country, especially near urban ghettos, to be used against blacks at some future time. It was precisely this fear that Huey Newton had voiced in his "Executive Mandate No.

1: May 2, 1967," when the Panthers demonstrated against the new California gun control law. Black people, he declared, cannot allow themselves to be "disarmed and powerless" at a time when the World War II relocation camps "are being renovated and expanded," presumably for "Black people who are determined to gain their freedom by any means necessary."[13] Cleaver, knowing that the Williams novel was the source of these rumors because it was excerpted in *Ramparts* in 1967, nonetheless believed that such an endeavor would be within the bounds of acceptability for the U.S. government and served notice that if such a plan were put into effect, blacks would not go passively to prison camps in a state of shock.

Clearly, Cleaver offered the coalition with white radicals as an insurance policy against such an outcome for militant blacks. His hope, and that of the Panthers, was always that such reformist measures as breakfast for children would take hold along with an increased radicalism among whites. Together, reform and radicalism would lead to (a) the passage of bills designed to promote the welfare of blacks and (b) the decrease of such racist atrocities as police intimidation of black communities. A decrease in the level of racist oppression, combined with a climate of goodwill that would create true equality of opportunity and result, would have been Cleaver's dream. The difference between his dream and Baldwin's was really the difference between individual and group success. Whereas Baldwin wanted a Du Bois–like acceptance of meritorious individual blacks, Cleaver pushed for the advancement of the entire race through the adoption of a new socialist-humanitarian program that would eliminate the need for long-range planning and working for education and achievement and promote a new order that mandated a complete redistribution of wealth immediately, not after two or more generations had painfully attained a middle-class level of income. To press for the instant satisfaction of these and other, more specific needs, Cleaver repeatedly stated that it was "possible, barely possible" to avert civil war if these desires were granted before it was "too late" (*Post,* 173). He insisted that the Panthers stood for "responsible action," and that is why they emphasized killing "specific targets" like police while discouraging young blacks from rioting and leaving themselves open to police retaliation. The goal was to unite with whites to create a "machinery" that would destroy the old structure and build a new one "fit to exist on a civilized planet inhabited by *humanized* beings" (*Post,* 198).

The Campus Speaker

One of Cleaver's set speeches, "A Word to Students," was given as part of a multispeaker course at American University that included Mark Rudd, Dick Gregory, Seymour M. Lipset, and William F. Buckley, Jr. All the talks were subsequently published in the collection *The University and Revolution* (1969).

Cleaver's pledge to keep his language impeccable held only on the Berkeley campus. After saluting Washington, D.C., the home of American University, as "the pigpen of Babylon," he announced that he had no expectations of occupying the White House "this time around." "As a matter of fact," he stated, "if I were elected, I would not enter the White House. I would send a wrecking crew there to burn the motherfucker down. Then we could build a monument to the decadence of the past on the ashes that would be left."[14] Cleaver's threat became so closely associated with him that Don Schanche used it, expurgated, for the title of his November 1968 *Saturday Evening Post* article: "Burn the Mother Down." The phrase succinctly embodied the negative side of Cleaver's position in its full extremism, while omitting his demands for equality and education. As such, it made good press.

In the midst of his somewhat poorly organized talk, Cleaver was careful to note that he was not going to return to jail, but he had "no present plans for going to another country." At Stanford he had specified that he would hide out in the homes of white radicals; here, he declared he would "seek refuge in the black community" ("A Word," 161). Assuming that there were "pig" agents watching him everywhere, he wanted to plant as many contradictory suggestions as possible. What he would actually do when the 27 November deadline approached was known only to him.

Ironically, in view of his later anti-Zionist stance, Cleaver twice drew an analogy between black Americans and Jews. Repeating his remark that black people would refuse to "play Jews" if the white people wanted to "play Nazi," he added that the American "pigs" were war criminals to the ghetto and that "we," presumably blacks, intended to prosecute them as such. "They need to know that. They need to know that just as the Jews hunted down Adolf Eichmann, we are going to keep a list ourselves and we are going to execute these pigs for crimes against the people" (157).

Finally, he called for a return of the troops so that they could help form a "people's militia" to defend Americans against "the pigs who

want to turn America into another Nazi Germany" (164). It's up to
"you," he told the students, to stop that process, for those like himself,
"who stand up and run our mouths off, they're going to rip us off,
they're going to lock us up, or they're going to shoot us down." He
encouraged college students to "make up your minds quick" and decide
"which way to go" before the police "blow your mind for you, and I
mean with a gun!" (164).

Cleaver readily admitted that he was paranoid, and everyone around
him acknowledged it (Swados, 149 and *Fire*, 100). The Panthers shared
his fears, and their sense of danger was mirrored by that of J. Edgar
Hoover. Cleaver later claimed that Hoover was justified in believing
that the Panthers planned destruction if they failed to achieve "total
victory" (*Post*, 202), for they were stockpiling weapons. And though
Oakland police chief Gain never considered the Panthers a serious
threat, they had taken California for the world, it seems, and believed
themselves truly dangerous. According to Cleaver, speaking of fall
1968, "Our conviction was that the government would become more
oppressive and more intolerable. The Vietnam war was sinking in its
own decay. Popular support had vanished, for even white grandmothers
were marching against the military. It was my contention that whites
would outnumber blacks in their revulsion for the war insanity and
eventually turn against the powers that sustained it. At that point, a
massive, bloodletting upheaval would take place, and the blacks as well
as enraged whites would seize ultimate power" (*Fire*, 102). Cleaver's
fantasy was fed by the presence of hard-core white radicals around him,
these persons in turn having been selected by Cleaver precisely because
of their extremism. At the 1968 National Peace and Freedom Party
Convention in Ann Arbor, for example, Cleaver, who had easily beaten
Dick Gregory for the presidential nomination, insisted that Yippie
leader Jerry Rubin have the vice-presidential slot, much to the disgust
and chagrin of the rank-and-file leftists in the organization, who were
planning to make a serious Marxist-style bid for the White House with
a black/white working-class ticket.

Erection Day

Stew Albert reported in the *Berkeley Barb* that at the convention
Cleaver attempted to present the argument for having a representative
of "the street people"—the white radicals that included "yippies, SDS,
[and] the lumpen dropouts of the urban streets"—as vice-president on

the grounds that they were the only whites "making revolution in their own lives and trying to revolutionize the American system," but Cleaver met a "crazed" group of "cerebral souls, men of the library," who "will watch the black revolution on TV, take sides with the heroes, and then switch channels and watch a panel discussion on Karl Marx" ("Then Eldridge Blew Their Minds," 23 August 1968, 5). Albert continued, "When he realized that he might just as well have been arguing with Pope Paul, Eldridge called the radical caucus a bunch of middle-class snobs and went on doing his own thing throughout, together with a Rubin Yippie caucus made up of blacks and 'white niggers.' It wasn't big, but it was the first bit of soul I'd seen at the convention" (Albert, 5). In the end, the national convention decided to allow each state to select its own vice-presidential candidate, and so in California, where he was stricken from the ballot for being underage, Cleaver ran with one-time SDS president Carl Oglesby, who was selected by the party in order to correct Cleaver's "ill informed" choice of Rubin ("Peace and Freedom Brass Out to Show Cleaver What," *Berkeley Barb,* 30 August 1968, 7).

Cleaver's cynicism toward the founding fathers and the current politicians was easily matched by that of white radicals who, having rejected Republicanism almost from birth, had faced the same antiblack establishment in sit-in days that many blacks had. They had dealt with racism in their own homes and hometowns and as a result had little respect for the intelligence of the average American, and many of them had previously worked for antiwar candidates like Kennedy and McCarthy, forcing Lyndon Johnson out of office only to have his vice president receive the nomination in Chicago. Few regarded Hubert Humphrey as a new candidate who represented a possible change in policy; hence, Election Day was to be treated as the farce it was, a scenario in which two machine-picked candidates opposed each other in a meaningless contest. There were to be day-long rallies and sit-ins and love demonstrations all over the United States as a "strike and boycott of the election" that "represents death" ("Yipanther Pact," *Berkeley Barb,* 4 October 1968, 9). "This may sound like a yippie pipe dream," commented Stew Albert, "but it's the second apparition of the multicolored negation to throw fear into American Babbitry [*sic*] this year. The first was Chicago" ("Vote in the Streets," *Berkeley Barb,* 20 September 1968, 3). Their candidate was a pig named Pigasus.

By the end of October, the term for Election Day had become "Erection Day," indicating the sort of alternative antipolitical activity favored for that day. On 1 November, the Friday before the election, there was a pre–Erection Day rally at the Berkeley Community Center. Cleaver, admittedly "stoned" on marijuana, delivered an incoherent speech containing elements of his former public speeches in a series of non sequiturs. He conceded the election to Pigasus, surprising none of those present, among whom were many of his students from the social analysis course at Berkeley; for their attendance he awarded all of them an A ("Friday Yip Night Leaves them Yipping," *Berkeley Barb,* 8 November 1968, 5). (On 21 December, the *Black Panther* printed the speech in full under the title "Pronunciamento," perhaps as a subtle hint that Cleaver was in Cuba.)

As 27 November, the date for Cleaver to report to his parole board, drew near, Cleaver stayed in his home much of the time, except at night, because it was impossible to sleep there (*Fire,* 141). Gradually, a group of people gathered around to keep vigil and to "protect" Cleaver. The size of the group varied considerably from time to time; by the end of the vigil, the *Berkeley Barb* declared that "over one hundred supporters of Eldridge clustered outside of his house at 2777 Pine Street, San Francisco" ("Pigs Stymied," 29 November 1968, 3).

Farewell

On 22 November, just days before time would run out on his freedom, Cleaver addressed an official farewell party in San Francisco. There, he stressed his refusal to return to prison, his frustration at being in more trouble with the police because of his activities in the movement than he had ever been when he was robbing and raping, and his support of the concept that the prison system was corrupt, more likely to educate people to crime than to cure them of an inclination toward it. In his comments about the prisons and his reflections on his own experience, Cleaver returned to his earliest concerns, some of which were to be the subjects of his autobiographical writings in exile. His 1965 essay on Malcolm X had made the point that convicts rarely feel an obligation to pay a debt to society, for they feel *they* are the ones who have been wronged. The leaders of a system that fails its youth are the criminals, he said.

In reviewing his own past, Cleaver pointed out its similarity to that of many other convicts. He mentioned the start of his "career" with other youths in Juvenile Hall at age 12, and he noted the presence of the same youths every time he returned to prison. The fatalism of their

lives, the seeming futility of escaping the treadmill, made an enormous
impression on him:

In the California prison system, they carry you from Juvenile Hall to the old
folks' colony, down in San Luis Obispo, and wait for you to die. Then they
bury you there, if you don't have anyone outside to claim your body, and most
people down there don't. I noticed these waves, these generations, I had a
chance to watch other generations that came behind me, and I talked with
them, I'd ask them if they'd been in jail before. You will find graduating
classes moving up from Juvenile Hall, all the way up. It occurred to me that
this was a social failure, one that cannot be justified by any stretch of the
imagination. Not by any stretch of the imagination can the children in the
Juvenile Halls be condemned, because they're innocent, and they're processed
by an environment that they have no control over. (*Post*, 154)

The roots of the revolutionary doctrines of the Panthers and the basis of
their appeal to so many street youth are revealed in Cleaver's sense of
hopelessness and the anger it generated.

Later, in his condemnation of "this piggish criminal system,"
Cleaver responded to Nat Hentoff's point during the *Playboy* interview
about the undeniable and inescapable criminality of the criminals:

When I speak up for convicts, I don't say that every convict is going to come
out here and join the Peace and Freedom Party. I'm not saying that. Or that he
would be nice to people out here. I'm not saying that. Yet, I call for the
freedom of even those who are so alienated from society that they hate everybody. Cats who tattoo on their chest, "Born to Hate." "Born to Lose." I know a
cat who tattooed across his forehead, "Born to Kill." He needs to be released
also. Because whereas Lyndon B. Johnson doesn't have any tattoos on his head,
he has blood dripping from his fingers. LBJ has killed more people than any
man who has ever been in any prison in the United States of America from the
beginning of it to the end. He has murdered. And people like prison officials,
policemen, mayors, chiefs of police—they endorse it. They even call for
escalation, meaning: kill more people. I don't want it. (*Post*, 158–59)

The prospect of a return to prison became more terrifying as the
deadline approached. Cleaver told author Gene Marine that he hadn't
minded being in prison so much before, because he was always in "the
prison of being alone" (Marine, 195). But his immersion into society,
especially being accompanied as it was by a level of fame and a sense of
being able to influence people and events, was too heady and fulfilling
for him to be able to withdraw from it suddenly and return to the social

silence and feeling of irrelevance that prison life brought. Cleaver said, "I've found people who really dig me, people I really dig. People care about me, people *like* me. I've never had that before, never at all. I can't go back in there now and leave all that out here. I've got friends—I've got friends for the first time in my life and man, I just don't think I can do without that anymore" (Marine, 196).

On 24 November, the Sunday before he was to report to his parole board, Cleaver was interviewed in his home by Henry Weinstein, a law student at Berkeley, for the *Nation*. Weinstein commented that Cleaver was more than "upset" over the thought of returning to prison; he was " 'freaked out' in a manner akin to Rubashov in Koestler's *Darkness at Noon*."[15]

The conversation ranged over a number of topics, although it was considerably shorter than the as-yet-unpublished Hentoff interview. Cleaver occasionally attempted to reach for his old intensity but failed. In response to Weinstein's query about "the meaning of some of your rhetoric," specifically the phrase that originated at Huey Newton's February birthday rally, "Free Huey or the sky's the limit," Cleaver stated, "When we say this we mean that Huey must be set free or the country will be destroyed; there should be no misunderstanding about this." But almost immediately he was comparing the "psychological warfare" value of such a remark before the trial with its value after Newton's sentencing in September: "It becomes a question of getting into a position to implement what you have to do" (Weinstein, 75).

Cleaver would return with full enthusiasm to the concept of "leveling the earth" as a way to bring about the new order, but on this occasion he merely suggested that activist whites help the working class to see how "miserable and dissatisfied" its members really are: "They are suffering spiritually as a result of the oppressive lies that have been imposed upon them. This deterioration of their condition is increasing. Politically conscious people have to make these working class people see how racism is affecting their lives and project a Left alternative to these problems. That is what it will take to get these 'comfortable people' to move" (76). On the subject of white students, however, he remained optimistic, at least to an extent. For students, "it doesn't matter if they are well-off materially because their values are affronted by what they see in society," except that they have only rarely committed themselves to real "revolutionary activity" by his standards. "It has been like an extended field trip to upset their elders and it has not gone far enough. . . . They probably won't be willing to take up guns and

execute the regents, as they deserve" (76–77). His almost casually
imposed death sentence was nearly lost as he continued to speculate on
the source of future revolutionary potential.

Ironically, Cleaver, who had been fond of marijuana since his early
teens and had been high on it in public shortly before this interview,
agreed with Huey Newton's warning to blacks to avoid drugs, especially hallucinogenics. In response to Weinstein's question about the
"different types of discipline" required by black militants and white
radicals, Cleaver declared that "the Black Panther Party can't be effective in dealing with the power structure if its members are high or
drunk. Some of the people who are getting high will have to stop. . . .
People will have to relate to a revolutionary mentality. . . . Sex and
LSD can't be used any more and the leadership must set an example"
(77). It is not certain how many Panthers had ever used psychedelic
drugs, but the counterrevolutionary effect of such mind-expanding
substances was a worry to Newton in particular, and in Algiers would
lead to a direct confrontation between Cleaver and hippie guru Timothy Leary.

Cleaver concluded the interview in a similarly low key, devoid of
both imagery and intensity:

> *Weinstein:* Any concluding remarks?
>
> *Cleaver:* I may be cut off from the movement here. I would encour-
> age people to develop an intransigent attitude toward the
> enemy. They should view the enemy and his efforts with
> contempt.
>
> Pain should incense us all the more to speed up the move-
> ment for liberation. But the people also must use their
> minds to understand the enemy and his tactics, to develop
> counter-tactics, and to break his strategy. Let the struggle
> continue. It should intensify, come hell or high water. I'm
> not going to say good-by because I'm not gone. (77)

But the day before he was due to report, he *was* gone. In what Don
Schanche later called "a carefully premeditated act that I can't help
characterizing as political and social suicide," Cleaver escaped the police, leaving "his civil libertarian supporters suddenly without a legal
cause . . . and his bail backers holding a $50,000 bag."[16] Ed Keating
was forced to sell his home, according to Schanche, but he felt Cleaver's
cause was "worth it." Schanche disagreed. What *was* Cleaver's cause? he
asked in a 1970 article in the *Atlantic*. Was it merely "his own liberty,"
or simply to free himself for "playacting as a revolutionary on a remote

stage, urging his homebound followers to bloody conflict?" ("Against Wall," 59). One suspects that Cleaver's decision was primarily emotional, not tactical, and that he ran like a "rabbit," just as Robert Williams had, strictly for self-preservation (*Ice,* 19). His move was premeditated but not calculated; as events were to prove, his exile was indeed to be his political and social death.

Up until the last day, Cleaver hoped for a pardon so that he could continue to live in California. When a last-minute appeal to Thurgood Marshall, the only black member of the Supreme Court, failed to win a stay for him, Cleaver resolved to leave the country. He missed his last class at Berkeley on Tuesday, which was to have been a big farewell party at noon in the Lower Plaza, and disappeared ("Eldridge Misses His Own Party," *Berkeley Barb,* 29 November 1968, 11).

The Escape

Cleaver had briefly considered a melodramatic "red light finale" such as Huey Newton had once requested and Cleaver had vetoed:

My plan was to take over Merritt College in Oakland and turn it into a fortress. It was an old two-story, concrete building, complete with towers and a commanding view of the surrounding terrain. I wanted to hole up there with some fellow Panthers and tell the white power-police pig structure to come and get me. We had plenty of military gear and enough volunteers to join me in this action that would forestall my imprisonment, give me a fighting chance, and at least let me die outside of prison.

It was Huey Newton's turn to veto this death extravaganza. He sent orders from his cell that nothing of the sort was going to happen and notified the Central Committee that they should do everything possible to get me out of the country. (*Fire,* 137–38)

Cleaver's plans for escape included far more than hiding among either black or white sympathizers, as he had openly suggested earlier; he agreed to every plan suggested, in an effort to throw off undercover operators, but in secret he already had his own plan.

What was undoubtedly one of Cleaver's rejected plans was reported almost two and a half years later in the Tel Aviv tabloid *Ha'olam Hazeh* by "a respected member of Israel's parliament," Shalom Cohen, and reprinted in translation in *Atlas,* a monthly review of the world press. According to the report, "a Jew of great influence in California leftist circles" paid "a short visit" to Israel "about two years ago, when Cleaver was wanted by the F.B.I." and was in hiding from "the detectives." The anonymous American told leftist columnist Amos Kenau, who thought the information important enough to relay to "a friend who has contacts among the greats of the Israel Establishment," that Eldridge Cleaver was seeking refuge abroad and was prepared to come to Israel to work for a period of time on a kibbutz; he asked if the Israeli government was prepared to grant him asylum. The friend Kenau told, in turn spoke with yet another friend, "a figure of greatest importance," who responded, as promised, within 24 hours: no ("Did Eldridge Cleaver Seek Asylum in Israel?" *Atlas*, April 1971, 24).

Considering the comically inappropriate image of Cleaver breathing revolutionary blood and fire from an Israeli kibbutz, espousing Marxist world revolution from under the protective wing of one of America's most reliably anti-Communist allies, it is inconceivable that Cleaver dreamed up such an alternative. It could only have been the brainchild of the "Jew of great importance" himself. In *Soul on Fire* Cleaver finally explained how he had escaped:

Escape was a very trying act. On the last afternoon in San Francisco prior to being hauled away to San Quentin, Kathleen and I drove up to our house, pushed through the chanting demonstrators and stand-by police, and spoke a few words from the front porch. Then I went inside and there was Ralph Smith—a Panther who was a near double for me. In a moment, he and Kathleen returned to the front steps and continued the revolutionary rhetoric about not going to the pig prison. A couple of Panthers in the crowd were cued to ask "me" questions which Ralph answered in grand style. Whites say that all niggers look alike, and Ralph and I fit the bill for the watchful authorities. As they continued this charade, I went out the rear door and over the back fence into a waiting car that took me to where I prepared for stage two of my goodby to America. (*Fire*, 142)

With $15,000 in cash in his pocket from royalties, Cleaver raced off to the San Francisco airport, flew to New York, changed planes for Montreal, and finally took a slow freighter to Cuba, hiding in a closet most of the way (*Fire*, 143). He arrived on Christmas Day of 1968, and anticipated a safe and successful new year. From the first, he planned to return; in the meantime, he looked forward to life in a revolutionary Communist republic, forming the kind of international bonds that the Panthers would need in order to play out their roles in the struggle against capitalist power, "setting up the big training camp" for revolutionaries "while preparing to deal with Nixon's American Dream" (*Fire*, 143).

Chapter Five
Exile: Message from Algiers

Not long after his release from Vacaville in June 1968, Cleaver, accompanied by Bobby Seale and others, visited the United Nations headquarters in New York City. The primary objective of the visit was to present the Panther demand for a black plebiscite so as to determine whether American blacks indeed wished to be regarded as a separate nation. Although this goal was never accomplished, the group reportedly spoke with several delegations from unnamed "Revolutionary Countries" and requested that U. N. observer teams be stationed in ghettos. In a 1970 article in *Black American Literature Forum,* San Diego State instructor Joyce Nower stated that the Cleaver-Seale proposal had "found support from sixteen [unnamed] nations of the Third World."[1] The action was necessary, the Panthers had declared, because "the racist power structure" planned soon to unleash "a war of genocide against her black colonial subjects." The statement, accompanied by a group photo taken in front of the United Nations building, was dated 24 July 1968 but not printed in the *Black Panther* until 14 September.[2]

Cleaver also had had occasion to speak to a Cuban delegate about the possibility of setting up a Panther branch in Cuba. He could not know, back in June, that his parole revocation would be put back into effect on 27 September and that he would be ordered to return to prison, and so no definite date was then set. It was only when all other alternatives were exhausted and Huey Newton ordered Cleaver out that the Cuban plan was actually put into effect. Cleaver writes,

Our highest hope was to have a center in the Caribbean that would prepare revolutionary cadres to slink back into the United States, many to blend with the urban scene and function as guerrillas on that sidewalk level. No major confrontations with the army and police, no battle at Little Big Horn or Gettysburg, but much disruption and chipping away at a decaying power structure that was becoming increasingly anti-democratic and invariably more fascist.

The other trained and equipped forces would be dropped into the mountain area of North America. The plan here was to have small mobile units that could shift easily in and out of rural areas, living off the land, and tying up thousands of troops in fruitless pursuit. What turned out to be fruitless was the reality of such a camp in Cuba. (*Fire*, 107–8)

In a 1975 interview, Cleaver first admitted his disappointment and sense of betrayal. "It was all programmed," he complained, that the Panthers would be given "a permanent, well-organized facility" there, which plan he took to include "a program on Havana Radio" such as Robert Williams had had when he was there, in order to broadcast to the United States. Further, Cleaver stated more vaguely, Williams used to "publish certain things, circulate information and various other things that you can do there that would be useful to our struggle," and Cleaver had expected a similar degree of freedom but received almost nothing. "Not only did these things not take place," he declared, "but the Cubans never had any intention of allowing them to take place."[3]

As Lee Lockwood pointed out in the introduction to his book-length interview with Cleaver in Algeria, the Cuban economy was in trouble when Cleaver arrived, and all effort was bent toward a record 10-million-ton sugar production by 1970. Because of this factor and because they were "perhaps unwilling to stir up fresh provocations of the United States," Cuban authorities insisted that Cleaver maintain a low profile.[4] Cleaver was at first cooperative and willing to rest after the traumas of the past several months. "For the first weeks," he told interviewer Curtice Taylor, "I read a lot and not much happened. They postponed meetings all the time but I thought that was cool—the Cubans had a nation to run and so I just cooled out. I was waiting for Kathleen, who was pregnant at the time."[5]

After about a month, however, Cleaver began to become irritated. Other Panthers were due, notably his old friend Alprentice "Bunchy" Carter, who on 17 January 1969 would be killed in Los Angeles along with John Huggins by Ron Karenga's black nationalist gunmen from United Slaves (US). Cleaver later blamed the Cubans in part for Carter's death, saying, "He wouldn't have been killed if the Cubans had allowed him to come when we had planned for him to" (Gates, 34). Of greater significance, however, was the Cuban deceit in handling Cleaver's communications with Bobby Seale, who was in Sweden at a "liberation conference" with David Hilliard and another Panther named Ray "Masai" Hewitt (Heath, 140), whom Cleaver later mistakenly referred to as "Mosiah" (Gates, 34).

According to Cleaver, he gave the Cuban delegate to that conference a verbal message for the Panthers that included an invitation to visit Havana "so we could get this thing going" (Taylor, 40). The Panthers did not arrive; however, they sent Cleaver "a lot of literature" (Gates, 34). Cleaver's account is somewhat sketchy. He told interviewer Taylor that along with "the reply," presumably from the delegate en route, were "some papers that I should not have seen" instructing the delegate "to tell Bobby that I did not think that it was appropriate for the brothers to visit me at that time" (40). Because of his early experiences with Spanish-speaking Chicanos on Rose Hill, Cleaver says he knew enough Spanish to translate the note before returning it to his "pig" bodyguard, Silva. Cleaver did not refer to this letter, which probably preceded the trip, in his interview with Gates but instead emphasized his discovery of a letter to "the Cubans" from "the Cubans in Sweden" stating that "the Panthers had wanted to come but that he ["this Cuban Embassy official"] had done what he had been told to do and told them it was not possible." What the Cubans had told him, Cleaver said, was that "Bobby didn't have time to come" (49). Lockwood makes no mention of the situation.

Kathleen did not materialize, either. Alternately, Cleaver was told that she "wasn't ready to come" (Gates, 34) and that she "was having legal difficulties leaving the United States" (Lockwood, 18). Cleaver accepted neither excuse: "We had everything programmed," he declared (Gates, 34), and he maintained an undercurrent of distrust toward the Cubans because of the delay throughout his stay there.

On the Home Front

Kathleen knew where Cleaver was, although she insisted to the press that she did not, even to the extent of telling *Berkeley Barb* reporter Phineas Israeli that Cleaver could be dead. On the day in December 1968 that the date was to have been set for Cleaver's trial, she, Edward Keating, and author Paul Jacobs held a press conference at the Alameda County Courthouse. Jacobs read a statement by the six who had guaranteed Cleaver's bail in June—the three present; Godfrey Cambridge, the black comedian; a Dr. Philip Shapiro; and another person whose identity was withheld but who was later named by Kathleen as Dr. Jane Aguilar (*Ramparts,* June 1969, 7, and *Black Panther,* 9 August 1969, 5). The loss of the $50,000 bail, which became official that day, was not mourned. "To all those who believe in freedom," declared Jacobs, "Eldridge Cleaver's life is worth much more than $50,000" (Israeli, 3).

Kathleen repeatedly insisted to reporters that she hadn't "the faintest idea" where her husband was. Reported the *Berkeley Barb:*

> We asked Kathleen Cleaver if she thought she might one day leave the Panthers and the Bay Area to rendezvous with her husband in say, Cuba.
> She smiled confidently and said, "I'll remain here forever." ("Is He Still Alive?" 27 December 1968, 3)

As the months wore on and the time for her delivery grew nearer, it appeared that Kathleen's stay in San Francisco would indeed be indefinite. Finally, in June 1969, she was told to fly to Paris to catch a plane to Havana. But she was never to land in Cuba, although her arrival there was announced by the Panthers prematurely in the *New York Times* on 3 July (4). By that time, the situation had deteriorated so badly that Cleaver was abruptly shifted to Algiers. It was up to Lee Lockwood, who happened to be in Havana at the time, to intercept Kathleen in Paris and reroute her to Algeria.

Cuban Racism

The events leading up to Cleaver's dismissal from Havana were varied, but all had as their common denominator Cleaver's loss of trust in the Cubans. He had met Castro once, briefly, and had been on a tour of Cuba (Gates, 38), but aside from those events he led an isolated life in his apartment under the eye of two guards, one black and one white, from the Cuban Ministry of the Interior (Gates, 33). He was given a large apartment on L Street several blocks from the Havana Libre Hotel; it was accessible "only by means of a hidden elevator located at the rear of the basement garage" (Lockwood, 21), a factor that greatly increased its value to a man on the run. In the beginning, Cleaver was in the constant companionship of the two Cubans, but later, as he met some Afro-Americans and various hijackers appeared, the place began to fill with new Panthers "lounging on chairs and chaises and quietly digging the blues sounds" (Lockwood, 22). When he was alone with the Cubans, Cleaver had tried to find out as much as he could about Cuba. Already suspicious of the purity of Cuban intentions, he began to ask about racism in Cuba, about the practice of sending black American hijackers first to prison and then to a work camp in Camaguey province, and about why the black guard never came by alone, although the white guard did. This last question provoked a tense response from the white man: "He's too busy." Cleaver was informed that he asked too many questions, and "the black guy never came around any more" (Gates, 33).

Cleaver tried to find the black agent at his apartment and left a note. He missed the "penetrating comments" the man had made, and wanted more contact. Moreover, the agent was the only English-speaking black person with whom Cleaver had contact in Havana at that date. The agent came by only briefly to say it was "impossible" for him to continue, because of the pressure that had now been put on him, and gave Cleaver Philip S. Foner's two-volume *Cuban History* (Gates, 33). It was here that Cleaver first discovered the little-known story of Antonio Maceo, black hero of the Cuban revolt.

The repression of the story of Antonio Maceo established for Cleaver the historical racism of Cuban society. The fact that all the materials concerning Maceo were locked up in a special room in the National Library made Cleaver suspect that the Cuban people preferred not to publicize the reality that the general who led the troops against Batista was black; instead, Cleaver found, all credit is given to Jose Marti. Toward the end of his stay, Cleaver went with a companion out to the countryside to see the monument to Maceo, on which was a record of the war showing Maceo's participation "to the end." According to the Cuban Congress, Cleaver said, "Jose Marti was the brain and Antonio was the brawn. That is bullshit because Marti died almost immediately after the war began, so there was nothing he could have said to carry the movement through. The white Cubans, historically, were constantly trying to sell out the blacks, to keep them from coming to power. That's the main historical fact." (Gates, 41). Cleaver's discovery of Maceo became "part of the process of solving the problem we had there" (42). It clarified his vision and made him defiant rather than patient. Indeed, Cleaver's identification with Maceo was so strong that he chose to name his firstborn son after him a few months later.

Cuban Deceit

At some point just before Cleaver's March 1969 tour of Cuba, he befriended a white American woman from Georgia whom he has referred to variously as Kitty (Taylor, 42) and Bunny (Gates, 36) Hearne. One of the hijackers Cleaver had met in Havana warned him away from her because she was "flipped out," but Cleaver, spotting the woman standing in line for some ice cream, and feeling in need of "some female companionship" (Taylor, 42), introduced himself, but as the deceased Bobby Hutton, for the sake of caution. Kitty/Bunny turned out to have been a Castro fan from years back who wrote to Fidel regularly during the revolution and was invited to come to Cuba after the war. According to Cleaver, she fully expected Castro to marry her, but it was obvious to all that he would not. What he did do was to send her lettuce every day for her pet rabbit (Taylor, 42). (The fact of her owning a rabbit may be the cause of Cleaver's confusion about her name in an interview he gave six years later.) Cleaver claimed to have carried on an "innocent" relationship with this woman for some weeks, during which time he became more and more deeply involved with various hijackers and more deeply suspicious. "I began demanding interviews and asking questions," he said (Taylor, 42), which behavior was partly why the Cubans thought a tour would be a welcome distraction. Cleaver said that immediately before the tour, he was in Kitty's apartment when a phone call came from "Commandante Pinato, the man directly responsible for my case" (42), announcing his intent to visit her. Kitty, never directly revealing that she was not alone, stalled Pinato by saying she had to get dressed first. Cleaver says he would have "split" had he "understood the implications of her implied nudity," but since he did not, he was discovered by Pinato, who had not met him previously, and was introduced as Bobby Hutton. Pinato, recognizing Cleaver and apparently fearing that he was being set up, ran for the kitchen, asked for coffee he did not drink, and left, assuring Kitty he would "take care of [her] mail." Kitty, her suspicions now aroused, made inquiries and discovered who Cleaver really was. Weeks later, in May, it was she who would reveal to a Reuters correspondent both Cleaver's identity and his residence in Havana, for what Cleaver called "reasons which had more to do with her conflict with the Cubans than with me" (Gates, 36). When he spoke with Curtice Taylor for *Rolling Stone,* however, Cleaver emphasized his own apparent complicity in the tip-off: "At this point Kitty really came through—she informed a Reuters reporter that I was there, so I had the protection that the press knew of my whereabouts and that I was in trouble" (Taylor, 44). Lockwood, though, reports that an unnamed "mentally disturbed young American lady . . . had conjured up the unfortunate delusion that [Cleaver] had tried to rape her" and gave James Pringle the information out of a desire for vengeance (Lockwood, 22).

It is not clear how this early account relates to the "implications of her implied nudity," but it may be that there was an attempt to set up

Cleaver himself, a plan that fell through when Pinato realized who he was and feared that perhaps he himself had nearly been lured into making a mistake. At any rate, the white guard, Silva, failed to show up for two days and then appeared, accusing Cleaver of trying to blackmail the commandante (Taylor, 42). It was then that Silva "got us some guns so we could go hunting in the mountains" (42), and the tour began.

When the trip was over Silva never returned the guns but instead stored them in secret in Cleaver's apartment. While on the tour, Cleaver heard that a man he'd known in prison, one Raymond Johnson, had hijacked a plane to Cuba in order to seek exile where he'd heard Cleaver was; Cleaver wanted to cancel the trip and return, "but of course [the authorities] advised against it" (Taylor, 42). Upon his return to Havana, Cleaver says, "it seemed that everything was happening at once"; he "heard over the radio that the UN delegate, who I had discussed the whole thing with in the first place, was denied an extension of his visa by the Americans, which meant he would be coming home." Relieved to have someone arriving with whom he could get "down to the fine points," Cleaver asked to see Johnson, but he was informed Johnson did not want to see him; "then I knew things were very fucked up. There was no reason why he would say that, but I had no way of knowing because he was out in the provinces at a camp" (42). Simultaneously, Cleaver said, Kitty informed him that the Cubans "had no intention of letting me work out my program," and the U. N. delegate, Jose Jimenez (40), admitted that "he had never really believed we would actually accept their invitation and that they had made it as a kind of public relations gesture" (42).

Defiantly, and out of a desire for allies, Cleaver "decided to start the program anyway, not to wait for any more people from the Panther program to arrive. So I started to recruit every Afro-American in Havana" (42). The Cubans began to refer to Cleaver's penthouse apartment as *"La casa de las panteras"* (Lockwood, 21).

"When they got to my pad," said Cleaver, "I would baptise them in the name of the Father, the Son, and the Holy Ghost, and make them Black Panthers. I told the Cubans that I was authorized by the Black Panther Party to induct Afro-Americans into the Black Panther Party anywhere, anytime, as I saw fit, and I took these people in" (Gates, 36). Altogether, Cleaver offered asylum, so to speak, to "about eight individuals"—all hijackers and their families. Primarily because of the Cuban treatment of these black Americans, Cleaver and the new Panthers were in "that siege frame of mind, that Afro-American, 'Cus-tardism [*sic*]—LAST STAND' frame of mind" that Cleaver was so familiar with from his recent days in Oakland. When Raymond John-son, the last to escape, made it to Cleaver's apartment, "guns were involved. . . . We told them that we were not going to let them take the dude and that we were going to resist. We made our last will and testament on tapes, sent them to the states through some Puerto Rican who was from New York" (Gates, 38). The guns in question were one pistol of Cleaver's and the two "hunting guns" checked out to his security man—AK-47 assault rifles.

It was at this point that Kitty tipped off James Pringle as to Cleaver's whereabouts. Pringle's account of their meeting contains little other than the fact that Cleaver was "visibly startled" and "refused to say much after being discovered," except for revealing that he was "work-ing on a sequel to *Soul on Ice*" (*New York Times,* 25 May 1969, 1, and *Time,* 30 May 1969, 23).

The Bum's Rush

The revelation of Cleaver's presence, however, was enough to compel the Cubans to "suggest" that he meet his wife somewhere else, specifi-cally Algiers. Cleaver made Byron Booth, who would join him in Algiers, and Mosiah Kenyatta (Earl Ferrell) coleaders in Havana; caught up with Lee Lockwood and arranged for him to intercept Kath-leen; and prepared to travel to the "center of liberation movements" under Cuban guard. Cleaver did not believe he would be returning. All he wanted by this time, he says, was to depart from Cuba, which had swiftly become "a San Quentin with palm trees, an Alcatraz with sugar cane" (*Fire,* 143).

A possible explanation for Cleaver's abrupt expulsion from Cuba is the imminent arrival of Angela Davis by air from Mexico, in time for the Day of the National Rebellion on 26 July.[6] The Cubans were probably aware that it would have been difficult to keep the two from meeting, and Cleaver's revelations would have created problems for them if they wanted Davis and her party to remain loyal and to con-tinue to promote communism among black Americans. While com-mon sense and our own national experience teach us that racism cannot be erased from a culture simply by official decree, even when the economic system is simultaneously changed, Castro did manage to convince many leftists, at least for a time, that universal love existed in

Cuba. Since it was vital to the leftist belief system for leftists to see a socialist state as a utopia by definition, it followed that without capitalist exploitation of blacks, racism would end, the reason being that all prejudice is really class prejudice and not racial at all, and so it cannot exist without classes. Marxism has always fared poorly among blacks in America precisely because it keeps telling them that prejudice based on race is an illusion, a distraction from the "true" conflict among people—class struggle—and black people, to put it simply, know better, with the exception of a few committed party members in every decade. Cleaver's skepticism is easily the opinion of the majority of blacks; it is not hard to imagine the Cubans panicking at the thought of Cleaver and his newly "baptized" Panthers confronting the black party regulars from the United States, and telling them some of the things he later told Henry Gates. It is no wonder that an airplane ticket materialized quickly; even the Algerians were left out of the planning.

According to Cleaver, when he was in Cuba he had sent a taped message "back to friends in the U.S.," saying, "The white racist Castro dictatorship is more insidious and dangerous for black people than is the white racist regime of South Africa, because no black person has illusions about the intentions of the Afrikaners, but many black people consider Fidel Castro to be a right-on white brother. Nothing could be further from the truth"[7]. No such remarks were printed in the *Black Panther,* although they do not sound out of character for the disillusioned and embittered Cleaver of late spring 1969. In Cleaver's 1976 *Newsweek* article on Castro, he tied the suppression of the story of Antonio Maceo to Castro's more generalized racist treatment of black troops. Although Castro had expressed solidarity with American blacks and protested their exploitation by the American military, which sent them "on the most difficult and dangerous missions . . . [t]o fight and participate in the adventures of imperialism outside of the U.S." (Saul Landau, "On Blacks," *Good Times,* 18 December 1969, 7), Cleaver declared that such practices were in fact typical of Castro himself, who sent off Cuban blacks in disproportionate numbers to fight and die in the African wars. One Captain Toro, a black Cuban officer whom Cleaver had befriended, told Cleaver that he viewed the policy of shipping off militant black officers as a safety valve: "By sending them off to fight in Africa, Toro said, Castro kills two birds with one stone: (1) he gets rid of an explosive element capable of causing him trouble at home; (2) he impresses black Cubans that he is a fighter for black people's rights, thus quelling opposition to his rule amongst blacks, who are still at the bottom of the Cuban pecking order" ("Castro's African Gambit," 13). Further, Cleaver reported, Castro had pulled Che Guevara out of the Congo just as he was about to link up with the guerrilla forces of Pierre Mulele, a follower of the assassinated Patrice Lumumba, in Katanga province. This action was, as Ange Diawara, Cleaver's Congo source, would have it, "the fundamental betrayal of the African revolution" (13). When Cleaver wrote about his 1971 visit to the Congo (he speaks of it in *Newsweek* as occurring in 1973), he omitted all references to this development, for ideological reasons. Everything he published until he left Algeria in 1972 was virulently leftist and avoided dealing with actual events.

In the Panther press, Cleaver followed the official line. When Mosiah Kenyatta (Earl Ferrell) failed to contact Cleaver in Algiers (Don Schanche had met Ferrell in the airport as he was leaving after the Cleaver interview, and reported that Ferrell had not been permitted to enter the country [*Paradox,* 180, 216]), Ferrell left for Paris. There, he asked for asylum and denounced Cuba in much the same terms as Cleaver, Smith, and Booth had done to Schanche. When a UPI story to that effect broke in the United States, though, the *Black Panther* countered with "Eldridge Cleaver Raps about Cuba," a Liberation News Service release available to a number of alternative-press publications. The article, based on a telephone interview between Cleaver and David Hilliard, denounced Ferrell as an "imposter and embezzler who stole money from the Party, violated security and fabricated the story about Cuban 'racism' " ("Eldridge Cleaver Raps about Cuba," *Black Panther,* 17 January 1970, 6). More to the point, Cleaver stated, the party had never made the claim "that if socialism is instituted . . . racism automatically ceases." More vital even than that, though, was Cuba's value to "some members of the Black Panther Party" who "used Cuba as a means of escape from fascist oppression in Babylon. It would not be in the interest of Cuba or the world revolution to launch attacks at Cuba because they have not been able to eliminate all forms of racism in the ten years since their revolution began" (6).

While in Cuba, Cleaver published nothing; officially, his location was unknown, and so the Black Panther party could not print any new items. Before he "broke his silence" in July, however, the party reprinted "The Black Man's Stake in Vietnam" from *Soul on Ice* and also printed a 1968 article or speech on "Community Imperialism" that made use of the black colony/white mother country dichotomy on a local level—"Urban Dungeons" versus "the imperialism of the white suburbs" (*Black Panther,* 20 April 1969, 14).

His remarkably nonviolent speech is accompanied by a large photograph filling the top third of the page. It shows Cleaver before a chalkboard, quite possibly in the act of lecturing to his social analysis class at Berkeley, from which "Community Imperialism" may have originated. The most interesting thing about the photo, however, is what is written on the chalkboard, which relates only slightly to the text; rather, it appears to be a six-item list of Cleaver's proposed schema for his own life:

1.   Robbery

2.   Rape

3.   Political Organizing

4.   Escaping

5.   Rebellion

6.   Murder

Items 2 and 4 specifically seem to particularize the list to the extent that it could serve as a guide not to revolutionaries of the future but rather to steps or stages in Cleaver's "public life" (14). Assuredly, his rhetoric from Algiers would contain extensive threats and a variety of violent prophecies, usually couched in uncompromisingly aggressive language.

Algiers

Kathleen's arrival in Algiers preceded Eldridge's, and the two immediately became established in the Victoria Hotel, which Lee Lockwood, who visited about two weeks later, described as "a hotel to be strictly avoided," a place whose only merit lay in the fact that it was "much better than sleeping on the sidewalks under the arcades as some Arabs still do in that area of the city" (Lockwood, 24).

The U.S. government had cut off Cleaver's royalties from *Soul on Ice* as soon as the *New York Times* published Pringle's sketchy report on 25 May 1969, the government declaring that Cleaver was now a Cuban national and that no funds could be collected "under the 'trading with the Enemy' Act" (Lockwood, 31). This situation prevailed until mid-September, when the Treasury Department finally informed Cleaver, "You may be regarded as a person who is not a designated national of Cuba" (32). Nonetheless, Cleaver told Don Schanche in Algiers that the money was still cut off (*Paradox,* 177).

There was little likelihood of financial support from the Algerians yet, because the Cubans had never notified them that Cleaver would be arriving. His visit was secret and unofficial. Immediately after his arrival in Algiers, he had been told by the Cubans that the Algerians had originally agreed to his residency there, but while he was in the air they "changed" their minds; he was no longer welcome. "The next day," said Cleaver, "the Cubans came to me with a plane ticket to Amman, Jordan. They said the Algerians wanted me to go to a P.L.O. camp where I could surface. It just sounded incredible" (Gates, 43).

Cleaver refused to leave his wife and began to make inquiries of his own. "The Cubans asked if I knew a girl called Elaine Kline [*sic*]. I said no. They said stay away from her, she's an American and she's dangerous. When they said that, I thought this was somebody with whom I should get in contact right away" (Gates, 43). Elaine Klein was a translator for the Algerian Ministry of Information and a member of the committee for the first Pan-African Festival, to be held in Algiers in July.[8] She had placed the Black Panther party organization and Cleaver himself on her invitation list, as it happened; "she just had been making this list at her desk, with nothing to do" (Gates, 43).

Strangely, Cleaver told Curtice Taylor that the Cubans had warned him away from a black American woman named Elaine Carter, because she was a CIA agent. "So naturally," Cleaver said, "the moment I was out of their sight I tracked her down. It turned out she was organizing an international Pan African Conference in Algeria. She had made up a long list of black artists to be invited from all over the world and she had included my name without a hope in hell that I would attend" (Taylor, 44). There is no clear explanation for this confusion; certainly the same woman is referred to in each case. According to Schanche, "Miss Klein was a Leftist in the late Forties who had moved from New York to Paris during the McCarthy era and become an active supporter of the Algerian revolution. She was now employed as an information ministry official by the government of Algeria. As such she had become unofficial Jewish den mother to the two-dozen or so international revolutionary groups which were formally sanctioned and sheltered in the

Arab country" (*Paradox,* 176). Klein discovered through inquiries that the Algerians had no idea Cleaver was there. "They didn't know and didn't care," said Cleaver (Gates, 43). Encouraged, Cleaver himself spoke with "an official" who assured him the Cubans had lied, but it was not until Ms. Klein had introduced him to the South Vietnamese representatives that he felt secure. One of them happened to be lunching with the president of Algiers, Houari Boumédienne, the day after Cleaver met him. "He said he'd tell Boumédienne we were okay. Next day, the Cubans disappeared; I never saw them again. It was very strange" (43).

The Vietnamese remained the most supportive of associates all the time Cleaver and the other Panthers whom he would accumulate lived in Algiers, three full years. Part of their motivation, of course, was to keep Cleaver and the party on their side in the war with the United States. As Cleaver put it, "We saw the Vietnamese as the spearhead of opposition against imperialism. . . . So at that time we planned a sort of Asian strategy and the Vietnamese were very receptive to this" (Taylor, 44). They were also fully cognizant of Cleaver's opinions on the war as stated in *Soul on Ice,* and knew of his influence with the white leftists. When the Vietcong became the Provisional Government of Vietnam, they were able to move into a better official residence, leaving their old embassy, "a handsome villa in the hill suburb of El Biar" (de Gramont, 30), to Cleaver and his organization as of September 1970.

The Lockwood Interview

But the move was months after Lee Lockwood met the Cleavers in the Victoria Hotel, or Don Schanche visited their somewhat more roomy accommodations several weeks after Antonio Maceo's birth on 29 July.

Lee Lockwood's interview took place in four sittings over three days in late June 1969; the tapes ran to five full hours, approximately half of which material filled a book, *Conversation with Eldridge Cleaver: Algiers* (Lockwood, 27). The discussion ranged widely, reaffirming every point Cleaver on earlier occasions had made about American society.

Cleaver declared that "the American Dream," the belief that all people are created equal and that they have inalienable rights to life, liberty, and the pursuit of happiness, was "the foundation of the American character" (60). He explained to his interviewer the vital importance of those values: "It's very significant that Huey P. Newton made

as an appendage to the Ten Point Program and Platform of the Black
Panther Party a section from the Declaration of Independence of the
United States that talks about all of this. He appended that because he
understood, as every revolutionary in the United States has always
understood, that he was struggling and fighting to implement that
dream. It's possible to be confused on this issue. But it's very important
not to be confused and to understand that" (Lockwood, 61). The same
Cleaver who had used the cynical Pledge of Allegiance he cites in *The
Black Moochie* could also tell Lockwood, "I remember as a child how I
used to choke up every morning—we used to have to line up and
pledge allegiance to the flag, you know" (61), because the juxtaposition
of the ideal and the reality of its implementation, or lack of it, is
exactly what spurs leftist radicals into fits of scorn and rage. It is not
hard to imagine the youthful Cleaver moved by a vision of equality at
one moment and cynical over the reality of racism the next.

A less romantic person might have insisted that "the foundation of the
American character" is greed, lust, envy, and hatred, especially racist
hatred, and that we can expect little else, given the propensity of a flawed
humankind toward the age-old Seven Deadly Sins. But an idealist never
gives up. "What we seek," Cleaver declared, "and what the world seeks,
and what has been the dream of mankind, is utopia . . . what we want to
do is bring heaven down to earth, you see. That is, to create the best
possible living conditions and standards of living that human knowledge
and technology are capable of providing. That's the aspiration of the
revolutionary, and that's the dream" (62–63).

The realization of that dream, however, is impossible as long as there
is capitalism ("a bad scene" {68}) and the resultant class structure, with
the government solidly in support of businesspeople. Speaking for
those at the bottom of society, Cleaver and the Panthers demanded not
that a system based on merit alone replace the present racist system but
that the present system be destroyed and replaced by one "that guaran-
tees to everybody the right to access on an equal basis to all that it takes
to make up the good life, and . . . this has to be socialism" (64). It is
not equal opportunity that Cleaver looked forward to; it is equality of
result in a land free of racist or ethnic bias.

A socialist system in a free democratic society that is fully committed
to individual rights is what Cleaver referred to as a "Yankee-Doodle-
Dandy version of socialism, one that will fit our particular situation"
(63). "The basic problem is the institution of private property" (77).
"What we need . . . is a war on the rich," he said, echoing his *Ramparts*

essay on Bobby Kennedy (64). And he reaffirmed his belief that this class war would have to be waged by revolutionary coalitions among "all oppressed people in America." Reiterating his statements to the Peace and Freedom party, Cleaver stated, "We need machinery in America that can move in two directions at the same time. What we need is a coalition between the forces in the black community which are working on the national question and the forces in the white community which are working on the class question, whereby they can make a common thrust against their common oppressor" (107). To create this implacable "machinery," Cleaver now went beyond coalition to advocating "a North American Liberation Front" that would "unite the revolutionary forces in all of the communities so that they could carry out their activity in a coordinated and disciplined manner" (108). And by "coordinated and disciplined" he did indeed mean a transfer of Black Panther party experience "not into the political arena, but strictly into the military arena where politics have been transformed into warfare" (54). In this manner would be brought about the "revolutionary struggle for the violent overthrow of the United States government and the total destruction of the racist, capitalist, imperialist, neo-colonialist power structure" (54).

Here Cleaver specifically rejects politics, as exemplified by his own candidacy and that of several others on the Peace and Freedom party ticket a year earlier, in favor of urban guerrilla warfare. Simultaneously, however, he urges the creation of a new constitution, which was one of the Panther projects, although its acceptance would be unimaginable without the preliminary destruction of the American "ruling class," given the values and social goals of the black and white radicals who were invited to draw it up. And Cleaver now had a timetable: he predicted that by 1972 there would be "full scale war going on in the United States" and it would be impossible to hold a presidential election; thus, a "military coup" would of necessity take place, followed by a "military dictatorship" (118). The war, in fact, had already begun. Without again identifying King's assassination as the event that changed the situation into open war (as in "Requiem for Nonviolence"), Cleaver declared, "I see that the last straw has already been placed on the camel's back, and the camel's back is broken, and the war is already going on" (118).

Somehow, the movement of the Panthers into the "military arena" was to produce a united front that would defeat the U.S. Army (which would certainly be called into play if a military dictatorship were running the country), by the ruthless employment of urban guerrilla warfare. Had not the Cuban leader in Hentoff's novel pointed out how effectively a small group (like Weatherman, the violent offshoot of SDS) could disrupt a technological society? How easy it would be to imagine a Christ-like, selfless, charismatic revolutionary like Huey Newton leading his people into Washington and finally letting Cleaver burn down the White House. As Lockwood pointed out, the scenario "is an uncompromisingly grim vision indeed: in order to have Utopia, we must have Armageddon first" (29).

Other remarks by Cleaver seem to indicate that he was not, to his mind, merely "selling wolf tickets," or "wolfing," making exaggerated claims about what he (or the Black Panther party) could actually do. When he spoke about Guevara, for example, he not only quoted his favorite and often-used passage, "wherever death may surprise us . . ." (92), which epitomized "my Che Guevara" to him, but also cited "the most important thing" he learned from reading Che. Surprisingly, it was a tidbit of practical advice: "It is the wisdom, when laying an ambush, of shooting the first man, and the position this places the second man in. This is something very important" (93). This valuable piece of information tells "how to intimidate the Army" when it sends out "scouting teams" (93). The idea is that the practice becomes instantly known, and "then problems develop about who's going to be the first man out" and soldiers begin to ask "who is it that has the right to send them out there to give up their lives, and for what?" (94) With enough of this sort of fear and other forms of harassment, such as having the noncombatants break out all the lights and "plunge the city into darkness, so the fighters can move about with a little more security" (95), the army can be turned into a "weak force."

Cleaver still held firmly to the dream he had when he left for Cuba— setting up training camps preparatory to invading "Amerika"—but nothing he did in Algiers bore any resemblance to that task.

The Pan-African Festival

The first distraction was the Pan-African Festival, which ran from 21 July to 1 August 1969. During that time, the Algerian government provided housing for the Cleavers, and they were able to move from their tiny cell into roomier quarters in the Aleti Hotel in time for Maceo's birth and a supportive visit from Mrs. Neal, Kathleen's mother.

Cleaver had mobilized a "huge delegation" (Gates, 43) through Panther artist Emory Douglas, who had accompanied Kathleen as a bodyguard, along with Richard Wright's daughter, Julia Wright Herve. The delegation included Robert Scheer; Dave Hilliard; one of Cleaver's lawyers from Charles Garry's office; Ray "Masai" Hewitt; and Byron Booth, who had arrived from Cuba. Douglas also brought "thousands" of newspapers, art, and propaganda. The Panther delegation called a press conference so that Cleaver could officially "surface," an event that provided quite a boost in publicity for the festival. Cleaver gloated, "At our press conference, there were Algerian officials, Al Fatah, representatives from other governments, and representatives from Liberation movements throughout the world. This freaked out the American press. They covered the whole thing. But to cover us, they had to place us in the context of the Festival" (Gates, 44). During the festival, the Panthers opened a two-floor Afro-American Information Center on Rue Didouche, the main business street, not far from the Al Fatah ("Al Fath," as the "political bureau" of the Palestine Liberation Organization is called) information center. Cleaver took the occasion to denounce Israel along with U.S. imperialism, which "uses the Zionist regime that usurped the land of the Palestinian people as a puppet and pawn." To alternating cheers of "Power to the people" and "Al Fath will win," he declared, "We recognize that the Jewish people have suffered, but this suffering should not be used to justify suffering by Arab people now" ("Eldridge Warmly Received by the People of Algiers," *Black Panther,* 9 August 1969, 3).

To Ericka

Although the *Black Panther* for 5 July 1969 featured the headline "Eldridge Cleaver Breaks His Silence," referring to a taped statement "from somewhere in the Third World" on the subject of Ericka Huggins, the earliest actual publication of a Cleaver article in exile was "On Revolution and Education" in the 28 June *Black Panther,* reprinted in the *Guardian* in July. He begins with a paragraph from V. I. Lenin declaring that "all the marvels of science and the gains of culture belong to the nation as a whole" now that the revolution is complete, and thus sets the tone for a standard New Left essay on the university. All leftists agreed that the "ruling class" dominated the universities and their boards of trustees, but most, like Cleaver himself in his Berkeley class or, more ambitiously, Angela Davis in her leadership role in the creation of a new college for the "oppressed" at San Diego State, seemed to want to use the universities for their radical educational objectives. Here, though, Cleaver disavows any such moderate aims: "We're not reformists, we're not in the movement to reform the curriculum of a given university or a given college or to have a black students' union recognized at a given high school. We are revolutionaries, and as revolutionaries our goal is the transformation of the American social order" (*Black Panther,* 12; *Guardian,* 19 July, 10). Almost incidentally, he denounced the Apollo project, which had just put a man on the moon, as "a misuse of public funds" better spent on the poor, an example of the way in which an imperialistic and power-hungry ruling class distorts social priorities ("Cleaver Denounces Apollo Project as Misuse of Public Funds," *New York Times,* 21 July 1969,40).

The official "Breaks His Silence" tape is addressed to "Sister Erica [*sic*] Huggins," wife of John Huggins, the Panther who had been murdered by US members along with Alprentice "Bunchy" Carter in January. In May, while Cleaver was still in Cuba, a recent Panther recruit named Alex Rackley had been brought to New Haven, Connecticut, from New York, tortured, murdered, and left in a river, supposedly by the order of Bobby Seale, who had recently been in town. Ericka Huggins was almost immediately arrested, along with four other Panther females, one of whom was pregnant, on charges of having participated in the torture phase of the killing, which purportedly took place in a Panther home. Seale stood trial in New Haven for conspiracy to commit murder and to kidnap, kidnapping resulting in death, and aiding and abetting murder. Ericka's charges were identical, with the addition of "binding with intent to commit a crime."[9] The case was to dominate Yale and New Haven until May 1971, when the state of Connecticut dismissed the charges against both Seale and Huggins.

The case was condemned by Panthers and sympathizers as yet another attack by police, or as Panther attorney Charles Garry put it, "agents of some armed agency of the government," adding that fully 29 Panthers had now been killed by police.[10] It was the case of Seale that kept the trial in the public eye. Indeed, the case became such a cause célèbre that at Yale, a May Day rally was held in 1970 that purportedly drew 20,000 demonstrators over the weekend before the earthshaking killings of four white students by Ohio National Guardsmen at Kent State on Monday, 4 May. William Sloane Coffin, the Yale chaplain, declared the trial to be "Panther repression," and Yale's president, Kingman Brewster, Jr., expressed doubt that black revolutionaries could receive "a fair trial anywhere in the United States" (Epstein, 52).

Cleaver's contribution in July 1969 was to emphasize the role of females in the party. With a loyally suffering wife nine months pregnant in the African heat, Cleaver declared that male chauvinism had to be purged from the minds of male Panthers. Twice he invoked the name of Huey Newton against "all manifestations of male chauvinism" and in favor of equality for "a revolutionary woman" who will receive "the same kind of injustice from the pig power structure that a revolutionary man receives" because the police recognize her to be "just as much a threat" ("To Sister Erica [*sic*] Huggins," *Black Panther,* 3).

This is the sole mention of explicitly feminist sentiment anywhere in Cleaver's work, and it would appear to owe a great deal to the influence of Kathleen. In a short summary of his public life written for a Times Books Volume on the sixties, Cleaver later mentioned having read "Simone de Beauvoir and Betty Friedan—*The Feminine Mystique*" at some point previous to his exile.[11] The chronology of the essay is unclear, but it seems reasonable to assume that Cleaver read these feminist authors after meeting Kathleen Neal in the spring of 1967, rather than during his stay in San Quentin. It is possible that this specifically feminist essay was designed to placate his militant wife, who was still officially communications secretary to the party. The theme soon disappeared from Cleaver's writing, however, to be replaced by decidedly reactionary male supremacist sentiments.

SDS/PLP/BPP and Nationalism

A week later, a second communication from "somewhere in the Third World" was taped from the telephone at Black Panther headquarters (Cleaver's telephone bills, he later told Don Schanche, were a source of irritation to the Algerians). After a lengthy introduction full of generalizations about the world liberation struggle against the capitalist system, Cleaver commented that he approved of the SDS resolution made at the organization's national council meeting in Texas in March; the resolution, as readers would have known at the time, praised the Black Panther party (BPP) as the "vanguard force" among black organizations. Those who disagreed with the SDS "right to comment on the struggle in the black community" were merely "reactionary" and their remarks not "worthy of discussion" ("Somewhere in the Third World," *Black Panther,* 12 July 1969, 12). The "reactionary" remarks actually had their source in only one person, black columnist

("From the Other Side of the Tracks") Julius Lester. Lester was incensed that SDS endorsed the Panthers at all, but he was particularly angry that the organization attacked cultural nationalists like Karenga as the "tool" of Nixon and the black capitalist bourgeoisie. SDS condemned them as "pork chop nationalists" (Lester, *Guardian,* 19 April 1969, 13). This condemnation, Lester insisted, was "white chauvinism" and "racist" because the SDS was interfering in a matter that was "none of its concern" (22).

The Panther who responded to this complaint was none other than Kathleen Cleaver, who denounced Lester's column in the 3 May issue of the *Guardian* as "a devious attack on the Black Panther Party in the guise of a racist criticism of SDS" (7). Kathleen's rebuttal was longer than the original column. Among other things, she pointed out that the phrase "porkchop nationalism" was a Panther expression "coined by Huey . . . to describe the phenomenon of black people using their blackness to better sell out their people to the pigs" (14). Lester, a "viper," is charged with being ignorant and "cowardly," his words "madness." The issue is coalition with whites, and in this case, the right of white radicals to express revolutionary solidarity with blacks. Anyone who feels that guilty cultural nationalists can't be attacked, she says, is "counter-revolutionary" and "a fool" who resides on "the other side of the tracks" with "a bunch of punks, sissies and cowards, so fuck them and fuck Julius Lester" (14). Kathleen's husband, quite naturally, supported her opinions.

In his July tape Cleaver also praised the various communities that were organizing "so rapidly," a statement that in part was praise for the action of the Mexican-American Brown Berets and the Puerto Rican Young Lords groups in supporting the Black Panther party effort to expel the People's Labor Party (PLP) group from the SDS on the grounds that PLP considered all nationalism of oppressed minorities "reactionary" ("SDS Ousts PLP," *Guardian,* 26 June 1969). The PLP was against not just "porkchop nationalism" but any degree of ethnic self-awareness as a basis for unity, and so the Panther position is not actually self-contradictory. Particularly, Cleaver points out, it is essential to organize each community first and then to "develop machinery that transcends each community" (12) so that the communities can focus on a "common enemy" (13). The SDS debate was soon to become irrelevant anyway, though, for in July white radicals failed to see why "community control" was so important to the movement, at least for white communities, and thereby alienated the Panthers during the

Panther-sponsored United Front against Fascism Conference in Oakland on 18–20 July, at which most of the 3,000 people attending were white radicals (Lawrence M. Bensky, "The Souls of White Folks," *Hard Times,* 28 July 1969, 3).

The disintegration of the 1968 coalition took up Panther energy at a time when the Panthers felt themselves to be under siege by police, under scrutiny by the McClellan Committee, and under attack by Stokely Carmichael following his departure from the party in June. Ironically, it had been Carmichael's position all along that it was a mistake to work with whites, and he disaffiliated himself from the Panthers.

The remainder of Cleaver's July tape was a sort of "test run" for some concepts Cleaver was developing for a "Note" to his friends from exile. He cited a concept corollary to the one mentioned to Lockwood about the prisons producing revolutionary guerrillas; this time it was the "pigs vamping on freedom fighters" and imprisoning them for "ransom" that would "create more revolutionaries" because the word would be taken into the prisons and spread. In a garbled metaphor, he declared: "It's no longer a case of one or two bad apples in a barrel, but it's a barrel of good apples who know that they're not bad apples, who now realize that the pigs are the bad apples in the barrel and it's time for some pruning. And so we're gonna do some pruning and we're gonna prune these bad apples, these pig apples, off the tree of life and put them into the garbage can of history where they belong" ("Somewhere in the Third World," *Black Panther,* 12 July 1969, 13). Cleaver ended with a theme he would develop fully in his "Note" and in the months to come. He never wanted to leave, he said, and he would return, because Babylon is "where my heart is. And that is where I will be returning to as soon as possible, and it's not far away, and do you dig it? Do you dig it? Do you realize that I will be back and that I'll be back soon? And that just as I was able to get out without the pigs being able to do anything about it, I will be able to get back in without the pigs being able to do anything about it" (13).

Three Notes from Exile

On 17 July, Cleaver took time out from preparations for the Pan-African Festival to finish "A Note to My Friends" and to write "An Open Letter to Stokely Carmichael." The two pieces were printed in *Ramparts,* along with "On Meeting the Needs of the People," an editorial essay about how the Panther Breakfast for Children program and the radicals' People's Park project, a plan to turn an empty lot into an ad hoc park despite the opposition of the Berkeley police, were both revolutionary actions; the trio of writings bore the title "Three Notes from Exile."[12]

The first "Note" was begun just before "surfacing" on 15 July, and it states emphatically that Cleaver has every intention of returning, primarily so as to be able to destroy "all this suffering" in Babylon ("Notes," 29), to "focus in . . . on the Babylonian contempt for the rights of others that stands between me and where I want to be" (30).

There is also an undertone, however—the homesickness of the disoriented traveler. Although Cleaver knew some Spanish that had helped him in Cuba, in Algeria and later in Paris he proved to have little capability for learning French. Now that he had surfaced, he was no longer "incarcerated in an anonymity, the walls of which were every bit as thick as those of Folsom Prison" (30), but he was isolated from the United States and from Algerian society: "And here we are in Algeria. What is a cat from Arkansas, who calls San Francisco home, doing in Algeria? And listen to Kathleen behind me talking over the telephone in French. With a little loosening of the will, I could easily flip out right now!" (30). Cleaver declared he was willing to face "my day in court on the charges on which I was indicted in Oakland" (30) following the 6 April shoot-out, but he could not return to jail. On the other hand he seemed to consider sneaking in again, "the quiet passage back," just as he had slipped out, merely in order to be in hiding on familiar turf: "They are unable to prevent me from returning, not knowing when, where, or how" (30). If he never returned, he admitted, he "would die of a broken heart" (30), but only, of course, because he would thereby "neglect the sense of duty that I have toward my people" (30).

He remarked that his travels had shown him "the poorest in the world, the victims of centuries of colonialism and exploitation" (29). Later, he would grow cynical about this poverty in the many socialist and Communist countries he visited in his "scooting around the globe"; at the time, though, he blamed the United States for all of it, for the people he saw were "being destroyed, starved and killed in our name." By contrast, he had already begun to realize that oppression in the United States was superior to everyday life in Third World countries "free" from the curse of capitalism: "It seems to me now, after seeing this deep shit, that those who are being squashed in Babylon are being squashed between two pieces of silk" (29). For the time being, and for several years to come,

Cleaver ignored the message that the poverty and police-state atmosphere of many countries sent to his mind. Emotionally, he felt himself one with the people and the leaders of the revolutions in all the once-colonized countries he visited; he identified especially with successful revolutionaries who became heads of state. Always a fan of Stalin, with a poster of him in both office and home back in California, Cleaver excused even totalitarianism for the sake of the greater good. All the time he was in Algiers, he stood for world revolution, and he became more convinced, after seeing Cuba, Algeria, North Korea, North Vietnam, China, and the Congo, that a small and intransigent cadre *could* take over even a large country like the United States. The first part of his "Note" concludes: "One last word. I think that we have all been sold a trick—this shit about us being powerless—by the pigs who benefit from the sale. In the formal sense, yes, we have been organized out of the power structure. But we still have the ultimate power: the power to overturn systems, to smash power structures, and to bring pigs to justice. We have that power, and the pigs tremble when they think of it because they know it's true, even if we don't" (29). He ended the "Note" with a reference to the upcoming Pan-African Festival and mentioned the presence of Hilliard, Emory Douglas, and Robert Scheer, along with a "rumor" that Stokely Carmichael would be there, this last information providing a transition to the "Open Letter," which was "previewed" for the *New York Times* reporters in a news conference on 18 July.

The "Letter" focuses directly on the issue of how the black movement should be conducted. From the first, even at the Free Huey rally on 17 February 1968, Cleaver pointed out, Carmichael had taken the occasion "to denounce the coalition" of the Black Panther party with the Peace and Freedom party and to demand instead "a Black United Front" that would have linked both Panthers and SNCC with nonrevolutionary "Cultural Nationalists, the Black Capitalists, and the Professional Uncle Toms, even though it was precisely those three groups who were working to murder your shit even before it broke wind" (32). Because of Stokely's "paranoid fear" and "habit of looking at the world through black-colored glasses," he shunned "unity based on revolutionary principles rather than skin color" in favor of closing ranks "with such enemies of the black people as James Farmer, Whitney Young, Roy Wilkins, and Ron Karenga" (32). Perhaps Cleaver still dreamed of a single black organization such as he envisioned in *Soul on Ice,* but his commitment to Marxism-Leninism and revolution barred him, for ideological reasons, from accepting most blacks as allies.

A secondary point is the unspoken fear of the uneducated portion of the black population that the more educated and talented blacks will move ahead and leave them behind forever. Cleaver, as the spokesman for the revolutionary Marxist portion of "the brothers and sisters off the street," articulates this point indirectly when he complains that "your old Black Power buddies are cashing in on your slogan. In effect, your cry for Black Power has become the grease to ease the black bourgeoisie into the power structure" (32). For the moment, the old "house nigger/ field nigger" dichotomy is merely implicit, but the split continued to influence Cleaver's mentality in the next few years, as he sided more and more with the unemployed and outcast lumpen portion of the proletariat, with the victorious guerrilla warriors of the Third World, with the fighters who would put their lives on the line for the cause.

Cleaver's sentiments in this letter, which he undoubtedly discussed with various Panthers at the conference, appear to have influenced Seale and Hilliard's response to the United Front against Fascism disputes over community control. In interviews with the *Berkeley Barb* and the *Guardian* on 4 August and 9 August, respectively, Seale and Hilliard were both intent on reacting to white recalcitrance as an "attack" and attempt to "dictate" what whites were willing to do "in the black community," indicating a possible desire to dominate black-white efforts on the community control issue. Determined to avoid the SNCC situation, in which whites became disproportionately influential, the two Panther spokesmen reacted with anger, threats, and insulting references to the SDS level of manhood (Jack Smith, "Panther Leaders Blast SDS," 16 August 1969, 4).

There were two things Cleaver had chosen to omit from his "Open Letter"—his recent experience with racism in socialist Cuba and his awareness of Stokely's hypocrisy on the question of dealing with whites, a matter he finally spoke about years later:

In a very demagogic way, [Carmichael] used this thing about white people. I traveled with Stokely as a journalist on his first tour of Northern college campuses in 1967, in January or February. We went, I think, to the University of Chicago, Penn, to New York and to Detroit. He would make his standard speech, pushing hard that white people work in the white community, black people in the black community. Then, in Chicago, he went to his white doctor's pad for dinner. So I said, "Why are you here, man; how can you be?" And he said, "This man has been a long-time SNCC supporter." You see, instead of associating with white people openly, he was doing it sneakily. He would do those kind of things. And this was a malady of that movement: running heavy lines about white people, then sneaking around fucking white girls. But we used to deal openly. We'd say it was okay to do this, then they would attack us for that. But they did it themselves. Because they were sneaky, they didn't have to deal with criticism. Finally, I thought that was immoral and not useful. (Gates, 44)

The seemingly endless permutations of black-white misunderstanding and intrablack conflict over various ideological and personal issues were a permanent problem for the New Left and the black movement throughout the entire period of sixties and seventies activism; ultimately, with the help of the FBI, distrust and intransigence would split the Panthers from their white allies and from one another as well. For the moment, Cleaver chose to blame Carmichael for the failure of the BPP-SNCC "merger," ending with a snide citation from Malcolm X: "Remember what Brother Malcolm said in his Autobiography: 'We had the best organization that the black man has ever had in the United States—and niggers ruined it!' POWER TO THE PEOPLE" (32).

A negative assessment of both Cleaver's and Carmichael's roles was subsequently made by Daniel H. Watts in the September issue of the *Liberator*. Focusing simultaneously on the debate over white involvement in the movement and on the current African residency of both men, as well as their support of the Pan-African conference, Watts suggested that neither was actively providing leadership to black Americans:

Stokely, Eldridge . . . the survival for 25,000,000 Americans of African descent is here in the other USA, not in Africa. Returning "home" to Africa as an individual solution to the racism encountered in America is fine, but unfortunately Africa today is neither psychologically, politically or economically ready to absorb millions of Afro-Americans. We must, then, get it together here, and any argument, whether public or private, over the ancient riddle of how Black is Black is thus pure folly indeed. For in reality, as long as we continue to live, to work and be financially dependent upon white Americans and white institutions, none of us can argue with any degree of logic about whether white America is or should be involved in the affairs of Afro-Americans. What we should be debating is our order of priorities: (1) if we choose to leave the USA, then we must prepare our "Noah's Ark" and plot our course as to where we want to resettle; (2) if we wish to remain here in the USA, we must decide which institutions to build to guarantee our survival; and perhaps most important of all, (3) we must stop massaging our egos with dreams of glory and bullshitting with each other, for the establishment peeped our game long ago—that is why they are taking care of business while we are still trying to discover what our business is.[13]

Watts's practicality had no effect on the quarrel between the two men; as has always been typical of the Left in America, ideological disputes took priority over any call to action.

The third and final of the "Notes from Exile" concerns the new Breakfast for Children program initiated by the Panthers and the People's Park campaign in Berkeley. The Panthers saw themselves as creating the groundwork for revolution by serving poor black schoolchildren breakfasts of food "donated" by somewhat reluctant area businesses. Although he (and most black radicals) had trouble seeing the establishment of a park as anything more than trivial, Cleaver ingeniously links the two efforts as revolutionary attacks on private property. When "the People" actually attempt to create the "rearrangement of a system" that takes "all the means of production, the institutions of a society . . . out of the hands of those who now have them and have abused them," then they move "beyond the racist pig cops to confront the avaricious businessmen and the demagogic politicians" who send the police and the National Guard in to protect their property and especially their ownership of it. For this, they deserve to die: "We must get it clear in our minds that we will shoot anyone who uses a gun, or causes others to use guns, to defend the system of oppression, racism and exploitation. . . . We must face the fact that we are at war in America" (35). All that is needed "to unlock and focus the great revolutionary spirit of the people" is to make them actually aware of the problem, and not just theoretically capable of comprehending "the relationship of struggle" between ruling class and ruled.

The Black Che Guevara

The overwhelming problem, as Cleaver told German journalist Stefan Aust in an undated interview later that week, was to awaken people to the need for international revolution and the reality of war when in fact, "even in the most oppressed areas,"[14] they are "oppressed between slices of silk" compared with those who live in poverty elsewhere.[15] When the people understand their true situation and also witness the actual persecution of Panthers who are arrested and held for extremely high bail, like the New York Panther 21, then they will be willing to join in with the "organizational machinery" that will make the revolution. Cleaver specified that the United Front against Fascism was "a very important move" toward creating solidarity but that he would prefer a North American Liberation Front, since, as he had stated in the Lockwood interview, "politics have been transformed into war" (Aust, 12). Cleaver's insistence on war as early as 1969 shows his basic disagreement with Huey Newton quite dramatically. While the Panthers at home were concentrating on defensive maneuvers and clear-cut, narrowly defined programs like Breakfast for Children, Cleaver was demanding armed confrontation immediately and assuring everyone that it could succeed. He considered the Weathermen and the Panther 21, who apparently planned to blow up major symbolic targets like Grand Central Station and the Statue of Liberty, to be on the right track, whereas the Panthers in California had sneered at the concept: "We would not waste dynamite on the blowing up of some jive statue" ("Scorned and Denounced," *Good Times,* 9 April 1969, 5).

Cleaver, however, seems to have begun to think of himself as kin to the successful revolutionary leaders of the world. Even *Newsweek* had labeled him "a sort of black Che Guevara" when he first went into exile,[15] and his visits to various Communist countries in 1969–71 would only serve to feed this fantasy.

During the festival, little Antonio Maceo arrived, his life as a revolutionary already planned for him. In the third of his July "Notes from Exile," Cleaver had referred to "our child" and commented, "I'm counting this Panther before he claws his way out of the womb" (34). The announcement in the next issue of the weekly *Black Panther,* dated 2 August, was headed "Another Problem for the Fascists" and began, "A new 'Rage' is on the set" (2). The 16 August issue features a family portrait in the militant style of the day. Eldridge wore a dashiki (in honor of Africa, one presumes, not as a gesture of friendship with black American cultural nationalists), and Kathleen, holding the child, wore her hair in an Afro "bush" at least six inches deep. Of the four short paragraphs announcing the birth of the new "revolutionary warrior," only the first refers to him; the other three sketch the life of the original Antonio Maceo, whom Cleaver had come to admire so much, "the best warrior of the 1895 campaign" against the Spanish (3).

On 23 August, Cleaver published in the *Black Panther* a short item entitled "Eldridge on Black Capitalism." In it, he condemned Richard Nixon's corrupting the concept of black power into black capitalism, on the grounds that capitalism in America was an evil, "constructed out of the slave labor of Black people; out of genocide of Indians; out of the forced labor of Chinese and the exploitation of poor Whites"; black capitalism, then, was simply "a neo-colonialist policy" in disguise. By using this "treacherous policy" to "buy off the black bourgeoisie and other black opportunists," Nixon merely gave them "the crumbs from the master's table" (5). Cleaver here made use of an image that had first appeared in *The Black Moochie,* and although the humble Negro in khaki has become the black middle-class entrepreneur, the concept of an obedient and servile black person is intact. But whereas in *The Black Moochie* Cleaver had had no specific idea of how to oppose the system according to which the white Omnipotent Administrators, as he called them elsewhere, divided up the cake among themselves, by 1969 he was convinced that the only solution for black people was to seize the cake, as it were. Yet neither in *The Black Moochie* nor anywhere else did he concern himself with the problem of the Little Red Hen in the children's tale—who would grow the wheat and make the cake? What Cleaver saw as the solution to all economic problems was for the other animals to take the cake away from the hen, whether she thought they deserved it or not. The evil, he always insisted, was in distribution.

Hard Times

When Don Schanche visited Cleaver in September, the family, which now included not only the baby but its maternal grandmother, who was on a two-week visit, was preparing to move from the Aleti, a former luxury hotel, to an apartment "above a malodorous auto repair shop on the main thoroughfare of Point Piscade, west of Algiers . . . a five room walkup." Temporarily, the entourage also included "Gwen and Amiri Akili [hijackers from Philadelphia whom Cleaver had met in Cuba] and their year-old child" (*Paradox,* 200). Each family had its own room; Mrs. Neal had one to herself.

Among the many stresses of life in a strange city, and with a new baby, was the fact that the Cleavers were low on cash. Most of the $15,000 Eldridge had taken with him out of the United States had been absorbed by a variety of expenses, among which was what seemed to be the support of the entire Panther contingent. Schanche reported Kathleen's confidential request to him for "as much as you can" (*Paradox,* 177) and Eldridge's reprimands of Byron Booth, Akili, and Rahim (Clinton Smith) when they requested funds of him. Later, in *Soul on Fire,* Cleaver said that even after the government had declared he was no longer a Cuban national, money was scarce. Although he had estimated to Schanche that he was worth "about a half million dollars" (177), none of that cash seemed to find its way to Algiers. Thus, it was necessary to "start hustling" (*Fire,* 150). Cleaver's "criminal background," as he put it, helped him in "trafficking in stolen passports and counterfeiting visas" (151) and, later, in selling stolen cars from Europe. "Someone," he reported, sometimes "Panther sympathizers" and presumably sometimes ordinary criminals, would steal, lease, or even "buy" for 10 percent down a car and get it to Algiers. "Cars we brought into Algeria," said Cleaver, "found their way throughout the Third World" (*Fire,* 153).

Cleaver's dream in late 1966 had been to cut off all contact with the criminal world and to work to benefit himself, his race, and his country. Now he found himself "back into gangster patterns" of behavior, including "the regular use or threat of firearms" and "the readiness for attack or a street corner shootout" (153). Actually, it was his Panther membership that had reintroduced him to those things, as well as "the protection of oneself in a very tense society" (154), and Cleaver participated in them now not to make revolution directly but only to survive. Further, the Algerians held him responsible for the behavior of what would amount to "nearly thirty" people at one point before the end came in 1972, an "assortment of revolutionaries, hijackers, bank robbers and revolutionary Communists" (154) that severely tested Cleaver's powers of command. It is little wonder that he complained to Don Schanche that he couldn't write, even in 1969.

In spite of Cleaver's lack of productivity, Schanche asked him whether he minded having become a "frustrated, exiled theoretician" of the revolution. Cleaver's reply revealed at least some of the fantasy or frustration behind his ever more strident calls for intensifying the struggle: "I would rather be a soldier . . . I have a real desire to pull some triggers. I'm not saying I want to get all fucked up, you know. I'm saying that out there are a lot of targets that I actually want to aim at and I want to pull the trigger. This is something that I want to do. At the same time, I want to do these other things. That's the way to take a long-range shot at them. I know that if I can really define this shit, it will be like shooting a thousand of them. It's not immediate, though. I need them both. I think we do need that" (188). What Cleaver did do was to expound to Schanche along much the same lines as he did to Lee Lockwood and in his few written (or spoken) articles: he attacked the Zionists, including all American Jews who supported Israel; he supported Al Fatah; he insisted on the need to bond with white radicals in a unity "based on revolutionary principles" (206), not on race; he called for escalating "the people's war," especially for members of the white community, whose "footdragging" constituted "the great sabotage to the revolution," in order to "smash and disrupt the machinery of the oppressors" (208). When Schanche left Cleaver, Cleaver and Byron Booth, bearing one of Schanche's "liberated" Nikons, were on their way to North Korea by way of Moscow. About two months later, *True* magazine printed Schanche's revised estimate of Cleaver.

While he has not yet pulled a trigger, he has written, but the quality of his writing has suffered terribly both from the chaotic life conditions of exile and from his own deliberate decision to disdain art for politics. *Ramparts* recently published two of his pieces, one of them a commentary on his exile and the other an open letter to Stokely Carmichael, whose violent anti-white feelings are anathema to Cleaver. In style and content, neither was much more than a hurried political tract. The slick, radical magazine followed in the next issue with the beginning of a partially completed autobiographical novella which Cleaver wrote while he was still in prison in 1966. The rhythm of the prose was commanding, style simple and bursting with power. To one whose admiration of Cleaver came through the strength and eloquence of *Soul on Ice,* also written in prison, the contrast was symptomatic of Cleaver's condition. He has lost power, both literary power and real power, as a result of his exile and his almost exclusive preoccupation with Marxism. If he remains in exile, a prospect which horrifies him, he will almost certainly fade away as a leader of the radical New Left. (quoted from *True* in *Paradox,* 217)

Schanche's later article in the *Atlantic* went even further. He delineated Cleaver as a man who had become "increasingly isolated inside a brain that simply isn't functioning as it used to." His evaluation of Cleaver's prose—"stumbling diatribe"—was also more negative ("Against Wall," 61).

North Korea

Cleaver's and Byron Booth's two-man contingent arrived in North Korea on 11 September 1969 and remained about a month. The principal reason for the trip was the eight-day International Conference on Tasks of Journalists of the Whole World in Their Fight against U.S. Imperialist Aggression. While there, Cleaver addressed the group in a lengthy anti-American harangue entitled "Solidarity of the Peoples until Victory or Death"; the speech attacked "the monster of U.S. imperialism," which was armed variously with "tentacles of aggression" and "talons of aggression," and the country itself, inhabited by "the freaks of mankind," the "bloodsucking capitalist vultures and the blood-letting warmongers who control the U.S. government and benefit from its barbaric policies" (*Black Panther,* 25 October 1969, 12). Cleaver said, "The American flag and the American Eagle are the true symbols of fascism, and they should elicit from the people the same outraged repugnance elicited by the swastika of nazi [*sic*] Germany and the rising sun of the Japanese imperialists" (12). His concession to the journalistic nature of the occasion was a call to "give meaning to the old saying that the pen is mightier than the sword, or else throw down the pen and pick up the sword," a turn of a phrase in which the Cleaver of old attempted to emerge. Essentially, however, the author was subordinate to the radical, even as he defined a journalist's task not as responsible reporting or analysis but an obligation to produce "articles . . . that will inflame the masses, that will spur on the revolutionary temptation to kidnap American ambassadors, hijack American airplanes, blow up American pipelines and buildings, and to shoot anyone who uses guns or weapons or causes others, directly or indirectly, to use guns and other weapons in the bloodstained service of imperialism against the people" (13).

A short article published in the *Black Panther* a few weeks later and entitled "Statement to All Reactionary Journalists and Pressmen of the United States of America" imposed a similar standard of partisanship upon "the members of the mass media" who were reporting on Bobby Seale's treatment in Judge Hoffman's court during the Chicago Eight trial. Any objective reporting that was critical of Seale's disruptive behavior was "lies" or "bullshit"; it identified the enemy: "Up against the wall for the men of words" (8 November 1969, 2). Cleaver declared that the only solution to such reporters' "evil" behavior, since "they know what they are doing and . . . will continue to do that no matter what you say," is "to take their heads" (2).

Cleaver also contributed an article to the *Pyongyang Times* while he was in North Korea, reprinted in the *Black Panther* as "We Have Found It Here in Korea" (1 November 1969, 11). "It," as Cleaver revealed late in the article, was the successful implementation of "international strat-egy based on [international] analysis" of the "struggle against imperial-ism," by which he meant success in maintaining a socialist state, as Premier Kim Il Sung had done following his "deep experience in guerrilla warfare" during the battle "against imperialism," the Korean War. Cleaver recounted a visit to the "execution chambers" of Sinchon, used by both Japanese and American imperialists "to mass murder Korean children," and one to the demarcation line at Panmunjon, where he and Booth confronted a black GI from Georgia. Cleaver and Booth told the soldier it was "absurd" for him to serve as a "mercenary" for the imperialists after having been "subjected to extreme oppression" at home. "We could see how weakwilled and confused he was," Cleaver reported. "It was disgusting." Cleaver concluded with assurances that "ardent battalions" of oppressed Americans, responding to Che Guevara's call for "an army of liberation," waited to join with North Koreans in the "sacred cause of our joint struggle" and carry it through to "the bittersweet end" (11).

On the way back from North Korea, Cleaver and Booth were surprised to meet *Time* correspondent Stanley Cloud in Moscow. Cloud, who remembered Cleaver from having covered the Panthers in California, recalled the face "from a steamy Oakland courtroom."[16] He described Cleaver, with his black leather jacket and single gold button earring, as "unchanged. The face was still hard and menacing, the bearing still rigid." What Cleaver had to say was nothing new to readers of the *Black Panther,* except for the complaints about the Soviet Union for its less-than-intransigent stand toward Western imperialism. He praised Kim Il Sung, criticized Stokely Carmichael, and predicted an American revolution "in our life times." Toward that end, he rejected "national dissent" and "re-evaluation" following the passage of the era of demonstrations. "There's nothing to re-evaluate," he declared, "except the choice of weapons" (27).

Radicals and *Radical Chic*

Cleaver returned to Algiers in October 1969 and began to write again. In November the Cleaver houseguests were white radical Stew Albert "and his rib [female companion] Gumbo."[17] The visit produced Cleaver's introduction to Jerry Rubin's book, *Do It! Scenarios of the Revolution;* it was a disjointed and chronologically incoherent collection of thoughts about the Panthers, Rubin, the Democratic National Convention of 1968, and the coming revolution, admittedly written after Cleaver had "turned on" with marijuana (*Do It,* 6). An interesting item of information is revealed in Cleaver's mention that he first met and admired Stew Albert, Jerry Rubin, and Jack Weinberg of SDS back in December 1966, when he was first paroled and Beverly Axelrod was introducing him to "her friends," people he had read about in prison. This first meeting preceded Cleaver's encounter with Huey Newton by two months and helped create the situation that would lead to the Panther-PFP coalition, the nomination of Cleaver for president (and his selection of Rubin, newly become a Yippie, as running mate), and the continuing, if thorny and stress-filled, Panther-SDS alliance, which was now doomed.

The other item that emerged from that visit was a short article by Cleaver called "On the Weathermen," printed, with Albert's "Introduction from Algiers," in the *Berkeley Tribe* for 29 November with the headline "Eldridge on Weatherman" (reprinted in the *Black Panther* of 22 November 1969). Albert assures us that Cleaver writes "from the clarity of world revolution" (*Tribe,* 3; *Black Panther,* 5). Not only was Cleaver living in Algiers, but he had recently visited North Korea and had "found there a nation of Newtons, tough brothers off the block who once built a mountainous barbecue which imperialism called Heartbreak Ridge." The connection with Weatherman, to Albert, is that Kim Il Sung's revolution, like any other, was "at some point unique"; hence, no orthodox criticism is likely to be relevant. Therefore, while some people were criticizing Weatherman and its black imitators, the Panther 21, for their foolhardiness, adventurism, and self-destructiveness, Albert pronounced, "I do not think the Weathermen can be criticized by quoting 1905 Lenin."

Cleaver's predictably pro-Weatherman statement rejects "a reactionary nape (essence of jackanape streamlined) like Julius Lester" and any others "who block the revolution with rhetoric." The victories will be made not "in courtrooms and at press conferences, but in the streets of Babylon, doing it in the road but doing it. As long as we kill pigs." He concluded, "In order to stop the slaughter of the people we must accelerate the slaughter of the pigs. Those who can't stand the sight of blood, especially their own, should stay home and pray for those who come outside to move, to do it, and pray for victory and not for an end to the slaughter. Pray for us to win, because if we win you will be safe. If we lose, then kiss the baby goodbye" (5, 3).

In late November Cleaver began efforts to return home. On 27 November and again on 6 December he met with U.S. diplomats in Algiers for the purpose of obtaining a regular passport. Since a passport would have allowed freedom of travel anywhere in the world, however, and since Cleaver was a fugitive from the United States, his request was denied. Consequently, Cleaver issued a press release in which he complained, "It proves they're racist, because there's a White lady here who also wanted a passport. They gave her a passport real quick, her name is Elaine Klein. They gave her a passport immediately. When all the Black people went up there, they refused them" ("On Denial of Passport," *Black Panther*, 20 December 1969, 9). The only possibility open to him or any of the other hijackers (Kathleen already had a passport) was a certificate of identity permitting him to return to the United States. ("And they even wanted to pay my way back, and get me a ticket. I don't need them to book me no flights.") Once back in the United States, he would have to return to prison as he had been scheduled to do on 27 November 1968. Further, Cleaver would be liable for a $57,715 tax lien that the IRS had filed against him in December 1968 for taxes owed in 1968, not to mention interest and penalties and subsequent taxes on royalties on both books (Earl Caldwell, "Cleaver Appeal Planned on Coast," *New York Times*, 21 December 1968, 16).

At some point in late fall, the Cleavers abandoned the apartment for a house that Cleaver later referred to as "a shack on the Mediterranean" (*Fire*, 150). When author and photographer Gordon Parks visited the Cleavers and their five-month-old boy in January 1970, he described it as "one of those yellowish-white concrete houses that line the Mediterranean coast,"[18] with five rooms and a kitchen. Besides the Cleavers, resident Panthers now included Emory Douglas, artist and Panther minister of culture, and Connie Matthews (an ex-secretary of Newton's and wife of New York Panther Mike Tabor), who "represented the Panthers in Scandinavia" (Parks, "Rage," 20).

Cleaver, whom Parks labeled "the most uncompromising individual I ever met," was angry over the recent killings of Panthers Fred Hampton and Mark Clark by the police in Chicago. Cleaver's prediction that the police would be found justified in the shooting was very nearly correct, but in spite of conservative belief to the contrary, investigation did lead to the conclusion that the men were killed as part of "a deliberately planned raid on a Black Panther headquarters" (Epstein, 73). The usual paean to the coming revolution followed, along with threats to "the cops who murdered them" (Parks, "Rage," 20), while Kathleen, "pale, strong, and intense," already pregnant with the next child, supported her husband: "Right on, Papa Rage." Cleaver's guarantee that white allies would be of value in protecting blacks from being "wiped out" was augmented by his belief that those allies would help after the revolution to establish "social justice" and to "replace racism with solidarity" (23). Parks was skeptical. "Social justice," he thought to himself later, "is much more difficult to come by than martyrdom" (23).

The most significant Panther event of January 1970 excluded Cleaver altogether but featured both Ray "Masai" Hewitt and Panther field marshall Don Cox, who had recently visited Cleaver to plan a way to raise funds ("February Trial Scheduled for Panther Late in Court," *New York Times,* 23 December 1969, 16). The event, a benefit for the jailed Panther 21, was immortalized by Tom Wolfe in *Radical Chic* (1970). As of fall 1969, Wolfe said, "Radical Chic," the compassion for the poor and downtrodden that is felt by the very rich and expressed in an elegant, socially correct manner by fund-raisers in penthouses, was the rage, "the new wave supreme in New York Society."[19] Even *Vogue* had a column on "Soul Food" as "a form of Black self-awareness and, to a lesser degree, of white sympathy for the Black drive to self-reliance. It is as if those who ate the beans and greens of necessity in the cabin doorways were brought into communion with those who, not having to, eat those foods voluntarily as a sacrament" (Wolfe, 36–37). Panther taste, on the other hand, is a source of comic speculation. What does one offer to the descendants of the cabin dwellers who are talking about armed revolution against one's own class? Wolfe writes, "Do the Panthers like little Roquefort cheese morsels rolled in crushed nuts this way, and asparagus tips in mayonnaise dabs, and *meatballs petites au Coq Hardi,* all of which are at this very moment being offered to them on gadrooned silver platters by maids in black uniforms with hand ironed white aprons . . . the butler will bring them their drinks. . . . Deny it if you wish to, but such are the *pensées métaphysiques* that rush through one's head on these Radical Chic evenings just now in New York" (5). Those were not exactly the white allies Cleaver had in mind, but they had money and a lot more to lose by a Panther connection than the Panthers did. And lose they did. Bernstein was booed at a concert when the *New York Times* printed the story about his "meeting" for the Panthers, and he was forced to assure fellow Jews that he did not support Panther violence, love of Al Fatah, or Arab desire to destroy Israel (Wolfe, 110). His only concern was the Panthers' civil liberties; actually, they were "a bad lot," he said.

The McGrath Interview

Cleaver would have enjoyed the party, but he also enjoyed, to a certain extent, his role in setting up what had become "an information center" instead of a guerrilla camp. When John McGrath interviewed him in February, he was still promoting the concept of a "people's army" that would develop and win the revolution through arms, although he inexplicably changed its name from North American Liberation Front to New World Liberation Front.[20] Cleaver's outspoken sympathy with the lumpen proletariat, the unemployable lowest portion of the "working" class, emerges in his condemnation of the American Communist party for its "diabolical failure" to deal with the "specific conditions of oppression of black people" (McGrath, 10–11). Cleaver's insistence on the special nature of the black experience in America, like that of Richard Wright, would have no impact on true believers among Marxists, and would serve to alienate him from yet another potential ally, although in reality the Communists in the United States had never seen eye to eye with Panthers anyway, partly on the issue of nationalism and partly on the use of violence both to create a revolution in the near future and to create confrontations with the police on a day-to-day basis.

The Communist party insisted that only the working class could function as the key to the revolutionary process, while Cleaver knew that middle-class union members would never revolt. His awareness that, in practice, the Panthers represented only the underclass prevented him from understanding that a revolution cannot be made in a country where most people support the system. His alliance with white radicals and his winning of more than 36,000 votes for president (when the voting age was still 21) made him believe that the groundswell was in favor of the revolution and that within a few years the younger generations would dominate. In spite of his claim, then, that the Panthers were Marxist-Leninist, he continually criticized the old-line party members for "lagging behind" (12) at the very least, when what black people really needed, he thought, was a "Kami-Kaze consciousness" that would make revolutionary suicide a real possibility.

Cleaver's distrust of the black bourgeoisie, the black capitalists, and all other nonlumpen blacks extended even to "educated people," who he felt were originally trained in order better to serve the slave master "and [who had] performed these functions well" into the present. Cleaver had dropped the old "house nigger/field nigger" designations, but his exclusive sympathy for the black masses, whether seen as field slaves or as lumpen proletariat, remained solid. As a result, he sided not with workers versus the capitalists who would rob them of their just share in the wealth but with the unemployed and outcast versus everyone else, who became "establishment."

Only those who could identify with a colonized, poverty-stricken people could consider Fanon's *Wretched of the Earth* to be their Bible and imagine an armed revolt led by a dedicated few from that group, as did Newton and Seale right from the beginning. They were really Fanonists, not programmatic Marxists. Cleaver told McGrath that he and others he knew in prison read Fanon along with Marx, Lenin, Mao, and "even some Fabian socialist essays" (12) but that Newton and Seale simply read Fanon and "something clicked inside their heads and they put the Party together" (12). The three found their common ground in the concept of blacks as a colonized people rising in revolt, not as members of a working class oppressed by capitalism. The later indictment of capitalism was inevitable, as was the linking of racism and slavery with the economic exploitation of black people.

It was Cleaver's concept at this time that the Liberation Front needed to move against the enemy establishment. The various black, brown, red, and yellow power groups, along with the white revolutionaries in SDS and Weatherman, would use any means necessary to attack all establishment, bourgeois persons, making use of ethnic bias when possible, as between Irish and Italian groups in large cities, and denouncing all educated enemies of the people, whatever race or color they might be. Cleaver's plan as of early 1970 was to attack where he thought the power was:

> *John:* In fact you're aiming for Washington or aiming to overthrow Washington?
>
> *Eldridge:* Washington, Washington, D.C. Because that's where the seat of power is. That's where the country is controlled from. Actually we're aiming for Long Island—Long Island controls New York, New York controls the country and the country controls the world. (12)

It is hard to imagine Cleaver seriously expecting to take over the country from Long Island, using the mountains to attack other major population centers, as he suggested elsewhere, but he seems to have convinced himself that "Fortress America" was really just a "skeleton in armor" (17), not a genuinely powerful armed force. "America is very vulnerable from within," he insisted, and declared that if enough people understood that and could be brought to "move on" it, then it might be possible to "avert disaster." If not, America would "take the world down the drain" (17). The next vital step, not surprisingly, was to "create machinery" that would get him back into the country so that he could lead the fight.

The Ideology of the Black Panther Party, 1970

As it happened, 1970 would be the last full year Cleaver would spend as a Panther. He wrote a number of short pieces for the *Black Panther*, notably a "Happy Birthday, Huey" tribute (*Black Panther*, 28 February 1970, 3) and the essay "Huey's Standard" as a gift to Huey Newton for his February birthday (*Black Panther*, 15 March 1970). In the months before he led a delegation of eleven radicals back to North Korea and on to North Vietnam and Peking, he wrote several similar items, which varied little in their themes and subjects. Briefly, among these were "Manifesto from the Land of Fire and Blood," an introduction to some pro–Kim Il Sung propaganda that attacked the "savage persecution of political parties and patriots," that is, Communists, in the Republic of Korea at the hands of "U.S. aggressor troops and their stooges" (*Black Panther*, 15 March 1970, 13), and "On Richard the Pig-Hearted Nixon," in which he (correctly) charged Nixon with having "unleashed the forces of repression upon the movement in general and the Black Panther Party in particular" (*Black Panther*, 19 May 1970, 2).

Actually, J. Edgar Hoover was the one who originated the crackdown, since he was the source of the orders to the San Francisco and Chicago offices. On top of telephone tapping, fully authorized by Attorney General John Mitchell, and police harassment and even killing, as in FBI agents' apparent collaboration with the Chicago police in the Hampton murder, Hoover's organization took advantage of the disagreement over tactics between Cleaver and Newton to create a permanent split through a campaign of disinformation such as might have been used during wartime to spread false information between an enemy country and its agents in the field, unknown to both. The first item in the effort to split the Panthers was "an anonymous letter to Cleaver which said Panther leaders were seeking to undercut his influence"; next was a letter from Paris to Oakland that made Newton and

Hilliard begin to distrust their European followers (Bergman and Weir, 48). The effort, which stretched for months until the breakup was complete in February 1971, would include innumerable calls and phony letters and intraparty directives.

On 31 May 1970 Cleaver published two articles in one issue of the *Black Panther*. "The Pentagon" linked the current campus atmosphere of fear and paranoia with the general crackdown on radicals. The killings of four students at Kent State by Ohio National Guardsmen had taken place on 4 May, and only 10 days later two black students were shot and killed at Jackson State in Mississippi when police fired into a dormitory. Students on nearly every campus in the United States went out on strike in protest (about 760, according to James Michener's *Kent State*),[21] for almost every student, black or white, could imagine being one of the victims of such a massacre, so frequent had been the riots and demonstrations of the preceding four years. These "murders," declared Cleaver, demonstrate "that an overall plan is in action" that calls for both political and judicial persecution and "slaughter in the streets." It is the Pentagon, "the headquarters for the policemen of the whole world," that must be dealt with, for "the domestic police—local police departments and National Guard—have all been programmed by the Pentagon" (14).

"Method, Time, and Revolution" is directed only at blacks and concerns, as its title indicates, "how" and "when" to have the revolution. For extremely clear reasons, "how" ought to be violent and "when" ought to be "now." The "only redeeming path" left open to black people other than "prison, death, the U.S. Armed Forces or a short, hard and bitter life" is "total war" against the oppressor (168). The "stone lumpen," the "stomp-down black lumpen proletariat," is "the backbone of the Black Panther Party," without which there could be no revolution. In the past, Cleaver said, blacks "begged for mercy" down on their knees in "the Martin Luther King position," but now the "pigs" have "provoked us to madness":

Madness. People are right when they say that Black people are not in a position to face down the pigs on their level. But we are in a position to implement head-up murder. We can guarantee the total destruction of Babylon—with a form of struggle that pigs will call madness. But madness is the Black man's hydrogen bomb inside Babylon, and we must unleash this hydrogen bomb, now, because pigs are carrying out a genocidal conspiracy of extermination against our people. And since we have everything in the pot, why shouldn't everything and everybody in Babylon be in the pot with us? The name of the pot is Babylon. ALL POWER TO THE PEOPLE—Eldridge Cleaver. (19)

In June 1970 the Panthers published a pamphlet by Cleaver entitled "On the Ideology of the Black Panther Party" and simultaneously printed it as an essay in the 6 June issue of the *Black Panther* (12–15).[22] Originally, the piece was intended to be the first of a series of articles, but the rest never materialized.

Cleaver's main topic is the definition of the black lumpen and a defense of its autonomy. Initially, he distinguishes it from the early, more strictly European Marxist concept of the proletariat and also from the specifically African refinement of Marx's and Lenin's theories by Fanon. Fanon, while at least black and therefore a more acceptable authority figure for Cleaver than Marx ("It's like praying to Jesus, a White man" [5; *Black Panther,* 12]), still did not provide "the last word" on Afro-American revolution. Only Americans could do that; "we must take the teachings of Huey P. Newton as our foundation and go from there" (5; *Black Panther,* 12).

In developing "a uniquely Afro-American" (6; *Black Panther,* 13) self-definition and the prerogative for action that goes with it, Cleaver next isolates the "Black Working Class and Black Lumpen in the Colony" from their counterparts in the "Mother Country," which was not an idea original with Newton but rather a concept popular with the Left and first embraced in print by Cleaver himself among the Panthers.

At any rate, Cleaver's point is to indict the white Marxist-Leninists in the American Communist party for their failure to perceive the reality of race in America, "assuming the existence of one All-American Proletariat; one All-American Working Class, and one All-American Lumpenproletariat," and then to reject the efforts of the black lumpen to revolt as "spontaneous," "unorganized," and "chaotic and un-directed"—probably, Cleaver suggests, "because they themselves did not order the actions" (10; *Black Panther,* 15). Cleaver's cynicism to-ward the Communists was part of an "objectivity of vision" such as had come to Richard Wright only after several years of enduring party scorn and bullying on top of intellectual narrowness. The Panthers, who had always insisted on their autonomy, were able to confront overbearing white radicals as easily as they did the police simply because of their group cohesion. Cleaver's insistence on the validity of Panther self-definition had behind it the united strength of the Panthers, who had begun as black nationalists and never ceased to believe in the relevance of ethnic and racial identity.

In his effort, however, to differentiate the black lumpen from all others, Cleaver went so far as to attack the entire working class, asserting that the lumpen were the "majority of mankind" as opposed to the "percentage" that has been bought off by capitalism "with jobs and security" (8; *Black Panther,* 14). His partisanship exclusively with those who have been labeled "parasites upon the Working Class" (18) and whom Marx himself called "the Scum Layer of Society" (11; *Black Panther,* 15) is consistent with his other statements to the effect that blacks, led by the Panthers, can destroy America if they can do nothing else and therefore have nothing to lose in an armed struggle. He embraces, in their name, the identity of lumpen:

O.K. We are Lumpen. Right on. The Lumpenproletariat are all those who have no secure relationship or vested interest in the means of production and the institutions of capitalist society. That part of the "Industrial Reserve Army" held perpetually in reserve; who have never worked and never will; who can't find a job; who are unskilled and unfit; who have been displaced by machines, automation, and cybernation, and were never "retained or invested with new skills"; all those on Welfare or receiving State Aid.

Also the so-called "Criminal Element," those who live by their wits, existing off that which they rip off, who stick guns in the faces of businessmen and say "stick'em up," or "give it up"! Those who don't even want a job, who hate to work, and can't relate to punching some pig's time clock, who would rather punch a pig in the mouth and rob him than punch that same pig's time clock and work for him, those whom Huey P. Newton calls "the illegitimate capitalists." In short, all those who simply have been locked out of the economy and robbed of their rightful social heritage. (7; *Black Panther,* 14)

Cleaver's difficult economic status in Algiers and the criminal activity to which he resorted to support himself and the rest of the Panthers undoubtedly contributed to his identity as an outcast; perhaps his knowledge of how much he could have earned made his sense of entitlement to a certain quota of goods as a "rightful social heritage" all the more intense.

Two years later, in a *Black Scholar* article entitled "On Lumpen Ideology," Cleaver was to correct his "mistake" in defining the members of the lumpen too narrowly; actually, "the Lumpen condition" is "basic" to all "dispossessed people," even though some "lift themselves out" and into "the proletarian condition," sometimes only temporarily.[23] Thus, the lumpen, "understood in its broader sense," is what used to be called the proletariat, some of whom were always unemployed ("Lumpen," 9). Such a mentality, he insisted, was "more advanced" than the old "job-seeking" one that assumed it was the norm to work. For the lumpen, it is the norm to demand "to be cut in on Consumption in spite of being blocked out of production." This, he declared, "is the ultimate revolutionary demand" (10). Wealth *is,* it would seem; no one needs to produce it. "The point is not," he clarified, "equality in Production, which is the Marxist view and basic error, but equality in distribution and consumption" (10). In some way, all future work will be done by "technological advances" anyway, and in the meantime, the unemployable have a right to consume.

The Anti-Imperialist Delegation

The return trip to North Korea and to North Vietnam and China could serve only to deepen Cleaver's concept of himself and the Panthers as allied with the great international downtrodden revolutionary humanity that was casting off its chains country by country. The respect with which the mostly white "Anti-Imperialist Delegation" was received by its "allies" made both Cleaver and fellow Panther Elaine Brown take themselves very seriously and accept everything they saw with absolute credulity. The group of 11, which included Cleaver and Brown as Panther representatives, also starred Robert Scheer and Ann Froines, who was both the wife of Chicago Eight defendant John Froines and a member of the New Haven Defense Committee. The trip began in Algiers in July 1970 and proceeded first to Pyongyang, North Korea; then to Hanoi; and finally to Peking.

Kathleen and Maceo were sent on ahead of the group so that Kathleen could give birth in North Korea without having to travel at the last moment (*New York Times,* 27 August 1970, 3).

It appears that originally the Korean trip was planned by Cleaver and the other two stops were added spontaneously. A radio interview with Elaine Brown on KPFA-FM in San Francisco in late September, after her return from Algiers, revealed the impromptu schedule when the host asked how the group happened to go to China. Replied Elaine: "Just as in Korea we had visited the Vietnamese embassy and had received an invitation to Vietnam, we visited the Chinese embassy in Hanoi and were invited to come to stay in China" (*Black Panther, 3*

October 1970, D). According to Elaine Brown, the group spent "over a month" in Korea and about a week in China. Although she never mentioned Kathleen, we know that the Cleavers' second child, a daughter named Joju (short for *Jojuyounghi,* Korean for "female freedom fighter"), was born on this trip in early August, soon after Maceo's first birthday on 29 July, and this event undoubtedly accounted for the lengthy stay in Korea. A photograph of the Cleavers at Maceo's birthday party accompanies, among others, the *Black Panther* reprint of the radio interview. A secondary result of Kathleen's confinement was her husband's relationship with one or more North Korean women, whom he later singled out for praise in a *Rolling Stone* interview. When Curtice Taylor asked Cleaver a general question about North Korea, he replied that he didn't "relate to [the North Koreans] as well as to the North Vietnamese," except for the women, who "have it very much together because they don't confuse sex with politics. I mean, they are liberated without getting all hung up about the sexual act" (Taylor, 46).

Earlier in the year, Cleaver had written an open letter "To My Black Brothers in Vietnam," which was reprinted (along with "The Black Man's Stake in Vietnam") in the *Black Panther* as a two-page spread surrounded by photographs of many Black Panthers, among them Bobby Seale, who had received a bad-conduct discharge from the Air Force *(Black Panther,* 13 September 1969, 17); Seale's brother John; and Elmer "Geronimo" Pratt, all in their army uniforms. In the letter Cleaver had pointed out that "you're either with your people or against them. You are either part of the solution or part of the problem," and had made it clear exactly how the black GI could "move" while still "inside the army." Aside from killing the "racist pig" officers, specifically "General Abrams and his staff, all his officers," one should "sabotage supplies and equipment, or turn them over to the Vietnamese people" and start "weeding out the traitors amongst you," who would include all those loyal to the army. Finally, "when you can no longer take care of business inside the army, then turn yourself over to the Vietnamese people and tell them you want to join the Black Panther Party to fight for the freedom and liberation of your own people" *(Black Panther,* 22 March 1970, 4).

A New Headquarters

Cleaver's work on behalf of the Vietcong cause did not go unrewarded; at the very least, it got him and his family out of the "shack" by the sea and into a villa. Once back in Algiers, the Panthers' main concern was in opening the official headquarters of the international section of the Black Panther party in the old blue-and-white Vietnamese National Liberation Front (Vietcong) house in the suburb of El Biar. Arriving guests saw two large brass plaques, one on each side of the gate, that featured the party emblem, a leaping black panther, and the words "Black Panther Party—International Section"; one plaque was in English, and the other in Arabic. At the September 1970 opening reception, attended by recent exile Don Cox, along with Scheer, Froines, Elaine Brown, and the rest of the delegation from the summer trip, Cleaver announced his plans to *New York Times* correspondent Sanche de Gramont: "Here in Algiers, we've set up an international section of the Black Panther party. Through this technique, we internationalize our struggle, we show that oppression is an international problem. We have been successful in making alliances with other movements. We are going to bring up the issue of our oppression in the international public forum. We will publicize our struggle, develop exchanges with other groups and receive assistance from them. Although we realize that the U.N. is only a puppet of the United States, we are going to lay a concrete proposal before the U.N." (31). The references to "other movements," "exchanges," and "assistance from them" allude to a Panther offer to recruit black Americans to fight in the National Liberation Front; to the earlier Cleaver plan to exchange "Pilots for Panthers," as one radical paper called it (*Harry,* printed in Baltimore, 2 December 1969, 4); and to the Cleaver–Al Fatah arrangement, first reported by CBS News correspondent Richard T. Hottelet in January 1970, to train Panther leaders "in actual combat against Israel" and to have them take part in various "Fatah operations in the Middle East." In this manner, Al Fatah would gain soldiers while the Panthers would learn "combat and sabotage," including the use of "bombs and other tactics" so as eventually to be able to carry out "quick and deep strikes in the United States," consisting largely of "assassinations." An Al Fatah spokesman with the alias Abu Bassem told Hottelet that Black Panthers "were already being trained in North Korea, Cuba and North Vietnam," in what can only be called a moment of considerable disregard for the strict truth, unless you count the visits of Cleaver and the others as "training."[24]

Cleaver appears to have been riding a wave of confidence. When a guest commented, "The French say that prisons are the antechambers of cabinet ministries," Cleaver "smiled and replied, 'We're not there yet' " (de Gramont, 112). Otherwise, none of the rhetoric was new, except to those who had skipped everything but the headlines over the preceding two years, for Cleaver's position had solidified in its militancy and expanded in its scope to include an international dimension that had only been foreshadowed in *Soul on Ice*. Cleaver still dated his dedication to "armed struggle" from the assassination of King (de Gramont, 128), while his ability to reach out to "other groups" was a by-product of another event over which he had no control, Newton's ordering him into exile.

Meanwhile, the FBI was at work, sending the newly released Newton a forged document praising Cleaver and Hilliard while dismissing Newton himself as a mere "drawing card" (Bergman and Weir, 48). Newton, who was actually an "almost mythical" figure after three years of propaganda, much of it written by Cleaver, reacted by purging the party of a number of members thought to be infiltrators and police agents. A vital expulsion was that of "Geronimo" Pratt and all his followers in his armed guerrilla group in Dallas, Texas; the "Panther 21," later the "New York 21," sided with Pratt, and Newton expelled them, too (47). The real police agent, ironically, was Melvin "Cotton" Smith, who informed the beleaguered Newton that Pratt was a police agent, when it was Smith himself who was an undercover informant for the Los Angeles Police Department (47). Subsequently, Pratt was arrested and imprisoned on the word of yet another LAPD undercover operative (47). Over the years, Pratt and Newton came to an understanding; when Newton spent time in San Quentin for parole violation in 1988, he refused to leave unless Pratt could go, too. Pratt was still in prison, Newton maintained, as the result of an FBI frame-up over a 1968 murder in Santa Monica ("Newton Leaves Prison," *Detroit Free Press*, 28 August 1988, 4A).

Cleaver, given his aggressive rhetoric, saw Pratt and the New York 21 not as traitors but as the vanguard of the revolution. What they and the Weathermen were doing was the only fit activity for real revolutionaries; on the other hand, Cleaver's personal loyalty to Newton was still strong to the point of worship. His "Huey's Standard," written the previous February, shows Newton as Cleaver saw him, frozen in time as a warrior with a gun, setting the standard of masculinity for black men. But since leaving the United States, Cleaver had been completely out of touch with Newton, receiving only second- and thirdhand messages, mostly over the telephone, and seems to have assumed that Newton shared his vision of taking on the "skeleton in armor," fighting from the mountains, conquering America from the stronghold of Long Island, leveling the earth and then creating utopia, all on his own. Cleaver was like a person in love who creates a perfect image of the remote or unattainable loved one without seeing how much of a fantasy it really is.

In early fall, Newton reportedly saw a film called *Eldridge Cleaver,* made in Algiers by William Klein at the request of the Algerian government. Although Irwin Silber's review for the *Guardian* stated that the film was more ideological than personal, the title and the actual footage both emphasized Cleaver over the Black Panther party. The beginning of the film presents Cleaver as a "complex mixture of profound political insight, socially crystallized ghetto cultural patterns and a multifaceted human personality," while part 2 places him in the context of Africa, specifically at the Pan-African Festival, and finally, part 3 uses Cleaver's narration over "footage of demonstrations and police riots in the United States" and McClellan Committee meetings (Irwin Silber, "Baez and Cleaver," 5 September 1970, 17). According to *Newsweek,* Newton "flew into a fury" when he saw Cleaver in the spotlight and speaking for the party according to his own version of its mission. [25]

When Newton, reacting to FBI insinuations and warnings, saw enemies and entrapment in every scheme, Cleaver was confused. He invited Newton to come to Algiers for a reunion, but Newton was "mysteriously denied" a passport for six months, after which the split had become definite and irreparable (Bergman and Weir, 47). It is not hard to imagine that such a maneuver would be well within the capabilities of the FBI, as indeed it was. The Los Angeles office was also busy writing to Cleaver, first to criticize Newton for failing to arrange enough press coverage for the Anti-Imperialist Delegation and then to attack his judgment when the Revolutionary People's Constitutional Convention in Washington, D.C., failed, although Cleaver had written in support of it in the 13 June issue of the *Black Panther* (48).

The Lone Ranger

A completely separate headache for Cleaver commenced on the day Timothy Leary, LSD guru, and his wife, Rosemary, arrived in late September 1970 to begin their exile following Leary's escape from a minimum security prison in California, the Men's Colony at San Luis Obispo, where he had been sent for possession. According to Cleaver, he had first obtained Huey Newton's approval for Leary to seek asylum with the Panthers in Algeria, and then made it clear to Leary that his politics were "not very sophisticated" and offered him some "political consciousness raising" more or less as a condition of his residence (Taylor, 46). The Panthers had regularly conducted "political education" classes for new recruits, and it would appear that Cleaver had much the same sort of thing in mind for Leary. Before any education could take place, however, Cleaver issued a "preliminary statement announcing an upcoming news conference with Timothy Leary and Miss Dohrn," permitting the press to believe that Weatherperson Bernadine Dorhn was in town when it was really her sister Jennifer. Cleaver referred to this misrepresentation as "a little media rip-off" on his part (Taylor, 46). He was unaware that the Algerians were then "leading a very important debate" in the United Nations, and they became furious when news coverage for "the Pope of Dope" overshadowed news about their delegate.

As a result, Cleaver said, "the next day the Algerians showed up with four airplane tickets to, of all places, Amman, Jordan, and they wanted Leary on the flight and out of the way" (46). Cleaver sent Jennifer Dohrn and "some others," whom Dohrn identified as "D.C. [Don Cox] and Marty Kenner, who's chairman of the Panther Defense Fund" (Jennifer Dohrn, "Getting High with Jennifer," *Good Times*, 8 January 1971, 6), off to Amman with Leary, stopping in Beirut. It is unclear whether any of the four knew what was going on. Dohrn commented only that "the Algerian government sponsored a trip for four of us to go to the Middle East to meet with the Palestinian guerrillas" (6), and they set off, only to have a reporter identify Leary on the Cairo-to-Beirut leg of the trip and leak the story. No one from Al Fatah met the quartet at the airport; consequently, they checked into a hotel "recommended by the Lebanese government" that turned out to be the one all Americans used—including the entire press corps. According to Dohrn, "CBS had the room next door" and reporters were on top of cars outside the hotel room "with telescopic lenses" (6). Leary, who feared extradition, panicked. "They finally found Leary hiding in a stall in the men's room," Cleaver laughed later. "He was blown away" (Taylor, 46).

The group managed to return without further incident, and Leary remained tractable for at least two months. Gradually, however, Cleaver began to regard him as a security risk of sorts. Leary was "turning on the world" with acid (LSD) and encouraging Cleaver to take some, too, on top of not "being careful" of adverse publicity.

"Also, Tim would do things like drop acid and go out to the desert with his wife Rosemary. The two of them would be out there, lying naked on the sand, and some sheepherder would come by, flip, and tell the first cop what he saw" (Taylor, 46). When a young musician fan of Leary's showed up with 10,000 tabs of acid hidden in his stereo, Cleaver confiscated the LSD and put it in the villa, "which was like, diplomatic and free from search," he said.

The relationship snapped when Leary planned a big "coming-out party to announce himself to the world," as Cleaver put it, and foolishly invited "all these people: informants, secret police, shaky press people, who we knew all about and who we avoided" (46). When Cleaver tried to talk him out of it, he said, Leary called him "a paranoid nigger" (46), and so Cleaver "busted" him—threw him into a Panther apartment under lock and key, or as Cleaver put it on a tape released later, "On January the 9th of 1971 I issued an order to Field Marshall D.C. [Don Cox], who works in our intercommunal Section here in Algeria, to go to Leary's apartment and to take Leary and his wife Rosemary to another location and to confine them there until further notice" (broadcast on KPFA-FM, 1 February 1971; printed as "Acid Fallout?" in *Good Times,* 5 February 1971, 10–11).

Cleaver went on to condemn LSD for what it did to people's judgment, particularly the Learys' ("There's something seriously wrong with both [their] brains"), and what it did to society: "strengthening the hand of the enemy" (11). He withdrew welcome from the "Hippies and Yippies and so forth tripping over here, making their pilgrimage to see their god. . . . [Y]our god is dead because his mind has been blown by acid" (11). He continued,

What I'm saying here also applies to the Jerry Rubins, Stew Alperts [*sic*] and the Abbie Hoffmans and the whole silly psychedelic drug culture/quasi-political movement of which they are part, and of which we have been part in the past, which we allied ourselves with in the past, which we supported in the past because it was our judgment that at that time this was what we had to work with from white America.

But we're through. We're finished with relating to this madness. We're through tolerating this madness, and we want everybody to know that the serious work of uprooting and destroying the empire of Babylon, with its vicious fascism and imperialism, this has to be dealt with.

And we want it dealt with in the only way it can be dealt with: by sober, stone-cold revolutionaries, motivated by revolutionary love, men and women who fit the description given by Comrade Che Guevera: cold, calculating killing machines to be turned against the enemy, people who have firm ideological foundations, who know what they're doing and who know how to do it, who know how to implement their ideology for the purpose of carrying out this revolution. (11)

Cleaver admitted to having "taken trips to check [LSD] out" but said, "That's not where we're coming from, and that's not where we're bound. . . . The drug culture is part of the death culture." The use of drugs, he said, is a result of the "pressure of the Babylonian social structure on people that forces them to seek escape from the awful confrontation that is upon us" (11).

In this single speech Cleaver did more to alienate the white radicals from the Panthers than any FBI agent could ever have hoped for, and the FBI got as much mileage out of it as it could by sending Newton an anonymous letter denouncing Cleaver for "divorcing the BPP from white revolutionaries" (Bergman and Weir, 48). For once, the charge was true. Cleaver's old friends Jerry Rubin, Abbie Hoffman, and Stew Albert retaliated personally. Rubin and Hoffman wrote ELDRIDGE IS A PIG. FREE TIM LEARY with spray paint in a number of different locations around New York City (Taylor, 46), while Rubin and Albert, in an interview at the *Good Times* commune in San Francisco, denounced Cleaver. "He's had his mind blown by exile," said Rubin; "I think we should rise to the defense of Tim Leary . . . when he got locked up by Eldridge for ego reasons, and Stalinist reasons, it's outrageous. Eldridge putting down the psychedelic culture is very bad" ("Jerry and Stew," *Good Times,* 26 March 1971, 9). Albert added, "Eldridge says that in order to become a revolutionary you have to become a killing machine. . . . Eldridge is attacking the whole culture, not just Tim Leary—but what he's doing is attacking the thing in himself, because he smokes dope, and he's taken LSD and he's already related to that" (9).

The Leary-Cleaver dispute alienated the white Left. The two made a videotape in Algiers on 12 February 1971 and sent it to KQED-TV, the Public Broadcasting System channel in San Francisco, which telecast it on Wednesday, 24 February. Each defended his position and claimed his allies, Leary insisting that the Weathermen and the White Panthers of Ann Arbor (a white radical group supporting the BPP and the Ten Point Program) endorsed "the use of acid to expand consciousness" and Cleaver asserting that if he had it to do over, he'd run for president with Bernadine Dohrn ("The Battle of Algiers," *Good Times,* 26 February 1971, 2–3).

The FBI had been extremely busy in February. They already had
Huey in such a state by the end of January that headquarters informed
its four relevant field offices that Newton would "respond violently to
any question of his actions or policies," and encouraged "priority attention" to the project. "The present chaotic situation within the BPP
must be exploited," the memo went on, and suggestions were welcome
for ways in which "to further aggravate the dissension" between the
leaders (Bergman, 48).

As a result, Cleaver received a phony letter from the "New York 21"
attacking Newton; Newton's brother received an anonymous letter informing him of a Cleaver plot to assassinate Newton with the help of
the expelled New Yorkers; late in February, Cleaver received a forged
letter from Elbert "Big Man" Howard saying he was "disgusted" with
the way things were going, and especially with the way Newton "ignored" Cleaver and "has to lie to you" (Bergman, 48).

It remained only for Cleaver to alienate himself from the man he had
most admired, Huey Newton. On 26 February, Newton appeared on
Jim Dunbar's TV talk show, and the host placed a long-distance call to
Algiers so that Cleaver could participate in the discussion. Cleaver took
the occasion to denounce David Hilliard, demanding his expulsion
from the party, and to support the Panther 21 in New York, whom
Huey had expelled, supposedly on Hilliard's recommendation. Embarrassed and outraged, Newton placed a return call to Algiers as soon as
the show was over. Elaine Brown, who was there at the television
studio, stated "Huey had tears in his eyes. He said, 'Eldridge, I
thought we had a *party*' " (Bergman, 48).

The next day, Newton officially expelled Cleaver and the entire
international section of the party. Further, he wrote a letter to Algerian
president Boumédienne informing him that Cleaver was "no longer
responsible to the party" and that the international unit was "dissolved"
(Taylor, 47). The Algerians, who were sick of the illegal activities of
the Panther unit, embarrassed by the Panthers' presence, and more
interested in gaining favor with the United States than in maintaining
Cleaver on his own, no longer wished to support him and his group.
The Chinese, who were courting Richard Nixon and Henry Kissinger,
Cleaver said, therefore "used any excuse to drop us" (47). Only the
Vietnamese, having no contact with anyone else involved, remained
loyal to Cleaver, but their concerns and questions were voiced "on many
occasions" (47).

Weatherman and the New York 21 sided with Cleaver, but the

White Panthers and their leader, John Sinclair, did not. "We recognize," wrote Sinclair for the party's Central Committee, "that there is only one Black Panther Party—the organization founded in October, 1966 by Huey P. Newton and Bobby Seale." Those in Algiers, he said, were too hasty with their "eve of the revolution" talk; Huey Newton and his concept of a "protracted struggle" were correct.[26] The issue was not Leary and LSD but breakfast programs versus urban guerrilla warfare; "survival pending revolution" versus Weatherman. The White Panthers, like many others, saw that they had been "rebels," not dedicated revolutionaries, "just . . . stumbling along doing whatever popped into our heads."[27] All their actions did was to get numbers of people busted; it got old; everybody was over 30; and "we had to get rid of the name White Panthers because it didn't fit anymore" ("Lessons," 350). On 1 May 1971, the White Panthers became the Rainbow People's Party and published the first issue of the *Ann Arbor Sun* (352). They still considered themselves free and politically radical, but they were no longer disruptive.

Cleaver, becoming even more isolated and disillusioned, saw what he thought had been serious commitments made on the basis of shared revolutionary principles all being renounced, many for what seemed to him a hypocritical expediency. The FBI had attained its objective. To underline the point, the FBI mailed Cleaver a copy of the *Black Panther* in which his expulsion was announced, and followed that on 25 March with a forged letter from David Hilliard to the Panther European offices, condemning Cleaver as a "murderer" and "a punk without genitals" (Bergman, 48). On that day, the operation was declared over.

Murder One

The term *murderer* as used in the FBI letter referred to a charge leveled by Elaine Brown in a special supplement to the 6 March *Black Panther.* The headline story, entitled "Free Kathleen Cleaver and All Political Prisoners," contained charges that the "Champion of Male Chauvinism," Eldridge, held Kathleen as a prisoner and beat her, even when she was a new mother in the summer of 1969. Brown stated that Kathleen had taken her into her confidence in tearful "clandestine (secret) meetings" in Korea in 1970, when Brown had formed part of the Anti-Imperialist Delegation. There, Kathleen revealed that Eldridge had sent her on ahead of him to "get rid of [her] for a while" so that he could pursue an affair with his new woman, "an 18 year old girl named Malika" (page B of the supplement). Further, when the delegation joined Kathleen in Korea, Cleaver "constantly harassed her with the statement that the baby she was carrying was not his" (B).

The man whom Cleaver supposedly considered the father of the second child was Rahim (Clinton Smith), who had escaped from Chino State Prison in California with Byron Booth and hijacked a plane to Cuba to be with Cleaver. He and Booth followed Cleaver to Algiers, where he met Kathleen and she "began relating" to him (B). Rahim, whom Don Schanche described as "a short powerfully built man of about 28" (*Paradox,* 168), remained in Algiers when Cleaver and Booth went on the first trip to North Korea. Presumably, a relationship could have been initiated at that time, with a second pregnancy resulting in December 1969, but there is no proof to that effect. Cleaver himself was back in Algiers long before December; it is impossible to determine why he would have decided the child was not his, unless he were simply expressing his anger.

What is even more confusing is the date of Rahim's supposed murder. Apparently, Rahim was already dead when Brown was in Algiers (and on the trip) in 1970. "When I last saw Eldridge," she claimed, "he was laughing about how 'we bury people here' (Algiers)" (B), and she assumed that it was his murder of Rahim to which he referred. Brown said, "in an act exemplifying the true nature of a chauvinist, a combination of cowardly terror and an inferiority complex, Eldridge snatched even this from Kathleen. He killed—which act he could never seem to be able to commit against any of the People's oppressors—killed this brother, Rahim. He murdered him and buried his body right in Algiers, because Kathleen had done only once what he had made an integral part of their relationship" (B). At some unspecified time in 1970, then, Cleaver was to have murdered Rahim and buried him there. Boumédienne, a "chauvinist and opportunist" himself, said Brown, "gave Eldridge the plot of ground in which to bury Rahim; and Boumédienne kept it quiet for him" (B). Brown supposedly kept it quiet, too, until after the Cleaver-Newton split, when she could damage Cleaver with the exposure of his alleged crime. No charges were filed against Cleaver. Although Kathleen rejected Elaine Brown's charges, Brown had already anticipated that response. For Kathleen to "speak otherwise," she claimed, would be a "death warrant. So we will understand" (B).

In the next issue of the *Black Panther,* 13 March, Emory Douglas published a full-page cartoon attacking Cleaver's manhood on the occasion of the 6 April 1968 shoot-out. At the top of the page we see the date and the address of the house where Cleaver and Hutton had been holed up in the cellar, "1218 28th Street, Oakland, California" (16). The right two-thirds of the page is filled with the dominant figure of a man, fully dressed and caped in camouflage clothes, armed with an assault rifle and aiming off to the right. He is labeled "Lil' Bobby Hutton." The left of the page is taken up with a naked figure of a man with no genitals, pants dropped around his ankles, arms raised in surrender. A photo of Cleaver in sunglasses forms the man's face; long hair is growing from his armpits; a peace sign hangs around his neck. The man's belly is hugely rounded from waist to groin, unlike a typically masculine "beer belly" and more like an incredibly out-of-condition sedentary man's "gut." The implication is clear.

On 20 March 1971, an open letter "To Eldridge Cleaver and His Conspirators" from the San Quentin branch of the Black Panther party appeared in the *Black Panther*. The convicts sided with "the Supreme Servant, Minister Huey Newton, who is the Soul Servant of the People," and against Cleaver, whom they labeled a "power crazy nigger" (11). They particularly repudiated the "propaganda bullshit" Cleaver had purportedly launched against Newton, and charged him with "treason and counter revolutionary tactics against your comrades," along with the murder of " 'Smitty' [Clinton Smith-Rahim] . . . who, along with Byron [Booth], you lied on about the theft of $20,000 . . . while you yourself had done the stealing" (10). (Actually, according to Don Schanche, it was Booth and one Louise Solomon Wibecan who were charged with the theft of $20,000 and with spreading "propaganda" against Cleaver early in 1970 [*Paradox*, 215].) The letter declined further discussion of Cleaver: "You're not even worth the space taken up here. The only space you should be given is 3 × 6 × 6 feet with a black apple stuck in your mouth" (11).

On 17 April, Newton published in the *Black Panther* an essay entitled "On the Defection of Eldridge Cleaver from the Black Panther Party and the Defection of the Black Panther Party from the People." The article, reprinted more than once, blamed Cleaver for the party's loss of its defensive posture and its adoption of the doctrine of armed revolution in its place, and for the subsequent alienation from the party of the black masses, simultaneous with their alliance with white revolutionaries instead; Cleaver was a traitor who wanted everyone "into the streets tomorrow to make a revolution," but that, declared Newton, was "a fantasy" (*Die*, 53).

Newton said that looking back, it seemed to him that Cleaver decided to join the Black Panther party under the false assumption that the organization was "*the* Revolution and *the* Party," whereas Newton and Seale intended only "to build a political vehicle through which the people could express their revolutionary desires," to "act as a guide to the people" by responding to "a concrete analysis of conditions" and then "mobilizing the people" to respond to the party, "leading them to higher levels of consciousness" (49). Newton admitted that he and Seale "had political and revolutionary objectives in mind" but knew they "could not succeed without the support of the people" (48). That fact, it seems, is what Cleaver did not know or did not care about. He responded enthusiastically to the confrontation at the *Ramparts* office, transforming it in his mind into the first skirmish in a revolutionary war like that fought in Havana (*Post,* 32). He already revered Malcolm X, who had declared everyone was either part of the problem or part of the solution, and he saw in Huey the solution. Newton writes, "When Eldridge joined the Party it was after the police confrontation, which left him fixated with the 'either-or' attitude. This was that either the community picked up the gun with the Party or else they were cowards and there was no place for them. He did not realize that if the people did not relate to the Party then there was no way that the Black Panther Party could make any revolution, for the record shows that the people are the makers of the revolution and of world history" (*Die,* 50). What Cleaver saw in Newton, as we have noted before, was the personification of black manhood, the setter of the standard for black males, the "baddest motherfucker" in all of history, an advocate and practitioner of violence, a five-foot-seven "shield" to his people, a Christ figure.

The many years in prison had not made Cleaver especially receptive to dialogue with the masses; he transformed a concern for concrete conditions into a Marxist-Leninist ideology with a global perspective. A small cadre of dedicated leaders at the center of the party seemed enough. Perhaps he even equated fame with having an actual following among the masses, and writing a best-seller with providing an example. Certainly, he needed a leader before whom he could lay down his life. All of this may be what Newton had in mind when he commented, "Sometimes there are those who express personal problems in political terms, and if they are eloquent then these personal problems can sound very political. We charge Eldridge Cleaver with this. Much of it is probably beyond his control because it is so personal" (50): Because of Cleaver,

The Black Panther Party defected from the community long before Eldridge defected from the Party. Our hook-up with White radicals did not give us access to the White community because they do not guide the White community. The Black community does not relate to them so we were left in a twilight zone where we could not enter the Black Community with any real political education programs; yet we were not doing anything to mobilize Whites. We had no influence in raising the consciousness of the Black community and that is the point where we defected. (*Die*, 51)

Newton also condemned Cleaver for starting his own "Free Speech Movement" in the party, a reference to the political movement at Berkeley and to Cleaver's notorious use of obscenities in his speeches and writings, a characteristic never found in anything of Newton's. Although Cleaver had clearly enjoyed profanity for shock effect and as a manner of personal expression, Newton knew that typical churchgoing blacks in the community were shocked by it, and thus the language "further isolated us from the Black community" (52).

In dismissing Cleaver, Newton insisted that "Eldridge was never fully in the leadership of the Party. . . . I knew that Eldridge would not do anything to lift the consciousness of the comrades in the Party, but I knew that he could make a contribution and I pressed him to do so. I pressed him to write and edit the paper, but he wouldn't. The paper did not even come out every week until after Eldridge went to jail. But Eldridge Cleaver did make great contributions to the Black Panther Party with his writing and speaking. We want to keep this in mind because there is a positive and negative side to everything" (52). According to Bobby Seale, not only was Cleaver a "hidden traitor" who had no interest in any community programs, but also he pulled the Party "into the radical hippy group of people," as a result of which the impressive Panther uniform disappeared.[28] When "it looked like we were following the white hippies instead of them following us," another step in the "alienation" of the black community from the Panthers had been taken. From then on, the community had no correct source of information about the Panthers' activities: "It was left up to the mass media to define what we were about—terrorists, bombs . . . we didn't have a lot of constructive programs" (Seale, 14).

With Cleaver gone, Newton concluded, the Panthers were "now free to move toward the building of a *community structure* which will become a true voice of the people, promoting their interests in many ways. We can continue to push our basic survival programs, we can continue to

serve the people as advocates of their true interests, we can truly become a political revolutionary vehicle which will lead the people to a
higher level of consciousness so that they will know what they must
really do in their quest for freedom" (*Die,* 53).

Right On!

Almost immediately after the various March 1971 attacks on Cleaver,
the Cleaver faction began the publication of a short-lived newspaper of its
own, *Right On!,* published in the Bronx by New York Panthers. The first
issue, dated 3 April 1971, contains material by Eldridge and Kathleen,
as well as by Michael Cetewayo ("Cet") Tabor, husband of Connie Matthews and an exiled member of the New York 21; all of it is devoted to a
leveling of various charges against the Newton faction and to a simultaneous defense of themselves. While the name Clinton Smith is never
mentioned, the countercharge of murder is brought against Huey Newton and his "assassins," who are said to have killed Robert Webb, deputy
field marshall of the Cleaver contingent, as he tried to prevent the sale of
the pro-Huey *Black Panther* on the streets of New York. The cover
features a photo of Webb in a wide-brimmed hat and armed. The "mad
dog assassins" who killed him were presumed to have been among the
"75 robots" sent east by "former Minister of Defense" Newton specifically "to murder Panthers" ("On the Assassination of Deputy Field Marshall Robert Webb," *Right On!,* 3).

Citing the "pathetic state of affairs" within the party and the "count-
less mistakes" made by David Hilliard while Newton was in prison, an
editorial from "Central Headquarters," probably written by one of the
Cleavers, calls for the dissolution of the entire Central Committee and its
replacement with a more democratic leadership that would be representative of the various branches "throughout Babylon," particularly, one
suspects, New York (2). The "contradictions" within the party were the
subject of a two-page essay by Tabor that in turn had been "excerpted and
edited from the discussions held in our political education class on
January 31" ("Michael Cetewayo Tabor on the Contradictions within the
Black Panther Party," *Right On!,* 13–14), or almost a month before the
public conflict between Cleaver and Newton on the Dunbar show. "Hid-
eous violations of all revolutionary principles" on the part of Hilliard,
which included "[setting] brothers up to be arrested" and being against
"all military activity" as well as spending "a considerable amount of
money" on clothes and "wallow[ing] in luxury," had taken from the party

its "true image" and made it "revisionist" (13). When Newton perceived that proper leadership could come only from Cleaver, Tabor charged, Newton cut off all communication with what was now called the "Intercommunal Section" in Algiers. Geronimo Pratt was defended, and artist Emory Douglas attacked as a "revisionist Al Capp" (15). One of the most damaging charges was made in a short "Editorial" on page 2, when Central Headquarters revealed that Newton now lived in "a $650.00 a month penthouse" and that Hilliard had just purchased "a $65,000 home"; the implication was that party money was used to pay for these things. Although in *Newsweek* (22 March 1971, 27) and in *Jet*[29] Newton defended his apartment as a security need and even explained that the money came from the sale of books by Seale and the late George Jackson, his credibility was seriously affected.

In May 1971 Kathleen and Eldridge visited the People's Republic of the Congo (Brazzaville) at the invitation of President Marien Ndouabi and the Congolese Worker's Party.[30] According to Cleaver, the visit was part of a program designed to show revolutionary Marxist-Leninist groups from other nations how to conduct a successful takeover of their governments. In a pamphlet entitled "Revolution in the Congo," published by Stage 1 for the Revolutionary People's Communication Network (Cleaver's group) in London later that year, Cleaver reported that "Guerrilla and training camps have been set up for a number of revolutionary organizations that are fighting to liberate their countries from the oppressive grip of colonialism and neocolonialism."[31]

Among these students were those representing "the Black Panther Party delegation" (cover), who produced out of the experience a seven-part, 48-page illustrated booklet that included interviews with Ernest Ndalla, first secretary of the Congolese Worker's Party; Pierre Nze, politbureau member in charge of organization; and Ange Diawara, political commissar of the National People's Army, whose role it was "to make the army a revolutionary tool" (29). Three of the seven sections—1) "After Brother Malcolm," 2) "The Number One Problem in Africa: Neocolonialism," and 7) "Afro-America and the Congo"—were published separately as "Culture and Revolution: Their Synthesis in Africa" in the *Black Scholar* in October of the same year. Those three sections, which for the most part are theoretical, speak about how an African example of a revolutionary government can heal the post-Malcolm rift between the cultural nationalists in the United States and those who "relate to the gun" (there is no reference to Cleaver's split with Newton); how Afro-Americans could count on the Congo as a "true, reliable ally" in "their own struggle for liberation" because the United States "is the chief enemy of freedom and liberation in Africa, just as in all parts of the world" (11); and how black Americans ought therefore to "proclaim solidarity with the African revolutionaries," especially the Congolese. "HANDS OFF THE CONGO must become our battle cry," Cleaver insists, adding, "We must DEMAND that the United States withdraw all of its troops from Congo-Kinshasa," which is where the CIA had its "main base of operations" in Africa (48), particularly those directed against the republic, or Congo (Brazzaville).

The lengthier interview sections, a political history of the Congo (Brazzaville), and a brief "Message to Afro-Americans" exhorting American blacks to "liberate themselves from oppression through violence" and not to "hesitate to pick up guns and use them" (27) complete the booklet. Of these, the how-to-do-it discussion with Ange Diawara is by far the most interesting. It serves as an African counterpart, one could say, to Che Guevara's *Guerrilla Warfare,* at least on a theoretical level.

Diawara's emphasis on the army as the "servile tool" of the people springs from the concept that the military ought to function as a "propaganda corps . . . capable of making the people adhere to the ideas of the Revolution," as well as "organizing the people politically" (30). The second function of the army, in order to avoid "the parasitic role" of past armies that depended "upon the budget of the State for money, for food and for clothing," is to serve as "a work corps" that can be "self-sufficient" and thereby "lighten the burden and diminish the sacrifices of the people" (31). Finally, the army must serve as "a combat corps, a battle corps" that has, despite its title, no "monopoly on battle" but must extend its responsibilities even unto "organiz[ing] the people militarily," presumably with weapons the army has purchased on its own, as well as providing instruction in "the techniques required for the struggle" 32). The regular army "is then nothing more than a group of people who deal with [the revolution] on a more permanent basis" than the people themselves do; such as a reality does not, however, "give [the army] the title of a professional military" because it is on the one hand complemented by "the people in arms" (33) and on the other "under the direction of the Congolese Worker's Party" (32). It is no wonder that "the Revolution must penetrate the Army from top to bottom" (33), for nothing but total dedication would be adequate for a group with so much responsibility and so few perks.

Possibly Cleaver here found a viable model for the takeover of America by force. Castro may have needed only 78 in *Granma,* his yacht, but Cleaver would certainly need more, and would be without any funds to pay them. As he reveals in the initial "After Brother Malcolm" section, he was inspired to find "a revolutionary Marxist-Leninist state" complete with a people's army and could now envision "the Afro-American Liberation struggle" at "a higher level, making possible an unprecedentedly tighter unity" (8) between the two factions of "the cultural nationalists" and "the revolutionary black nationalists." It seems that Cleaver hoped to disregard the existence of Huey Newton and his followers, to ignore the Panther split, and to bid for an alliance or even a merger with those "back to Africa" types he had previously scorned, provided that he could convince them that the example of the Congo was relevant to the United States. No alliance with white revolutionaries is mentioned, unless we assume the U.S. Army could one day be fully converted. This new idea might help to explain Cleaver's enchantment with the U.S. military upon his repentant return in 1975; although by then he professed an antirevolutionary stance, it is possible that he thought it would not be a waste of time to proclaim his "love" for the military (Taylor, 48).

Almost a year after the abridged version of "Revolution in the Congo" was published in *The Black Scholar,* Socialist Workers' party member Tony Thomas attacked the tract solely on the basis of Cleaver's remark that the Black Panthers had become so Marxist-Leninist that "it even negated our nationalism."[32] The real point, to Thomas, was that both Cleaver and Earl Ofari, a Newton loyalist and author of the pamphlet, "Black Liberation: Cultural and Revolutionary Nationalism" (1969), considered black nationalism as counterposed to the struggle of "African-American workers against class exploitation" (Thomas, 48). Thomas argued that this separation of race and class struggle was a misreading of Lenin's true position on national liberation struggles, which had been "suppressed by the leadership of the Soviet Union and the Communist parties since the 1920's" (48). Thomas blames this inevitable confusion for the Panthers' "retreat from the black nationalist principles that they had been founded upon" and in turn for the error when "the Panthers launched the national presidential campaign of Eldridge Cleaver" (51) and thus "diminished rather than increased their support within the African-American nationalist movement and in 'the community' " (Thomas, 52). It was, of course, not the Panthers who launched Cleaver's campaign but Cleaver, who not only dissociated himself from most of his Panther friends during the campaign but also alienated the serious Left with his selection of Jerry Rubin as his running mate.

Thomas zeroes in on Cleaver and "the section of the party loyal to Cleaver" in commenting that they substituted "themselves as an armed vanguard for the power of the whole black nation" rather than helping to unite the "people" in a program of "mass nationalist action" (52). Such a "view of terrorism and armed struggle," says Thomas, "is completely contrary to everything Marxism has to say on the subject." Such antinationalist sentiment was in fact the source of Cleaver's long-standing disgust with the American Communists. Thus, far from recognizing or discussing Cleaver's major point about the relevance of the Congo example to black Americans, Thomas insists that the "primary task" is to organize "a mass African-American political party to direct our struggle on all fronts" and thereby ultimately to bring about "the destruction of American imperialism" (52). Hence, Thomas is back where Malcolm had been 15 years earlier, calling for Afro-American unity but ignoring Cleaver's point about a Marxist-Leninist state in Africa for the sake of correcting a footnote, as it were.

The Beginning of the End

In October 1971 Cleaver's "Message from Algiers" appeared in the leftist press exclusive of the *Black Panther.* The "Message," less than 1,000 words long, consisted of an urgent warning to "Afro-American People" that "various countries we thought were our friends and allies to the end are now making a separate peace with our sworn enemy, the fascist imperialist U.S. government and ruling class," which is to say that the People's Republic of China was involved in "dialogue and negotiations" with the United States (*Good Times,* 15 October 1971, 12). This betrayal is part of a "global plan to carve up the planet," says Cleaver, according to which plan "a white racist empire" consisting of "the customary grouping of Western Capitalist sweetheart nations and including Spain, Portugal, South Africa, Southern Rhodesia, and Israel" will be formed, with Afro-Americans "trapped inside and at the mercy" of the United States, with no Third World allies. "In return for this," Cleaver explained, "the United States is going to pull its forces out of Asia—South Korea, Indo-China, Japan, the Philippines, Thailand, and Taiwan, etc." (13). The logic of many of Cleaver's positions was always questionable, but here coherency falls apart completely. He had been dismayed to see that Chou En-lai had agreed to Nixon's visit.

Cleaver's assumption that Mao and Nixon had agreed to establish something like the "spheres of influence" that Walter Lippman had once called the respective areas of power that would inevitably surround Soviet Russia and the United States was premature but not paranoid; Cleaver's conclusion that this state of affairs would lead first to the isolation of American blacks and then to "a final genocide for us" (12) was extreme, as was his urgent insistence that blacks arm themselves and "come together in a United Front . . . with all the other oppressed people inside Babylon and the world who have not made [*sic*] their human rights" (13):

To cope with this situation, we have one and only one path to us; to arm and organize ourselves into a powerful, deadly, invincible block inside the United States so that the United States cannot do anything of which we do not approve. There is no other path open to us. Only an Afro-Amerikan People's Army can guarantee the Civil War. Our first battle is for the right to organize our People's Army. Again, there is no other way. Our People's Army must come into being through combat, fighting from its inception for its right to be. . . . There is a world of difference between 30 million unarmed niggers and 30 million niggers armed to the gills.

> Eldridge Cleaver
> Minister of Information
> Algiers, October 1, 1971
> (13)

Although Cleaver already knew the Chinese were no longer supporting the Panthers, he was not prepared for Mao to betray the Third World revolution as openly as he did in February 1972. Writes Cleaver:

The final shock came the day I saw Richard Nixon shaking hands with Chairman Mao. When you see Nixon and all that he stands for shaking hands with Mao and all that he supposedly stood for—well, it marks a turning point in history and a personal turning point for me. It completely exploded the political spectrum that has dominated the world since 1850—since the First International—when Marx defined the nature of the capitalist system, provided an ideological framework for the restructuring of society and, most importantly, gave people an alternative to capitalism. Well, it had gone through a lot of changes. The Russians could even become revisionists and betray that ideology but as long as you had Mao proclaiming the people's struggle, an alternative still existed. But after that visit and Chou En-Lai's apparent dominance in China, it's all just gone. (Taylor, 48)

Kathleen Cleaver was in the United States with her children and
Elaine Klein in the fall of 1971. While in the country, she placed her
children in the care of her mother and set up "headquarters" in New York
City, traveling around from there to explain the "position" of the Revolutionary People's Communication Network (Thompson, 24). Among the
stops was the Southern People's Revolutionary Conference at the Malcolm X United Liberation Front base in Tallahassee, Florida. Both she
and Elaine Klein spoke before a Thanksgiving-weekend crowd of 125
assorted radicals, both black and white, representing the Socialist Workers' party, the People's Labor party, and the Republic of New Africa,
among others, but no Panthers from either coast. A notice in the *New
York Times* (17 October 1971, 22) and a brief article in *Jet* announced her
visit; *Jet* showed her with her mother and the two children. It would seem
that Kathleen's visit had two purposes: (a) to prepare for Cleaver's possible return and (b) to leave the children with her mother because of the
deteriorating situation in Algiers. Besides explaining the "position" of
the Revolutionary People's Communication Network, she declared her
intent to work on "restructuring and reorienting some of the organizational and revolutionary forces that are presently in a state of chaos."
Simultaneously, she said that Cleaver had "decided to leave Algeria and
come home" in order "to devote himself to guerrilla warfare in the U.S.,"
although she would reveal no specific plans.[33]

When Kathleen was interviewed by her friend Julia Wright Herve
for the *Black Scholar* in the fall of 1971, she had quite a bit to say about
violence in the relationships of black men and women in general. When
"black men move to assert themselves, . . . to regain a sense of dignity,
to regain a sense of manhood, to regain a sense of humanity . . . they
many times take out resentment of their position against their own
black women," she said. At the same time, she noted, they invariably
use white males as their role models, "following the European model of
suppressing the woman."[34] Both motives, though, originate in the
"colonization" of the black race; black males are not, by implication,
fully responsible for "the violence . . . the brutality, the hostility, the
bitterness, the antagonism, and . . . resentment" they heap upon their
women. Therefore, in order to resolve these interpersonal problems,
"the whole system of colonialism must first be destroyed" (Herve, 59).
Sexism, like racism, is seen as economic in origin; under socialism,
society would be perfect, or at least perfectible.

Elaine Brown and her partisans would regard remarks of this nature
as proof that Kathleen had endured beatings and was attempting to

rationalize them for the sake of maintaining the marriage. If this were the case, it would fit the pattern of abused women, but the comments do not in themselves constitute proof. Kathleen's appearance in the United States is also inconclusive evidence as to whether she was in fact usually forbidden to travel, since in this instance and again in 1973 she was on an errand to help her husband return home; such a benefit would surely outweigh any husbandly suspicions, if they existed.

In January 1972, Cleaver responded to increasing conflict within the Panther group by moving out of the blue-and-white villa and into an apartment downtown. Simultaneously, he officially left the Panthers to form the Black Liberation Army, giving over the leadership of the Panther international section and its propaganda arm, the Revolutionary People's Communication Network, to Peter O'Neal. O'Neal himself departed from Algiers rather abruptly late in September, abandoning the leadership of the remaining fragment of the group to Roger Holden, a black Vietnam veteran who had arrived as a hijacker in June, along with a young white girl named Catherine Kerow (Henry Giniger, "Black Panthers in Algeria Halt Operations in Rift with Regime," *New York Times,* 9 September 1972, 28).

The Panthers had been having increasingly tense relations with the Boumédienne government, mostly over the huge telex and telephone bills they had run up, but also over their flamboyant life-style. *Time* magazine referred to "all night parties and loudspeakers blasting out hard rock, . . . hashish smoking," and Algerian disapproval of Cleaver when he "took up with a teen-age Arab girl called Malika while his wife Kathleen was away."[35] This would seem to be the same woman Cleaver had been involved with more than a year earlier, according to Elaine Brown in the March 1971 *Black Panther.* The relationship would seem to have been either continuous or renewed in the fall of 1971.

Throughout 1971 and 1972 the Cleavers became ever more steadily isolated. It was soon clear that the New York 21 did not command the loyalty of those radicals who were still politically inclined, with the exception of the Weathermen and the SDS branch in Stony Brook, who had endorsed the Cleaverite Panthers in the first issue of *Right On!* In Algiers, the situation became increasingly tense as the Algerians realized that Cleaver represented only himself, and not the revolutionary vanguard in the United States. Cleaver's claim that the New York 21/ Black Liberation Army group, which he now headed, was the true black revolutionary group did not win favor, partly because of Cleaver's behavior and partly because of Newton's influence.

Cleaver spent 1972 trying to raise money in Algeria and trying to find a place to go. In view of the remarks made by the San Quentin Panthers in 1971, one would assume that the Panthers had been sending Cleaver money to supplement the $500 monthly stipend the Algerians supplied. In accusing Cleaver of having stolen the money he had accused others of stealing, the San Quentin group had said, "you stole from those little Black babies, who are dying every day of hunger, and freezing right now because they have no clothing. . . . And you need to be dead" (11). The cash, however, was not from Oakland or even U.S. Panther coffers; rather, it was made up of direct contributions from wealthy European sympathizers. Back in March 1970, Cleaver had sent the Panthers a letter, complete with photographs, expelling six persons from the party: (James) Amiri Akili, Gwen Akili, and their baby, Tanya Kathleen Akili, all designated as having the "slave name—Patterson," along with Byron Booth, Louise Solomon Wibecan, and Clinton (Rahim) Smith. In the photographs, Booth and Wibecan have WANTED under their names. While all were expelled "because of activity and consistent behavior that cannot be tolerated," Booth and Wibecan were specifically charged with "absconding [*sic*] with party funds," among other nameless objectionable activities. They were believed to be in Nigeria (*Black Panther,* 21 March 1970, 18). Later, in the 9 May issue of the *Black Panther,* David Hilliard wrote a short article, "Repudiating Lies of Renegade Bandits Byron Booth and Louise Wibecan," in which he criticized the two for having spread "propaganda" against Cleaver as well as for having taken $20,000 that Wibecan herself had raised by "waging fund raising parties throughout Europe" (9). Presumably, the party assumed that such money was to go to it and not to the international section, at least for the purposes of attacking Cleaver in 1971. Whether the nature of the "lies" told by the bandits—who had last been seen by Panthers in New York City—had involved murder or not is impossible to say.

The Blowup

With the Panther money gone and the royalties from his two books held up, Cleaver's only sources of steady money were the Algerian stipend, or *permanence,* and criminal activity. According to Cleaver, the Panther delegation had already made "plans to leave" Algiers in late spring. Since Nixon's visit to China, they had felt the balance of power to be shifting against them even in the other socialist countries, and they had begun to hear people "saying that the Americans at the Swiss Embassy there—that we were going to be cooked in six months . . . that we were just living on borrowed time. . . . [T]here was a constant menacing atmosphere."[36] Cleaver was back to his "Custard's [*sic*] last stand" frame of mind again, as he had been in Cuba. "We saw absolutely," he declared, "that the days of the Wild West Liberation Movement were over. Not over, but numbered on a shortscale" (Gates, 53).

Cleaver writes, "At that time we started making plans to leave. We already had our plans to leave. In fact, some people had already left when to our surprise people started hijacking planes to Algeria, which completely turned everything around, retarded everything, created a situation which had to be dealt with. . . . I felt I would be able to get out of Algeria and still retard leaving long enough to see after these people, which finally took about six months" (53). It was in June and July 1972 that the apparent bonanza hit Algiers. First, two hijackers, Holden and Kerow, arrived with $500,000 in ransom money; then five adults and three children from Detroit hijacked a Delta flight and demanded and got $1 million in ransom (Henry Giniger, *New York Times*, 28, and *Jet*, 17 August 1972, 9). But the Algerian government, eager to sell gas to the United States and hoping for an investment loan from the Export-Import Bank, planned to return all of the money ("On Ice," 32). Delta's payment was made on 31 July, and on 2 August, Cleaver, fearing the loss of the money, wrote an "Open Letter" to President Houari Boumédienne. First flattering Boumédienne and praising him as a "hunted man" who had returned in triumph, "a revolutionary warrior for the liberation of his people" to sit "at the head of the government" (*Fire*, 157), Cleaver then attempts to persuade Boumédienne to give the Panthers the money by arguing that their existence in Algiers marked "an historic advancement for the Afro-American Liberation struggle," for it established "machinery" to serve the "struggle" and created "a vital link" between black Americans and "our brothers and sisters in Africa" (*Fire*, 158). The appeal to an Arab people as Africans is technically correct, of course, but also stretched. Not only were both Cleaver and Boumédienne aware that only sub-Saharan Africans are black, but Cleaver had noted the presence of black servants in many Arab homes.[37] Further, he later claimed that he was referred to as a "slave" (*kulasha*) in North Africa,[38] and that black Americans were criticized for being too "arrogant" because of "the way we move and carry our bodies" (Taylor, 44). Nonetheless, in the hope of persuading Boumédienne to give him the money, Cleaver found no remark too insincere or exaggerated.

Cleaver devotes at least a paragraph each to several interrelated arguments, beginning with the statement that "the Afro-American people" will "carry out" their struggle so as to avoid "[betraying] the blood of our people" (*Fire,* 159). To emphasize the vital nature of the revolution Cleaver wants to launch, he declares "our struggle" to be "a profound contribution to the struggle of the other oppressed people of the world," and states that (just as had been true for Cleaver since 1968) the moment is at hand. "The Afro-American people fully recognize that this is their historic moment of opportunity to strike a final blow for their complete freedom. And we shall not hesitate" (159).

The letter weakens rhetorically from that point on, until Cleaver arrives at the real point: "We must have money. There are no ifs, ands, or buts about that point" (*Fire,* 159). Without the money, "there will be no freedom," and that is why the "ruling circles of the United States are going crazy" over the possibility of the international section getting its hands on so much money (160). Cleaver asks Boumédienne not to fight for "the ruling circles" and to remember "the value of assistance and support" in a struggle for freedom.

"Finally," Cleaver says, it is the task of the Algerians to resist the power of the U.S. government: "To give in to it will only feed its greed in its lust to compromise others and suck them into the pit of reaction in which it has trapped itself by its own deeds and actions." It is hard to imagine that Algeria could resist the lures that had converted even the militant Mao, but Cleaver found it irresistible to point out "in humbleness" that it would be logically "consistent with Algeria's traditions of struggle and revolutionary principles to continue welcoming American revolutionaries and Afro-American freedom fighters" to their "shores— or . . . airfields," especially because "it is a part of Africa—the Afro-American people—who are asking you for this help." Cleaver ends with a fairly standard exhortation: "Let it not be said that Algeria has turned its back on the struggle of the Afro-American people" (161).

Boumédienne was furious with Cleaver for his effrontery. The letter was an embarrassment to him as an ex-revolutionary who hoped to maintain the image of a Third World radical leftist leader, especially among the black African nations; he had every intention of returning the money and was aware that Cleaver represented no more than 50 revolutionaries, let alone "the Afro-American people." He wanted to get Cleaver out of Algeria, but not in such a way as to appear fascistic.

Instead, on 15 August he ordered a raid on the villa, complete with search warrant, during the course of which a gun was taken that had been a gift to Cleaver from Ange Diawara of the Congo (*Fire*, 170); simultaneously, Boumédienne turned off the telephone and the telex machines. A summons for Eldridge Cleaver was delivered by one Si Salah, head of the Renseignement Général, the second division of the Algerian Political Police, which is the equivalent of the FBI (*Fire*, 162).

The next morning, Eldridge and Kathleen and two Panthers (whom even several years later Cleaver identified only by pseudonyms) went to police headquarters for the *coup de sémonce* (literally, "warning shot"), or scolding, from Salah ("Panthers on Ice," *Time*, 33). Salah began by telling them they were forbidden to hold a press conference as scheduled on Friday, 18 August, at the El Biar villa. In Kathleen's lengthy description of the meeting (published in full in *Soul on Fire*), she includes, idea for idea, if not verbatim, each complaint of Salah's and each response of the Panther group. In this case she took two paragraphs to deny that a press conference had been called. Actually, 18 August was the day designated by the Organization of Solidarity of Peoples of Africa, Asia, and Latin America, or OSPAAL, as the International Day of Solidarity with the Afro-American People, and the Panthers were merely holding an open house (*Fire*, 163). This brand-new organization seems to have been formed by liberation groups in Algiers that supported the Panthers in the ransom dispute; the "International Day" was simply an excuse to call in the press. In *Soul on Fire*, Kathleen and Eldridge remark, "We intended to make a statement analyzing our liberation struggle and the revolutionary movement in the world" (164), undoubtedly along lines favorable to their financial interests.

Salah apparently dropped the question of the "open house"; for him, it was already settled in his favor. He proceeded instead to castigate Cleaver and his companions for having "gone beyond [their] prerogatives as a liberation movement" (164). He informed them that the hijacking was Algeria's affair and not theirs at all; furthermore, if they needed money they would have to "confine [their] robberies and ransoming to [their] own land," reported Kathleen. Eldridge, apparently believing that Salah was open to persuasion and also able to affect policy, argued that the leaders of Algeria had "created the problem" by daring to place "their national interests above the interests of an oppressed people, and acting as if their interests were the only ones that counted" (166). He even explained that Algeria ought not to worry about American pressure because the United States needed its natural gas and would have to "back off." Salah was not interested in advice; he responded angrily that Algeria would sell its gas to anyone it liked—"capitalist or communist, it doesn't make any difference" (166). This non sequitur was no doubt prompted by the Cleavers' suggestion, omitted by Kathleen, that Algeria ought to sell its gas only to properly revolutionary countries.

The interview degenerated into personal insults. Salah denounced the Panthers as "Palace Revolutionaries" who actually did nothing, were "too materialistic" and greedy when they needed to be waking up their sleeping people, and were users of "marijuana" (168). Further, he had three complaints against Cleaver for "kidnap and death threats," had heard about the group's drug use for "three years" now, and had already once requested Cleaver's expulsion from Algeria, two years earlier, "based on his behavior" (169). The date would place the request somewhere around the time, perhaps, of the Leary episode and the disappearance of Clinton Smith. Kathleen recorded no details of the objectionable "behavior." The interview was soon terminated on an unpleasant note, with the issue of the open house left dangling.

On the eighteenth, there were no open house and no statement. The Algerian police arrived at the villa, confiscated all film, and chased the guests away. By the end of the month, the ransom money had been repaid and Cleaver was not in sight. *Time* speculated, encouraged by Bernice Jones of the New York Panther group, that Cleaver might be in "one of the revolution-minded African states, such as Guinea or Libya, which like Algiers, have no extradition treaty with the U.S." ("On Ice," 33). The *New York Times* thought Tanzania a possibility ("Panthers Appear to Have Left Algeria," 28 March 1973, 24).

Cleaver took a chance at offending Boumédienne out of desperation; he needed money to leave Algiers and he also felt a sense of responsibility toward the two sets of hijackers. Because he had already resigned as head of the international section, Pete O'Neal (the new head) and the others would not let him speak with any of the hijackers until all of the hijackers' money was gone—"the hijacking money plus the money they had with them in their pockets" (Gates, 54). After Algeria took the ransom money, "they had a few hundred dollars and they gave these cats [the other Panthers] some. And after that was over, they were treated like dirt. In the end, [Cleaver] started talking about getting their papers together" (54).

With ten hijackers and two Cleavers—only one of whom had a passport—and no money and no more "Wild West Liberation Movement," money was desperately needed to fund thei₁ evacuation. The attempt to get the hijacking money failed, but considering how shredded relations with Algeria were already, it is unlikely that Cleaver's letter really made the situation appreciably worse. Cleaver writes:

Kathleen was not a fugitive, but I was. We were the only two left there; everybody else had gone. And there were all these hijackers with no passports. We didn't have enough money because we figured it takes at least two or three grand per person, and we didn't have enough. We needed a passport and we didn't have that much bread for all those people. We did have enough to organize a passport for one person to go back to the United States to get some more bread. This was successful and it all worked out. Plus I used advances from my books to help. We were able to get passports and bread for everybody. We didn't lose anybody; everybody got out. When you look now at what had happened—I think the question was why did we leave—we saw the handwriting on the wall. Now the United States has re-established diplomatic relations with all the Arab countries, more or less, including Algeria. This is no place for an Afro-American liberation movement. There is no place for it now. (Gates, 54)

Cleaver left Algiers on a false visa of his own creation,[39] probably in January 1973. In *Soul on Fire,* he gives both August 1972 (183) and January 1973 (240) as the dates of his entry into Paris. The second date seems more likely, because the *New York Times* reported both that he had been seen in Algiers on 10 December 1972 at a news conference "by President Salvador Allende of Chile" and that he had not been "noticed" since January 1973 ("Panthers Appear to Have Left Algeria," 20 March 1973, 24), when he had had surgery in Algeria for an intestinal disorder (James F. Clarity, "Notes on People," 24 January, 47). Further, his remark to Gates that it took "about six months" to "see after" the newcomers, who began arriving in June 1972, would place his departure in January 1973. It may have taken some time to decide where to go next. Presumably, Paris was selected partly because Kathleen knew French and partly because it was easier for them to hide in a cosmopolitan center.

A more personal reason for the delay in departure might have been Cleaver's inability to decide whether to carry on as a Lone Ranger of the Left, running to various Third World revolutionary countries for refuge from American law enforcement agents, raising money through forging papers and dealing in black-market goods, and indefinitely cut off from family, or to hide in a Western nation and drop the revolution, spending all his energy on attempting to return to the United States without having to go to prison. Clearly, the second choice was as much an ideological decision as a practical one. The only identity Cleaver had had outside prison was "The Revolutionary"; that he was far more The Revolutionary than "The Writer" was obvious from the fact that his life and his writing had been consumed by his politics since late 1966, when he first met Jerry Rubin, and other white radicals he would befriend, through Beverly Axelrod. When he met Newton and Seale in February 1967, the die was cast. Now, little more than five years later, there had been no 1972 coup, as Cleaver had predicted there would be back in 1969 (Lockwood, 118), and he felt abandoned. As he told Curtice Taylor, Tim Leary had felt betrayed because no one attempted to get him out of prison back in the old days. Cleaver complained, "At one point [Leary] said that he had been ripped off by the new Left, the old Left, the sideways Left; and he does see it like he was ripped off, and, man, we all were" (Taylor, 47). The question must have been, at least for a while, whether the "Wild West Liberation Movement" was over only in Algiers or everywhere on earth.

In *Soul on Fire,* Cleaver revealed that he had "slipped out of Algeria alone, leaving Kathleen behind, and was reunited with her in Paris" (186). At the time, he still hoped to avoid a return to prison, but he was having no luck in negotiating parolee status. Though Cleaver recognized that there would have to be a trial on the charges stemming from the 6 April 1968 police shoot-out, he wanted to await trial out on bail, as he had from June to November 1968. This kind of arrangement would have required a court order canceling the 27 September order that had rescinded Judge Sherwin's release of Cleaver in June and required Cleaver to report to prison on 27 November 1968. It is possible that a lawyer might have been able to persuade the court that a repentant Cleaver would never run again after surrendering himself; however, Cleaver was in disfavor with Charles Garry and his associates, who remained with Newton and Seale, and lacked the funds to hire his own counsel. The few devoted revolutionaries who wanted to see him return home to head the Black Liberation Army were poor and altogether without political influence; few others cared. From France, where he lived with forged documents, Cleaver tried to arrange something for himself, but only became increasingly isolated and embittered.

Chapter Six

The Return: "One Black Face in a Sea of White"

In fall 1972 the *Black Scholar* published "On Lumpen Ideology," which Cleaver had submitted from Algiers. Indeed, the November–December issue noted that Cleaver, "internationally known as a black revolutionary and theoretician . . . is now head of the International Black Panther Party in Algeria, and actively involved in Third World liberation struggles."[1]

This essay is the clearest and most extreme statement of Cleaver's antiproletarian, prolumpen bias, which dates back to at least 1968. Here, as before, he declares the members of the working class to be "a part of the system that has to be destroyed" because of their very success in claiming their share. "The real revolutionary element of our era is the Lumpen, understood in its broader sense" ("Lumpen Ideology," 9), that is, as "the vast majority" of mankind (10). True "Lumpen consciousness" assumes that "the Lumpen, humanity itself, has been robbed of its social heritage by the concentration and centralization of technology" that really belongs to "the people" (10). Thus, all the wealth technology produces belongs to the people, too. "The point is not equality in Production, which is the Marxist view and basic error, but equality in distribution and consumption" (10). In other words, those who produce nothing have as great a "right to consume" as those in the working class. This view, says Cleaver, is "more advanced" than the "job-seeking, fringe benefit consciousness of the AFL/CIO/Communist Party/Working Class accommodationist movement"; this is "the ultimate revolutionary demand" (10).

Cleaver was not satisfied with thus alienating all the members of the proletariat; an essential part of his argument is the thesis that all ordinary citizens of the earth (including the extremely poor he saw in postrevolutionary Third World countries) are fundamentally lumpen. It follows, then, that even Marxist countries oppress their masses, and worse, the leaders copy the capitalist leaders and join them "in the common task of repressing and blocking revolutionary forces in the world" (3). They, like the capitalists, have become "gigantic and powerful, conglomerated into Superpowers," and they have no interest in "the oppressed people" (3). Clearly, Cleaver's disillusionment with Red China, which now appeared to him to be as revisionist as Russia had ever been, was complete, and along with his condemnation of those "Superpowers" went his loyalty, it would seem, to the dream of Third World liberation.

This indictment drew a response from C. J. Munford, a history professor from the University of Guelph in Ontario, Canada, in the pages of the *Black Scholar* the following summer. Munford's article, "The Fallacy of Lumpen Ideology," served both to refute Cleaver's views and to recant Munford's own opinions in his companion article in the 1972 *Black Scholar*, "Social Structure and Black Revolution." In his earlier essay, Munford had excitedly taken the "ghetto explosions in the latter part of the sixties" as a sign that Fanon was right in designating the lumpenproletariat as the ultimate revolutionary force.[2] "Unfortunately, I neglected the classic works of Marx, Engels, and Lenin for lesser lights. This is a grievous fault. I hope I have now overcome it, and I intend never again to fall victim to it" (Munford, 51). Thoroughly chastised and repentant, Munford now admitted that "premature advocacy of armed struggle—and I admit that I have been guilty of this—is counterproductive" (51).

Cleaver's case, although leading equally to "adventurism and provocation," said Munford, was different. On the theoretical level, his ideas are "counter-revolutionary and extremely dangerous to the black community" (47). "There is nothing even vaguely scientific and Marxist about the designation 'Superpower' " (50), says Munford; in true orthodox fashion, he rejects the reality of any entity not already described by Marx in the previous century. More concretely, however, he zeroes in on Cleaver's advocacy of the right to consume; in a rather clever maneuver, he turns Cleaver's antiproletarian stance into a procapitalist position, even while complaining that "Eldridge would never admit that in order to consume society must produce" (49).

Perhaps from sheer spite, [Cleaver] wants to keep American workers unorganized, disunited and hence weak and defenceless [sic]. If so, then, objectively, Cleaver is an agent of the monopoly capitalist class. He is not at all shamefaced about his hatred of workers; he states in so many words in the article "On Lumpen Ideology" that the working class should be destroyed (p. 9). He dreams of negating, of pulverizing proletarian class consciousness. In its place he would put donothingness, a "gimme-gimme" mentality, the ultimate in a consumerism which denies the human need for labor. According to Cleaver, the destiny of man is not to become human through creative labor, but to become "lumpen" through parasitism. (50)

Because of these offenses, it is clear that "Cleaver's doctrine is anti-communist, and despite the form or camouflage anti-communism is always the subterfuge of the scoundrel. Behind each and every black anti-communist hides a head-scratching, feet-shuffling Uncle Tom. Through years of being subjected to virulent anti-communist slanders like these we have grown accustomed to looking for the hidden influence of the CIA whenever it crops up" (48). These charges would be remembered only two years later, when Cleaver returned to the United States. Journalists with no overt link to the American Communist party or the Socialist Workers' party, apparently impressed that Cleaver was not shot to death when he deplaned in New York, would insist that he had cut some kind of deal with the FBI or the CIA even as he went off to prison.

The fact that Munford could even consider charging a man with Cleaver's past reputation with being a CIA operative shows how isolated and unpopular Cleaver had become, or worse, how irrelevant. It is not surprising that no one came to his defense. In fact, when we see how conservative his ideas became, we realize that Munford was inadvertently correct when he labeled Cleaver "anti-communist." What he meant was that Cleaver was anti–working class, which is to say, anti-Marxist and therefore not a true Communist, but in view of Cleaver's later support of Christ and the flag, the charge is actually funny.

Cleaver's final publication from exile was "The Crisis of the Black Bourgeoisie," which appeared in the *Black Scholar* in January 1973. The article was accompanied by the same biographical information used the previous November, since Cleaver was not yet officially in Paris, not yet having been granted asylum.

The title of Cleaver's article is misleading, for the bulk of his writing concerns not the crisis but the success of middle-class blacks in adapting from a) educated Negroes who merely wished to dissociate themselves from the black masses to b) relatively wealthy blacks who benefited from social programs designed, in postriot America, to increase poor blacks' income through black participation in the economy. The crisis is really that of the lower classes and the few remaining radicals, who suffered from the "benign neglect" of governmental reduction of social services[3] and from an inability to participate more than vicariously in black capitalism ("Crisis," 10). Cleaver avoids the use of loaded terms like *lumpenproletariat* here, but he does insist, in line with his characteristic distrust of the professional class and his impatience with slow change, that only "a few thousand" Afro-American people "out of the 30 million" get any of the "few hundred million dollars" available, which means that the entire scheme is only "a gigantic fraud and a cruel deception" (10).

Insofar as this money "binds" the black bourgeoisie to "the ruling class" while simultaneously the government represses the "militants" through "an unprecedented reign of terror" in black communities, it returns control of "the mass movement" to previously "rejected" middle-class "black Christian preachers, politicians and opportunists." Nixon thus created, said Cleaver, a situation analogous to that mentioned in *Revolution in the Congo:* neocolonialism.

The analogy is imperfect. Whereas the African model had provided for the physical departure of administrators and military personnel from the various imperialist countries and their replacement with indigenous puppet rulers, there is little evidence in America of a white presence surrounding the ghetto while middle-class blacks "take over" rule from them. Rather, there is bemoaned here a simple reversal of the phenomenon Cleaver had announced in "The Fire Now": "field nigger-ism" had had its brief day in a social group noted, as Cleaver had prophetically pointed out in 1968, for the "transitional nature" of its organizations. Things were back to normal again; Du Bois's "Talented Tenth" provided the leadership and the spokespersons of the black race, and the masses concerned themselves with survival. Cleaver was right about one thing, though: the concept of blacks as a colonized people within a white mother country was no longer viable. In that sense, the "colonial" period was indeed over. What he could not admit was that the revolution was over, too.

While some "back-sliding militants" (11) like "the reactionary wing of the Black Panther Party, led by Huey Newton and Bobby Seale" were bought off, he claimed (10), other still-revolutionary radicals had been the victims of "selective genocide" (2). Here Cleaver seems to blur the years from 1967 to 1972 into one, moving swiftly from police attacks on Newton, Seale, himself, and Fred Hampton, among others, to the period of quietude and co-optation that followed his break with Newton, blending them into one simultaneously occurring set of phenom-

ena. Actually, Panther Breakfast for Children programs, free health
clinics, and other reformist projects like free shoes for children and free
bags of groceries had all begun in late 1968 and 1969; well before their
participation in the $4 million Model Cities Program, the Oakland
Panthers had established their "community concern." Although Cleaver
insisted that Newton was repaying the government for his inclusion in
such programs by making "a public statement in support of Black
Capitalism, Christianity, White Capitalism, and an end to revolutionary violence," all that Newton was really doing, he himself said, was
working to "meet the needs of the people," which had been his (and
reluctantly, Cleaver's) phrase all along. In fact, Cleaver used the phrase
as the title of one of his three "Notes from Exile" in *Ramparts* in
September 1969, before he lost interest in all but violent struggle.

Cleaver's idea that Nixon hoped to "destroy the liberation movement" (11) is correct. The FBI worked to split up and nullify the Black
Panthers on the one hand, and on the other, Nixon gave the BPP
money, which is partly what the movement had been about to begin
with, among blacks. Cleaver, like the Weathermen, had no interest in
economic opportunity; that was not why he had become a revolutionary. He concluded his essay with the threat of revolutionary "votes" in
the form of "guns and bombs" directed at both the newly reelected
Nixon and "the Afro-American bourgeoisie" (11). While the government believed the movement was dead, it also appeared to be readying
a last "gigantic apparatus of repression" against the revolutionaries,
who were at that moment "regrouping, reorganizing, laying in supplies, and girding [themselves] for waging war." The troops returning
from Vietnam, as Cleaver had insisted before, would form a people's
army and destroy the entire "ruling class," and the black middle class
with it. Their destruction, apparently, is the "crisis" the black bourgeoisie would have to face.

Paris

Cleaver has said very bluntly that when he left Algiers he "had
decided to come out of the Third World and the Communist/Socialist
world altogether" (*Fire,* 195), with the clear implication that he had
abandoned his self-image as a revolutionary leader in exile who would
one day return to lead an army of assorted oppressed peoples to victory.
His disappointment with the revolutionary governments he had seen,
his awareness almost from the first that even very poor Americans were

being "squashed between two pieces of silk" in comparison with the plight of the poor in Asia and the Middle East, and finally his knowledge that radical fervor was decreasing daily in the United States combined to convince him that revolutionary Marxist-Leninist ideology was not the answer to American problems. Perhaps he realized that the provision of social welfare programs within a context of capitalism was as close to "Yankee Doodle Socialism" as the United States was likely to get, and that Newton may have been right to emphasize small-scale manufacturing. During the next several months, Cleaver would change his ideas dramatically; by the time he reentered the United States in November 1975, he had accepted Christianity, conservatism, and apparently even capitalism, this last to the extent that he had begun his own business: the manufacture of gender-specific men's trousers of his own design.

When the Cleavers first moved into their little "two-room walkup apartment on the Rue St. Jacques" (*Fire,* 194), Eldridge had lost his radicalism but not his naïveté. He had learned that "people's" governments are not necessarily dedicated to the people, but he had forgotten his older awareness that democratic governments are often less than single-mindedly devoted to the cause of democracy. When he explained to radical playwright Jean Genet, a longtime Panther sympathizer, that he wanted to apply for political asylum in France on the grounds that France had once granted such asylum to Benjamin Franklin and Thomas Paine, Genet "burst out laughing" at him (195). "Not only are you a child," said Genet, "you're white!" (196). Ironically, Genet's radicalism made the white author's ideas a negative image of those the ex–radical black author held; while Cleaver, "disillusioned, angry at the Third World in general," was "in no mood to hear them praised," Genet espoused "total condemnation of the white race and total absolution of people of color" (196).

In spite of his scorn for Cleaver, Genet agreed to help him. Not only did he introduce Cleaver to the socialist lawyer Roland Dumas, purported to be "a part of François Mitterand's inner circle" (193), but he extracted from Dumas a promise to stick with Cleaver "to the end." In April he began to work for Cleaver's asylum on the grounds that Cleaver had been "persecuted because of his action in favor of liberty" ("Cleaver Seeks French Asylum," *New York Times,* 4 April 1973, 39).

Genet's petition, addressed to Premier Pierre Messmer, never mentioned that Cleaver was already living clandestinely in France (*Fire,* 197), creating false documents for himself and others much as he had in

Algiers. Along with the official petition, according to Cleaver, "Roland Dumas sent an appeal to the government signed by many outstanding French personalities, including Jean-Paul Sartre and Simone de Bouvoir [sic]" (197). The only obvious holdout on the Left was the French Communist party, which Cleaver claimed resented him not because he was "anti Communist," but because he had "dared to criticize Angela Davis" (197). In actuality, Cleaver had been critical of the "Free Angela" movement on the grounds that it detracted from the emphasis the Panthers needed to place on freeing Bobby Seale (and secondarily, Ericka Huggins); at any rate, he was unacceptable to the French Communist party because he was unacceptable to the American Communist party, which instructed the former not to sign (197). The *New York Times* reported that the petition was filed in April and the appeal, signed by French Socialist party deputy François Mitterand in addition to various celebrities, was issued in August (James F. Clarity, "Notes on People," *New York Times,* 7 August 1973, 31), after Interior Minister Raymond Marcellin had rejected the request in May, arguing that Cleaver faced "no particular risk in his present country of residence because of his political convictions or ethnic origin" ("France Rejects Request from Cleaver for Asylum," *New York Times,* 20 May 1973, 17). Or, as Cleaver rephrased it, "He's doing fine in Algeria. So let him stay in Algeria" (*Fire,* 197). The decision was appealed, and "there the matter rested" (197) for the time being. As things stood, Cleaver could be extradited at any time if he appeared in public "without assurance of asylum" (*New York Times,* 20 May 1973, 17).

Failing to Meet Huey's Standard

In May Cleaver's life worsened upon the appearance of the Huey Newton interview with Lee Lockwood in *Playboy.* Those who were not already aware of Newton's blaming Cleaver for the "filthy speech movement" in the party and for the use of inflammatory rhetoric that brought police persecution down on the Panthers read it now. Bobby Seale, in an interview published in the *Black Scholar* the previous September, had already dubbed Cleaver "the hidden traitor," and now Newton went so far as to say that Cleaver, who had videotaped himself calmly smoking as he chatted on the telephone with a hysterical and unwitting Newton after the Dunbar talk show, was "a very disturbed and unhappy person" who "probably hates himself very much."[4] Cleaver, he said, had "to destroy those he respects" because he was "insecure" and that is the way a person like him tries to "assert his masculinity" (Lockwood, 84). He pointed out that Cleaver had been sent to prison "as a rapist." (Actually, though Cleaver admitted to rape, the charge that stuck was attempted murder.) Newton went on: "When I was imprisoned, I quickly learned that guys who would come in with many counts of rape ended up as homosexuals a large percentage of the time. I think it was no accident that Eldridge had the rape conviction or that when he came out of prison he became so attached to the Panthers and the idea of the gun. I think the gun was a substitute for his penis; he called it his 'rod.' That's what the party meant to him: a masculine kind of demonstration that he needed in order to reinforce his very shaky sexual identity." (84). When Lockwood pressed Newton for "factual evidence" that Cleaver is "a repressed homosexual," Newton replied:

Well, there was something that happened on the occasion when he and I met Baldwin. We met Baldwin shortly after he returned from Turkey, I guess in 1966 or the early part of '67. Eldridge had been invited to a party to meet him, and he asked me to go along. So we went over to San Francisco in his Volkswagen van and we got there first. Soon after, Baldwin arrived. Baldwin is a very small man in stature: I guess about five-one. Eldridge is about six-four, you know: at the time, he weighed about 250 pounds. Anyway, Baldwin just walked over to him and embraced him around the waist. And Eldridge leaned down from his full height and engaged Baldwin in a long, passionate French kiss. They kissed each other on the mouth for a long time. When we left, Eldridge kept saying, "Don't tell anyone." I said all right. And I kept my word—until now. (84)

This first reference to Cleaver's supposed homosexual inclinations would resurface in November 1976, when Elaine Brown would remind *Black Panther* readers of Cleaver's "nine years of penitentiary love" ("Whatever Happened to the Black Panther Party," 20 November 1976, 20). She would further claim, in order to unload all the blame on him, that he had "mesmerized everyone, as if he were a god, or perhaps Beelzebub" (10).

Finally, Newton explained his earlier comment that Cleaver's "exile was in large measure staged by the exile himself." As opposed to Cleaver's repeated claim that Newton had ordered him into exile, Newton insisted that Cleaver wanted exile as a part of his "fantasy."

Cleaver never responded to either of Newton's allegations. The interview was detrimental to swinging public sentiment toward helping

Cleaver return; the destruction of his image as a macho, black-leather-jacket-and-sunglasses revolutionary who had been hounded from the country by fascist types bent upon his destruction was complete. When Huey measured Eldridge by "Huey's standard," Cleaver failed; his attack in *Soul on Ice* on Baldwin and on homosexuality as a "sickness" was really an attempt, said Newton, "to project his own femininity onto someone else and to make someone else pay the price for his own guilt feelings" (Lockwood, 84).

It is easy to interpret Cleaver's customary insistence on black manhood as compensatory, and there is certainly considerable discussion of masculinity in his work, from a demand for aggressiveness to the mockery of King's nonviolence as effeminate; from the praise of the maleness of muscular menial men to the assumption that "administrators" and even nonviolent bourgeois blacks were effete; from the presentation of "street" manners, the behavior of "the brothers off the block," as admirably tough and action oriented to the evaluation of the manners of the boardroom or the academy as accommodationist and passive. Now Cleaver, always a man of letters at heart, was forced to embrace a mode of living that had to be quiet and submissive; he could petition but not demand. It is possible that this passivity contributed strongly to Cleaver's depression, as well as to his admitted abusiveness (which may have been mostly verbal) toward Kathleen, supposedly in an attempt to drive her away and back home out of exile for her own good (*Fire,* 210).

The months of 1973 dragged on; the Cleavers found a five-room house in the 13th Arrondissement right behind the Hôpital Salpêtrière, at 9, rue Bruant (*Fire,* 185). "The heavy pedestrian traffic between the Metro Station and the hospital, including workers, patients, and visitors, provided a perfect atmosphere of anonymity," noted Cleaver, "ideal for someone living illegally in Paris, with a false I.D. and an assumed name" (187). Joju and Maceo had been in the United States for most of a year for their own safety—from the time "the sky began to fall in on us in Algeria" (186) until mid-1973. Their parents hoped the children could join them once they had a home.

The Hidden Traitor

In July 1973 Ross K. Baker of Rutgers, writing in the *Nation,* presented the Newtonite version of the Black Panther party's history. His evaluation of the 1971 split accepted without question a "more conservative, pre-Cleaver orientation of the Panthers which placed a greater premium on community service than on revolutionary commitment,"[5] an orientation to which the party returned after an inevitable break between the leaders of the "two rival factions." According to Baker, following the "party line" in Newton's 1971 statement on the "defection" of Cleaver, Newton and Seale had been interested only in self-defense all along:

In early 1971 it became clear that not only were the differences between the factions irreconcilable, but that, in fact, there was not one party but two. It could even be argued that there had always been two parties—that there had been severe cleavages of ideology and tactics ever since Cleaver's accession to the Panthers. The concept of self-defense articulated by Newton and Seale and based on the ostentatious display of firearms was an artifice which covered the essentially reformist and community-oriented inclinations of the founders. Cleaver saw the guns and inferred from them that Newton and Seale were revolutionaries. Newton and Seale were also, for a time, captivated by the guns, but the difference was that for them guns were a temporary obsession; for Cleaver they were the embodiment of the Panthers. (Baker, 49)

This is not the place for a full analysis of the development of the Black Panthers both ideologically and organizationally between 1966 and 1971, but a few salient points ought to be considered nonetheless in the context of the charges against Cleaver. First, Newton and Seale were strongly influenced by Fanon's *The Wretched of the Earth,* which speaks positively of revolution and the moral and psychological justification of killing on the part of oppressed colonial persons. While they called their group the Black Panther Party for Self-Defense, at least for a time, it is clear that they were militaristic in their emphasis on guns and uniforms and that they planned to organize the local lumpen in Oakland and in nearby communities into gun-bearing vigilante groups to show force against local police. Whether they initially intended the group to spread to all the major cities in the United States is not possible to say, but such a plan seems likely, considering the Ten Point Program and the credo "What We Want, What We Believe." No such program could exist in a single city; most of the demands require a massive reorganization of society and a rethinking of such basic issues as the right to property and the criminality of criminals, along with a consequent reorganization of the nation's economic and judicial systems in a manner favorable to the lumpen and to what are regarded by most as dangerous felons ("political prisoners"). The Ten Point Program was

intact before Seale and Newton met Cleaver in February 1967, and they
carried guns before he met them.

Newton's charge that Cleaver had hooked the party up with white
leftists and thereby lured it into "defecting" from the black community
is both hypocritical and ungrateful, considering that he and Cleaver
both knew that white money and influence were needed to get Newton
out of jail and that Cleaver was the only Panther with any contacts in
that group. It was probably a mistake for Cleaver to run for president
on the predominantly white Peace and Freedom party ticket, but it was
also a mistake for Newton to antagonize the police as he did; it was
Newton's self-consciously "macho" role-playing that made him a target
and got him into the kind of trouble he created for himself in October
1967, a skirmish that ended with a police officer dead and Newton in
prison throughout the tumultuous years of 1968 and 1969, and a
skirmish without which the Panthers would not have been so dependent on the white Left to begin with. In effect, Newton and Seale (and
Baker) were claiming that the party made no mistakes of its own;
Cleaver, partly because he was disturbed and partly because he was led
astray by white radicals, was responsible for everything.

Baker's uncritical acceptance of Newton's analysis is disturbingly
nonscholarly in its willingness to take Newton's version of events as
history rather than ideology or self-serving justification. Baker concludes his article with remarks to the effect that the new, "safe" Panthers will quite possibly become a local Democratic organization:

> It is well to recall that the great ethnic urban political machines of the past
> began in much the same fashion as have the transformed Panthers. How
> different, after all, are the Panther shopping bags of free food from the bags of
> coal and the Thanksgiving turkeys that served to build the urban machines of
> the Irish and Italians? The defeat of Bobby Seale for mayor of Oakland consti-
> tutes a minor, temporary setback. The Panthers have put down the gun and
> taken up the shopping bag, but in so doing they appear to have learned that
> the acquisition of community power is a process that can take many forms. No
> longer dependent on radical allies for their approbation and no longer fearful of
> the retaliation of authorities, the once angry Panthers have decided that poli-
> tics is an extension of war by other means. The result may be the creation of
> the first important black political machine in American history. (51)

Ironically, when Cleaver returned from exile, he would charge that the
Panthers had sold out to the extent that they were simply a part of the
local Democratic machine.

The Expatriate

In June 1973 Cleaver had renewed his appeal for asylum in vain; in August, Mitterand and the others appealed to the government on his behalf, but to no end. In the fall, Kathleen returned to the United States to discuss not only Cleaver's possible return as a parolee out on bail but also the need for a defense fund so that Cleaver could cover the legal expenses entailed by his return ("Cleaver Is Writing a New Book," *New York Times,* 27 December 1973, 7). Meanwhile, Cleaver had two lawsuits in the works: one against the French government's decision to deny him asylum and the other against the U.S. government's continued freeze on his royalties from *Soul on Ice* and *Eldridge Cleaver: Post-Prison Writings and Speeches,* still withheld under the Trading with the Enemy Act of 1917. Cleaver was no longer a "national" of Cuba in the government's eyes, and had not been since late 1969, but he was now considered a national of "China, North Korea and North Vietnam" (*New York Times,* 7). During this time, Cleaver was under contract to Viking to produce a book on his experiences in exile, and he retained the little two-room apartment as a retreat in which to write, in addition to using the study in the house and, later, a small place "in Rocheville in southern France on the fringes of the French Riviera" (Oliver, 207).

Besides his dealings with Rolande Dumas, Cleaver was negotiating with an influential female acquaintance named Fanchon, who was apparently an intimate of Valéry Giscard d'Estaing. In fact, it has been said that Fanchon was originally d'Estaing's mistress, and had an affair with Cleaver as well during this time.[6] If so, that would explain her concern and enthusiasm for helping him solve his problems. Against Cleaver's wishes, for he feared a quick, unsympathetic extradition, Fanchon spoke to the minister of finance and economy about him; she told the truth about his being in Paris already and also about his "desperate" situation (*Fire,* 191). She gave d'Estaing a copy of *Soul on Ice* and obtained a promise that he would speak to Minister of the Interior Marcellin and tell her his reply. Cleaver kept this information from his lawyer in case it was all merely a fantasy or an empty promise, but he soon received word that he and Kathleen were to meet d'Estaing at Fanchon's for breakfast the following Sunday. In case the meeting was a trap, Cleaver explained everything to Dumas, who remained "on call" over the weekend.

As it turned out, d'Estaing was indeed sympathetic to Cleaver and arranged with Marcellin's replacement, Jacques Chirac, to "normalize" the Cleavers' situation, despite the fact that Cleaver's file called for his immediate expulsion from France were he ever to enter the country. According to Cleaver, the French had him "classified as a dangerous terrorist associated with airplane hijacking" (*Fire*, 202), a listing that was not surprising, considering Cleaver's associates over the preceding five years. Nevertheless, d'Estaing's influence was sufficient to procure "the magic papers" granting residency (206), with the proviso that Cleaver take part in "no political activity of any kind."[7] Years later, when Cleaver, in *Soul on Fire*, revealed d'Estaing's role, d'Estaing insisted he had aided the Cleavers "on strictly humanitarian grounds," in order to keep his record spotlessly neutral on the subject (Albin Krebs, "Notes on People," *New York Times*, 6 July, 1978, sec. 3, p. 2).

Thus, by 1974 the Cleaver family was reunited and safely legal in their Parisian residency, but they had no future; in particular, Eldridge felt disoriented and depressed. His writing was going poorly (he had canceled the contract and returned the $40,000 advance to Viking),[8] and no one in the United States had any interest in him anymore. As he put it, "the Nixon administration was satisfied to let me 'twist slowly in the wind' of Southern France" (*Fire*, 207).

The alternative to returning to America was to become a lifelong expatriate, an option that made Cleaver feel only despair. He had never become fluent in French, having surrounded himself with Americans and translators in French-speaking Algiers and in Paris; now he felt threatened that his children learned French in school, and he wanted "to keep English number one around the house" (*Fire*, 208). He who had once planned to play high school football was dismayed when his son began "talking and playing soccer" instead of "the premier American sport" (209). He later said he attacked "the minor league gloating" of French friends who "eternally . . . lifted a glass to the Eiffel Tower," telling them that "it was America which built the electric typewriters, and until they had something like IBM, they had better stick with busts of Napoleon"(208). "One good buddy," says Cleaver ironically, "flew over from the States and told me face to face to forget about [returning]" (210). Eldridge had ended up on the wrong side of the Panther split, and there was nothing to be gained from his return; no one would associate with him. As Cleaver phrased it, "There is no place for you, so why don't you just settle down and become a black Frenchman and enjoy all those French pastries. It was like a sentence— another era of serving time" (210).

A rumor stated that old pal Jerry Rubin, long over his snit about

Cleaver's insensitive handling of Tim Leary, visited Cleaver in Paris in 1974, bringing with him est founder Werner Erhard (born Jack Rosenberg). Some believed Rubin's plan was to get Erhard to finance Cleaver's legal defense fund; if so, it was a fruitless trip (Art Goldberg, "Changing Times Changed Cleaver," *In These Times,* 13 April 1977, 20). One cannot help but consider, however, what sort of minisession Erhard (who was himself sort of born again when he left his parents and changed his name) might have had with Cleaver. The essence of est, the acceptance of life as it really is and a determination to accept and enjoy it ("What is, is. What isn't, isn't"), involves such things as looking behind one's belief systems, dropping one's defense of nonnurturing or nonvaluable belief systems, and adopting an honest relationship with others and with oneself. When one experiences life as it really is, one reaches satisfaction. Erhard's ideas can be seen, possibly, in Cleaver's willingness to drop his role as a revolutionary and become simply an author and a backer of the U.S. government, and as such may have had a role in Cleaver's subsequent decision to accept the fact that he would have to go back to prison, at least for a time, if he hoped to return to America.

By September 1974 Cleaver's ideas had begun to shift quite dramatically. It would seem that his disaffection for Third World leftists made him a political conservative on the issue of foreign policy. Curtice Taylor discovered Cleaver at a café in Paris and persuaded him to be interviewed. Cleaver made it clear to Taylor that he had "a completely different perspective" now and that he was "not a member of any organization" (Taylor, 40). Further, he noted, he "plan[ned] to be back in the United States by July 4, 1976," in order, one assumes, better to celebrate the bicentennial. Cleaver said the Republicans were a "discredited" party after Watergate, and he looked forward to the possibility of a new "New Left," a coalition or "new force" made of the "left faction of both parties" in the future (Taylor, 64).

A major result of Cleaver's changed perspective was his strong support for the U.S. military. He told Taylor, "We have to be prepared to do some turnarounds. For example, after all my travels and seeing the socialists' world up very close, really seeing how the Soviet Union and China function, well, I now think that the U.S. should be second to none militarily, that we have to strengthen, not demise [*sic*], our military, and that really causes a lot of people's mouths to drop open" (48). Taylor, his mouth "gaping," protested, in the name of many leftists, "I consider them madmen. . . . I consider them to be as evil as the

Soviets. . . . I think that the military mind so dominated the CIA that what we have now is, well a can of worms that is so fascistic I can't see any hope for them" (48). Cleaver did not contend against these remarks; rather, he blamed the left for "turn[ing] its back" on the military. As we move into the seventies, he added, it is "the responsibility of the left to initiate" a post-Vietnam détente with the military. "I, for one, intend to develop a new relationship with the U.S. military. I'm on a honeymoon with them myself. I love 'em [*much laughter*]" (48).

The ulterior motive behind Cleaver's "love" is not hard to discover. Never forgetting that political power grows from the barrel of a gun, he noted, "If we are going to really talk about progressive change in America, then we have to talk about moving on the military, not excluding it. Because without that support, brother, there ain't goin' to be no revolution" (48). Cleaver's politics became conservative on specific issues, then, particularly foreign policy, while remaining left of center on the question of the redistribution of wealth. He saw the insincerity of Third World governments in their concern for their citizens and in their commitment to world revolution; the one thing they did want, it seemed, was to destroy the United States. "You see," he later told an *Encore* interviewer, "The Communists aren't plotting just to wipe out the right (wing) in America, they're talking about doing in the whole thing. And I can't subscribe to that. I want the U.S. vastly improved, not done in. We have to maintain a vigilance against people who want to destroy the United States."[9] The revolutionaries within, however, are critical of the efforts of the Communists. Seemingly unaware of the influence he and the international section of the Black Panther party had had on the various "generals from the Soviet Union and marshalls from China" whom they had met in their travels, Cleaver noted how confidently the foreigners spoke of the "internal disintegration of the United States," taking it "for granted that they can count on certain elements inside the United States" for help. "The revolutionaries abroad have a slogan," he told the *Reader's Digest,* " 'We will destroy them from without; they will destroy them from within' " (Bartlett, 70). If J. Edgar Hoover believed everything the Panthers and the Yippies said, it is not surprising that Third World leaders were convinced. It is dismaying, however, to see the effect of Cleaver's fiery rhetoric upon himself, for it is certainly the Panthers and their ilk whom "the revolutionaries abroad" had in mind; the American Communist party is no closer to launching a violent revolution than the John Birch Society, in the long run.

One result of Cleaver's new allegiance to the United States was an acceptance of American political democracy over the forms of government found elsewhere, but a continued rejection of the economic system. He told Jerome McFadden for *Sepia:* "Whereas, in the United States you don't have economic democracy, which hasn't developed, you have just the opposite situation in the Soviet Union and the other socialist countries. Political democracy is zero in those countries, but they have outstripped the West in economic democracy, in terms of more benefits for more people."[10] Cleaver's feelings about the inequity of "distribution" had not changed from his fairly recent *Black Scholar* articles in which he urged "the right to consume" and condemned the black bourgeoisie. Even after his return, he condemned black capitalism as a right-wing ploy to spend millions instead of billions and to incorporate promising black individuals into the establishment, ignoring the masses and their problems, and he advocated "nationalizing the system of distribution. . . . To give more people access to the product of the economy . . . would be revolutionary. And I think that has to happen" (Douglass, 14).

Late in the spring of 1975, Cleaver's father died in Chicago. The man who may have been responsible for creating an antiauthoritarian, anti–father figure revolutionary, whose son once longed to be big enough to kill him, died pathetically alone in his apartment; the body was not discovered for several days.[11] Predictably, Cleaver was at least temporarily saddened by the reality of his father's death, but he was also finally and permanently relieved of the need to do battle; he himself was now the authority figure. That he had been far away from his father and had never had a chance to reconcile their relationship was yet another part of the price he was forced to pay for the years he spent as a radical and in exile. Interestingly, the father appears to have paid his son homage by producing what he called "an older man's version of *Soul on Ice*," entitled "Babylon in Retrospect," at the age of 73. The manuscript was never published.

Early in 1975 *Newsweek* reporter Kim Willenson found Cleaver and his family in Paris. They had "fallen on hard times," she reported. Their "small house in a working-class district" was smothered in "memorabilia of [Eldridge's] Panther days: newspaper clippings, photos of himself and his wife and black notables like Dr. Martin Luther King Jr. and Malcolm X, a pair of worn black combat boots, bookcases full of tapes and stacks of papers that he says are notes for a new book, 'Over My Shoulder' " (Willenson and Friedman, 40).

Cleaver told Willenson some of the same things he had told Curtice Taylor in the 1974 interview, which would not be published until September 1975. She reported that he had "cooled on Communism" and now believed that the U.S. needed "a strong defense establishment" against a possible "surprise attack" by Russia. He confessed to a feeling of distance from the Africans ("the whole skin thing didn't stand up too heavy") and from the Palestinian cause ("We learned what some of these [Arab] governments were doing. It's more complicated than we thought it was"). He rated Watergate as "America's greatest contribution" and hoped that the new leadership, especially in California, where Ed Brown had replaced Reagan, would make it possible for him to return to America. "He is willing to stand trial on the assault charges," said Willenson. "All he wants before he returns is an assurance that he won't be slapped back in prison until the trial ends." Cleaver's optimism, however, was not matched by Panther lawyer Charles Garry: "It doesn't look good" (Willenson and Friedman, 40).

Signifying

Once Willlenson's article appeared in print, comments began. In May Nikki Giovanni wrote in *Encore,* "The news from Paris, France, that Black fire-eating, anti-racist, anti-sexist, anti-middle-class militant Eldridge Cleaver is considering a return to the United States is not surprising. That he left in the first place and the circumstances of his leaving are perhaps the real news story."[12] Her one-page article contained a series of innuendos that led the reader to suspect Cleaver's collusion, from the beginning, with various law enforcement agencies.

It was "intriguing," Giovanni wrote, "that Angela Davis couldn't get to Cuba . . . while Cleaver could go all the way to Algeria without being noticed" (Giovanni, 26). Actually, Angela Davis's 1974 *Autobiography* gives a full account of her July 1969 trip to Cuba; not only did Davis use a valid U.S. passport to enter Havana, but she flew on a regularly scheduled Cuban airline, visa in hand, after having been photographed by "Mexican immigration officials" along with the entire planeload of passengers (Davis, 202). Certainly her chances of being noticed exceeded those of Cleaver, who made the trip in a closet and on the run from the police. Giovanni, of course, was well aware of these facts. Further, Cleaver was indeed "noticed," perhaps according to his own wishes, in Cuba during May 1969, and then disappeared, to resurface officially in Algiers in July.

Giovanni's most damaging remark is the implication that Cleaver survived the 6 April shoot-out by prearrangement: "It is curious to those who knew them both that Hutton, a mere 17-year-old boy, could be mistaken for Cleaver, one of the oldest members of the Panthers, but stranger things have happened when the police go gunning." Even the fact that *both* Mark Clark and Fred Hampton were killed in Chicago, while only one Panther was killed in Oakland, is held against Cleaver, but again, only by implication. The speculation, with its hint that it would have been more "normal" for the police to have gunned both men down, is "answered" by the probability that there is "a difference in how police squads operate in different parts of the country" (26), a feeble explanation, and therefore subtly damning.

Cleaver's desire to return is seen as "strange," since there is "no difference in this country now and when he left" in terms of racism or police persecution. Among Cleaver's "colleagues," only Stokely Carmichael has not been "silenced either through death or prison," and Rap Brown's trial is still not up for "review," even though he was "exonerat[ed]" by the Kerner Commission. (Actually, the commission's official report mentions only that in both Cincinnati and Atlanta in June 1968, Brown "attempted to capitalize on the discontent" provoked by a "minor police arrest" and failed).[13] "Is Cleaver returning because he thinks he will be given a fair trial?" Giovanni asks. Her penultimate paragraph contains perhaps the most subtly damning hint: "The resisters to the wars in Southeast Asia and especially Vietnam have been proven right both legally and morally, but they are not welcome back. Yet a few people who fled are coming in from the cold, and it's reason for concern" (26). The phrase "to come in from the cold," after John LeCarré's successful novel, *The Spy Who Came in from the Cold* (1963), implies that Cleaver is a spy. The analogy is imperfect, since a spy out in the cold is on assignment, not in exile. Throughout her essay, however, Giovanni succeeded in "signifying"—making serious trouble without any direct statements—and thereby planting suspicions in people's minds six months before Cleaver would actually arrive in the United States, if indeed he still wished to do so, after reading Giovanni's article, for she concluded with a veiled threat: "No one should deny Cleaver the right to return to America. But perhaps Cleaver should rethink his plans. People get hurt playing with fire, and that's the root of the matter" (26).

Whether Giovanni meant Cleaver could "get hurt" in the same way as the Panther convicts at San Quentin had meant it is not possible to establish, but her remarks almost certainly added to Cleaver's sense of insecurity upon his return, when he feared prison, he said, for exactly that reason. Even if she were only "wolfing," Giovanni clearly felt safe both socially and politically, as well as legally, in making all her innuendos about Cleaver, for he now had no friends on the Left and her movement credentials had been solidly established since at least 1971, when she published her autobiography, *Gemini.* An ex-conservative herself, Giovanni attacked Cleaver with all the zeal of the born-again radical. As a friend of James Baldwin, with whom she published *Dialogue,* a discussion on race in America, in 1973, she had yet another motive for her malice.

The next December, conservative columnist William Buckley echoed Giovanni's cynicism about Cleaver. Ironically, he also stated that nothing had changed in America in the years since Cleaver's departure, although Buckley's remark was without the note of bitterness expressed by Giovanni. What really happened, Buckley said, was that Cleaver had "come round." His belief that he could obtain a fair trial, said Buckley sarcastically, placed Cleaver "to the right of Kingman Brewster [President of Yale]." Once a radical "crypto-liberal" who, like other radicals, simulated his rage in "a form of Stepin Fetchitism," Cleaver had now become "sufficiently rational," Buckley thought, to see the evils in society the way Buckley and his cohorts did.[14]

During 1975 Cleaver was interviewed by several Americans, including Henry Louis ("Skip") Gates, whose lengthy interview contains invaluable information about Cleaver's life in Cuba and Algiers. In the second part of the interview, published in 1976, Cleaver and Gates discussed the possibilities of an American revolution in terms considerably more radical than those found in the Taylor or Willenson articles. While continuing to reject Third World revolution as "a skin game" (Gates, 54), Cleaver still discussed such issues as the value of the lumpen to a revolution and the significance of "economic class" in the formation of a "political strategy" (55). The best thing with which to replace the "skin game," at home or abroad, said Cleaver, is "relationship to the means of production" or class; "class struggle is politics [and] so is National struggle politics."

Speaking of black Americans, Cleaver told Gates, "You see, in our situation in the United States we had a class problem and a national problem. *Both* had to be dealt with. I always thought this: that by intensifying our struggle around the national question, it would also contribute to a resolution of our class problem because you eliminate certain particular grievances of our group. Other groups have particular grievances as well that are peculiar to them, that involve their history and their traditions—as so do we. Ultimately, all struggle is Class struggle; but you cannot overlook national questions" (55). To Cleaver's mind, black unity would best be achieved by an elimination of classes within the race; in terms of cause and effect, however, he seems to say that unity on the "national question," the identity of blacks as a nation, would somehow "contribute" to eliminating income anomalies. Given Cleaver's earlier reasoning, he might have presumed that the members of a unified race would all understand themselves to be proletarian, if not lumpen, and therefore not exploit one another; in other words, black unity would yield socialism.

What Cleaver wanted was a new version of socialism that didn't necessarily involve reverence for Marx (or even Lenin and Mao), particularly since Marx was "a racist" (56). It doesn't "do violence to socialism" to point out that fact, said Cleaver, "but I *do* think it does violence to black people to try once again to shove a white super-hero off on them, like [an]other Jesus . . . so I don't want to be involved in pushing Marx for that reason" (55).

Cleaver explained socialism as "a very simple doctrine" (56), one teaching that all "national resources—the mountains, the waters, the forests," as well as "mankind's heritage," or our "social heritage," all the "technology that goes back beyond the wheel"—should be "the common property of the people who are dependent upon it for their existence." There should be no private property and no accumulated wealth. The problem lies not in understanding this argument but in making it relevant to real life: "How can someone," Cleaver mused, "make this applicable to black economics?" The task, he admitted, "seems simple, but it is not so simple."

As elsewhere, Cleaver spoke of revolution in terms of "nationalizing the system of distribution," but never in terms of creating a competent proletariat that could function in a service-based, technologically sophisticated society. He spoke of America's present "system of distribution" as being rooted in a "frontier society" (where, presumably, only the fittest would survive) and as owing its continued existence to "laissez-faire economics" (57). The only concession "they" make to our "highly complex society" is in "welfare or social security," he explained. Cleaver's version of economics is more or less on a par with John Steinbeck's in *The Grapes of Wrath* when Cleaver laments, for example, a food shortage: " 'Inflation' and 'unemployment' have nothing to do with the objective natural resources or the concrete means of production—the machines, the mines—have nothing to do with that. It only has to do with the paper work, with what's going on inside Committee rooms and Board rooms and balance sheets. It has nothing to do with the objective existence of the physical things that people need to survive. Inflation is so bad you can't buy apples, but the apples are there. It's just the system" (56). To Cleaver, socialism meant giving away not only the apples but anything else people want. In 1975 he was no closer to envisioning an adequately trained and rewarded proletariat than he had been in 1968. "From each according to his ability; to each according to his need" still meant that those who lack skills are excused from making any contribution to society, but they deserve nonetheless the full measure of what they "need," and their needs don't stop with welfare. What is apparent here is that Cleaver's partisanship was still with the lumpen nonproducers among us and still set against the upwardly mobile, let alone the "ruling class" or the professionals. That is why he questioned the "applicability" of the "dictatorship of the proletariat" to "various societies"; he meant that the concept is useless as a means of demanding a sizable increase in benefits for the underclass. "A doctrinaire Marxist-Leninist," however, would not accept Cleaver's dramatic alteration in the definition of the term *class* to include the lumpen "scum" within the proletariat. Further, Cleaver wishes to create a black economics that includes some blacks within the ranks of the enemy "oppressor" while still promoting the concept of black nationhood. There is nothing here that is essentially Republican, that fits the Cleaver who avowed his desire to return in time for the 1976 bicentennial. As of 1975, he remained committed to socialist revolution and cast a speculative glance at the army; what was gone was the rhetoric, the anger, and the sense that he was part of a worldwide, historic uprising of the "colored" masses.

Another major theme temporarily dropped during Cleaver's exile was sexuality. His ideas about masculinity and femininity, as found in *Soul on Ice,* stressed an original oneness that had been sundered by a combination of race and economics; later, he became a partisan of feminism, at least briefly, when he supported Ericka Huggins, but his credibility was seriously undercut by his previous use of the phrase "Pussy Power" and his condemnation as a male chauvinist by Elaine Brown, not to mention his record as a rapist; finally, Huey Newton's charges of "repressed homosexuality," which Elaine Brown would resurrect after Cleaver's return, hinted at a confused sexuality haunted by the same demons that made Cleaver's religious and sociopolitical concepts so intense.

Human Sexuality and the Tantric Guru

In a September 1975 interview in his two-room retreat in Paris, Cleaver explained to reporter Jacqueline Simon that he had recently been interested in reading Eastern erotic literature. The apartment was appropriately done up in a style one could label "sixties hippie": "music, incense, pillows on the floor, books, very little furniture."[15] In discussing the watercolor designs of his new clothing covering the walls, Cleaver spoke of having been drawn to tantric literature, to the Etruscans, and then to "erotic art," whose universal symbols are found everywhere. "This is from Iran, that's from Mexico or Latin America, and that's from Nepal and this is from Rome . . . that's the way people used to be, in other words" (Simon, 43). He declared, "My whole motivation is because . . . I've always been keen about sex. I like it. So you know the whole thing about the Kama Sutra. There's something to learn there, right?" (44). The Kama Sutra and the tantric stories formed his reading until he "became a tantric guru." When questioned about the phrase "tantric guru," Cleaver said it was "a label I bestowed upon myself, because I know who I am. I've mastered it. That's why I made these pants" (44).

Cleaver's new role as a "guru," the first of several attempts on his part to establish himself as a quasi-religious leader, gave him the credentials, in his own eyes, to teach people what was wrong in their traditional approach to men's clothing and to offer his own typically eccentric, extremist solution. His new pants design offered him such a sense of accomplishment that he spoke of being "reformed," not in religious or political terms but because of the work he had done on his men's pants as part of a total ensemble. He proclaimed, "Something has happened to me, see, as a part of all this. You know, it's changed me, how I approach things. I really feel much more confident, . . . all kinds of things, just because of what I've been doing" (43). The new design was, to Cleaver, an example of working for freedom "within this institution of pants" (43); he would retain pants but change their oppressive qualities. His objection to men's pants was not made clear to Simon, and Jerome McFadden, who interviewed him soon after, found the theory boring; his only comment was that the pants "flaunt[ed] the male sex organ so brazenly that no photo can be printed in a family magazine" (McFadden, 69).

Rolling Stone has never considered itself a family magazine; not surprisingly, in October 1975 it ran a full-page item, illustrated with Cleaver modeling his own pants in three different poses, which purported to be an advertisement for the line. The design may be Cleaver's, but the accompanying copy is pure *Rolling Stone*. "Walking Tall," the headline reads, ". . . Walking Proud . . . Walking Softly but Carrying It Big . . . You'll be Cock of the Walk with the New Fall Collection from Eldridge de Paris."[16]

The high-waisted style modeled by Cleaver features a light-colored central front panel that includes all the fabric from where the front pleat of the trousers would be to the seam inside the leg, and from the waist to the hem. The zipper is on the side, so as not to break the line of the solid panel. The codpiece portion, a tube for the penis plus an area about four inches square around it on the front panel, is in the darker tone of the sides and back of the pants. The dark "appurtenance" accentuates the male sex organ as completely as possible, presuming one is to wear clothing at all. *Rolling Stone* calls these pants "for men only . . . real men . . . the three-fisted variety." Cleaver's plans, they reported, included "a red and white-striped appurtenance for the U.S. Bicentennial," presumably attached to navy blue pants. "Up your revolution!" cheered *Rolling Stone*. "And don't forget . . . heavy on the starch"!

Cleaver told Simon that the pants would "abolish . . . the crime of indecent exposure. Because now we'll have decent exposure, see" (Simon, 55). The interview came to a rather abrupt and inconclusive end when Simon and her companion, editor Terry Karten, began to ask him about his assessment of his life at 40. Immediately, Cleaver became evasive to the point of incoherence, briefly dragging his bewildered interviewer along with him. The conclusion of the discussion reads:

TK: Very often at your age, it seems that men write autobiographies and self-portraits perhaps not because they want to recapitulate their past, but just because they want to find out where they are now. To express that. . . . not to find out who they are but. . . . almost to create metaphors for themselves. Maybe that's what this has been, this interview.

JS: You're in a unique position. As you say, you've tried all the other things. What do you do about all the people who want to try all the other things?

EC: That's kind of general, and well, I think I'm withdrawing from the general, and I want to deal with just specifics, you know, so I can't respond to that, except. . . . you were talking about certain people. If you break down the categories, like . . . There's one crime that these clothes will abolish, and that's the crime of indecent exposure, see; maybe that's not too helpful to society, that's not the major crime. But I'm interested in the crime of rape, and why people rape. It all goes back to the problems of human sexuality and of . . . what I call the right to fuck . . . because of the consequences.

JS: Well, I . . . it occurred to me yesterday that you have moved professionally away from "rape-ology" into "seduct-ology." I was thinking, in your sociology you've discovered the joys of seduction.

EC: Well, because, if you feel that rape is not right for many reasons, you know, including the fact that it's not really satisfying . . .

      It's based . . . I mean, the rapist has a profound ignorance of the nature of woman. I think if most men really understood . . . the real reaction they provoke in women when they rape them, they would never do it, never do it. They would be horrified . . . to really know that at that moment the women had really hated them, because in fact what they want most of all is love, you see. If they really understand that, they would recoil from the very idea. But that's all complicated, you see, that's not . . . no one is talking to each other. . . .

JS: Well, we spoke. (55–56)

Cleaver's insistence on dealing only with "specifics," rather than anything personal or "general," was noted by Dan Schanche early in Cleaver's Algerian sojourn, when he reported Cleaver's refusal to discuss anything but "policy." Cleaver stated: "All the psycho-social analysis—'Why did that happen?,' 'Why do you feel this way?'—all that is obsolete. It's even insulting, you know?" (*Paradox,* 194). That quality, along with the tendency to make few remarks that "linked rationally together" when he was pressed (196), remained with Cleaver through the years, as did his basic socioeconomic beliefs.

Over My Shoulder

The difference in tone and subject matter between the Gates interview and the Simon interview is marked. What happened in between was the rejection of Cleaver's manuscript of reminiscences, "Over My Shoulder," by Viking in June 1975. This in turn meant his giving up and returning the $40,000 advance (largely spent). But worse, it almost destroyed Cleaver's image of himself as a writer. Although he had always had a genuine gift for writing insightful turns of phrase, he was never a meticulous craftsman, and probably, judging from the many disorganized pieces that were published in the *Black Panther* and that displayed little more than unity of topic, he had no concept of structure.

How, then, to account for *Soul on Ice?* The following exchange with Jacqueline Simon offers insight:

> *JS:* Did you know when you were writing in prison, you were a writer?
>
> *EC:* Absolutely not. It was a long time, you know, before I stopped thinking that people were pulling my leg. I just couldn't understand what they were saying. They were making comments that were very extreme, you know, in terms of compliments, you know what I mean. And there was nothing in my life that had prepared me for that. I wasn't prepared to understand that or accept that and it's a long process before you believe it.
>
> And I will take it even further and say if I did, if I had been consciously trying to write a book, you know, I don't think I could have done it, because I did, I've done that, I've sat down and tried consciously to work, you know, and it's a completely different thing than what I was doing. What I was doing before was I had no idea that it was going to end up being a book, I was just passing my time and fooling around with words, and tripping out, you know.
>
> *JS:* But you must have seen you were getting better. You got much better; you moved from an emotional level of writing to a more systematic level in the second section [of *Soul on Ice*] for example.
>
> *EC:* . . . [L]ike the second section . . . it's only a second section because of the way that McGraw-Hill packaged it, you see, but I'm not really aware of the chronology of the actual writing of those pieces, you see, because what they did was take a rather large manuscript and make selections. Some of the things that appear in *Soul on Ice* as essays are just parts chopped out of other essays which mostly legal opinion controlled. This couldn't be said because Jackie Kennedy would sue me or James Baldwin would sue me, or it's not nice to do this. This kind of thing. So the final result to me is like that *Rolling Stone* article last week, a highly edited version. (Simon, 51)

Actually, the only comparison to be made between the editing of *Soul on Ice* and the cutting of Curtice Taylor's interview was that some of the material had to be eliminated from both because of the threat of potential lawsuits. Cleaver attempted in the interviews to make the job his editors did on his manuscripts from prison seem like little beyond proofreading, but his remarks in fact reveal a shapeless, "large manuscript" that had not been subdivided into chapters or sections, or in fact conceived holistically at all.

As Cleaver admitted, planning and writing an actual book involves a different approach, one he had never used. In fact, in his description of his attempt to produce an essay called "Turning Forty," he recounted what is clearly the first stage of writing, in which one either "brainstorms" or simply begins to write, with the intention of shaping the material later:

You see like it's not taking place in your conscious mind always. What takes place in your conscious mind is I think the refinement of your thoughts, you know, but other than that, it's just, you don't know what you're doing, you're just there, you know. I mean if you prepared yourself to be a writer, you know, you know how to write. The next thing is to sit down with your writing tools and be quiet and stop doing other things and let your computer just compute. Not compute, print-out. It's in there, you see, you can have faith in that. I know that absolutely just because of some of the things I've gone through. I know that if when I sit down to write or even doing new stuff, it's print-out, that's what happens. But you have to know how to get all the stuff we were talking about, like programming and scheduling, this is creating the conditions for your print-out mechanism to work. That's what the writer has to do, see, and once something prints out, then he starts fooling around with it, that's what we usually call thinking. (Simon, 51)

What Cleaver called "print-out" is a rough draft; he seemed to have no idea how to get beyond it, except for "fooling around."

Cleaver was an untrained writer with a natural gift, someone whose lack of education and ability to organize material in a methodical manner finally caught up with him. What he had needed somewhere in his life was writing classes, but he probably could not take many in prison and would never have considered doing so later, when he was a best-selling author and desperately involved in Panther-police conflicts as well. In exile, there would have been no question of his being tutored while working to stage the American phase of the world revolution. When he had to produce a manuscript on his own, he fell apart;

but Viking expected a polished manuscript from a professional writer, not a pile of material from which to "make selections."

In some way, Cleaver's failure to produce an acceptable manuscript probably led to his escape into erotic literature and from there into a new, nonliterary scheme for self-support, one that would permit him to make a name for himself anew and return home with a career and a means of paying his bills. The new pants, however, were so eccentric that they made him a laughingstock rather than earning him respect as an innovator.

The Return

Certainly, Cleaver was confused and ambivalent when he spoke to Simon and Karten, for very soon afterward he abruptly decided to leave France on U.S. government terms and go to jail, something he had been trying to avoid ever since he left Algiers. Sometime in October 1975 he spoke to the appropriate people at the U.S embassy in Paris, and in "about three weeks" (*Fire* 215) had the necessary papers and arrangements to return. Cleaver was still denied a passport ("I thought this was ridiculous because I had access to all the passports I would ever need" [214]), but he was offered instead a letter that would permit him to enter the United States, where he would be arrested.

There was "a lot of red tape," inevitably, that had to be "waded through" before Cleaver would be able to fly home: "I was told that Judge Harold Tyler, the number two man in the Justice Department under Attorney General Levy, had taken personal charge of organizing my surrender. From the moment I entered American custody to my final destination in the Federal Prison in San Diego, California, at least half a dozen bureaucracies had to be coordinated, including the Justice Department, the Federal Bureau of Prisons, TWA, the California Department of Corrections, the offices of the Alameda County District Attorney and the California Attorney General" (214–15).

The suspense and the fear that something might go wrong, that he might be refused entry after all, haunted Cleaver's dreams while he waited. He dreamed that he awakened "in the wee hours" and rushed to the bars of his cell, "grabbing hold of them, giving them a futile shake" (216). He was afraid of being locked up in prison, but it is also likely, considering the way he spoke about his experience in exile, that he feared being "sentenced" permanently to life abroad.

Finally, on Saturday, 15 November 1975, the two Cleaver children,

Antonio Maceo ("Ceo"), age six, and Joju, age five, departed yet again for the United States. This time they headed for Pasadena, to stay with Grandmother Cleaver. Although the *New York Times* said that Kathleen would be accompanying Eldridge, she actually stayed behind to close up the house in Paris (*Fire*, 216). Cleaver was a half-hour late getting to the airport, but since there was also a delay in takeoff, he made the flight on time, only to land three hours late in New York, at about 5:00 P.M. rather than the scheduled 1:55 P.M., on 18 November (John F. Burns, "Cleaver Seized on Return," *New York Times*, 19 November 1975, 20). Cleaver's companions were two FBI agents, one black and one white (*Fire*, 218). When the plane landed, "there were no demonstrators or supporters at the airport. Neither, to all appearances, were there any relatives or friends of Mr. Cleaver" (Burns, 20). There were, however, "about 100 newsmen" who were pushing and shoving to get close enough to ask a question. "Tempers flared and punches were thrown as one man, engulfed by the mob, lost his balance and dropped his camera" (20).

Cleaver, who had been arrested and handcuffed with his hands behind his back as soon as he stepped onto American soil, became frightened at the crush. He said the agents "plowed a path through the center of the journalists, using me as the plow" (*Fire*, 208), while the *Times* reporter concurred: "At times the agents had to use considerable force to clear a path through the newsmen" (Burns, 20). Cleaver, whose paranoia was in full bloom (he had mentioned to Jacqueline Simon during their interview on the previous 12 September that he often feared someone might try to poison him), could think only of how vulnerable he was in handcuffs. "I kept thinking of how Lee Harvey Oswald got assassinated while wearing them" (*Fire*, 218), he said, inadvertently revealing how unpopular he felt himself to be at that moment. But no one made any hostile attempts, and after covering 150 yards from the customs area to a car, he was driven to the federal building at the airport, where booking took another hour; then to court, to be arraigned before a U.S. commissioner on the federal fugitive charge (Burns, 20); and last to a federal detention facility in Manhattan, to spend the night before being taken to San Diego's Metropolitan Correctional Center. It was evening before Cleaver, whose body was still six hours ahead on Paris time, could finally collapse on a cot and sleep. That much of the turmoil and stress had been predictable is the reason the children were not traveling along; their fear and exhaustion would have turned the already-difficult situation into a nightmare even worse than the ones Cleaver had experienced.

Besides jail, there were the incessant charges of a "deal" Cleaver had made in order to get a light sentence. These accusations had been further fueled by Cleaver's being served, while at the airport, with a subpoena signed by Mississippi Democratic senator John Eastland, chairperson of the Internal Security Subcommittee of the Senate Judiciary Committee, and ordering Cleaver to appear at a 20 January 1976 hearing "to testify on terrorist and subversive activities in the United States" (Oliver, 232). There is, however, no evidence that Cleaver ever did so.

Cleaver's "official announcement" of his return appeared in the *New York Times* on 19 November 1975. "Why I Left the U.S. and Why I Am Returning" appeared as a column on the same day as the straight news announcement from Paris headlined "Cleaver Returning after 7-Year Exile" in an inner section. A smaller item reported his scheduled arrival at Kennedy International Airport on TWA flight 803 at 1:55 P.M. on the same day. Cleaver's article, which the *Times* said had been written "several weeks" earlier, was probably mailed as soon as he decided to return and held until the copy was actually newsworthy.

Cleaver opened his article with an explanation of how he went into exile, so that people would not believe "I left because I preferred to go live in a Communist country," had changed, and was now "locked outside the gates of the paradise I once scorned, begging to be let back in" (C37). There follow about 10 paragraphs that more or less parallel Cleaver's "Affidavit #2," written in prison right after his arrest on 6 April 1968. He ends by revealing that on the day he was to have "surrendered" to the law, 27 November 1968, "I was in Montreal."

There follows a passage summarizing Cleaver's version of the events leading up to Richard Nixon's resignation:

History shows that when the American political system is blocked and significant segments of the population are unable to have their will brought to bear on the decision-making process, you can count upon the American people to revolt, to take it out into the streets, in the spirit of the Boston Tea Party.

During the 1960's, the chips were down in a fateful way, uniting the upsurge of black Americans against the oppressive features of the system, and the gargantuan popular opposition to the Indochina wars. . . . In the end, the system rejected President Nixon and reaffirmed its own basic principles. (C37).

Cleaver's real point is that the post-Watergate era offers new hope for
everyone, "a brand new ball game." In this new game, the old teams, so
to speak, are no longer contenders; it is time to choose up sides again.
"We cannot afford to refight battles that have already been won or lost."
In a non sequitur, he concludes by pointing out that had Nixon "accepted the verdict of the people at the polls in 1960" there would have
been no Watergate, because Nixon would not have refought that "battle" (and won) in 1968. "But the truth is," Cleaver commented, "that
nations do get the leaders they deserve," implying that it isn't so much
Nixon's fault that he was elected as it was that of the American people,
who in an expression of overwhelmingly poor judgment chose Nixon
over Hubert Humphrey (and, let us not forget, the author himself).
Even so, Cleaver evaluates at last, in what became his most-quoted
postexile remark: "With all of its faults, the American political system
is the freest and most democratic in the world." Cleaver's avowal of
faith and allegiance was mitigated only in passing by the remark that
"democracy" needed to be spread to "all areas of life, particularly the
economic," as long as the changes are "conducted through our established institutions." Now that the old (unspecified) battles have been
fought, the new fight will be one "to defend [the 'values . . . worth
conserving'] from the blind excesses of our fellows who are still caught
up in the critical process. It is my hope to make a positive contribution
in this regard." It was Cleaver's intent to make the New Left appear as
out of date as possible in 1975, a faction characterized by "excesses" he
had disavowed, and to align himself solidly with the far more right-
wing defenders of the unnamed "values worth conserving" he wanted
them to think he would uphold.

On 19 November Cleaver, in federal custody, was flown to California
in order to avoid any extradition problems that could occur between
New York and California (Wallace Turner, "Cleaver Is Flown," *New
York Times,* 20 November 1975, 1). He ended up in San Diego rather
than the San Francisco area because of the ease with which Federal
Bureau of Prisons guards could transfer him from federal to state care in
a federal corrections center rather than a state-run prison. His ultimate
destination, for the time being, was to be Chino State, the facility from
which Clinton Smith and Byron Booth had escaped together. The
various agencies were waiting to pounce. The California Adult Authority, responsible for parole, said through administrative officer William
Leon, "He owes us three years, four months and twenty-three days" (1),
while Alameda County District Attorney Lowell Jensen announced he

was "waiting in line" to prosecute Cleaver on the 6 April 1968 charges. Meanwhile, Garry had declined to represent Cleaver because of "other commitments" (1).

There had been one agreement in advance that Cleaver admitted to, one guaranteeing his "security" against "the California Department of Correction, the Oakland Police Department, and other state and local agencies" in exchange for "agreeing to testify before Senator Stennis's Internal Security Subcommittee" (Allman, 11), because Cleaver was afraid to leave federal custody for a state prison (Wallace Turner, "Cleaver Fearful of Jail Transfer," *New York Times,* 22 November 1975, 35). (*Soul on Fire* contains no mention of this self-protective agreement.) Cleaver's sister Wilhelmina told the press the family feared for his life because of potential threats from prison guards, ex-Panthers, or "militant black prisoners such as the Black Guerrilla Family, which has been linked to several prison stabbings in recent years" (Gregory A. Gross, "Cleaver's Sister Fears for His Life," *New York Times,* 20 November 1975, A6). Ironically, Cleaver had people to fear from his past for conflicting reasons: guards still hated him as a Panther, Panthers hated him as an anti-Newton "traitor," and revolutionists hated him because he'd "sold out." The one agency Cleaver had forgotten to include in the "security" agreement was "the Alameda County Sheriff's Department, into whose hands [he] ultimately fell" (*Fire,* 217); nevertheless, he was at least temporarily safe in San Diego until 2 January 1976.

On 29 November 1975, two editorials concerning Cleaver appeared in the American press. The *New York Times,* quoting Cleaver's most-quoted remark, declared that, in spite of his views "either before or after his recent conversion," Cleaver was "entitled, first, to the full protection of his personal safety and, subsequently, to full protection of his rights in court" (26). The *Black Panther,* on the other hand, called for "justice" for Cleaver, "a fair trial before a jury of his peers," one in which he would "face the judgment of the people" for whose "allegiance" he had once "appealed" (2). Beyond that, declared Editor in Chief David G. DuBois, "Eldridge Cleaver's return is of little political importance to the Black Panther Party." In other words, Cleaver would not receive even verbal support from the party or its sympathizers: "Each of us must accept responsibility for his actions." And Cleaver's actions were unacceptable. Alluding to the FBI's suspected role in creating "disinformation" among Panthers, DuBois (or Elaine Brown, perhaps editorializing in his stead for the occasion) insisted, "It does not matter that our actions are based on incorrect information, wrong interpretations or faulty analyses. . . . One is either with the people or against them. At every moment of human history the choice is the same. The real test of commitment is consistency" (2). Somehow one senses that Cleaver is "on trial" for a different set of offenses from the ones the *New York Times* referred to; as judged by "the people" on his "consistency," Cleaver is already condemned. At this point, the penalty is not set, but the charges are not complete, either. As "new evidence," so to speak, or new interpretations of old information, was brought in, Cleaver's crimes would escalate far beyond mere inconsistency.

Nikki Giovanni's May article in *Encore* had not been helpful, but the damage was as limited as *Encore's* circulation. A worse blow by far was struck by Margaret Montagno, a *Newsweek* reporter who wrote in the 1 December issue that Cleaver had decided to return "a fortnight ago"[17] and had "[taken] the precaution of first dispatching his lawyers to Washington." The hint of bargains and influence was clearly present. Cleaver's lawyers, said Montagno, "insisted that they made no deals, but when Cleaver appeared at the American embassy in Paris, embassy officials quickly produced a special one-way travel document and a ticket for a flight the next day" (Montagno, 42). It was clearly Montagno's intent to imply that prearrangement included promises on both sides, a charge Cleaver always denied, offering as evidence his $100,000 bail and his months in prison. In frustration, he once burst out, "People say I'm a CIA agent, an FBI agent; but look, I'm in a fucking penitentiary" (Ray Riegert, "The Return of a Radical Ghost," *Berkeley Barb,* 16 January 1976, 5).

In retrospect, it would seem Cleaver was telling the truth on that point; he returned because he simply could not stand exile anymore. As Kathleen put it, "he's 40 years old and he wants to go home" (Montagno, 42). And elsewhere she added, "Exile is an endless process . . . so he decided once and for all to put an end to it. . . . He just told me, 'well, this can go on forever.' He just decided he'd go back to the United States and work it out from there" (Riegert, 5). Cleaver had already told reporters Peter Kalisher and Lou Cioffi, in a joint news conference in Paris, that he was returning for a variety of reasons, among them the end of the Vietnam War, the rise in the status of blacks, the conviction of the Watergate conspirators, and the lessened reputation of Ronald Reagan (CBS-TV and ABC-TV, 17 November 1975), but his enemies chose to sneer at every one of these motives in preference for a "deal" that would brand Cleaver as a turncoat and a traitor to "the people." Ida Lewis, editor and publisher of *Encore* and friend of Nikki Giovanni (Lewis wrote the introduction to the Baldwin-Giovanni *Dialogue*), published a December editorial with the punning title "What's the Big Deal?"[18] Using the same "evidence" as Montagno but adopting a question format, Lewis wondered, "Was a subpoena waiting [in New York] because Senate investigating committees just happen to draw up subpoenas in case ex-revolutionaries come back?" Or, she suggested, were there likely to have been "understandings" formed? "The question is: what deal did the U.S. government make with Eldridge Cleaver?" There are quite a few "concerned people" who are "fearful and suspicious" of what Cleaver will say "to save himself." We can imagine who some of them were; perhaps they had believed that if they refused to help Cleaver return on the terms he preferred, if they told him to stay where he was, he would have to do so, as if he had been sent to outer Siberia. As absurd as it may seem, they acted as though Cleaver were safely dead. No wonder they felt fear when an embittered and knowledgeable dead man reappeared, as Cleaver phrased it to Ray Riegert. "I'm in the position of a ghost coming back and a lot of people wish I'd just go away" (3).

As Elaine Douglass put it, if Cleaver meant "nothing else" to people, "he is the 1960's returned to torment many of his early followers. . . . His return sent many people burrowing through the fields of their memories" (9). When he was in exile, she noted, "he gradually disappeared as a topic of conversation in radical and black nationalist circles in the United States. The press rarely carried stories on him, and his exploits in Algeria were little known here. Now Cleaver is back in the news and everyone, it seems, has an opinion on him" (10).

Some of those opinions were strongly negative and had been so for several years. Nonetheless, Cleaver seemed unable to accept the reality of his rejection, even as he languished in prison over the Christmas holidays. Desperately lonely, he attempted to call Panther headquarters in Oakland on New Year's Eve. Evangelist George Otis recorded in his 1977 book *Eldridge Cleaver: Ice and Fire!* part of a 1976 "Interview with Eldridge Cleaver" in the little magazine *Radix.* There, in response to a question about contact with the Panthers since he returned, Cleaver recounted the episode:

Around New Year's Day of this year, I called the Black Panther office to wish them a happy new year. I called collect from the federal prison in San Diego. A man answered the phone, and the operator said, "I have a collect call from Eldridge Cleaver; will you accept the charges?" The guy laughed and said,

'Wait a minute.' There was about 10 minutes of silence. A couple of times someone came on and said, 'Wait a minute.' Then the guy came back and said, 'We will not accept the call.' I was in jail, but I laughed because it was the phone number of the newspaper I had started; that part of the Black Panther Party refused to accept a collect call from me; and I was in jail. I thought, 'Well, maybe they're right; but I can't go along with their politics now.' Then I found out that they were part of Ron Dellum's [sic] machine in the 8th Congressional District. On top of that I found out that the black judge named Wilson was part of that group and that I had to go before him on my case. And then I found out that John George, who was part of that group, was a candidate for supervisor—and that he had just won the election. (Otis, 168–69)

Cleaver's claim that the Panthers refused to speak with him because they were "part of . . . [a] machine," and not because of bad blood, indicates an inability to accept the situation as it really was. The speed and thoroughness with which everyone repudiated and scorned him after the spring of 1971 seem to hint at relationships that were shallow and based on pragmatism, as befits a political organization. Cleaver had no friends in evidence dating from before his parole in 1967, and those whom he had befriended in 1967 and 1968 now had no sympathy for him at all.

For example, Roy Innis of the Congress of Racial Equality bluntly labeled Cleaver "a psychopath and a thug" (Douglass, 10), while David DuBois, writing in the *Black Panther* that same week, referred to him as "an addicted media freak" who had just come out in a "not-so-new 'red, white and blue' Bicentennial model" as a "publicity stunt" ("Cleaver: 'Red, White, and Blue,' " 31 January 1976, 2). And Paul Jacobs, who had stood part of Cleaver's bail in 1968, now felt safe in referring to him as "a Bicentennial Coon—proof that the system works" (Allman, 11).

Arabs and Racism

The specific item that had most angered DuBois was Cleaver's state-ment on the United Nations General Assembly vote equating Zionism with racism, a statement "distributed by the Black-Jewish Information Center in New York." (2). Whereas Cleaver (and other Panthers) had long ago wounded committed leftist Jews with a pro-Arab stand that was strongest when he lived in Algiers, he now repudiated Arabs as "the most racist people on earth" because of their use of "black slaves to do their menial labor."[19] Jews, on the other hand, "have not only suffered particularly from racist persecution, they have done more than any other people in history to expose and condemn racism. . . . To condemn the Jewish survival doctrine as racism, is a travesty upon the truth" ("Racism," 224). Whether this new sentiment was a return of Cleaver's old feeling of empathy with a land-hungry Jewish nation that one can see in his earlier writings or was simply, as DuBois called it, "a last ditch, desperate appeal for Jewish funds" (2) is hard to say. Certainly Cleaver repeated again and again that he was penniless, and only in January Alameda County Superior Court Judge Lionel J. Wilson had set his bail at $100,000, while reportedly some lawyers had asked that much to defend him ("Bail," *New York Times,* 10 January 1976, 26). With all royalties "impounded by a civil suit and the Internal Revenue Service," said Kathleen, "I'm flat broke" (Riegert, 3). It is not incredible that Cleaver might have chosen to release a pro-Israeli statement for personal reasons.

Whether Cleaver's statement had any effect on the composition of the interracial committee that created the Eldridge Cleaver Defense Fund in the same month is uncertain, but the group did include Albert Shanker, president of the American Federation of Teachers, who generously overlooked Cleaver's 1968 attack on him, and Nat Hentoff, one of Cleaver's favorite authors when he was in prison (Laurie Johnston, *New York Times,* 18 February 1976, 50). The committee, headed by Bayard Rustin of the A. Philip Randolph Institute, also included A. Philip Randolph himself; Julian Bond, who was then a state senator in Georgia; Fredrick O'Neal, president of Actors Equity; and lawyer Joseph L. Rauh, Jr. As created, the group planned to raise bail money for Cleaver and to provide for legal defense at his trial, as well as to aid the children financially. The initial meeting, at the home of Mary Temple, a "civil rights activist," was attended by Kathleen, who was "working full time to rally support for her husband," and "nearly 70 potential supporters" of the fund (50). Radical chic was not yet altogether dead, although the cause had now become considerably less radical and more purely constitutional in its aims.

As a result of the committee's efforts, George V. Higgins, Boston lawyer and author (*The Friends of Eddie Coyle*), agreed to represent Cleaver at his trial, but the liaison lasted only a few months. In June, Higgins withdrew from the case, citing "profound differences of opinion between my client and me on how to proceed with the case" ("Trial Of," *New York Times,* 15 June 1976, 42) but offering no details. In the absence of any comment from Cleaver, it is impossible to speculate on the nature of the lawyer-client disagreement except to note T. D. Allman's remark that Cleaver had attempted to obtain FBI documents that "he believes would prove the Oakland shootout was provoked by Federal authorities" (Allman, 11). If that were what Cleaver insisted on as a trial strategy, one can easily understand Higgins's desire to avoid taking on the FBI and to stick with the actual events of the evening, with a resultant impasse between the two men.

As part of the effort to obtain FBI documents regarding Cleaver, Kathleen traveled to Washington, D.C., in the spring of 1976. While it cannot be established that Cleaver ever testified before the Internal Security Subcommittee, that Kathleen did is a certainty. On 8 April 1976, in executive testimony, she described the negative effects of FBI COINTELPRO (Counter Intelligence Program of 1967–71) efforts against the Panthers, specifically those aimed at splitting the party in 1970–71. Her testimony, used in part to document the charges being investigated against the FBI, was not intended to incriminate colleagues. A typical remark concerning the disruption in Algiers was this: "We did not know who to believe about what, so the general effect, not only of the letters but the whole situation in which the letters were part was creating uncertainty. It was a very bizarre feeling."[20] It seems unlikely that such information was instrumental in bringing about her husband's release on bail four months later, but fear of her unpublished testimony did provoke a vicious Panther counterattack in less than 10 days.

On 17 April, the Panthers went far beyond mere questioning of Cleaver's "consistency" and printed a statement "condemn[ing] and denounc[ing] Eldridge Cleaver as an active and willing agent in the FBI's COINTELPRO plan to destroy Black organizations by creating internal dissension" ("Eldridge Cleaver Denounced as F.B.I. Agent," *Black Panther,* 17 April 1976, 3). This accusation is a long way from charges of "deal-making" with the various law enforcement agencies in 1975; it refers back to an indefinite time when Cleaver supposedly first became a double agent.

Murder Two

But even the spy charge is not enough. If Cleaver had always been an FBI agent, then Nikki Giovanni's suspicions about his surviving the 6 April 1968 shoot-out would have been well founded, even if such suspicions had never occurred to anyone before. Hence, the party statement continues, "The Black Panther Party formally condemns and denounces Eldridge Cleaver for the murders of Bobby Hutton, the first member and Treasurer of the BPP, Samuel Napier, the Circulation and Distribution Manager of the *The Black Panther* newspaper, and other dedicated Party members who sacrificed their young lives in the cause of freedom and liberation" (3).

The statement becomes quite explicit:

On the night of April 6, 1968, while emerging from the burning ruins of what had been a family residence at 1218 28th Street in Oakland, the frightened and naked wreckage of what was once a man, Eldridge Cleaver, shoved 17-year-old Bobby Hutton in front of him, intentionally pushing the half-blinded, brave Black youth into the sights of dozens of police shotguns and rifles ready to kill without hesitation anything that moved.

On April 17, 1971, on Cleaver's orders, agents entered the Black Panther Party's Distribution Center in New York City with guns drawn to murder Sam Napier. Doing as they were told to do, the agents of Cleaver tied Sam's hands and feet, put cotton in his ears and over his eyes, proceeded to shoot him six times in the head with a .357 magnum and to burn his body. (3)

Sam Napier had indeed been killed by Cleaver adherents among the New York 21, but not necessarily at Cleaver's request. Certainly Cleaver didn't think the Oakland Panthers held such a thing against him when he attempted to place the collect call to Panther headquarters, and as late as 6 April 1976 he had complained that he was abandoned by old Panther colleagues even though he was in jail in Oakland: "I'm right here in the community and they won't come to see me. That's kind of heavy" (Laurie Johnston, "Notes on People," *New York Times,* 6 April 1976, 29). It must therefore have been an incredible shock to be charged with murder by the party again. (The old Clinton "Rahim" Smith murder charge was not resurrected now or at any later date.)

The same 17 April issue of the *Black Panther* contained an editorial headed "No 'Split' with Police Agents" (2), which began, "Flash! A 'revelation' from Kathleen Cleaver, interviewed by a KPFA Radio reporter in Washington, D.C.: that the FBI's COINTELPRO operation created and fostered the 1971 'split' between Huey P. Newton and Eldridge Cleaver through false communiqués sent to Algiers before Cleaver decided that American 'democracy'—KKK racism, spiraling unemployment and heightened imperialism—was 'the best there is' "

(2). The implication of the article is that, as the lead article stated, Cleaver was an FBI agent all along, and therefore any "split," whether documented with FBI papers or not, was phony.

The lead article concludes with mention that Cleaver's name would be included in the party suit "against the FBI." This referred to more than one case (the Cleavers had also filed suit against the FBI) in which Panthers sued for harassment in the late sixties and early seventies based on information being revealed through open hearings of the Senate Select Committee. At the time of this article and editorial, the party was involved in a "$47.7 million Fred Hampton murder case" ("Fallen Comrade," *Black Panther,* 10 April 1976, 3) in which "five present and former FBI agents" were found in contempt of court for refusing to yield approximately "4 cartloads" of COINTELPRO documents to the Panthers, although ordered to do so by Judge Joseph Sam Perry (3). While it is unlikely that any Panther case would be strengthened by the addition of Cleaver's name to the list of defendants, it was a symbolic move that felt politically right.

On 24 April, a statement that had been "issued by Black Panther Party chairperson and leading member Elaine Brown" three days earlier appeared in the *Black Panther* under the heading "Cleaver Treachery Exposed" (3). (The 17 April statement had been "issued" three days earlier by the party as a whole, and not attributed to any one person.) This article offered "as a service to the community . . . further information we have discovered concerning the past and present activities of Eldridge Cleaver" (3). It sets forth three new pieces of evidence against Cleaver.

First, an unnamed "witness, whose name will be revealed in an upcoming lawsuit to be filed against the FBI," claimed to have been present in Algiers when the news of Sam Napier's death in New York City was telephoned to Cleaver on 17 April 1971. The report says that Cleaver "gleefully jumped up and down," gloating simultaneously, "My people in New York got Sam Napier." The motive was to stop the sale of the Panther newspaper and thereby the major source of Panther cash flow to the headquarters in Oakland. This person's identity is impossible to guess, for not all the names of the members of the Panther international section in 1971 are known. Supposedly, Smith was dead and Booth and Louise Wibecan gone, accused of theft by Cleaver; possibilities include Connie Matthews Tabor, her husband Michael (Cetawayo) Tabor, Field Marshall D. C. Cox, and Richard (variously, Dharuba or Dhoruba) Moore.

Second, "a number of reliable sources, including attorney Howard

Moore," had informed the party that Cleaver had appeared before a secret session of the Senate Judiciary Internal Security Subcommittee headed by Senator Eastland of Mississippi "in early February of this year." Cleaver's "complicity" was questioned, although the content of his testimony was unknown.

Finally, a counsel to the Senate Select Committee Investigating Intelligence Community Activities, Arthur Jefferson, "admitted that Cleaver's wife was recently flown to Washington, D.C. at their expense and allowed access to unpublished COINTELPRO documents" while "most" of a "wide variety of organizations" had been denied access. This, along with the other "evidence," makes it "apparent" that "Eldridge Cleaver is the Black community's Patty Hearst" (3). (Hearst, granddaughter of publisher William Randolph Hearst, who had been kidnapped and forced to participate in holdups and other illegal acts in the company of the black-led Symbionese Liberation Army in 1974, later repudiated any allegiance to them. The 1979 commutation of her sentence by President Carter was not warmly received by the left. *People's World,* for example, referred to it as "all the human rights that money can buy" ["Patty Hearst," 9 February 1979, 2].)

Cleaver had never been able to stand being alone and without a group with which to affiliate himself; when he had been in prison in his youth, it was the "solidarity and brotherhood" of the Muslims that had "kept [him] going" (*Fire,* 74). Before that, it had been the gang, and after prison it had been the Panthers and then the international section. Now he had no one, and those with whom Kathleen tried to discuss his case "gave her the cold shoulder" (*Fire,* 222). Ironically, the quotation from Yochelson and Samenow's *The Criminal Personality* (1976) that Cleaver used in *Soul on Fire* to describe his early imprisonment in fact portrays far better his situation in the year he read the passage. It states, "A criminal is most vulnerable to change when he is locked up or is about to face a period of confinement, when his options in life are considerably reduced and he is more likely to reflect on his past" (*Fire,* 70). Following this formula, Cleaver again reverted to religion to fill the void in his life. This time it was back to the original Protestantism of his childhood.

Conversion

At some point in his San Diego stay, from November 1975 to early January 1976, Cleaver was visited by George Stevens, a black assistant

minister of an unnamed denomination who had once been "closely
involved with the Black Panther Party and other organizations during
the sixties" (*Fire,* 220). There seems to have been only one visit, during
which Cleaver "poured out to him what was on [his] heart" and mentioned "the spiritual sparks going off in [his] life" (221). The conversation ended rather abruptly when Stevens "introduced" Cleaver to
Christ: "George took the Bible and held it up before my face. 'Eldridge
Cleaver, this is Jesus Christ,' George said, 'Jesus Christ, this is Eldridge
Cleaver' " (221). Cleaver, not yet accustomed to the cornball piety so
common to some evangelical sects, was "baffl[ed]" and insulted. He
was afraid Stevens might be "putting me down or something," and his
reaction ended the ministration. But the experience, Cleaver said, left
him "transfixed": "I began to think more about God; I began to read
about Jesus Christ and to really think on a profound level about him"
(221).

According to Cleaver, he had met a man named Glen Morrison, who
was a member of a prison ministry group calling itself the God Squad;
Glen had given him a Bible that he "read avidly," but Cleaver had
never joined in a prayer group. It is easy to see why—the group members met not in a church but in the open. Cleaver writes, "When Glen
and the others would form a circle, close their eyes and hold hands and
pray, the hostile guys in the tank would throw bars of soap at them or
flick water at them with a brush that had been dipped in the commode.
You could see the hate in their eyes, and their obscene comments
clashed violently with Glen's soft-spoken prayers. There was no way
then that I could bring myself to be a part of that circle—the tough
guys would think I had an angle or was a softy. And I wasn't about to
turn my back on them or close my eyes; I'd been in too many jails for
that" (223). Sometime in the second week of February, "tired of running
away," Cleaver joined the circle. He listened to Morrison talk about a
"personal commitment to Jesus Christ" (224), a concept that probably
fitted Cleaver's personality perfectly. Even in his autobiographical story
"The Flashlight," an older mentor named Chico had set Stacy/Eldridge
on the right path; in prison it had been Malcolm X he valued more than
he did the Muslims as an organization; and in the public years of 1967–
71 it had been Huey whom he valued more than the Panthers. Now he
felt the need not only for the Christian religion as an institution but
especially for a leader. He began "actually talking to God" (224): "Late
that night I confronted the reality of my intense need, and my resistance
evaporated. I confessed the name of Jesus Christ. I asked him into my

life. I asked him to be my personal Savior. I laid all my sins at the foot of his cross and he set me free" (224). Apparently, as soon as he was "set free" Cleaver contacted the press, and soon thereafter Russell Chandler published an article in the *Los Angeles Times* on "the wave of conversions taking place in many jails as a result of various prison ministries" (225). The publicity had the desired effect.

Omitting for the moment any reference to the press, Cleaver makes the response seem to follow on the heels of the commitment: "As I began crying tears of joy, God then began unraveling the mess. In my isolation he sent me brand new friends, brothers and sisters in Christ. My mail exploded. My old friends sent me hate letters, condemning me, calling me a traitor and a turncoat, rejecting me. Some expressed hope that I would rot in jail. But this was more than overbalanced by all of the wonderful people who sent me letters of love and encouragement (224). Now Cleaver had a new leader and a new group, as well as a new politico-religious worldview that fit together as neatly as his Muslim/militant one had before, and this new "Christian grapevine" (for it consisted largely of letters while he was still in jail) "kept [him] going" (224) exactly as he felt the Muslim solidarity had 15 years earlier. How much was based on emotional and psychological (and even economic) need and how much on a bona fide acceptance of Christianity is impossible to say. Among his old associates there were only derision and cynicism; black Christians avoided him; only white evangelicals took him at his word, and among them, almost unbelievably, there was one who had the balance of the $100,000 still needed for bail. His name was Arthur DeMoss, and he was president of National Liberty Corporation in Valley Forge, Pennsylvania.

The money was not offered all at once, and it would not have helped matters if it had been, for even if Cleaver had been able to raise bail, the California Adult Authority still had a "hold" on him as a parole violator; according to Cleaver, it took nine months "to file a writ of *habeas corpus* and get it before a judge" (222). In the meantime, Cleaver and DeMoss "started a series of exchanges" of letters, while Cleaver continued to alienate his old colleagues.

Cuba Redux

As mentioned in the discussion of Cleaver's sojourn in Cuba, he claimed after he returned that he had sent a tape recording home from Havana stating that "the white racist Castro dictatorship is more insidious and dangerous for black people than [that of] South Africa" because blacks believed in Castro and had "no illusions" about South Africa. In a full-page article in the "My Turn," guest-editorial series in *Newsweek,* Cleaver made the point that Castro was not to be trusted on the issue of racial equality. The closing remark was that Africa would soon run out of wars and Castro out of "dumping grounds for his black troops"; then Castro would "have to face the Captain Toros [militant young black officers], who have learned much and forgotten nothing" ("Castro's African Gambit," 13).

The response from the *Black Panther* was typically dogmatic. No one on the paper had any idea what Castro's African policy was, but the editors knew Cleaver was wrong. "Cleaver openly mouths the thrusts [*sic*] of right-wing reaction. Therefore, Cleaver stands in ideological opposition to the Black Panther Party because we support the revolution of the Cuban people" (*Black Panther,* 22 May 1976, 2). Among other things the party supported that were anti-Cleaver, stated Elaine Brown in her editorial, were the "liberation struggles in Africa [and] the struggles of the Arab people," especially the Palestine Liberation Organization. The things to be "denounce[d]," she wrote, sounding more like Cleaver in his prime than the Huey Newton of breakfasts and golf bags, were "the activities of the American capitalist, imperialist and racist government which fosters wars of aggression around the world and maintains oppression within its own boundaries." She continued: "We do not believe, like Cleaver, that the U.S. government should build its defenses and move toward a better and bigger Bicentennial, but that it must be uprooted, transformed and turned over to the people. Unlike Cleaver, we know that Black and poor people in the U.S. have nothing to celebrate in this country's Bicentennial as we daily face many forms of oppression and live with the knowledge that the U.S. still maintains colonies abroad, like Puerto Rico" (2). And with that, Brown concluded, "[the party] refuses to spend any more time on the subject of Eldridge Cleaver," a promise the organization did not keep.

A more specific response to Cleaver's *Newsweek* editorial appeared in the leftist press in the form of a guest column by Lennox S. Hinds— identified as the national director of the National Conference of Black Lawyers and the permanent United Nations delegate of the International Association of Democratic Lawyers—in the 17 July 1976 issue of *People's World.* Hinds's essay was reprinted from *Venceremos,* the official publication of the Venceremos Brigade, an American volunteer group that patterned itself on the Abraham Lincoln Brigade that fought on the leftist side in the Spanish Civil War, only here volunteers "fought" by working in the cane fields of Cuba instead of taking up arms. Like Angela Davis, Hinds insisted, "What I observed in Cuba was . . . a country where racism has been defeated" (6).

Hinds notes, "In order to understand Mr. Cleaver's commentary, we should keep in mind that he voluntarily surrendered to federal authorities last November, and is now in a California prison awaiting trial. It is also relevant that Mr. Cleaver will soon appear before Senate hearings on international terrorism. Under such circumstances, we would hardly expect a critical analysis of United States policy in Africa" (6). Actually, the Senate subcommittee had disbanded in February 1976; the hearing, entitled "Trotskyite Terrorist International," was held on Thursday, 24 July 1975, while Cleaver was still in Paris, and was published soon thereafter. Cleaver is mentioned in the publication in an appendix, which is a reprint of a Socialist Workers' party *Discussion Bulletin* dated June 1971. It was, in short, impossible for Cleaver to be scheduled for a summer 1976 appearance.

Hinds concludes by pointing out that "we will have to contend with unreliable and self serving sources" like Cleaver until the day the United States "lifts its blockade against Cuba" and the truth can shine.

According to right-wingers, of course, the truth already shone. William Buckley, who had never been a Cleaver fan, now observed that Cleaver had become educated about the "free world" outside the United States when he went to Cuba and "noticed that . . . all the generals were white, and all the privates were black."[21] Unfortunately, criticism of Cuba was still unpopular in some circles, and "at Northwestern, [Cleaver] was booed when he criticized Castro's Cuba—by students who had never lived in Castro's Cuba." Buckley hadn't lived there, either, but like them, he knew he was right. Ironically, Cleaver, once himself the most devout of ideologues, seemed to have forgotten the power of dogmatism over fact.

The Press

Sometime in June 1976 attorneys were able to arrange for Art DeMoss to visit Cleaver in his cell. He and DeMoss talked, Cleaver said, for "almost two hours, and during that time I came to know without question that Art cared for me in the Lord in a very special way" (*Fire*, 226). In July, while DeMoss and others were working to raise Cleaver's bail and "unravel the legal maze" (227) that kept him in jail, an article appeared in the *East Bay* (Oakland) *Voice* recounting a jail interview with Cleaver and an assessment of his image in the Bay Area. Reporter Robert Schaeffer presented Cleaver as both isolated and fragmented, much as he'd presented himself through "the narrow, thick, green face plate" in the "steel wall" of the visitor's booth. Both physically and psychologically, Schaeffer said, Cleaver "never presented more than a fraction of himself at a time" (Robert Schaeffer, "Wrapping Himself in the Flag," *East Bay* [Oakland] *Voice,* July 1976, 1). At the end of the month, another interview, this one with Rob Fruchtman and Carol Blue of Pacific News Service, was printed in the *Berkeley Barb* ("Eldridge Cleaver: Inside Speaking Out," *Berkeley Barb,* 30 July 1976, 7).

In response to Schaeffer's question about his current lack of support, Cleaver introduced a new issue: the specific political opposition of black leftist representative Ron Dellums of the Eighth Congressional District, a longtime Panther sympathizer who had held office since 1970. Cleaver said there were two reasons he lacked support, the first being that "people aren't supporting political prisoners these days" and the second that he was languishing "in 'Boss Tweed' Dellums' [*sic*] jail, with his judge, Lionel Wilson, and there's been a lot of misinformation and slander spread following my return" (Schaeffer, 1). Somewhat confusedly, Cleaver declared that Dellums didn't "want to rock the boat because he no longer represents the community. . . . He built his machine on what the Panthers began. I get down on people like him because it has to be done. If he didn't exist I would have had to invent him."

Cleaver still embraced some recognizable concepts from his past. Referring to the spring Senate Select Committee hearings that revealed FBI-inspired and -directed harassment of the Panthers, he commented, "I was describing [COINTELPRO] without knowing what it was called, in a speech at American University in 1968." The truth of that remark, that nearly all leftist "paranoia" in the late sixties and early seventies was actually an accurate reading of the political situation, still did not endear him to the Left of the bicentennial year, and neither did his loyalty to the Carter Democrats. "We," he said, speaking as if he were united with a left-of-center group of liberals, "should aim for 1984, . . . when we can win power through existing institutions, through the electoral process." His inability to judge the mood of the majority of Americans, though, was intact: "The Republican Party is finished. Jimmy Carter will preside over its demise. The Democratic Party will take in all the progressive elements, because the Right has historically been the dumping ground of old political ideas and the Left the repository of new ideas. The Democratic Party, pregnant with these new elements, will give birth to a new opposition on the Left" (Schaeffer, 1). Schaeffer commented dryly, "His self-conception conflicts sharply with other people's opinion of him. . . . His inability to raise money and retain a lawyer is evident, the trial now postponed indefinitely. But what's more striking is his inability to dispel the suspicions and command the attention he once had."

As an illustration of that remark, Schaeffer moved on to describe a rally by Cleaver supporter Julian Bond at Marin Junior College. Bond, one of the first to declare his willingness to help Cleaver, spoke for an hour in introducing Kathleen, who was there to garner support for her husband by refuting various charges made against him. Insisting that he had not made "a deal," she reiterated much of the information already printed in the *New York Times* (and some that was to be revealed in *Soul on Fire*) regarding whom he had spoken with in Paris and when, "the time and flight number of his plane back to the U.S.—times, dates, names, all meticulously recorded and entered on his behalf. Her refutation, chock full of facts, revealed nothing, pointed nowhere" (Schaeffer, 16). Kathleen bored her audience, which was both "restive" and "inert." Sensing this response, "she became shrill, almost frantic. . . . Her voice echoed the length of the court, rebounding off the wall behind the far hoop."

In Dellums's office, Schaeffer spoke with administrative aide Lee Halterman, who blamed Cleaver's lack of support on "suspicions" about him. "But a lot of it is that he has really been off the wall." According to Halterman, Dellums had visited Cleaver when he was first moved to Oakland, but "we can't meddle with the judges. They get angry and vent their anger on the defendant" (16). The implication was that Cleaver rejected that argument and presumed that Dellums had sold him out. Halterman pointed out that Cleaver ought to have been able to show what "stands" Dellums was taking that "indicate[d] some change for the worse" if he intended to attack him. Barring that, Cleaver was "irresponsible" and hard to understand. "He's burning his bridges behind him." Considering Dellums's long tenure in office, which extended through the eighties and beyond, it would seem that he "represented the community" quite accurately. Certainly there was no pressure from his constituency for him to intercede for Cleaver.

Whether the anger of Judge Wilson (or later, Spurgeon Avakian) was another reason for his demurral is impossible to say.

To get "a historical perspective" on those burned bridges, Schaeffer visited Black Panther party central headquarters on East Fourteenth, where he spoke with someone who preferred not to be identified. Why, Schaeffer was asked, would anyone on the Left even do a story on Cleaver? "I said that whatever he is, there remains amongst many on the left a fascination with him, a mystique surrounding him that changes its form over time, yet, like a drop of oil in water, never dissolves. 'That's all too true' commented one member of the party" (16). In summary, indicated Schaeffer, Cleaver had come a long way from the Malcolm X he once admired. Where Malcolm had once said, "I don't see any American dream; I see an American nightmare," Cleaver had become "a lover of the American dream." And perhaps that's why he had so little support: "People no longer see him as a victim" (16), Schaeffer remarked.

Cleaver no longer wanted to *be* a victim, either. Even as he repeated his continued concern for the poor and the imprisoned, he had lost any desire to sacrifice himself for "the movement." While collections for the defense fund lagged, Cleaver bridled at any suggestion that he owed anybody anything more: " 'A man told me the other day,' says Cleaver, 'Young black children need you up there as a symbol. I say, Fuck you. You go up there. I'm coming down, you dig?' " (Fruchtman and Blue, 7). Even the born-againer's halo can slip. As his patron, Art DeMoss, would remark, "Eldridge . . . is not perfect—just forgiven" (Epilogue to *Soul on Fire,* 238).

The Social Principles of Jesus

At the same time as the Schaeffer and Fruchtman-Blue interviews appeared, another saw print in the *Reader's Digest*. There, Cleaver told Laile Bartlett that during the period of "emptiness" (*Fire,* 210) and drifting in Paris in 1974 and 1975, thinking about what he could have been writing but wasn't, about "the God that failed—or even the Mao that failed" (207), he turned to reading Martin Luther King again, and from there to Walter Rauschenbusch, although he doesn't say whether he followed up the Rauschenbusch lead in Paris or in jail. Rauschenbusch was a "social-gospel preacher/teacher of pre–World War I" (Bartlett, 70); in Rauschenbusch's *Social Principles of Jesus* (1916), Cleaver found, he said, the activist Christ that King had found, "the

Jesus who was concerned about the social situation, and was really like the voice of the greatest revolutionary" (70).

Rauschenbusch's outlook provides the basis for an early twentieth-century form of "liberation theology." The most relevant portion of his slim volume, at least to the mind of a revolutionary, might well be chapter 3, "Standing with the People: The Strong Must Stand Up for the Weak."[22] In chapters 1 and 2 Rauschenbusch establishes the "sacred" nature of each "human life and personality" and the "solidarity of the human family," according to which ideas war "is a rupture of fellowship on a large scale" (Rauschenbusch, 26) and "social unity" the most desirable of goals. American racism is never mentioned; rather, one ought to realize "intelligently" that "the Chinese and the Zulu" are "his brothers with whom he must share the earth" (27).

Rauschenbusch's missionary concern seems more foreign than domestic. Nonetheless, his concepts of social obligation and of the inherent evil in wealth and its pursuit could provide someone with Cleaver's originally socialist leanings with an establishment formulation of concern for the poor and the oppressed. In his reading of Matthew 25:31–46—the separation of humankind at the end of the world into two groups, the "sheep" destined for "eternal life" and the "goats" damned "into eternal punishment"—Rauschenbusch comes closest to opening a discussion of racism by including it in a list of social evils, but he does not develop the issue to any degree:

Whence he shall come to judge the quick and the dead. Think of it—absolute justice done at last, by an all-knowing Judge, where no earthly pull of birth, wealth, learning, or power will count, and where all masks fall! By what code of law and what standard shall we be judged there? Here is the answer of Jesus: Not by creed and church questions, but by our human relations; by the reality of our social feeling; by our practical solidarity with our fellow-men. If we lived in the presence of hunger, loneliness, and oppression, in the same country with child labor, race contempt, the long day, rack rents, prostitution, just earnings withheld by power, the price of living raised to swell swollen profit— if we saw such things and remained apathetic, out we go. *You and I—to the right or the left?* (38).

Rauschenbusch saw the Jesus "with his arm thrown in protection about the poor man, and his other hand raised in warning to the rich" (40) as the direct heir of the teachings of "The Old Testament prophets . . . his spiritual forebears" (41).

It may even be that, through Rauschenbusch's linkage of the Hebrew prophets with the social activism of modern Jews, Cleaver was able to recover from the anti-Semitism he had espoused during his Arab sojourn and to return to his original identification with Herzl and the need of a people for land. Writes Rauschenbusch: "Now, the Hebrew prophets with one accord stood up for the common people and laid the blame for social wrong on the powerful classes. . . . We cannot belittle the moral insight of that unique succession of men. Their spiritual force is still hard at work in our Christian civilization, especially in the contribution which the Jewish people are making to the labor movement" (41–42).

Rauschenbusch is at his most outspoken in chapter 10, "The Conflict with Evil" (151–66), where he unambiguously identifies "socialized" evil first with youth gangs and then with classes: the "leisure" class, which controls the wealth, is united "against the class of toil" and takes "tribute from the labor of many" (161). Rauschenbusch further clarifies the value of the working class and the sins of the rich in terms which clearly point out who is on the side of the devils: "The fundamental sin of all dominant classes has been the taking of unearned incomes. Political oppression has always been a corollary of economic parasitism, a means to an end. The combination of the two constitutes the largest and most continuous form of organized evil in human history. . . . The existence of great permanent groups, feeding but not producing, dominating and directing the life of whole nations according to their own needs, may well seem a supreme proof of the power of evil in humanity" (162–63). No radical of the sixties could condemn "the establishment" more sweepingly.

It seems possible that reading King—who was strongly influenced by Rauschenbusch's idea of the church as a socially committed institution—in conjunction with reading Rauschenbusch could have given Cleaver an entirely different concept of King as a highly principled, courageous prophet who gave his life for his people and who was thereby no less a man than a Panther. Whereas both Cleaver and Newton used to speak of the short life expectancy of the revolutionary, with nods to Bakunin and Guevara, in an almost Byronic manner (*To Die for the People, Revolutionary Suicide*), King's death made it clear that nonviolent people, too, can die for their beliefs and that King was just as aware of this possibility as the more radical young blacks were. Cleaver, who had been outraged at King's death (the title "Requiem for Nonviolence" probably refers to the death of any nonviolent, cooperative impulses he held within himself as much as to the end of the pacifism of the civil rights movement), must have been impressed by King's courage, recalling his words only a short time before his death: "I may not get there with you, but I have been to the mountaintop, and I have seen the Promised Land." Whereas in his earlier days Cleaver had seen King as effete and even cowardly, and had referred to the philosophy of nonviolence as "self-flagellating," he had had time since then to reflect on King's actual character and to find in it an acceptable role model. In 1974, Cleaver was pushing 40 and had two children; he was disillusioned with leftist revolutionaries and their doctrine and had no coherent worldview. Following King's example, Cleaver could see himself, perhaps, as a fiery speaker just as he was in the old days, still championing the poor, demanding racial equality, and standing up for brotherhood, but allied with a new group, the evangelicals. Unfortunately, his role as advocate faded, possibly under the influence of the conservatism of his evangelical peers, and he never referred to Rauschenbusch again.

In July 1976, despite her insistence that the party was sick of Cleaver, Elaine Brown returned to the subject in the conclusion of a *Black Panther* article that was reprinted from *Counterspy* magazine and that centered on the COINTELPRO operation. "Let us look at the Eldridge Cleaver business for a minute," she said ("Ideas of Freedom Are Always Dangerous . . . ," *Black Panther*, 10 July 1976, 2). Her claim was that during the time she was "part of what was purported to be a Progressive American Delegation to Korea" put together by Cleaver in 1970, she was, she implied, dragged off to several other countries, but worse, "Cleaver . . . personally threatened my life because I would not agree on phony ideological points that the Party was a 'Breakfast for Children' organization" (22). He was in favor of "more killing" and had "no other program," she said. He wanted Panthers to be killed "for the purpose of media attention (while he safely sat in Algeria)," and, she snarled, when they were all dead "he could describe to history the meaning of our deaths" (22). As before, when she questioned his new politics, Brown discounted the effect of the FBI operation on Cleaver. There were never any "letters . . . any misunderstandings on the level of leadership." She adds, "Today, it's all out—the closet door opened: Cleaver denounces Cuba, China, African liberation struggles and joins hands with Kissinger and Uncle Sam. All of this because the FBI sent notes? It is my belief that Cleaver too was as much a part of COINTELPRO then as now, as Karenga, as Roy Innis" (22). Brown's surprising inclusion of Ron Karenga and Roy Innis as agents, which not only charges them but in effect charges the Senate Select Committee with whitewashing the investigation, adds yet another twist to the double helix of black radical–undercover interrelationships.

No finger, by then, was left unpointed; no one but Brown herself (who had been a 1976 delegate to the Democratic convention) pure in radical credentials. The only person not charging and countercharging was Cleaver: at no time did he claim to have been entrapped by undercover agents among his former colleagues.

Art DeMoss saw Cleaver as both praiseworthy and pitiable; fortunately for Cleaver, he was also a "born-again gambler" (*Fire,* 227). On Friday the 13th of August, 1976, DeMoss sent a representative to the jail with "adequate securities to obtain the $100,000 bail." Although the judge refused at first to accept some of the highway bonds, Cleaver reported that "a flurry of activity" on the part of the representative and of his own attorney, Patrick Halliman, produced the requisite sum from a bail bondsman by 4:45 P.M. He was thus able to be released for the weekend, time he spent with Kathleen at the Fairmont Hotel in San Francisco.

On Monday, 16 August, Eldridge and Kathleen flew to Los Angeles, where Eldridge saw his mother for the first time since 1968. She had been far from sympathetic with the Panther point of view and "had been praying for thirty years," and especially since Leroy Cleaver died in 1975, that her son would "become a Christian" and return home. Eldridge had seen his children in prison only once, up in the Alameda County Jail, but the experience had been so upsetting for everyone it was not repeated. Now he was reunited with them "in the driveway of [his] mother's home" (*Fire,* 229).

Although Cleaver leaves the reader of *Soul on Fire* with the impression that DeMoss had raised the entire bail, he had in fact raised only "half," which is still a considerable sum (Laurie Johnston, "Notes on People," *New York Times,* 18 August 1976, 47). Christian biographer John A. Oliver reports that DeMoss raised $41,000 in 1976 (272), while he quotes an article in the *San Diego Church News* claiming that "contributions from the Christian community" had paid the bail. The defense fund had raised only $5,000 by mid-April, and the Cleaver finances were too desperately slim to permit the family to help themselves, especially with the huge legal fees and travel costs for Kathleen's coast-to-coast endeavors. (Oliver says one estimate of legal fees was $250,000 [265]). Paul Jacobs, writing in *Mother Jones* that month, mentioned that Daniel Patrick Moynihan had chipped in $500, and reported that Norman Podhoretz had held a fund-raising party "for the conservative and the reactionary chic."[23] After T. D. Allman repeated the statement in the *New York Times* the next January, Podhoretz wrote a letter to the

Times denying that he had done so (30 January 1976, sec. 6, p. 42). Perhaps he was now embarrassed at being associated with Cleaver. If Cleaver hadn't quoted Podhoretz's Maileresque "My Negro Problem— and Ours" at the head of his "Convalescence" essay in *Soul on Ice,* the world would probably have forgotten it. But now, recorded in hard-cover in the 1968 Book of the Year rather than in an obscure February 1963 issue of *Commentary,* is Podhoretz's already-laughable veneration and envy of black folks, with the key line italicized by Cleaver for emphasis: "Just as in childhood I envied Negroes for what seemed to me their superior masculinity, so I envy them today for what seems to me their superior physical grace and beauty. I have come to value physical grace very highly, and I am now capable of aching with all my being when I watch a Negro couple on the dance floor, or a Negro playing baseball or basketball. *They are on the kind of terms with their own bodies that I should like to be on with mine, and for that precious quality they seem blessed to me"* (*Ice,* 191). The fact that Cleaver used this passage to illustrate the healing of white racism is no help; by the seventies, even white folks could see the inherently racist stereotyping in it, and read it in the same light as Baldwin read Kerouac. Podhoretz did not approve of Cleaver's new role, but others who rejected Cleaver's ideas helped him anyway. Undoubtedly, it was important to reject Cleaver in order to reject "My Negro Problem" implicitly, just for the record.

Free at Last

Once out on bail and finally, gloriously free, Cleaver set about mak-ing a career out of being "born again," while pressing for defense spending aimed at protecting the United States from the Communist nations. His new associates were astoundingly different from those whose friendship had flattered him in 1966 and 1967. Then, his big break had come through Robert Scheer at *Ramparts;* now, Scheer was replaced by his antithesis, the conservative Christian businessman De-Moss. Then, Cleaver's supporters and fans had included Huey Newton, Norman Mailer, and Jerry Rubin; now, he would cultivate Billy Gra-ham, Pat Boone, and Charles Colson.

Two days after the family reunion in Pasadena, the nuclear family "sought refuge" from the press in San Diego, where Billy Graham was conducting a crusade (*Fire,* 229). Cleaver managed to meet first Gra-ham's "associate evangelist" Leighton Ford, and then Graham himself, a man Cleaver admittedly had "actually hated most of [his] life" (230).

Some years earlier, said Cleaver, Graham had visited San Quentin but Cleaver had refused to attend the rally. Now he was eager, even delighted, to be able to be in the same room with him.

Graham made Cleaver welcome and set him at ease. The two men "talked and prayed together," apparently without Kathleen, for more than an hour. Cleaver exulted, "His acceptance of me as a person and Christian brother at that time was precisely the kind of encouragement and affirmation I needed desperately" (230). Curiously, Cleaver claimed that the "most significant thing" he gleaned from his long conversation with Graham was the admonition "Eldridge, . . . one thing you must never forget—never embarrass the Lord" (230). Perhaps Graham had seen a picture of Cleaver in his "Cleavers" and prayed over it so that he would know how to keep Cleaver from wearing them on Sunday mornings. It is safe to assume that most of the audience for evangelistic rallies and television shows would be stunned to see a man appear in blue pants with a red-and-white striped bicentennial codpiece. Surely the costume would constitute an effective barrier against spreading God's word. If that was Graham's intent, he failed, for Cleaver clung determinedly to his new design for several more years, in spite of the counsel of friends.

About two weeks after Eldridge's release, the Cleaver family flew east for a stay at the home of Art DeMoss in Pennsylvania, where they spent a week relaxing. But first, Cleaver appeared on NBC-TV's *Meet the Press* on Sunday, 29 August. The questioners on the show included Ford Rowan of NBC, Robert Novak of the *Chicago Sun-Times,* and Paul Delaney of the *New York Times,* with Bill Monroe as moderator. Because the establishment press had printed little about Cleaver since his return, the news of his conversion came as a surprise to many.

Among the first questions asked was whether Cleaver had made a "deal" before his return. As usual, Cleaver denied that he had, pointing to his jail sentence as proof. He had had, he declared "deep transformations in my own personal life" (Oliver, 239, and transcript) that created "a change . . . toward how change should be approached in this country" (240). Asked whether he felt himself to be "less of a man" for having surrendered himself to authority, he insisted, "I have never felt stronger or more manly in my life" (240), but remarked that he had no need of prison, either. Further, he emphasized that his motivation was to "straighten up my life, to clear myself . . . to raise my family in the United States" (242), and thus he avoided a direct response to his questioner's probing about his "present posture" as "a big con game to help you in your trial." He declared that his hopes for leniency were based entirely on the "very different climate" that existed in the United States in 1976 as opposed to 1968–71, when his codefendants in the shoot-out had gone to trial and been found guilty of all charges. Then, he said, "people were not willing to question the behavior and . . . motivation of police . . . before the exposés of . . . Watergate . . . and the COINTELPRO activities" (241–42). But he hastened to excuse the police agencies, which were under "pressure" to spy on the Panthers, protesting only the "illegal activities" that he said ultimately drove him out of the country.

His most sweeping absolution, however, was reserved for the Panthers themselves. In response to a question regarding the Black Panther contribution to the black movement, Cleaver replied, "There was some good in what we did and there was some bad" (243).

Q. What was the bad?

A. I think that we were a little naive in our approach . . . that we were excessive in our language . . . that we scared a lot of people, not so much by our practices, our activities, but by the way that we described certain situations, and if I had it to do all over again, with hindsight, I would do it differently (243)

To say that Hoover was "scared" by the Panthers is an understatement; as the 1976 Senate Select Committee hearings made clear, Hoover, Attorney General Mitchell, and probably Richard Nixon himself were gripped by a racist paranoia that focused on the blunt-spoken, gun-toting Panthers as the single most formidable foe in an era of violence and polarization. To be sure, Cleaver's uncensored rhetoric helped to create the impression, "by the way [he] described certain situations," that the Panthers were a murderous gang fully capable of doing everything Cleaver had said they would. The actual gun battles conducted by other Panthers could only reinforce the concept.

Now, though, Cleaver declared himself "a person with a heart full of goodwill" who had "experienced religious conversion" and was "interested in whatever good contribution that [he] could make" (243). His new state of calm included an acceptance of both "the will of the Lord" as to the outcome of his trial and, after his expected acquittal, "whatever work the Lord brings to me" (244). Actually, Cleaver already had an exact idea of what that work would be; his own ministry was about to begin.

Chapter Seven
Soul on Fire

On 14 September 1976 Cleaver announced that he was "going on the lecture circuit" as an evangelist. He had "signed with a national speakers' bureau," reported Russ Chandler in the *Los Angeles Times*, "and with a major publishing house for a book detailing his philosophical and spiritual evolution" (Oliver, 274). One of the men he would see a lot of on the tour was Charles Colson, whose 1976 book, *Born Again,* hot off the presses in February, had been on Cleaver's recent prison reading list. According to Cleaver, he had selected the book merely because he was "bored to death," since he still hated Colson for his role in Republican politics, but then had become "strongly attracted" to Colson, who impressed him as "a real man" (*Fire,* 232). Cleaver actually met Colson "immediately following" the stay at the DeMoss home (*Fire,* 236), along with former liberal Democratic senator Harold Hughes and former Alabama Ku Klux Klan leader Tommy Terrants, a motley crew indeed. DeMoss later commented that he believed "the angels in heaven rejoiced to see such a disparate group as this praying together and loving together" (236).

Colson's book may have contained one hint for Cleaver besides the concept of Christian regeneration. Colson writes that after he confessed to his belief in Christ in December 1973, he was criticized in part for his "sudden coming to Christ" and in part for mentioning it. Colson said: "Onetime Trappist monk, turned liberal philosopher-journalist, Colman McCarthy, likened the Colson conversion to Rennie Davis's profession of faith in Guru Maharaj Ji of India. It was my willingness to speak publicly that offended McCarthy: 'In the history of authentic conversion . . . the new members of the faith always kept silence at first.' And so it continued for days and weeks to come."[1] The idea of testing a sincere conversion according to one's initial silence may have been behind Cleaver's reported concern over a "premature" announcement of his conversion in the press in mid-March (Oliver, 257). The Reverend Glen Morrison had revealed to *San Diego Evening Tribune* reporters that Cleaver "embraced Christianity shortly after entering the

Alameda County Courthouse in early January" (257). Further, another
account in the *Los Angeles Times*, two days later (the story also mentioned Colson), revealed that on 4 February an ex-Panther minister
named Shadrach Meshach Lockeridge had told a gathering of 600 Baptist ministers in Jackson, Mississippi, about Cleaver's conversion (258).
Reportedly, the reason Cleaver sought to conceal his conversion was
that he did not "want to use it as a lever to secure favors or to appear
that he [was] doing so" (259). Ironically, he would later repeatedly
blame the conversion for his shortage of funds, on the implied grounds
that his old friends disliked him for his spiritual outspokenness, and
would thereby play upon the hoped-for sympathy of Christians who felt
equally misunderstood. George Otis's 1977 book contained a full-page
plea for donations to be sent directly to the Cleavers at a post office box
in Van Nuys, California, the ad citing "some $200,000 in unpaid bills"
(Otis, 161). Presumably, Otis believed the timetable he presented,
which was headed by the statement that previously "Eldridge's needs
were supplied by his former communist and leftist friends," but "upon
his return," when Cleaver "began to speak out for God and for those
things which are worthy about America," two "large sources of income
dried up completely." The two sources, each prominently numbered,
were as follows:

(1)   His former friends stopped all support to him.
(2)   All royalties from his previous books were impounded. (161)

The chronology is exactly backward, as any "former friend" or IRS
employee could testify. Further, Otis seems not to have asked himself
why the federal government would impound the earnings of a Christian
and a patriot on the grounds that he flaunted those two roles. Nonetheless, Otis obligingly requested his readers to mail a check "today" and
assured them of God's blessing for such a "sacrificial expression of love"
(161)

Gestures like this do not serve to reassure the objective observer of
the Cleavers' sincerity. Rather, they offer evidence that the Cleavers
were willing to support such fraudulent claims in order to bilk gullible
and trusting readers out of their money. It is not certain that this
advertisement succeeded, of course, but on other occasions the "help a
persecuted fellow Christian" approach did. Whenever Cleaver spoke at
rallies, the hat was passed, as newspaper accounts testified. On one
occasion, Cleaver went home with $16,500 when he hit up well-to-do

Orange County residents at a barbecue in February 1977 (Oliver, 277). Because of the desperate financial situation in which the Cleavers found themselves, no other course could have seemed possible. There was no way to earn or borrow such sums as were needed for expenses; hustling was all that was left. Becoming a self-styled preacher was one of the few things Cleaver could actually *do;* previously, his noncriminal career had consisted only in making highly rhetorical speeches and in writing essays of a similar, though usually superior, sort. Now he suffered from writer's block. Lacking an education, he was qualified only for entry-level jobs he would never be able to bear, and it was obvious that all his old contacts were useless; no one would give him a second "main chance" such as *Ramparts* had in 1966. The one alternative open to someone with Cleaver's talents and qualifications was a contemporary version of what Grandfather Cleaver used to do as a circuit-riding preacher: television evangelism and college speaking tours.

Initially, Cleaver's ex-celebrity status and his born-again experience were enough to get him a spot on a show or in a "crusade" on stage somewhere. Problems, however, surfaced almost at once. While gut-level Christianity provides a full set of true-believer clichés and prefabricated phrases to be strung together, much as political extremism does, Cleaver had trouble expressing himself with the same charistmatic fervor as of old. Although he traveled the revival circuit with Charles Colson and even shared a pulpit with Jerry Falwell once,[2] he disappointed potential fans. One reporter wrote: "Cleaver's espousal of Christianity probably can be taken with a few grains of salt. . . . Watching him on TV, I've noticed that he speaks of his religious experiences without the fire of passion he exhibits when he talks of some of his social and political concerns. This is where I believe his real interests still lie, probably more as a centralist social reformer than as a radical or revolutionary" (Goldberg, 20). Neither in speech nor in prose could Cleaver make his newfound faith sound convincing enough to parlay it into fame.

Cleaver's second problem lay in the simultaneous promotion of Christ and "Cleavers." It would seem that Cleaver was so far out of touch with his audience that he was unable to comprehend how "sexy, shocking and insufferable" his pants would be to sexually conservative evangelical Christians, questions of taste strictly aside (Chuck Fager, "Born Again Media," *In These Times,* 18 February 1978, 24). When he attempted to publicize them at the Thirty-fifth Annual Convention of the National Religious Broadcasters (NRB) in 1978, he was quickly counseled and canceled, as was a world-premiere showing of the film *The Eldridge Cleaver Story*. The next morning, reporters were told that Cleaver had left Washington, D.C., for California after some "soul-searching and discussion." What he needed, said NRB executive Ben Armstrong, was "heavy introspection and consideration about the direction he's going to go" (Goldberg, 20).

Sometime in the fall of 1976, Cleaver met television evangelist George Otis and appeared along with Kathleen on Otis's show "High Adventure," the occasion being one of a number of services, shows, and rallies Cleaver addressed. In his book on Cleaver, Otis quotes "the new Cleaver" from a mélange of sources that includes not only his own show but Jim and Tammy Bakker's "The PTL [Praise the Lord] Club," "The 700 Club," and Robert Schuller's "Hour of Power." Otis's "edited composite of recent interviews and lectures" (Otis, 129) includes the following exchange:

QUESTION: Now after your encounter with Jesus, what do you think of the Bible? Many say it is a book of poetry, folklore and history. What do you believe the Bible to be?

ELDRIDGE: I believe that Book to be God's message and guidance to mankind.

QUESTION: Do you actually believe it is still relevant here in the 20th century? It was written thousands of years ago. How can such a book be practical and relevant in this modern day?

ELDRIDGE: I can just tell you from my own personal experience—a very recent experience—that the Bible is both practical and alive in my life. I have taken it as the guide for the rest of my life; and if this present moment is relevant, the Bible is absolutely relevant.

QUESTION: Eldridge, I would like to ask you who you believe Jesus Christ was—or is?

ELDRIDGE: I base my opinion on what is taught in the Bible. The Bible teaches us that Jesus is God manifested to us in flesh. And Jesus is the Son of God sent to mankind here on earth. And Jesus is the Saviour of those who believe on Him. I do not quarrel with that definition. When I placed my faith, Jesus entered my life. I have had the personal experience of being picked up and salvaged by Jesus, so now I take Jesus as my personal Saviour—as the Son of God, sent to mankind for salvation of the world. (132–33)

Leftists could read such a passage only with anger and derision, hearing Cleaver mouth the standard phrases of Bible-oriented Christians. It is doubtful, however, that language is genuinely a key to sentiment in such a case. The tendency to revert to clichés was always strong with Cleaver, who spoke in standard Third World revolutionary phrases as a general rule in exile, and used, as most politicians do, a fairly set speech in his 1968 "tour" that consisted of little more than assorted catchphrases and epithets. No one doubted him then. If staleness of phrase or imagery were regarded as the hallmark of insincerity, millions of uncreative believers and their pastors would stand condemned as hypocrites. It may be that Cleaver was purely an opportunist as charged, but his integrity cannot be questioned merely on the basis of his choice of words.

Hot Dogs and Malted Milk Reconsidered

Through George and Virginia Otis, the Cleavers met Pat Boone and his wife, Shirley, at the Boone home. There was dinner for 10, including all four Boone daughters. Boone was a personality that Cleaver had not only hated but publicly mocked; Boone, as a straitlaced singer of a watered-down form of WASP "rock and roll," had once symbolized for Cleaver the "Hot-Dog-and-Malted-Milk norm of the bloodless, square, superficial faceless Sunday-Morning atmosphere that was suffocating the nation's soul" (*Ice,* 193). When the "inner need and hunger" of the "white youth of America . . . was no longer satisfied with the antiseptic white shoes and whiter songs of Pat Boone," Cleaver had once written, "Elvis Presley came, . . . sowing seeds of a new rhythm and style" into the youth (*Ice,* 194). In the sixties, when Elvis was making films, "the Beatles were on the scene, injecting Negritude by the ton into the whites" (202). They represented for the Cleaver of 1966 "soul by proxy, middlemen between the Mind and the Body. A long way from Pat Boone's White Shoes" (204).

For his part, Boone had once refused to let a teacher assign *Soul on Ice* to his 16-year-old daughter, Debby, on the grounds that it represented, as he wrote to George Otis, "militant, vulgar, and antisocial thought" (Otis, 126). When he met Cleaver, Boone told him the story but graciously omitted any reference to the insults directed at him therein. In fact, Boone knew the insults were there, for he had taken the trouble to read the book before he condemned it.

Cleaver had a confession of his own, one that comes straight out of the youthful gang experiences he had recounted in his story "The

Flashlight," in which the boys from Rose Hill went on escapades into the wealthy areas of Los Angeles, breaking into homes and stealing from cars. Boone recounted Cleaver's words: "This is just blowing my mind, he told us. I can remember some of my buddies in L.A. coming around and looking at this house and others in Beverly Hills. We were sizing it up, planning to break into this place, y'know? Of course that never happened, but here we are in this same house—getting ready to pray together. It's just blowing my mind."[3] It blew Boone's mind, too. He told his readers that Cleaver's revelation "began a very meaningful prayer experience for us all" (Boone, 79). Before dinner, said Boone, "Eldridge Cleaver led us to the throne of God in prayer," and later, "we all wound up on our knees in our den, praying and weeping together and praising God with the kind of joy I've rarely experienced before" (80). They all sensed, Boone claimed, "that Eldridge and Kathleen's experience was particularly dramatic and awesome—a sovereign act of an all-powerful, all-loving God" (80).

From 1976 to 1978, Cleaver's "set speech" was a recounting of how he became a born-again Christian. He made it clear that his disenchantment with world communism had been gradual, beginning with his seven months in Cuba, but undoubtedly realized that an equal and opposite reaction, in the form of a gradual turning to patriotism and especially to Christian faith, would, whether it were true or not, produce difficult copy for an evangelical preacher to spin into gold. It was also important to offset the appearance of opportunism by dating the beginning of his conversion before his return to the United States. The fact that he had never mentioned anything like it at the time of his return would work in his favor; thus he could spare himself from the charges directed against Colson.

Accordingly, it would seem, there appeared something very like a vision an Old Testament prophet might have seen. It is tempting to imagine that Cleaver identified himself, if only fancifully, with Ezekiel, who prophesied among the Jews when they were exiles in the original Babylon and who saw visions in the heavens. (Cleaver had stopped calling the United States "Babylon," though he reminded his readers of his use of the term in *Soul on Fire* [80–81]). But where Ezekiel saw hallucinogenic visions of otherworldly animals and chariots, apparently during the day, Cleaver saw only a parade of human heroes in the moon. Beginning in prison, Cleaver made reference to this phenomenon, sometimes referring to it as a "vision" and sometimes denying that it was anything more than the way the shadows looked.

During the late summer of 1975, Cleaver said, he was nearly over-whelmed with despair. He reported sitting at a candlelit dinner with the family in Paris, with all the other lights in the house out. Then, he says, "I was suddenly struck that this was a perfect metaphor for our life: our life was empty—there was no light in our life. We were going through an empty ritual, eating in the same spirit in which you might drive to a gas station and fill up the tank. It was meaningless, point-less, getting nowhere" (*Fire,* 211). Almost immediately after that, as he tells it in *Soul on Fire,* Cleaver returned to his apartment in Rocheville to try to write. He began to contemplate suicide. One night, he said, "brooding, downcast, at the end of my rope" (and possibly, considering his history, in the process of some form of substance abuse), he looked up at the moon and "saw certain shadows" that took form as his own profile—"a profile that we had used on posters for the Black Panther Party—something I had seen a thousand times" (211). His reaction was extreme.

I was already upset and this scared me. When I saw that image, I started trembling. It was a shaking that came from deep inside, and it had a threat about it that this mood was getting worse, that I could possibly disintegrate on the scene and fall apart. As I stared at this image, it changed, and I saw my former heroes paraded before my eyes. Here were Fidel Castro, Mao Tse-tung, Karl Marx, Frederick Engels, passing in review—each one appearing for a moment of time, and then dropping out of sight, like fallen heroes. Finally, at the end of the procession, in dazzling, shimmering light, the image of Jesus Christ appeared. That was the last straw. (211)

Cleaver reported sobbing and praying and turning to the family Bible, which his mother had given him as the eldest son and which Kathleen had packed when she left California, to find the Twenty-third Psalm ("The Lord is my shepherd"). He looked "desperately" for the Lord's Prayer but failed to find it. Soon, overcome by fatigue, he slept.

When he awoke, he said, he saw "a path of light that ran through a prison cell" that was "a dark spot" on the path but not its end. Accord-ing to Cleaver, he understood then that he could end his misery and isolation if he wanted to. "I had it within my power to get back home by taking that first step, by surrendering; and it was a certainty that everything was going to be all right" (212).

Cleaver's account of the experience in George Otis's book, as taken from episodes on his show and others, was very similar to that in *Soul on*

Fire, except for Cleaver's allowing Otis to draw him significantly further into melodramatic intensity. As usual, Cleaver first pointed out that this "precious moment" was "the beginning of my life turning around," although at the time he had thought only that he was "coming unglued" (Otis, 131). But Otis knew that television viewers and rally-goers relish experiences more along the Saul-into-Paul line. He probed:

> QUESTION: After Jesus looked at you, did everything seem to melt? Did you have any feeling of a contact with God?
>
> ELDRIDGE: It was a focus on God, a focus on Jesus—because it was a rejection of the others. And I could see that I was rejecting them. These were the false gods that I had been through and I was rejecting them, yes, I was seeing that.
>
> QUESTION: Now you were really in a critical position. Suddenly the world you had given your life to—the cause you believed was the answer—the world in which you had become a leader, suddenly to see that old world crumbling must have been shattering, but in this moment of deepest despair, God sent you His Son in a vision.
>
> ELDRIDGE: Yes, but I didn't understand what all this meant for many months. (132)

This experience was, then, the foundation for what might otherwise seem abrupt. He told Laile Bartlett, "I don't like the idea that I've been 'born again in my cell.' I'm certain that people would see that as some kind of opportunistic gambit on my part. Also, there's nothing 'sudden' about it; it has been a very painful change that has taken place over a considerable period of time" (Bartlett, 71). He told Russ Chandler that that night on the balcony was his "conversion experience because I was not the same after it as before" (Otis, 139).

Controversy: Saint or Fraud?

Cleaver generated a fair amount of publicity in 1977 and worked on securing a place for himself and Kathleen in the evangelical establishment. Articles and even books about him tended to adopt one or the other of two extreme positions, as exemplified by the subtitle of Reginald Major's *Berkeley Barb* article ("Eldridge Cleaver: Fraud or Hoax?") and the subtitle of one in *Minority Voices* by assistant editor William P.

Warnken, Jr., "Eldridge Cleaver: From Savior to Saved." Both 1977 books, George Otis's *Eldridge Cleaver: Ice and Fire!* and John A. Oliver's *Eldridge Cleaver Reborn,* accepted Cleaver's new self without reservation, but an article in the alternative press *Portland Scribe* on 21 April 1977 was sardonically entitled "Saint Eldridge" (Alon Raab, 19). T. D. Allman's balanced essay in the *New York Times Magazine* in January raised, among other questions, the issue of Cleaver's inability to connect with young blacks, while James S. Tinney of Howard University focused entirely on Cleaver's lack of contact with the black church in a *Christianity Today* interview later that year.

T. D. Allman's article "The 'Rebirth' of Eldridge Cleaver" bluntly asked in its subheading, "Is he a convert or an opportunist?" Of the "strong reactions" felt to Cleaver's "political and religious conversion," Allman cites first Elaine Brown's and Paul Jacobs's denunciations of him and then the alleged contributions to his defense fund by Moynihan and Podhoretz, as well as Robert Schuller's provision of "valuable fundraising exposure" on his "Hour of Power" show. Some, Allman noted, believe that Cleaver is insincere: "This is so transparent," said one. And finally, citing the evidence of those fancy pants as so many would, Allman offers, "Others go so far as to suggest that Cleaver is losing his mental balance." Such terms as "schizophrenic" and "divorced from reality" (Allman, 11) were mentioned as assessments of the kind of man who would, at alternate moments, testify about his conversion experience and design highly suggestive clothing suitable for a Frederick's of Hollywood catalog.

Allman quotes Cleaver's defense of his reversal as well, but not in the most flattering terms. "I'm a master strategist," he had Cleaver saying; "I don't sign loyalty oaths with anyone, and some people are angry because I'm not afraid to change my mind" (31). It was exactly the "strategist" concept that caused Cleaver to be so cynically regarded by so many.

Allman's summary of Cleaver's October 1976 visit to Tulane University in New Orleans, which, as Cleaver pointed out, had once been "a slave plantation" (10), was lukewarm. Cleaver presented a right-wing line that was unlikely to win support. "They heard him praise Henry Kissinger's diplomacy, decline to support the NAACP, warn of the Soviet threat, denounce the Cubans and Arabs as racists. Nor could he refrain from taunting the women's liberation movement" (32). But Allman did not quote his jibes. The reaction of the "young affluent blacks" was "neither veneration nor hatred, only suspicious curiosity" (32–33).

Upon Cleaver's return, said Allman, he and Kathleen boarded a flight from San Francisco to Burbank and headed for the Arrowhead Hotel, where celebrations honoring the twenty-fifth anniversary of the Campus Crusade for Christ were in full swing. While they were there, Eldridge and Kathleen were baptized by immersion in the hotel swimming pool on Sunday, 10 October 1976, while Art DeMoss smiled down upon them (33).

Kathleen's baptism was the culmination, as it turned out, of a crisis-within-the-crisis of the threat of bankruptcy. At an early point, she had denied that Cleaver had had a vision or been converted. When George Otis asked Cleaver about this denial, he replied that Kathleen's reponse had been recommended by their lawyer so that Cleaver would not lose the sympathy of his former supporters. Since we know that support had mostly been lost in 1971 and during Cleaver's Paris period, it seems inescapable to conclude that Kathleen said what she did because she believed it. When Cleaver announced their joint baptism, he revealed that just as "old friends had forsaken him" when he turned to Christianity, "at first one by one, and then by the dozens, and then just in droves," he had also briefly feared that "Kathleen was going to decide just like a lot of other people had said, 'Man, you're going crazy, I'm going to get out of here' " (C. Gerald Fraser, "Cleaver 'Testifies' as an Evangelical," *New York Times,* 12 December 1976, 48). But since their baptism, he declared, they were "companions in the Lord" and their children were in a Christian school in Los Angeles learning math by counting "angels, crosses and churches, things like that" (48).

Allman concluded his article "a few days" after the baptism, when Cleaver, eating in a Chinese restaurant in San Francisco, gushed, "Imagine! Me baptized! I'm wearing my baptismal trousers now. I bet they bring good luck. . . . Oral Roberts. I'm going to go speak to Oral Roberts." To his wife's "Oh, Eldridge," he replied, "Why not? These people wouldn't have listened to me ten years ago" (Allman, 33). Allman's unspoken comment seems to hang in the air. He concludes with an oblique suggestion as to Cleaver's ultimate motives, in answer to the rhetorical question he'd posed at the beginning of the article. When he first met Cleaver, he said, he asked him what he would do if he had no more legal or financial problems and didn't have to "pursue a public survival strategy." Cleaver replied that what he wanted most was family life in a "dream house" with "all the electronic stuff." And, Allman suggested, probably the beefsteaks he'd praised even as a revolutionary. All those things, agreed Cleaver, "and a couple of good watchdogs" (33).

For some time, Cleaver stayed among the white evangelical Christians who patronized the Grahams and Otises and Robertses of the country, and in spring 1977 he branched off to found the Eldridge Cleaver Crusades, based in Stanford, California. There, Kathleen could become reacquainted with university life, now that much of the immediate pressure for survival was off, and the family could maintain contact with Ray Stedman's Peninsula Bible Church next door in Palo Alto while luxuriating nearby, on Art DeMoss's money, in "a $100,000 home in the plush Los Altos Hills" (Raab, 3; Albin Krebs, "Notes on People," *New York Times,* 2 April 1977, 12).

Kathleen, Eldridge, and DeMoss were the officers of the newly incorporated crusade. It seems that Cleaver spotted a gap in the evangelical ranks that would allow room for a black Jim and Tammy Bakker act that could potentially pull in millions, just as the Bakkers did on the PTL club. Such a crusade could not limit itself to an all-black congregation, even nationwide, if it were to flourish; a majority of the fans would have to be white. With Cleaver's old charisma working again, and Kathleen, who had at least once been styled as an "actress" in a biographical dictionary of black celebrities,[4] at his side, how could they fail? They were attractive, articulate, and endorsing Jesus. Their photogenic golden skin and pale eyes would not serve as hindrances, either. This plan was to fill Cleaver's mind for approximately two years. In May 1979 he went so far as to purchase 80 acres of Nevada desert in the hope of establishing a "multimillion dollar facility" there as a base for the ministry, even as he maintained his Hollywood pants boutique.[5]

Responding to criticism from those blacks who were not too disenchanted to listen at all, Cleaver began to diversify his audiences in the summer of 1977. He had been appearing at places like the San Diego Sports Arena, where in February he and Charles Colson spoke and where local organizer Ken Overstreet, whom Cleaver had met at the federal facility there, gave Cleaver all of the after-expenses take on the evening's collection (Bill Ritter, "Cleaver and Colson Praise the Lord," *In These Times,* 13 April 1977, 24), and the Portland Coliseum, where on Easter morning Cleaver held 7,000 "lily white" Christians spellbound during the dawn service of the Portland Christian Layman's group (Raab, 3). When he was challenged by a reporter in Portland,

Cleaver at first refused to respond to any questioning of the authenticity of his conversion, but then "he understood why some people did not believe his conversion because some 'didn't believe Jesus Christ, either' " (Albin Krebs, "Notes on People," *New York Times,* 12 April 1977, 38). In mid-May, Cleaver felt the wrath of the Vancouver-based Anarchist Party of Canada (Groucho-Marxist), members of which "pied" him during an "I Found It" rally in that city with an Oreo pie, selected because "Oreo cookies are black on the outside and white on the inside, just like Eldridge Cleaver" (Martin VanLubin, "Pie People Find Cleaver," *Open Road,* Summer 1977, 4).

Returning from Vancouver, Cleaver began to book himself into black churches. One of the best known was the Providence Baptist Church in San Francisco, whose pastor, Calvin Jones, was a sponsor of the Eldridge Cleaver Crusades (Reginald Major, "I Have Not Made a Deal with Anyone Except Christ," *Berkeley Barb,* 8 July 1977, 3). Cleaver's testimony there contained not only his account of his metamorphosis but a list of complaints about his treatment since his return, particularly by those black politicians who didn't "lift a finger" (3) to help him when he needed it. He even named some of them: State Assemblyman Willie Brown, Lieutenant Governor Mervyn Dymally, and Los Angeles Mayor Tom Bradley (3). Every black person in power seemed to be as much against Cleaver as Thurgood Marshall had been in 1968; even Judge Lionel Wilson, who had doubled Cleaver's bail when he arrived in the Alameda County Jail in 1976, had since become mayor of Oakland, with the backing of the Panthers and the Dellums "machine." Black rejection of Cleaver undoubtedly made him feel bitter about criticism that he was ignoring blacks, and his complaints helped to get his side of things straight.

Cleaver's partnership with white evangelicals was to reveal yet another area of conflict with other blacks. Whereas black Americans would react to the liberation struggles of black Africans by supporting the blacks without reference to their actual politics, whites (and Cleaver as well, since his rejection of Third World communism), would look at the Communist sympathies of such groups and opt for "uncritical support for the white minority governments of Rhodesia and South Africa" (3). Such a stance would invariably be perceived by blacks not as anti-Communist but as antiblack, especially when Cleaver was quoted criticizing as "racist" any partisanship toward "those niggers trying to push our brothers into the sea" in the southern part of Africa (3).

James Tinney's interview came out on 8 July, the same day as Reginald Major's snide assessment, although the audiences of the day probably didn't overlap. When he was asked why he saw more of white Christians than black ones, Cleaver, leaving out the politicians this time, again voiced his grievances against his "former friends and associates in the black community" who had called him "an FBI or CIA agent" and "asked black people not to help me."[6] He refrained from blaming the black clergy for rejecting him, regarding them as "confused" or lacking "adequate information," but, he noted, "many white preachers . . . came to see me" (Tinney, 14).

When Tinney asked what could be done "to reach young blacks with the Gospel," Cleaver pointed out a need to "strike a balance," giving them religion in "a language they can understand, relevant and contemporary and yet full of the truth of Christianity." Specifically, he commented on his own failure in using the "Four Spiritual Laws" of the Campus Crusade for Christ, insisting "they could not communicate to black people" (15). The Crusade's booklet, "Have You Heard of the Four Spiritual Laws?" had been in print for twelve years at the time. According to its author, Bill Bright, "approximately 1,000,000,000 copies . . . have been printed"[7] to date, indicating that the Crusade has seen a measure of success with it. The four "laws," each buttressed with two or three Biblical quotations and embellished by further commentary toward the end of the booklet, read as follows:

(1) Law One—
God **loves** you, and offers a wonderful **plan** for your life.
(2) Law Two—
Man is **sinful** and **separated** from God. Therefore, he cannot know and experience God's love and plan for his life.
(3) Law Three—
Jesus Christ is God's **only** Provision for Man's Sin. Through Him you can know and experience God's Love and plan for your life.
(4) Law Four—
We must individually **receive** Jesus Christ as Savior and Lord; then we can know and experience God's love and plan for our lives.

                                                      (Bright, 2–8 passim)

The language is not the parlance of the streets; moreover, it is abstract and colorless, as that of "laws" always is. The speaker must bring these laws to life by demonstrating, in specific ways that relate to the experiences of the members of his or her congregation, how it is that those members experience sin and separation, and how a conversion experience would change that. Presumably, bringing the words to life is what Cleaver could not do, either because he was out of touch with the sort of youth he was trying to reach or because, as others indicated, he lacked conviction and therefore charisma this time around.

Cleaver might have done well in a prison ministry, as Charles Colson did (although William Warnken reported a speech at the Wisconsin State Prison that did not go over well [58]), or among young gang members, but he does not appear to have cultivated such audiences, except for ex-Muslims. When we look at the contrast between points like the Crusade's emphasis on sin and the typical black prisoner's sense of his own innocence in view of the wrongs done to him by society (as described in *Soul on Ice*), we can see the potential for either a complete rejection of Christianity or a meaningful dialogue. It is possible, in addition to these two likelihoods, that Cleaver felt both sides of the argument equally; such ambivalence might well undercut the efficacy of one's testimony.

Another obstacle for Cleaver himself might have been the de-emphasis on emotion. In the Crusade booklet, accompanying the admonition that "the Bible—not our feelings—is our authority" is a small drawing showing a locomotive marked FACT pulling a coal tender marked FAITH and a caboose marked FEELING (12). The text assures the reader that "the train will run with or without the caboose," which is a fairly conservative stance theologically but also one that is anticharismatic and anti-Cleaver, in the final analysis. One need only look back to Don Schanche's account of a typical Cleaver speech or read a transcript of a talk or telephone communication to become aware that when he was speaking before an audience Cleaver usually fell back on clichés and rhetoric in the form of a series of one-liners or short set pieces. It is not hard to see why he would have dropped the Campus Crusade rather quickly and branched off on his own, where he could "adapt" the "Four Spiritual Laws" (Tinney, 15).

A *Newsweek* update on Cleaver and Seale in September, belatedly entitled "The Party's Over," signaled to the American public both that Cleaver and Seale had ended their action-filled careers as revolutionaries and that the Black Panther party had come to an end, "withered back to its roots in Oakland, California."[8] While Seale merely quit, "an engagingly unembarrassed deserter" who was "broke and unemployed" in

1977, Cleaver, it was implied, had to stage a "coming to Christ" to account for his abandonment of the cause and to avoid the degree to which Seale had become insolvent. Hence, Cleaver's "sawdust-trail ministry as pastor of his own Third Cross Church of the Holy Ghost." Of his return, Cleaver was quoted in perhaps the most damaging words since he had arrived. "People say I crawled back," he told *Newsweek* with "a trace of scorn," but "I thought I did a rather imaginative little three-step. I was in an impossible position" ("The Party's Over," 29). He did not say exactly what the "little three-step" was, but many were undoubtedly ready to believe that he referred to his newly found political and religious conservatism, as well as to his supposed arrangements to testify before the Internal Security Subcommittee of the Senate Judiciary Committee.

Advertisements for Himself

In 1978, the long-promised book appeared, entitled, in an obvious allusion to *Soul on Ice, Soul on Fire.* The title didn't help to sell books, however; the audience for born-again testimonies was limited and remained so, Cleaver's name less of a draw than that of Charles Colson, whose 1976 *Born Again* went through nine printings before coming out as a Bantam paperback in March 1977. Evangelists had awaited the book as salable documentary proof of the power of Christ to change lives. George Otis had gushed, "What a book that will be!" (140) but when it came out, only Christian believers found anything of interest, let alone of value, in it.

Jeffrey S. Goldsmith's three-paragraph review in *Christian Century* referred to the book as "a fascinating story of intrigue and political maneuvering."[9] "To read this story," declared Goldsmith, "is to watch the struggle of a soul to be born, the struggle of a man coming to grips with himself and his God." Barbara Nauer's review in the Catholic periodical *America* recommended *Soul on Fire* while dooming it as "disappointing."[10] A more demanding critic, Nauer faulted Cleaver for "the disjointedness of this book as a whole," noting that it was made up of pieces from several other "would-be books. The black child's story, the Panther's story, the religious believer's story, the loving husband's and father's story, etc.," "loose and vaguely related chunks" of which were all "pull[ed] together . . . into one rather confused telling." The complaint is apt, but Nauer blames "Word company's editors," not Cleaver, for both the disorganization they "encouraged" and the "grammatically sloppy or obscure syntax" they permitted. The subject, she asserted, deserved "more careful thought and clearer prose than this" (Nauer, 458). The one area on which Nauer departs from mainstream critics is her acceptance of Cleaver's "obviously sincere" involvement with Christian groups; she declares that "the Christian believer easily recognizes Cleaver's turning to Jesus Christ as an authentic event of grace" (458). Her own faith and enthusiasm for Cleaver's "gradual discovery of Communism's philosophical wrongness and overall baseness" probably account for her lack of cynicism.

Richard Gilman, whose 1968 review of *Soul on Ice* became a contentious topic in itself, sadly declared that the question of whether whites could accurately assess "political and ideological material" by blacks that was intended not as art but "as a source of morale for blacks" had become "academic" in this case. There was no need, in Gilman's view, to make a special niche for an amoral, self-interested genre that rejected the very concept of consensus. *Soul on Fire* was simply bad: "A slipshod, ill-written, spiritless piece of work from any point of view."[11] While accepting Cleaver's conversion as "doubtless honest," Gilman lamented his "complete loss of eloquence" and his heavy reliance on "clichés and platitudes" (31).

The dismayed critics asked themselves, in effect, "What happened?" Gilman selected a passage from an early chapter in the book: "Young people . . . trekked to the Haight to escape the cacophony of Babylon, the clank and clatter of a trussed up butcher shop of a society busy slaughtering the innocence and conscience of its youth in sleek, swift sacrifice to the dead gods of avarice and power" (31; 80 in *Fire*). This writing, lamented Gilman, is "gnarled and pretentious." Elsewhere, Gilman found "obvious and simple minded" (31) prose that either told the reader incredibly juvenile facts like "The Louvre houses the world's largest art collection" or fell into awkward biblical clichés like "It must have rained for 40 days and 40 nights." "It is all very sad," concluded Gilman, suggesting that perhaps Cleaver's "erratic and wayward talent" might have bloomed only when he was directly plugged into the "pressures and dramas" of his day (31). Out of the headlines, Cleaver dealt now with the right-wingers who were not in the mainstream of social activity but "at the cocksure, self-righteous edge of it" (32). Cleaver, like Charles Colson, had become, Gilman adjudged, "a footnote to the history of his time" (30).

There are two major problems with *Soul on Fire* that seriously affect its credibility: the first concerns outright lies or omissions, the second a clash of tone between the material written in Paris and that added later. Some of that newer prose, written to bring the account up to date, was simply inserted into earlier passages about Cleaver's criminal or postprison Panther days.

The misrepresentations exist purely to create a palatable "Born-Again Cleaver" for the presumed audience of the book. Thus not only are the sorts of intrigues and machinations described to Henry Gates and Curtice Taylor omitted (including every word about Tim Leary), but Cleaver goes out of his way to deny that he was naked when he came out of the cellar with Bobby Hutton on the night of 6 April 1968. His new, greatly attenuated account of that evening lacks all the detail, imagery, and drama of his earlier version in "Affidavit #2: Shootout in Oakland" (*Post*, 80–94). In *Soul on Fire* he says, "As I limped forward (reports of my being naked were exaggerated), one cop called me a name and told me to run to the paddy wagon" (23). Why would anyone have thought he was naked? Because he said so himself! Recounting the impact of a tear gas canister against his chest in the dark of the cellar, Cleaver had noted, "It knocked me down and almost out. Little Bobby, weak from the gas, was coughing and choking, but he took all my clothes off in an effort to locate a wound in the dark, patting me down for the moist feel of blood" (*Post*, 90). This summary of the events immediately preceding his exile, along with his reactions to ending it, opens the book. There follow the two chapters on youthful life already discussed in chapter 1 of this study, and then abruptly he is in prison.

The prison chapter, "3,285 Days Equals Prison," concerns two topics: Cleaver's sessions with a psychiatrist and his membership in the Black Muslims. I have already discussed his alteration of the occasion of his seeing a psychiatrist, as well as his reaction to the doctor's diagnosis; possibly a blend of the two versions is closest to reality, but Cleaver preferred to eliminate from *Soul on Fire* any reference to his lust for white women. It was, however, acceptable for one who had found Christ to have committed various crimes (in Cleaver's case, in fact, it was essential for him to establish himself as a degenerate in his former life), and so he readily admits to having been stoned on mace and raving as the immediate cause of his referral to a psychiatrist. Such an incident may have actually occurred in isolation or at about the same time as the "nervous breakdown" Cleaver relates in *Soul on Ice* (11). In each case the topic of his ravings included racism (and in *Soul on Ice* only, "white women in particular") (11) and resulted in the diagnosis that Cleaver hated his mother. In each book, Cleaver indicated that he rejected the diagnosis, but for different reasons. In the earlier version, he emphasized "the racial question" while the psychiatrist asked him repeatedly about "my family life, my childhood." Cleaver's psychological defenses did not permit such introspection then or later in life; thus, he insisted that it was the doctor who was avoiding unpleasant reality, not himself. The political and racial issues were the "real" ones that were hard to face: "This was a Pandora's box [the doctor] did not care to open" (11). In *Soul on Fire,* however, Cleaver's old political ideas are treated ambivalently. They are endorsed indirectly, in the relish with which he describes Panther life and condemns "pigs" and Richard Nixon, but not overtly. Hence, he expresses only confusion over the diagnosis: "I never understood why he said I hated my mother, because it wasn't true. Father hate, yes" (73).

On the one hand, there is something so important about this experience that Cleaver needs to tell about it twice, bowdlerizing the objectionable sexual material the second time. On the other hand, he resists the diagnosis both times, indicating that he had not gained a deeper insight into himself that he wanted to share; there is no reevaluation of the psychotherapy. The one thing he does add is his claim that the doctor ended up in prison for falsely declaring a man insane, thus firming up Cleaver's own refusal to see rape, male chauvinism, or his "phallocentric trousers," as one writer has called them,[12] as signs of a hatred for all women that began at home. Another possibility also exists: that Cleaver did not review *Soul on Ice* before he wrote *Soul on Fire,* and that he forgot he had included the psychiatrist episode in his essay "Becoming." This likelihood comes to mind because of the opening paragraph of the short (four-page) segment that contains that material in *Soul on Fire.* It reads: "Since I covered so much of the Black Muslim routine in *Soul on Ice* and my deep attachment to the personality and teachings of Malcolm X, it is important here to discuss some topics that I purposely avoided in that first book. Prison psychiatry is one. By far my most harrowing experience was with the shrinks and what they were trying to do to Negroes on the inside. But when one is still serving time, it doesn't advance the hours to reveal the awful truth about penal practices" (70). The reasoning of the first sentence is unclear, as is its structure; to say that it is important to discuss prison psychiatry because the Muslims and Malcolm X were covered in *Soul on Ice* is imprecise, when Cleaver seems to mean he'd rather discuss something other than those two topics in this new book. The key phrase, however, is "topics that I purposely avoided," when in fact he did not avoid the topic of prison psychiatry at all. Further, in this brief section prison psychiatry was the only topic, not one of several. This is the sort of disjointedness of which Barbara Nauer had complained; in this case, apparently the author and a much less competent set of editors than those at McGraw-Hill "made selections" from a larger manuscript or two. But the discontinuity extends beyond the lacunae in this text to contradictions and inconsistencies within the body of Cleaver's published work. It is as if the older material, even things from the last days in Paris, didn't exist and need not be taken into account, as if they disappeared along with the "old" Cleaver.

The Black Muslin section of the prison chapter, the third of four, takes up six pages. In them, Cleaver touches upon discovering Elijah Muhammad through the mundane process of copying Elijah's paid advertisements in the *Los Angeles Herald Dispatch* into the prison newsletter, the use the Panthers made of the Muslim antidrug creed, and the practice of police departments to arrest all black males in the ghetto in order to have their fingerprints on file. In between, Cleaver hits on two points: that Malcolm was his role model and that he now wishes to take the Eldridge Cleaver Crusades into the prisons to minister to "these bewildered Muslims" (78).

In the Footsteps of Malcolm X

Cleaver's identification with Malcolm X was always obvious. In *Soul on Ice,* he spoke of him as a role model for all black prisoners, "a symbol of hope" because he had "risen from the lowest depths to great heights" (58). In *Soul on Fire,* however, he identified with Malcolm on a more personal level, tracing that sense of kinship back to his own Muslim days. Malcolm, in addition, had been the only radical role model who was not explicitly rejected by Cleaver in the "vision in the moon" episode of which he had made so much. Ironically, he speaks of having "closely modelled my thinking and action after Malcolm X" during the time he was in prison and refers to this period as "those years of metamorphosis from reckless criminal to respected leader in the black community" (75). His use of the phrase "respected leader" with reference to his "off the pig" Panther days cannot stem from a desire to convince his audience of evangelicals and their flocks, but it reveals his self-image rather well. "Like me," he says, Malcolm "had been a gangster (in Chicago), ruthless and gun-toting" (75). Actually, Malcolm's criminal career had had its center in New York and Boston. When he was arrested, it was in the latter city. Chicago was Elijah's (and Leroy Cleaver's, finally) home base, a possible source of "father figure" confusion in Cleaver's mind.

Malcolm had rejected the racism of Elijah Muhammad's Muslimism in favor of the egalitarian Muslimism of Mecca while Cleaver was in prison, a change that fitted Cleaver's basic personality far better than the Nation of Islam's wild theories about the origin of the "white devil" in the schemes and crossbreeding experiments of a mad scientist called Yacub on the island of Patmos 6,600 years ago.[13] Cleaver's decision to follow Malcolm instead of Muhammad when the split occurred was based as much on his own early interracial experiences as on his respect for and identification with Malcolm. As he points out in *Soul on Fire,* he had been not only "in the center" of the Muslim split in prison but also central "in the division of the Panther Party" (76). Since it was Cleaver who announced the split, in as public a way as possible, over an international line on a television talk show, it is tempting to speculate that he had made the decision to break up the party at least partly because he was emulating Malcolm's successful move. As Newton and the Oakland group moved more toward reformism, Cleaver may have felt, in his increasingly militant isolation, that it was he who was Malcolm's heir and that the original Panthers had sold out. He seems to draw such a parallel in *Soul on Fire* when he begins to speak of the two splits. "Malcolm . . . was the living sign of the future for thousands and thousands of blacks. Increasingly, Elijah and his inner circle became uncomfortable with the hard line that the heir apparent was taking" (76). In his case, Cleaver didn't wait to be expelled; he moved first. Like himself, "Malcolm was the realist to follow and eventually to fight for" (77), was "all politics and economics, something that was practical and visible" (76). It was his followers who chose the correct side of "the doctrinal split" (77), just as Cleaver had probably assumed in 1971 that his own followers had, too. By the time he was writing *Over My Shoulder,* however, parts of which became the early portions of *Soul on Fire,* he had already abandoned the idea of militant leadership. Hence his summary remark, "And when you split, things don't always multiply, sometimes they divide and fade" (76).

The death threats issued against both men by the other side offer another parallel in their lives and may have added considerably to Cleaver's fear of return. Malcolm's enemies made good their threats, and Cleaver knew, as Malcolm had, that among his doctrinal and personal adversaries were plenty of vengeful people with criminal pasts and skill in the use of arms. It is not mere paranoia that led Cleaver to fear taking food with Jacqueline Simon in Paris or having his wrists cuffed behind him at Kennedy Airport but, rather, an objective assessment of his situation.

In *Soul on Fire* the discussion of Malcolm segues into Cleaver's discussion of "disillusioned Black Muslims . . . especially in the Bay Area" and their need for a special ministry (78). They live in "psychological chaos," he says, because they are losing faith in Black Muslimism but "they cannot accept a white Jesus" (78). Perhaps this situation is part of the problem Cleaver alluded to in *Christianity Today* when he spoke of the difficulty of making the "Four Spiritual Laws" of the Campus Crusade relevant to black people. He had already made it part of his mission to meet with these Muslims. In a four-paragraph footnote to the paragraph cited earlier, Cleaver remarked that Wallace D. Muhammad, Elijah's son and heir, had created a "new theology" and "completely outmaneuvered his rivals," while helping considerably to "heal the theological and spiritual divisions plaguing black Americans" (78–79). By his insistence on removing "all racial images from religion," says Cleaver, Wallace "is challenging both white and black racism," and even "white theology and black theology stand indicted" (79). It is easy to see how a rejection of the "white devil" doctrine could help heal splits, but Cleaver is altogether vague as to the crime of "white theology" in this regard, unless perhaps it is the centuries-old Christian assumption that Jesus was Caucasian. Asking his white Christian supporters to reject a "white Jesus" in the name of "theological metamorphosis" (79) is probably the least winning of Cleaver's ideas in this chapter, not to mention the least promising. It would appear, however, that Cleaver aimed at something like that in his attempt to "reach out to these brothers and sisters" (79). Within two years, Cleaver had canceled the Eldridge Cleaver Crusades and set up what *Mother Jones* magazine called "his new Oakland, California, born-again-cum-Islam church, which is called Christlam."[14] A typically eccentric Cleaver creation, the "metamorphosis" died at birth. Cleaver, however, apparently having been thus weaned from Jesus, then began to "study" Mormonism.

Meeting the Panthers Again

The final short section of "3,285 Days Equals Prison" describes the Haight-Ashbury district and Cleaver's entry into it on parole late in

1966. It is this weak transitional segment that is cited with dismay by Nauer and Gilman (quoted earlier), with perfect fairness. It ends with Cleaver's correlation of his own negativism and confusion with those in the Haight. He wanted, he said, "the red rose of a real revolution . . . that would kill" anyone in "the ruling class" who opposed the change from capitalism to socialism, from private property to ownership by "all the people" (83). He hated "prisons" and "all social controls as they existed," which included even "jobs." "They were all like cells of the same cancerous tissue" and at the same time "a sickening brew," the "digital calibrations of the contours of a monstrous system in which we existed—walking, stumbling as though in a dream, seemingly through a maze, which nobody seemed to understand, caught up in a social entity, situation, and process that was as abstract and formless as the spiral in the tail of a galaxy spinning through a universe of space" (83–84). This is not clear and gripping writing, but it is probably an accurate depiction of Cleaver's state of mind before he met Newton and acquired a purpose in life.

The fifth chapter of *Soul on Fire,* "Panthers and Power," covers 17 pages, about half of which are devoted to explaining the use of Panther terms and doctrines. The opening section begins with the comment that the fall of 1967 was "ripe for the sudden rise of the Panthers" and then shifts immediately to "the other major civil rights group," the "Student Non-violent Coordination [*sic*] Committee" (87). There follows a blended sort of discussion of Cleaver's meeting and marrying Kathleen Neal, a "black bourgeois" college dropout who may have worked for SNCC in order to purge herself of privilege and authenticate her blackness, and of the Panther-SNCC "merger." As a gesture toward black unity, the marriage was "a perfect match" (88), the merger "a natural but not easy hookup" (89). It was perhaps the identification of the two unions in Cleaver's mind that was behind his insistence on the term *merger* even when the SNCC membership rejected it. Cleaver's assumption that Newton and the Panthers were the ones to be taken seriously because they were the "real men," the "brothers off the block" who should be accorded respect and deference, shows clearly in his condescending assessment of SNCC (and, probably unconsciously, of Kathleen, at the time).

The death of King in the spring of 1968 shook Stokely and Rap and James Forman right down to their sneakers. They had grown up within the safety and protection of the black middle class, the black bourgeoisie—and while they

could use some daring language and point to threatening events, it all was
played out on the secure carpet of a college dormitory, a student union ball-
room or campus parking lot. (89)

The SNCCs had come out of the Southern rural tradition; we were off the
ghetto pavement and rather prepared for the sound of gunfire. When Stokely
and Rap and some others first appeared at the Los Angeles airport following
the final merger, I had a delegation meet them, like bodyguards and a big
show of rifles and shotguns. They gulped as much as the airport security
personnel. . . . Well, we gave them plenty to think about. The only way to
deal with violence which was shedding its grace all over the United States—
and rather thoroughly in Vietman—was to pack some ourselves. I was very
much at home with this, and my swift rise in the Panther leadership circle
came from two sources: my celebrity status as the best-selling author of *Soul on
Ice* and my ghetto background which never choked at the sight or sound of a
gun. (90)

Cleaver's elucidation of Panther principles includes his taking credit for
steering the party away from racism (but not into Marxism-Leninism,
as Huey had charged); it does not, however, discuss the Ten Point
Program or any personal details of his life in those two years—that
information occurs later in the book. He refers to his own advocacy of
black urban guerrilla warfare and quotes himself from the final paragraph of "The Land Question and Black Liberation," but then halts for
a three-paragraph conclusion to that section on how much worse Communist countries are than the United States, a complete alteration of
tone that serves as a counterbalance, apparently, to the material from
1968–70 that has been quoted in the chapter without reassessment.

I had lived defiantly so long and in such seething hatred of all governments,
people in power, people in charge, that when I came under the shelter of
Communist powers, I sadly discovered that their corruption was as violent and
inhuman as the people they "victoriously" replaced. "Up against the wall" was
a trendy slogan of the underground movements around the world—but I later
learned that without inner control, a moral perspective, and a spiritual balance
that flowed out of Christian love, justice, and caring, the Communist promises
were to become the largest fraud of all.
    Pig power in America was infuriating—but pig power in the Communist
framework was awesome and unaccountable. No protection by outbursts in the
press and electronic media—the Reds owned it. No shelter under the benevo-
lent protection of a historic constitution—the Marxists held the book and they

tore out the pages that sheltered you. No counterweight from religious and church organizations—they were invisible and silent.

My adult education began in prison and was ruefully completed in the prison that is called Marxist liberation, "power to the people": that was meant for the party in control, writing the script, and enforcing the rules. I did mean it deeply when I said seven years later I would rather be in prison in America than free somewhere else. (97—98)

The last short portion of four pages pokes fun at J. Edgar Hoover, for whom the Panthers were "bread and butter" (100) for several years, as he demanded increasing funds to meet their threat, and assures us that Hoover was actually right; the Panthers were "more and more on the defensive," and grandiose schemes (none of which are identified with Cleaver) were being proposed. Cleaver mentions Newton's desire for a "red light finale" attempt to spring him from San Quentin, but not his own desire for a siege at Merritt College when he planned to refuse to surrender in November 1968. He refers to his and Huey's "paranoia" and also to the arms pileup "in our armory," fed by leaks at "military depots and national guard armories" (102). "It was happening all over America, and the government was aware that our gear was in a state of readiness" (102). Abruptly, just as he is speaking of the "massive, bloodletting upheaval" he expected, Cleaver stops and jumps to Watergate, ending the Panther chapter in a manner that could scarcely be more discordant and unconvincing:

It is my belief today that the court sentencing of John Mitchell, Bob Haldeman, and John Ehrlichmann did more to restore the affection and support of blacks for their government than anything else in the last twenty-five years. Everyone in the ghetto was saying, "Well, Mitchell won't go to jail. Rockefeller will get him off; the fix is in." But Big John is in the cooler, the Constitution proved stronger than the cries of San Clemente, and the whole lying crowd was thrown out of office. Must have made Moscow shudder and Castro cough. There are times when America is just plain beautiful. (102–3)

The relish with which Cleaver speaks of his Panther role as minister of information and the Panthers' "vanguard" status (SDS's disputed term for them) as the leaders in the fight against "pig power in America" (98) is not atoned for by his abrupt endorsement of the Constitution. The chain of reasoning and experience that could explain such a reversal is missing. In his interview with Cleaver in Paris, Curtice Taylor had suggested that perhaps the sixties were "a time to react and experience, not to reflect." Cleaver had countered: "I disagree with that. It was a time to reflect, it's just that we never did it. We don't have to reflect so much now as to reanalyze a lot of the shit we believed in at that time. . . . We have to do some turnarounds" (48). Cleaver turned around, but the process of reassessment and reanalysis is not conveyed in *Soul on Fire*.

The events of 1968 having been dealt with summarily in the intro-duction, Cleaver disposes of the Cuban experience in a few paragraphs at the beginning of the chapter on communism and in four other paragraphs scattered elsewhere. Cleaver contrasts his original expecta-tion of training a guerrilla force to wage war in the United States with his condemnation of Cuba as printed in *Newsweek* in May 1976. There is a solitary transitional passage: he hoped, he said, for mobile units to be able to tie up the regular army "in fruitless pursuit. . . . What turned out to be fruitless was the reality of such a camp in Cuba. I sat in my apartment wondering if I was the enemy in the eyes of nervous Cuban security guards" (108). So much for the intrigues and betrayals revealed in interviews a few years earlier. The months in Havana were not to be described here at all. One might think that the justification for the omission would be the irrelevance of such machinations to a book about the spiritual odyssey of a reformed enemy of the state, but the three chapters "Communism: Its Flowers and Thorns," "Blood and Wine Are Red," and "Algiers" dispel any hope for such conscious planning on the part of the author and editors. Here we find out, in more detail than anyone could care for, the exact wording of the dispute between Cleaver and Algerian president Houari Boumédienne on the topic of the hijack-ers' ransom money in 1972, for example. Cleaver reproduces in full his "open letter" to Boumédienne and Kathleen's nearly verbatim account of the Panther confrontation with Si Salah in his office on the eve of the Panther eviction. These two segments and their context cover 17 pages.

The disorganization of the first of these chapters is disconcerting, for much of the material actually belongs in "Panthers and Power" but is instead placed in the post-1968 Cuba segment on the tendentious assumption that any discussion of Panther use of or response to Marxism-Leninism or Chairman Mao's "Red Book" belongs under Cleaver's "response to Communism" rubric. Some of the references are to 1969 purges of individual members of the party in the name of Maoist discipline, but Cleaver also includes at last, halfway through the book on page 113, the components of the Panther 10-point program,

although "they were not fashioned from the Little Red Book nor written in Moscow" (113) but were merely intended to "redress the injustices of the black community, suffered for more than two hundred
years" (114). A three-and-a-half-page recap of the party from its origins
to the Sacramento confrontation follows, followed in turn by a separate
one-and-a-half-page segment certifying that the Panthers could not
"work" with the "two windbags," the Socialist Workers' party and the
American Communist party (119). After concluding the chapter with
his disillusionment over communism stemming from the 1970 trip to
North Korea and China (he does not mention the delegation), he opens
"Blood and Wine Are Red" back in Oakland in 1968 and tells us now,
far from his account of how he, the "aged convict" (101), had vetoed
Newton's "red light finale," that he had wished to hold Merritt College
as "a fortress" against the police who would try to take him in, to
"jump straight into a final shootout scenario" (137). It was Newton
who vetoed that idea, he says, and then mentions the plan that he go to
speak at Knoxville and hijack a plane to Cuba. Yet "before Tennessee
came an appearance at Stanford" (139), and we find ourselves in the
middle of a description of that speech and its setting. The account of
his escape, which continues in a new subsection on the next page,
recommences after a brief comment on the "ironies" of "being a black in
white America" (139). The "latest" of these, predictably and dismay-
ingly, has nothing to do with race. It is that Cleaver, once the fiery
critic, is now, in 1978, "a part of the Palo Alto Peninsula community"
to the extent that he was offered, he claims, "a teaching post" at
Stanford University (140). He thanks God for the "changes in [his] life
that made these happenings come about" (140) and opens a new segment, on the next page, with a reference back again to 1968: "The day
before I was to return to prison . . . " (141).

Stranger in Paris

The final chapter, "Finding God—Finding Eldridge," covers the
period from the beginning of Cleaver's residency in Paris in January
1973 (or August 1972) to the time of publication, 1978. Most of the
story concerns his attempts to acquire the status of legal alien and his
feelings of insecurity created by his state of "free-fall," as it were: an
unscheduled life with no clear future, no prospects for dependable
income, all questions about his status left unanswered, and no sense of
belonging where he was. It is as though Cleaver's life up to 1967 had

been so rigidly confined and structured as to make adaptation impossible when he was free, on top of which situation he had been without a fixed dwelling for more than a few months at a time during all that period, even in California. For one who had been accustomed to "cage life," to be out first on parole and then, in exile, completely on his own, with no assurance of food and shelter, was enough to keep blood pressure up and adrenalin pumping, even without the reality of political maneuvering taking place around him in a language he could not readily understand. It is not surprising that even by 1975 Cleaver had not settled in and become a permanent expatriate. His second concern, after survival, was a return to home and an end to the insecurity and uncertainty of the free-fall state.

Cleaver focuses completely on his dealings with Fanchon (insofar as she helped him, but not romantically) and with Giscard d'Estaing, except for the inclusion of his "vision" of the faces in the moon in the fall of 1975. The "vision" material is included for tactical reasons; he had already explained elsewhere that sometime before he left Paris, he had had a religious experience he didn't fully understand. He presented his decision to return as though it were motivated primarily *by* the vision, all in one moment of perfect clarity and understanding. There is, on the other hand, no reference to the famous pants, the "Cleavers," although he had told Simon in September 1975—only nine weeks before his return—that their creation had been chiefly responsible for his sense of well-being at the time.

In *Soul on Fire* Cleaver tells us that, far from being self-assured, he was on the verge of suicide all along, and that what saved him from despair and showed him the brightly lighted path home was Jesus. One could conclude that Cleaver's words to Jacqueline Simon were empty assurances of serenity and hope that masked a profound fear of the future, and that Cleaver's more authentic sense of an empty and meaningless life ahead of him was bound to assert itself. But such a conclusion fails to account for his decision to omit from his autobiography all reference to the pants, especially since he continued to manufacture them until 1979. One likely possibility is a decision of the editors at Word to cut all references to the "Cleavers" on the grounds that they adjudged the pants to be offensive to evangelistic readers, regardless of Cleaver's own opinion.

A more surprising omission is the account of Cleaver's discovery of Rauschenbusch's activist Christ, a discovery brought about by his rereading of Martin Luther King. According to his 1976 *Reader's Digest* interview, Cleaver had read King again during the dark days in Paris and had read Rauschenbusch either then or in prison in 1976. The possibility for creating a credible link between the old and the new Cleaver through his new insight into Christ as a "socialist" who loved the poor seems perfect; for Cleaver to go from being a revolutionary out of a misguided atheistic humanitarianism to being a reformer out of a Christ-based social ethic would be elegantly symmetrical and quite believable, but the opportunity is thrown away. There remains the temptation for the reader to wonder whether its omission meant that the material was forgotten or disregarded, and was so because it was untrue. At the least, Cleaver's religious reassessments are no more adequately described than his political ones were.

One thing Cleaver did not omit from his closing chapter was his assurance to his readers that he had made no "deal" with anyone, aside from the provision that he would be protected from the Oakland Police Department and the California Department of Corrections, or state prison system, because he feared for his life if he fell into their hands (217). This is an occasion for born-again gush that he could not pass up.

> Many people have looked at what happened and concluded that I must have made a deal with the authorities. This is very intriguing to me: what they are saying is that such things just do not happen, that the whole surrender event was extraordinary and therefore a pay-off was involved. They had to insist on this—otherwise they would have to consider the miracle of salvation involved.
>
> Yes. They are right. I did make a deal; I made a deal with Jesus Christ! Yes, as well as I was able to understand it at that moment, I sold out; I sold out to Jesus! When I surrendered, I was stumbling ahead on faith and a vision, on assurance of the reality and truth of God, but I was still stumbling.
>
> Little did I realize how totally I was surrendering. Nor did I understand I was surrendering on two levels—to the civil authorities and to God. I am harping on this point, screaming out what seems to me a very vital fact—the act of stepping out on faith—because I clearly did not know what was going to happen. All I had was the assurance that things were going to turn out all right. (216–17)

If speaking engagements are an index of success, then things were indeed looking rather good in 1978. Since his release, Cleaver exulted, he had been invited to speak "on approximately fifty university campuses and eight Christian college and university campuses" in addition to "scores of churches and service clubs, on television programs, in prisons" and to individuals (231). Of all the occasions just listed, we may be reasonably sure that all but the personal discussions "with former friends and followers" carried an honorarium of some sort.

The negative verdict of the critics is certainly warranted, but as we have seen, the flaws in *Soul on Fire* go beyond stylistic or structural concerns to the core of the book itself. As a spiritual odyssey of a man who has rethought the basic assumptions of his life and become a new person, the book fails because it does not present the process by which the author realigned himself with society, became a reformist rather than revolutionary, and returned to the Christianity, specifically the Bible Belt Protestantism, of his youth after flirtations with Catholicism, Muslimism, and atheism. As a story of how a twentieth-century political figure fared in the most crucial decade of his life, it is an insipid misrepresentation of Cleaver's life as told elsewhere, in bits and pieces, by himself. The book can only be perceived as a poorly written cut-and-paste job, a self-serving version of events that is designed as a lengthy résumé, so to speak, that will get him even more speaking engagements and perhaps a career as a televangelist. For an intelligent and well-informed audience, it is insulting.

Two other planned books never appeared, quite possibly for reasons related to the varied failures of *Soul on Fire.* When Word Books first announced *Soul on Fire,* there was also mention of another Word book in the works, *Letters to My Children,* which was never published (Albin Krebs, "Notes on People," *New York Times,* 15 December 1977, C2). And in 1980, after he had folded the Eldridge Cleaver Crusades, Cleaver was reported to be at work on a study called *Divine Deception,* about "spiritual manipulation—not only in cults but also on 'acceptable levels' " (Alan Rumsey, "Did Cleaver Find God Just in Time?" *Berkeley Barb,* 21 February 1980, 7). Presumably, after his abandonment of evangelism Cleaver planned to expose the industry and turn to politics. That book, though supposedly completed, never broke into print either.

The Famous Pants

In 1978, Cleaver continued to promote both sides of his personality. In September, not long after *Soul on Fire* appeared, *Jet* ran a major article on the pants. Surprisingly, *Jet* illustrated the article with a photograph of Cleaver modeling his pants in front of his boutique; the article also contained a further interpretation of his philosophy of clothing design.

Soon after Cleaver's return to the United States, he had explained to *Jet* interviewer Gregory Simms that the "fig leaf mentality," or the decrees of "elders and priests" of old that the penis ought to be covered, was actually an attempt to eliminate the "content of erotic art forms" (the genitals) from view because their visibility and the sexual interest they generated had "a slowing down effect on efficiency and production." Thus, the "luxurious sexuality" of the East had to be subordinated to the exigencies of early capitalism, so to speak.[15]

The second *Jet* article on the pants appeared two years later and carried a more elaborate discussion of Cleaver's theory. In this 1978 article Cleaver confessed to having been "very sexually warped" in the past but said he now viewed himself as having "studied as much about human sexuality as professional sexual therapists."[16] Part of his plan to help others included a "finishing school for boys to teach them various things like manners . . . a modern version of the Chase—that is, how to go about getting themselves girls without having to resort to rape." Another consisted of "a 24-hour rape hotline for men who either have committed rape or are on the verge of rape," sort of a Rapist's Anonymous. And finally, there are the pants, which *Jet* describes as featuring "two types of eye-catching pouches: one is oval shaped like a football player's jockey cup and the other features a tubular shaped extension for the man's penis and an adjoining smaller pouch for his testicles" (22). According to Cleaver, men have been "castrated" by pants; "pants were originally designed to corral the penis" (22). Today, however, there is more at stake than eroticism. Having had more time to contemplate his pants, Cleaver announced that "heat had a decomposing effect on the sperm and traditional pants press the penis underneath the belly. My pants take it back out" (23). The fact that sperm are not produced in the penis is apparently disregarded as a boring detail in favor of the emphasis on masculinity that the "revolutionary pants" provide.

In 1977 Cleaver had told T. D. Allman that the pants were designed to "honor" the sex organs, whereas most clothing had given such honor only to "the intellect—the head and face" (Allman, 11). In this remark we seem to hear an echo of the barbaric yawp of the Supermasculine Menial from *Soul on Ice;* ready to join the subdued and presumably undersexed ranks of the Omnipotent Administrators, Cleaver had to declare, even if in the most bizarre and tasteless of ways, that he was still a sexual being. Perhaps even more important, Cleaver may have been responding to the Panther charge that he was a coward and a "punk without genitals," as depicted by Emory Douglas, especially now that Cleaver was moving to the right politically.

Cleaver's commitment to his "Cleavers" was serious. Unable to obtain financing in France, where good taste is still manifest in the fashion industry, he invested $42,000 of his royalties into their manufacture when he returned home and was finally in control of his finances again. With this money he established Eldridge Cleaver Ltd., which included both the small factory that made the pants and a retail store in West Hollywood (22). The pants, which sold for $20 to $30 apiece in 1978, were considered by Cleaver to be "one of the best ideas I've ever had," an item that would "open up the relationship between men and women" (Ray Riegert, "The Return of a Radical Ghost," *Berkeley Barb*, 16 January 1976, 5).

Probation

During the period that Cleaver's trial was repeatedly postponed, and Cleaver was battling to suppress evidence against him that he insisted was gathered illegally, he continued to claim that he would accept "the will of the Lord" as to his fate. Finally, with his trial on the original six felony counts set for January 1980, Cleaver saw that it was his will, if not the Lord's, that he make a deal. In the summer of 1979 he had already had a "vision," ignored by all, that California would soon be struck by a "natural disaster" and that "immediate steps" had to be taken "to evacuate the state" (Keerdoja, 12). When that failed to distract the California officials, Cleaver's insight presented him with a new phrase: plea bargain. With a potential 72-year prison term waiting for him, he chose in November to plead guilty to three charges of assault in exchange for the dropping of attempted-murder charges against him ("Cleaver Pleads Guilty to Assault," *New York Times*, 18 November 1979, 26).

Right after New Year's 1980 Cleaver was placed on probation and ordered to do 2,000 hours "of undetermined community service," the time later cut to 1,200 hours. Judge Winton McKibben, who had also approved the plea bargain, listened to Cleaver's claim that he wanted to work "with children and the unemployed in Oakland in the hope of cutting the crime rate" and pronounced him cured. "I believe," McKibben said, "people should have a chance to rehabilitate themselves. I feel you have changed for the better and I feel it would be

highly vindictive to send you to jail" ("Eldridge Cleaver Given Probation for 1968 Assault," *New York Times*, 4 January 1980, 6).

While Cleaver awaited sentencing, an article on him appeared in
Christianity Today indicating the kind of help he meant to give the
unemployed. He proposed the institution of a Debtor's Bank of America, in which the poor would deposit bills rather than money, accept
the "union" as their bargaining agent, and send all bill collectors to the
"bank," where a coalition of the government and the philanthropic rich
would make the troubles go away. [17] In this manner, one could declare
bankruptcy weekly, it would seem, while continuing to live on perpet-
ual credit. Cleaver's old obsession with the conflict between poverty
and materialism among what he used to call the lumpen had created a
new way to guarantee "the right to consume" that went beyond welfare,
as he had in the past said it should, to the "blank check" concept of
federal aid.

Meanwhile, Cleaver had begun a relationship with the Unification
Church of the much-maligned cult leader, the Reverend Sun Myung
Moon. He attended a six-week session at the "Moonie" ranch in Southern California, and returned willing to work for the cause. In the
process of phasing out his own unsuccessful religious entrepreneurship,
he began to attend Moonie gatherings in Oakland and to work with the
Unification group called Project Volunteer, which was involved in
social service projects in Oakland (Maust, 49). And he no longer attended Ray Stedman's Peninsula Bible Church in Palo Alto, declaring,
"I follow no man" (50).

With the free-fall condition he had endured for so long now over, at
least with regard to his legal affairs, Cleaver could settle down to
finding a place for himself in the economy. He had run up legal bills of
more than $350,000, and even though much of that had been paid by
donations, he still had debts. [18] He retained his born-again status, but
he moved from the mainline Christianity he had been patronizing over
to the fringe, where he had always felt more comfortable. He also
retained his old interest in politics, and in the eighties ran for office
again, first as an independent, then as a serious candidate on the
Republican ticket.

He began to travel on the lecture circuit with the Moonie campus
organization called the Collegiate Association for the Research of Principles, or CARP. In February 1980, accompanied by ex-Communist
Moonie Nadine Hack, he gave a guest lecture back at his old favorite,

the University of California at Berkeley, where the two visited a class on the "Theory of Collective Behavior" taught by Professor Bruce Fireman (Rumsey, 7). Presumably, they spoke on the collective behavior of leftists from the viewpoint of those who had been "on the inside," although they would serve as well as classic object lessons on the human tendency to switch from an authoritarian left-wing worldview to an equally authoritarian right-wing view in middle age; however, it is not possible to ascertain whether demonstrating the latter had been the teacher's intent. There were no crowds at the unpublicized event, but the inevitable *Berkeley Barb* reporter made an appearance and interviewed Cleaver briefly for the paper. Cleaver used the opportunity to announce his support for the Reverend Moon and to indict the "TV ministries which divert contributions into their own coffers," unlike the Unification Church, which involved itself in community affairs (7). The Reverend Moon, Cleaver admitted, was "open to charges of interfering in the internal affairs of the U.S." government in his effort to help "save the world from Communism," but "Billy Graham has sanctioned far more heinous sins of the government," although these remained unnamed. Ironically, Cleaver announced the completion of his *Divine Deception* manuscript on "spiritual manipulation" of the various faithful while denouncing the deprogrammers who tried to "un-brainwash" young Moonies. "I disagree strongly with people willing to violate the First Amendment rights of others," he stated, pointing out that he himself served as a "go-between" to "bridge the gap" between parents and converted children (7). *Divine Deception* never saw print; if it had, the public might have learned what specific incidents led to Cleaver's disillusionment with mainstream evangelism in general and to his reversal of his estimate of Billy Graham in particular.

While working as a Moonie volunteer, Cleaver continued to toy with a ministry to ex-Muslims and his "metamorphosis" of Christianity into Christlam. While he had abandoned the Eldridge Cleaver Crusades and the "Cleavers," he continued to formulate increasingly outrageous theories.

His remarks hit a paranoid, male-chauvinist low in a September 1980 *Mother Jones* item on the "Frontlines" page. In a phrase echoing the "precious bodily fluids" of the general in *Dr. Strangelove,* Cleaver asserted that "the dwelling place of God" was not in the North African desert in Mecca, as traditional Muslims believe, but "in the male sperm"; accordingly, he instituted "the Guardians of the Sperm," a "social auxiliary" to his new church in Oakland.

To Cleaver, the enemy—"ignorant scientists and lesbian propagandists"—used a variety of weapons "to murder sperm": "artificial chemicals, nooses, traps inside the female body" exist to prevent the sperm from completing its godlike task of reproduction. Because sex is the necessary means of reproduction, Cleaver saw his church's mission clearly as a sex facilitator. Expanding beyond his 1978 "finishing school" concept, Cleaver said his church would "teach a course called 'Urban Geography' to young men" (Klapper, 8). Explained Cleaver, "You see a good-looking woman on the street corner. Immediately you want to screw her. But you let her get away because you don't know how to follow her. We teach pursuit" (8). The now-defunct pants would have fit perfectly with Christlam's devoutly sexist outlook. According to ex–*Ramparts* editor Warren Hinckle, who was writing for the *San Francisco Chronicle,* Cleaver even alluded with pride to the old Panther charges that he had beaten Kathleen. Without openly admitting anything, he declared, "I don't mind being known as a wife-beater. There are all kinds of institutions to serve these so-called battered wives. What nobody's saying is that most of the time the bitch needed her ass kicked" (8). While Hinckle implied that these remarks were made during a free-ranging conversation in a barroom, they still reflected badly upon Cleaver's image.

To Huey

In the summer of 1980 Cleaver also wrote another of his open letters, this one addressed to Huey Newton (now as *Doctor* Newton), with whom he still vainly hoped to achieve a reconciliation. He began by asserting that "unity, trust and brotherhood need fostering on an emergency basis among American Blacks" and that "one of the best things that could happen in America is if you and I would bury our old hatchets, which in fact have been buried by time and events, and help constitute a force in America dedicated to serving our needs at this juncture."[19] The nature of the crisis: "Ronald Reagan is running for President. . . . Gas, Food, Water and Time are running out." And in a typically Cleaver-like mixed metaphor, he insisted, "We must put forth a step of unity that comprehends both the victories and defeats of our past struggles, that comes to grips with the choices of the present, and weighs the options of our future" ("Brother," 43). More specifically, blacks in 1980 lacked what Cleaver called a "leadership capable of digging in it's [sic] heels and going for the jugular vein of the beast of oppression."

The newly reunited pair would be the perfect nominees. As a plea for nostalgia, Cleaver referred to all they had endured together in the old days: "We have been slaughtered and traumatized by the onslaughter [*sic*] of Co-Intelpro and by our own mistakes and shortcomings." In the past, they suffered, but now that the pressure is off, Cleaver suggests, "We are in a growth stage" (44).

We made the supreme sacrifice in the Sixties, when we confronted the guns of the Establishment. Our blood was shed. Some of our Comrades died in battle. We shed the blood of our enemy. Our sacrifice was not in vain. When we laid our lives on the firing line, we knew that some of us would not take them up again. We fought the good fight. Our legal cases have been terminated. We have no more appointments with Tom Orloff [deputy district attorney of Oakland] in front of the judge. There are no warrants out for our arrest—for the first time in history! (44)

The two should demand amnesty, said Cleaver, for "everyone imprisoned under Richard Nixon," and "we must declare an amnesty among ourselves. Because we must reconstitute ourselves. And take our place amongst men of influence and reknown" (44). Like the Guardians of the Sperm, however, this new "force" in American politics would exclude women. Cleaver does not state openly that women are not permitted; he simply declares that the new need for self-definition, the "new consensus," the "new synthesis," would consist of males alone. His choice of words, in fact, almost seems to invite Newton, who had accused Cleaver of "repressed homosexuality" in 1973, to join Cleaver in a homosexually tinged macho camaraderie: "There is yet one more skeleton in America's closet: THE BLACK MAN. It's time for us to come out. We need dramatic examples of conciliation and reconciliation amongst Black men. Our common denominator is our **ethnic gender.** Our standard is one drop of Black blood and a set of balls to be eligible for membership" (43). Cleaver's sudden stress on the old Panther solidarity may be traceable to his discovery that Newton had received his doctorate from the University of California at Santa Cruz in June. His topic had been "War against the Panthers: A Study of Repression in America" (Albin Krebs, "Notes on People," *New York Times,* 16 June 1980, sec. 2, p. 4). The awareness that "the old days" were still on Newton's mind might have created a strong feeling of nostalgia for Cleaver, especially now that he had come to see the white evangelists he had respected as avaricious and self-serving rather than humanitarian.

Sometime over the summer, probably after the Republican National Convention was over in July 1980 and Reagan's candidacy was certain, Cleaver made his last-ditch-Democrat overture to Newton. Perhaps Newton's lack of interest in Cleaver or in the overtly sexist-racist basis of his appeal caused Cleaver to abandon the Left for good. By September, he had endorsed Reagan for president. A *New York Times* article on the FBI "moves" against the Panthers came out in October, specifying that in anonymous FBI letters to *Ebony* and the *Village Voice*, Newton had been named as the "fingerman" who helped incriminate Angela Davis 10 years earlier (C. Gerald Fraser, "F.B.I. Files Reveal Moves against Black Panthers," *New York Times*, 19 October 1980, 1, 16). Cleaver is not recorded as having responded to this revelation in any way. His first effort rebuffed, he had moved to the Right from either expediency or despair.

Step to the Right, Please

Considering Cleaver's increasingly unlovable eccentricities of belief, as well as his failure to support his family, it is no wonder that Kathleen began to investigate a return to college. She had remained loyal to her husband throughout the poverty and insecurity of the years from 1967 to 1980; now, "the revolution" was as old to her at 35 as it was to her husband at 45. With the consequences of the 1968 shoot-out settled at last, the pressure was sufficiently off for her to assess where she was at midlife. Both academically and in career terms, she had lost 15 years; with luck, she could still graduate at 40 and begin a career, much like a middle-class suburbanite housewife who had dropped out of college to marry a graduating senior and start a family. It took Kathleen a year to find a good school that was willing to give her a full scholarship, but she finally settled on Yale.

In August 1981 she moved with the children to New Haven, Connecticut, leaving Cleaver behind in California. There, with the house in Menlo Park gone and Art DeMoss a memory, Cleaver worked for a Mormon tree surgeon in San Jose while he "investigated" the church and lived "in a house shared by nine other employees" (Baranski and Lemon, 83).

Kathleen entered Yale as a junior-level history major and quickly achieved an A average. In addition to her studies and her responsibilities at home as a single parent of an 11-year-old and a 12-year-old, she worked at the Connecticut Afro-American Historical Society and began her autobiography (83); sometime in the busy first year at Yale she decided to go on to law school, and by June 1988 she had graduated from Yale Law School and begun to study for the bar.

Eldridge, who never gave up wanting to write, spent his free time revising *Divine Deception,* designing original flowerpots, and working out his sentence through various community services, such as helping the handicapped (83). He completed his 1,200 hours of service in June 1982. Sometime in 1982 he joined the Mormon Church,[20] although he continued on the CARP lecture circuit, presenting a set speech entitled "America's Future and the World Revolution."

Cleaver's politics continued their rightward swing. He had supported Carter in 1976 because he still saw himself as a Democrat (along with 90 percent of voting blacks in the United States), but by 1980 he'd declared that he was disappointed in the Democrats and especially Carter himself. "After watching him over the past four years I feel he hasn't lived up to expectations," he stated ("Black Panther Figure Supports Reagan Drive," *New York Times,* 17 September 1980, 24). Complaining that Carter had "turned his back on black Americans," Cleaver endorsed his old enemy, Ronald Reagan, for president.

Cleaver's religiopolitical outlook had finally moved 180 degrees from where it had been 15 years earlier. From Black Muslimism he changed to Mormonism, a religion that does not permit blacks to hold significant offices in the hierarchy. Among major American religions, it is the only one with an overtly antiblack creed. And from the Panthers and the Yippies, he came to support the man who had opposed the Civil Rights Act of 1964 and the Voting Rights Act of 1965 and who had been so repressive a governor of California, following his election in 1966, that Cleaver had once dubbed him "the father of the Black Panther Party." Only six weeks before Cleaver's endorsement, Reagan had visited Philadelphia, Mississippi, where three civil rights workers—James Chaney, Andrew Goodman, and Michael Schwerner—had been murdered in 1964, and told the white audience at the Neshoba County Fair, "I believe in state's rights" (Anthony Lewis, "A Nice Guy Contest?" *New York Times,* 22 September 1980, 27). There was barely a recognizable remnant of the old Cleaver left on earth. He really *was* "born again" into a new set of assumptions and values that bore no relationship to anything he had once held. In fact, one could interpret this acceptance of Mormonism and Reagan Republicanism as a complete rejection of a positive black identity. By 1982, he had abandoned even the pants and his various ministries, including Christlam, and become a conservative activist.

Cleaver's continued affiliation with CARP gave him contact with a number of rightist groups in a loosely held together Coalition for a Free World, which provided Cleaver with a specifically political (read anti-Communist) forum (Katherine Ellison, "Moonies Join Fight for 'Free World'," *In These Times,* 26 January 1983, 2). Through the coalition, newly formed in 1982 with Cleaver's help, he gained support from new friends among Bay Area émigrés from Cuba, Poland, Vietnam, Afghanistan, the Ukraine, Nicaragua, and El Salvador, some of whom were actually illegal aliens. Because of that fact, and because the Reverend Moon, as the newest edition of Jesus the Savior, had pledged to "conquer and subjugate the world" and to set up a world government to his own liking, Cleaver's new organization was the subject of the sort of surveillance that probably made Cleaver feel things were back to normal. The police watched the group because of its cult connections, and the Immigration and Naturalization Service copied down license numbers from cars parked near the group's meetings (Ellison, 2), just as the FBI had done to the Panthers 15 years earlier.

Back on Campus

In February 1982 Kathleen, with the help of Henry Gates, who was now an assistant professor at Yale, set up an occasion for Cleaver to visit the campus and give a speech at the Afro-American Students Center. Amid "boos and hisses" Cleaver endorsed Reaganomics and declared he was "very happy to see the Democratic Party swept out of the White House into oblivion" (Albin Krebs, "Boos for Cleaver," *New York Times,* 25 February 1982, C-22). He stated, "Ronald Reagan has said that no longer will the Federal Government house, clothe, and feed black people. I am glad about that because it will force blacks to unify and lobby for their needs" (C22). Reagan has delivered to black people a "Biblical message," joked Cleaver: "Lazarus, go for yourself."

Cleaver seemed to equate Reaganomics with the empowerment-of-individual initiative that would let the dead man (race) leave his tomb and walk. The phrase is clearly a comical allusion to Christ's words in John 11:43; it is interesting to speculate, however, whether Cleaver unconsciously echoed his own use of the name Lazarus in *Soul on Ice.* There, in the subsection of "Lazarus, Come Forth" entitled "the Mu-

hammad Ali-Patterson Fight," he equates Lazarus with "Uncle Tom"
and has Elijah Muhammad playing the role of Christ.

The New Testament parable of Jesus raising Lazarus from the dead is inter-
preted by the Black Muslims as a symbolic parallel to the history of the Negro
in America. By capturing black men in Africa and bringing them to slavery in
America, the white devils killed the black man—killed him mentally, culturally, spiritually, economically, politically, and morally—transforming him
into a "Negro," the symbolic Lazarus left in the "graveyard" of segregation and
second-class citizenship. And just as Jesus was summoned to the cave to raise
Lazarus from the dead, Elijah Muhammad has been summoned by God to lift
up the modern Lazarus, the Negro, from his grave. (*Ice,* 94–95)

Muhammad Ali, "born again," so to speak, from the Lazarus-like Cassius Clay, beat the Christian Floyd Patterson, or in Cleaver's confused
phrasing, "pounded a die-hard Lazarus into submission" (95). Even
more than that, Ali, as "the black Fidel Castro of boxing" (92), beat the
"leader of the mythical legions of faithful darkies who inhabit the white
imagination" (92). It was, in short, "the victory of the autonomous
Negro over the subordinate Negro" (91).

In Cleaver's new allusion to the Lazarus tale, it is Ronald Reagan,
once considered as "white" as Pat Boone and infinitely more malevo-
lent, who takes the role of Christ; his message is the self-reliance of
Emersonianism and the struggle for survival of Social Darwinism.
Cleaver's insistence on taking a positive view of the Reagan administration's abandonment of minority causes had to put a strain on his
relationship with college audiences. At Yale he was only booed, but
when he returned to Berkeley in May, this time as an advertised CARP
lecturer in Wheeler Auditorium, he was also insulted and even threatened with violence (Wallace Turner, "Cleaver Returns to Coast Campus," *New York Times,* 20 May 1982, A25).

At Berkeley, Cleaver reportedly displayed such poor judgment as to
insist, "The youth of America is crazy because they want to destroy the
country" (A25). He seemed to believe that time had stopped on campus
and that the students of 1982 were essentially the same in their basic
assumptions and attitudes as those of 1968. Those few who were as
leftist as the sixties students had once been called themselves the Revolutionary Communist Youth Brigade, and they did what they could to
disrupt Cleaver's talk, including marching around with a sign proclaiming Cleaver a "world breaking belly crawler." An independent student,

wearing a T-shirt proclaiming his devotion to the rock group the Dead Kennedys, told the crowd that "Malcolm X is more alive" than Cleaver. Perhaps this student represented more people than he realized; the *real* dead Kennedys, especially John, symbolized idealism and hope, while Malcolm was the "shining prince" of black manhood. Much of the anger and contempt directed at Cleaver on that occasion and many others stemmed from the conviction that Cleaver had betrayed all the best impulses of sixties activism. If Reagan was Cleaver's new Christ figure, then Cleaver was, by the standards he helped set in 1968, the unrisen Lazarus.

Three days after the Berkeley talk, Cleaver represented CARP at a Coalition for a Free World rally in Civic Center Plaza in San Francisco. One of the rally's sponsors was a new group founded by Cleaver calling itself the Fourth of July Movement (A25) and appearing to be a specifically American unit designed to balance those which were composed of foreign nationals. Among the day's activities on 22 May was "a flag burning ceremony in front of the Soviet consulate in San Francisco" (Ellison, 2). The flag burned, of course, was the hammer and sickle, in protest over Communist curtailment of rights in the various countries represented at the rally. And this from the man who refused to support Carter again in 1980 on the grounds that his human rights–based foreign policy had made him "the laughing stock of the international community" ("Black Panther Figure Supports Reagan Drive," *New York Times,* 17 September 1980, 24).

As part of a two-month CARP tour in the fall of 1982, Cleaver visited a number of college campuses. At Michigan State University, wearing a small flag pin in his lapel, Cleaver told a gathering of about 300 curious spectators that "a fascist or left-wing dictatorship could take over" unless the United States developed "a new consensus of democracy" (Marlene Hess, "Cleaver Slams Communism," *State News,* 20 October 1982, 1). Although his language echoed that in his 1980 letter to Newton, Cleaver's "fresh analysis" as described in East Lansing has no relationship to the concept of an excusively black male group consituting a new "force" in America. The only specific recommendation he made, aside from the basic anti-Communist line, was for the reform of the U.S. banking system. He declared the Federal Reserve system to be "unconstitutional" (12) and called it the nation's "No. 1 evil." "Our" job, according to Cleaver, is to "insulate the political system from the economic one," for the "capitalist economic system" is responsible for all of our contemporary social problems. This condemnation of capitalism and communism together left Cleaver, technically speaking, a Christian Democratic Socialist, if such a party were to exist in this country, although such a position would not be fully acceptable to most of those whom Cleaver depended on and supposedly respected. In this area alone one can detect the Cleaverite sympathies (and biases) of old, without the rhetoric appropriate to Marxism.

The one issue on which Cleaver never wavered, even at his most conservative, was the inequity of class in America. He learned to alter his diction adequately so that he consistently substituted *poor* for *lumpenproletariat*, *reform* for *bloodbath*, and *Federal Reserve System* for *ruling class* or *fascist octopus*, but his sympathy for the underclass point of view remained. Politically, although he had endorsed Reagan, he still maintained an independent stand, referring to the Republicans and Democrats as "Tweedledee or Tweedledum. . . . The Democrats postpone problems and the Republicans aggravate problems" (12).

TV and the Panthers

During the same fall, Kathleen published an article in *Channels* magazine blaming television reporters for the destruction of the Black Panther party. Naming no specific Panthers, she declared that "sensationalized coverage . . . encouraged the Panthers to see themselves as television portrayed them—as revolutionaries—and to exploit the impact of that image."[21] Coverage "subtly legitimized" the Panther image, she stated, simultaneously making the Panthers "loom far more glamorous and ferocious than they actually were" ("TV," 99) and helping to destroy "the organization's cohesiveness" through rampant and nearly unregulated growth. While the Panthers deliberately created situations designed to "exploit television's power to publicize their aims and programs," inevitably their "fundamental concerns" for "justice for blacks" were lost in the flashy imagery. The new Panther recruits were unable to distinguish "being on TV" from achievement in "organizing a movement for social change" (99). Particularly in 1968, during the period of time bracketed by the assassination of King in April and the riots outside Democratic convention headquarters in Chicago in August, the "crescendo of violence" in America society kept the Panthers in the "national spotlight" and "convinced radical whites to support the Panthers' cause" (99). What America saw on TV, she said, was "so extraordinary that belief in the feasibility of revolution grew" (98); "the revolution became like television itself—slightly unreal" (99).

Ms. Cleaver's analysis is at least partly correct; at the same time, by placing the blame on publicity and particularly on its effect upon "new recruits" and "radical whites," her analysis serves to temper Newton's and Seale's old charges against her husband as "the traitor" who led them away from reform and into revolution. According to the Cleavers themselves, there were hardly two Americans more firmly revolutionary than they. It is hard not to read Kathleen's article as an attempt to edit our recollection of the past, to recant fiery rhetoric by insisting it was misunderstood. In this sense, by portraying all the Panthers as victims, she attempts to accomplish approximately what Eldridge tried to do in his appeal to Newton—erase differences and offer a basis for reconciliation.

Actually, her position here is rather insulting, even to herself. Martin Luther King, for example, was widely televised, and condemned by many in the process. His stoning in Cicero, Illinois, demonstrated as clearly as anything could that he was not universally loved by white people, for all his message of peace and Christian love. He was considered a troublemaker and even a violent man because violence followed him; a John Birch Society film attempted to "prove" that he was a Communist. But King knew who he really was, and no media distortions confused him. For Kathleen Cleaver to attribute Panther use of the term *revolution,* for example, which every Panther leader used, to confusion caused by media coverage implies an appallingly low level of intelligence and maturity on all their parts. While it is undeniable that the Panthers were overawed by themselves when they began to believe their own publicity, it is simply not true that the Panther leadership remained faithful to its original "humane dedication to protect an abused community" (99) while the undisciplined new recruits believed they were supposed to work toward burning down the White House. Even her remark that the new recruits piled in as "nationwide police repression eliminated experienced leadership" doesn't hold up, for Eldridge Cleaver was on the scene as an extremely vocal spokesman during almost all of 1968, "the year of the Panther," as he called it, and only Newton was in prison. By 1969, when Cleaver was in exile, Seale under arrest, and Newton still in prison, the damage had been done and the era of maximum Panther recruitment had ended. That television coverage played a role in creating the Panthers from their May 1967 visit to Sacramento right to the end of 1968 is indisputable, but to insist that it was really TV fame that "wrecked the Black Panthers" is to oversimplify for the sake of absolution.

The Politician

Throughout 1983 and 1984 Eldridge Cleaver continued to work with CARP and the Coalition for a Free World. Seemingly, in the interests of battling communism he had come to accept aliens as allies. In his 1980 letter to Newton, one of the many crises he had noted in speaking of America's problems was that "our borders are being overrun by aliens, who are streaming in here and pushing us aside, with the connivance, sometimes, of some of our fellow Americans" ("Brother," 45). It would seem that he referred to capitalistically inclined Latins who arrived in California seeking work but not right-wing political involvement. It is unlikely that coalition members from the Nicaraguan Contras, for example, had to listen to any of his speeches about taking jobs away from inner-city youth.

It became obvious that Cleaver's evangelical career was history. In April 1984 *Christianity Today* published an article entitled "Whatever Happened to Eldridge Cleaver?" Cleaver's life from *Soul on Ice* forward was quickly recapped, with the comment that he had now become "an ultraconservative independent" after failing to find "a home in the evangelical world" (Frame, 38). The scandal of the "jeans highlighting the male genital organ" was resurrected, with the remark that Cleaver's Christian friends had tried to dissuade him from that venture, as well as from the attempt to combine Christianity and Islam, but that Cleaver had "regularly offered what he believed was a sound explanation for everything. Eventually his friends grew weary and gave up" (38f). And even in 1984 Cleaver was unreconstructed. He complained that his jeans venture had been "unfairly portrayed as frivolous and risqué. Actually it was a statement against the unisexual ideology that has been structured into our clothing and is being pushed by organized homosexuals. I felt it was necessary to establish a line of demarcation between male and female." He described Hinckle's account of his drunken bragging about wife beating as "an absolute hatchet job done by a former left-wing associate who set me up and betrayed me." When writer Randy Frame mentioned remarks by those "close to Cleaver" that he "never matured spiritually because he rejected opportunities to become grounded in the faith," Cleaver retorted, "This is not a time to be issuing each other report cards. Communists are pouring millions of dollars into an effort to destroy this country." When asked whether he would ever be the sort of person evangelicals had once hoped he would be, Cleaver responded in a characteristically evasive manner: "Evangelicals are gonna be dead. Evangelicals are gonna be nuked like everyone else" (39).

While he made flowerpots and continued trying to write books, articles, and even a screenplay, Cleaver still craved the spotlight. Finally, in February 1984 he simultaneously made a bid to run as a conservative independent against Representative Ron Dellums and attacked Dellums's friend Jesse Jackson as an opportunist in yet another "Open Letter," this time in the *National Review*.[22] The immediate occasion of his letter was the freeing of a black hostage, Lieutenant Goodman, from Syria by Jackson's negotiations. Probably correctly, Cleaver charged Jackson with being motivated less by humanitarianism than by "playing politics," "running for President" by "pretending you were more concerned about Goodman than the President was" ("Letter to Jackson," 33). Incredibly, Cleaver seemed to refer to his futile and stress-filled exile in equating himself with Jackson as a statesman: "Extragovernmental diplomacy is a process which you, along with many others in the black movement, myself included, used to great advantage for progress. Indeed, lobbying for the support of international public opinion is a respectable tradition—resorted to in pursuit of redress of grievances by people the world over" (33). The difference is that Jackson was not a dedicated revolutionary but a "ruthless politician on the make" and as such "should be arrested and prosecuted." Further, insisted Cleaver, Jackson, by acting specifically to free a black serviceman, made a bid for black votes and also implied "that the Administration didn't bother about Goodman's case because he is black. This is a dangerous postulate."

By running as the *black* candidate, "the quintessential expression of 'black politics,' instead of simply a man, who is also black, running for President," Jackson was making "a woeful error" and even alienating some blacks. Cleaver declared, "You have just played your race card. . . . It means you are still a prisoner of color in your view of the world." And he had a suggestion worthy of a "ruthless politician" himself: "Maybe you should purge the ranks of your advisors, many of whom are unreconstructed Sixties radicals, U.S. haters, ex-SNCC racists, and outright pro-Communists, like my congressman, Ron Dellums" (33). Cleaver's remark about Dellums set the tone for his unsuccessful red-baiting campaign.

Cleaver kicked off his candidacy for Ron Dellums's congressional seat by serving as the star attraction at a CARP-sponsored "Save the Flag" rally on 4 February in Berkeley (Paul Rauber, "Cleaver Chases Dellums' Seat," *In These Times,* 22 February 1984, 2). The origin of both the rally and the congressional campaign was a flag-burning incident (this time of an American flag) that took place upon the invasion of the island of Grenada in October 1983. At a protest demonstration involving some 4,000 students in Berkeley, a flag was burned. Alameda County supervisor Charles Santana, on vacation, was enraged by the events and by the image of his home they presented. Upon his return, he attempted to prosecute the students involved "under a federal law that had been ruled unconstitutional back in 1972" (Rauber, 2). Although he failed, he received a complimentary note from Ronald Reagan.

The next link in the "bizarre chain of events," as reporter Paul Rauber called it, was that right-winger Leo Bach of the All Berkeley Coalition (moderate/conservative) portion of the Berkeley City Council demanded that the council demonstrate Berkeley's patriotism by re-instating the Pledge of Allegiance before each meeting. (The pledge had been dropped in 1971, when three newly elected council members had refused, as a protest against the Vietnam War, to stand up for the pledge. To end the standoff, the existing council members, including the conservatives, canceled the pledge.) Bach's motion was rejected, out of fear that the leftist Berkeley Citizens Action side of the council would refuse to stand and thus put the city back on the front page again.

As punishment for the council, Santana persuaded the Alameda County Board of Supervisors and the Alameda County Training and Employment Board (ACTEB) to kick Berkeley's representative off ACTEB. Since the ACTEB distributes federal funds, $660,000 of which had been earmarked for Berkeley, the two boards thus conspired to violate federal law. In retaliation, Berkeley offered to sue, temporarily blocking all job funding in the county, unless Governor Deukmejian gave Berkeley the authority to administer its own money.

Into this "ideological circus" (8) came Cleaver, charging Dellums and his cohorts, including Berkeley mayor Gus Newport, with "acting in interests other than those of the U.S." (8). Never one for moderate remarks, Cleaver charged Dellums with being "a pliable tool in the hands of the Marxist-Leninist puppet masters of Berkeley, which has become an ideological cesspool of anti-American intrigue, where even the City Council refuses to pledge allegiance to the American flag" (2). Whereas in his heyday Cleaver had referred to Ronald Reagan and California School Superintendent Max Rafferty as Mickey Mouse and Donald Duck, now he tried the same device with less success against Dellums and Newport, dubbing them "Parrot Ron and Teddy bear Gus" (8). He urged the crowd at the February rally to "get rid of the Communists who sit on the City Council, this megaphone of a mayor and Ron Dellums, who is a puppet of the left" (8). The confusion of images (puppet/parrot, megaphone/teddy bear) reflects the decreased verbal acuity of the new Cleaver. When he was charged with using McCarthyite tactics, Cleaver countered, "Everything Joe McCarthy said wasn't wrong. You just have to look in a mirror to see he wasn't all wrong" (8). Presumably, the critic, whose un-American bias had been revealed by his attacking Cleaver, would see in the mirror the Commie sympathizer McCarthy would have seen.

For Cleaver to run against Dellums was futile to the point of political suicide. Although Dellums had originally moved from the Berkeley City Council to the House of Representatives in 1970 with Panther support, he continued to win elections and to serve on the Congressional Black Caucus. Dellums, a foreign policy adviser to the Jesse Jackson campaign at the time Cleaver ran against him, had the respect of his colleagues as someone who represented a constituency far broader than the members of the Black Panther party, which had been officially disbanded in 1982 by Newton, or the "Marxist-Leninist" interests of Berkeley radicals. By contrast, Elaine Brown had failed to win a seat on the Oakland City Council in 1973 and 1975, and Bobby Seale had lost the race for mayor of Oakland in 1973. Despite Cleaver's claim that leftist radicals held the area and made a "puppet" of Dellums, it is obvious that something more than leftist, or even Panther, connections was required to win an election even once.

When Dellums ran in 1970, he was appropriately outspoken and somewhat radical in his choice of words, especially when he was interviewed by *Black Panther* reporter Roland Young. Then, Dellums supported community control of the police and predicted that, given "the crisis of our cities" and "pollution—not only of our minds, but of our air and water"—as well as the war in Vietnam, "there are going to be some unlikely people who become revolutionaries," but he did not say that he was one of them. His most radical comment was that "the real question in this society has to do with crude raw exploitation of human beings that cuts across social lines and cuts across class lines" (Roland Young, "Interview with Ron Dellums," *Black Panther,* 31 January 1970, 6). He advocated tearing down "the walls between the races" and "between the classes" in order to avoid "a confrontation in this country which AmeriKKKa may never come back from." Dellums cannot be held responsible for the spelling of *America* with three K's (demonstrating a writer's opinion of the dominance of the Ku Klux Klan in our society), since he spoke, but did not write, the word. Whether he would have used that spelling or not, he was careful to avoid advocacy of violence or revolution. What he did was merely to predict that, given the situation in 1970, "this country will either bend in the winds of change or be broken in the storm of revolution" (6). Cleaver, who had disliked Dellums at least since his return from exile, persisted in seeing in him not a mainstream politician who was left of center but a Communist tool who hoped to destroy America.

After his congressional campaign failed, Cleaver made one last try for political influence when he attempted to win the Senate seat of Democrat Alan Cranston in 1986. He entered the Republican primary as one in a field of 13; *Time* reporter Dan Goodgame labeled him the "most unlikely" candidate of the group but noted that he received the "most enthusiastic ovation of any Senate candidate" at the California Republican Convention.²³ Goodgame failed to quote Cleaver, but in an interview with Gannett News reporter Jeannine Guttman shortly after he lost the primary election (he received 1.2 percent of the vote) on 3 June, Cleaver made it clear why some Republicans would cheer for him. For one thing, he reiterated what he had said at Yale about Reagan's wisdom in getting black people off welfare; the Democrats, he said, "have not helped blacks" (Jeannine Guttman, "Cleaver Now a Loyalist of the Reactionary Right," *Lansing State Journal,* 22 June 1986, 7A). Rather, the Great Society and its attendant programs "have made blacks dependent on welfare." Eliminating welfare payments (and especially the taxes required to fund them) has long been a preferred Republican position. Rather than blaming lack of education and opportunities for poverty and blaming poverty for welfare dependency, conservatives have usually chosen to blame welfare dependency for poverty and lack of education. Opportunity, preferably without affirmative action reinforcement, is thought already to exist in sufficient supply for those who will "work," or as Cleaver had put it, "Go for yourself." His advocacy of an end to welfare, as well as his "pro-death penalty, anti-abortion" stance, could hardly fail to win cheers in Southern California.

He did not miss the opportunity, either, to appeal to fears of a tidal wave of cheap Mexican labor. Cleaver proposed issuing all native-born Americans security identification cards in order to broaden police powers, fight communism, and stop the flow of illegal aliens, who wouldn't have the cards. "That way," he asserted, "we could find them and get rid of them" (7A). For one who had once advocated community control of the police to push for more police power is surprising enough, but for one who had once specialized in forging identification papers and passports to suggest a card system for controlling the flow of aliens from Mexico and Central America is astounding. Nonetheless, Cleaver, who was calling himself "a Ronald Reagan Black Panther," presented as seamless as possible a facade for the voters. Reagan was his hero, he declared, "and I only have two others: the Pope and John Wayne" (7A). After he lost the election, he remarked that he would be unlikely to run again. "I want to spend my time writing and get involved in really important issues, like the plight of retarded children" (7A).

The End of it All

The year 1986 was the last one in which Cleaver saw Kathleen, from whom he was finally divorced in early 1988. His contact with Maceo has been insignificant, but there are still ties with their daughter, Joju. He had no contact with Newton and Seale after the Panther split in 1971, except for a brief time a few years ago when he said Bobby Seale, perhaps hoping to make some extra money by going on the lecture circuit with Cleaver much as Jerry Rubin and Abbie Hoffman did together, proposed a speaking tour. The plan fell through, and they did not maintain contact ("Whatever," *Ebony,* 68). Seale still maintains the anti-Cleaver stance he adopted in 1971: "Eldridge Cleaver? I refuse even to talk to him. . . . He's not a true representative of the Black Panther Party. Eldridge was always trying to start a shoot-out while I was trying to organize breakfasts for children."[24]

In 1986, Acme Greetings of Chicago issued a humorous card by Kevin Pope depicting three shoulderless, jug-eared male figures on the front—two white, one black—under the caption "The Cleavers: Wally, Beaver and Eldridge." Inside, the card read, "Happy Birthday from Ward, June and the boys." Cleaver's once-fearsome image had become a joke, remembered just enough to make his juxtaposition to Beaver Cleaver incongruous; he is the only one not smiling.

Since 1986, Cleaver has remained in Berkeley, surrounded by memorabilia of his Panther days, now blended with Bibles and conservative texts. He earns a living by lecturing on conservative issues and by making flowerpots and other ceramic items. He appears to live a rather quiet, isolated existence. He told Jeannine Guttman: "I don't have any real friends; I never did. People you met in the heat of a struggle—the Black Panthers—those aren't your friends" (7A). It was a painful admission for the man who once told Gene Marine that he could not bear to return to prison because "for the first time" he had found real friends and was able to escape the prison of his solitude.

The Criminal Personality

Although still a member of the Mormon Church, which forbids smoking and drinking, Cleaver was arrested on a cocaine-possession charge in the fall of 1987 (Parks, 32). In February 1988 he was again arrested, in what he referred to as a case of "police harassment," for burglary. He insisted he was only "moving furniture for homeless people" (32), but the court did not believe his story; in June he was put on three years' probation ("Probation for Cleaver in Burglary Case," *San Francisco Examiner,* 29 June 1988, A15).

Cleaver's arrests put his born-again status into question, even for those who had never doubted his sincerity. Does his recidivism indicate that the cynics were right all along, that it was Cleaver himself who was the most cynical and manipulative of all? Did he play Art DeMoss and his other supporters for suckers just as heartlessly as he had caused Keating to lose his home when he jumped bail in 1968? Is he still what he impressed Peter Collier as being back in the "old days"—"a freelance nihilist" and "a hustler"? (171). The answer is probably as complex as Cleaver's personality; a significant clue to his 1976 conversion, though, may be found in one of the books he read in prison that year, Yochelson and Samenow's first volume of their study *The Criminal Personality* (1976).

In *Soul on Fire,* Cleaver quoted from the opening chapter of the book, regarding the susceptibility of a criminal to change "when he is locked up" (*Fire,* 70). Cleaver notes that the authors list three choices open to the newly incarcerated criminal—"crime, suicide, or change." But

Cleaver, instead of telling us what was probably the truth, that he finally decided to change his life when he read the book in prison, goes on to describe his temporary fourth option in an earlier period many years before: "going crazy." Thus he introduces the second variant of the raving-that-led-to-psychiatry-that-led-to-being-told-he-hated-his-mother story. The fact that he mentioned the study at all, though, indicates that he read at least the first chapter of the 530-page book. What it recommends, as the result of 15 years of clinical work by two professors of psychiatry at George Washington Medical School, is "a total destruction of a criminal's personality, including much of what [the criminal] considered the 'good' parts," if there were to be rehabilitation.[25] They insisted on a "conversion," but not necessarily to a religion—rather, it would involve "a whole new life style." In order that a self-centered, manipulative, and exploitative criminal be willing to understand and adopt a responsible attitude toward himself and his relationships, it would be necessary for him to "surrender," as they put it, to an "agent of change," in this case themselves as life mentors (Yochelson and Samenow, 36). All of a criminal's usual thinking patterns (discussed in detail in the fourth chapter) had to be altered, so that his "basic character structure" (35) would become that of a law-abiding person. Rejecting, after years of therapy with many criminals, all "psychologic and sociologic excuses" for crime, the authors demanded instead that the criminal accept what he was and resolve to make "a radical change" (35). And it would not be sufficient for the criminal merely to learn to verbalize his emotions, or to enter into a temporary "nonarrestable phase" in which he committed no new crimes but still retained criminal thought patterns. He would have to transform his personality into something positive—crimelessness alone, they said, was "a vacuum" (38). They write, "The criminals developed an understanding that their position was similar to that of alcoholics. A 'crack in the door' would spell destruction for either. Thus, 'once an alcoholic, always an alcoholic' we changed to 'once a criminal, always a criminal'; the criminals should never regard the job as completed. Just as a committed member of Alcoholics Anonymous never considers himself an *ex*-alcoholic, neither should a criminal view himself as an *ex*-criminal" (38).

Without the complete "metamorphosis" (35) engineered by Yochelson and Samenow, a criminal might enter a "nonarrestable state" lasting "for months," but the authors predicted invariable failure in the long run. The important element aside from "self-understanding" was an education in how to deal with "the outside world" and how to develop nonexploitative relationships. Emphasis was placed on choice and will; the criminal, before he was accepted into the program, was forced to make a decision to change, and he was then trained in "the decision-making process," "careful evaluation of money" (49), and sensitivity to others. The criminals were treated as beginners who had to learn attitudes that socially adapted people acquire early in life; "they were much like stumbling children who had a lot to learn from experience" (44).

The techniques according to which Yochelson and Samenow operated when transforming prisoners into socially responsible people are not important here, because Cleaver never became their patient. He read their book, or at least the beginning of it, and gained one vital piece of information: he needed to change completely if he wanted a new life. His criminal nature had indeed pursued him after prison; although he planned to go straight when he left prison on parole in 1966, it was not long before the excitement so loved by criminals (38) became available through involvement with the Panthers. In prison in 1976, Cleaver could see, and admit in *Soul on Fire*, that he had not only remained a criminal throughout his Panther years but even in France continued to raise money selling falsified identification papers. What's more, in the unrevised early chapters of *Soul on Fire*, Cleaver's pride in his street toughness and his love of melodramatic encounters show through clearly. His advocacy of what in some of his essays he calls the lumpen mentality embodies nothing more than what Yochelson and Samenow would consider basic criminal lack of responsibility, along with a classic sense of victimization and a desire for power (chapter 4, passim).

Even if Cleaver had wanted the kind of help described in *The Criminal Personality*, it would have been unobtainable, because most psychiatrists still adhere to the amoral position Yochelson and Samenow rejected as nonproductive. Further, most subscribe to the psychosocial causal factors Yochelson and Samenow discarded when they realized they "were finding the same patterns among ghetto-raised blacks and suburb-raised whites." They state, "Not only did we have men from a number of different environments, but we learned that even within a given family there could be two children whose paths in life were totally different" (16–17). Given these restrictions, it seems likely that Cleaver decided to transform himself by an act of will, exactly as Yochelson and Samenow recommended. Their refusal to accept psychological "excuses" for crime fit Cleaver's own predilection for an avoidance of probing into motives and unconscious causes for behavior. That was exactly the sort of questioning that he had told Don Schanche was "insulting."

For Cleaver, who had previously sought to remake himself through religious commitment at least once in Black Muslimism (and possibly twice, if we count his conversion to Roman Catholicism at puberty) and through political commitment once in Marxist world revolution, it was natural to turn to the Protestant evangelism that was offered to him in prison and to make a conscious decision that he would believe in it and accept it because only in this way could he save himself from himself. He never trusted therapists anyway, and in religion there is no probing to discover why the bad person has been bad. The same sort of reasoning it took the two psychiatrists 15 years to develop is automatic in church; except for the religious element, the two systems concur in placing full responsibility for one's actions upon oneself, even while allowing for the existence of negative influences. Where Yochelson and Samenow required no religious commitment, however, and insisted instead on a "surrender" to the superior knowledge and coping ability of the "agent of change," a Christian church presumes faith in Jesus and recommends that one surrender to and lean on God, with the priest or minister functioning as God's representative on earth. The concept of handing over one's judgment to a higher authority, however, is consistent. Furthermore, it fit both Cleaver's background and his personality.

Cleaver, then, made a decision to become a Christian because the conversion was a lifeline. Perhaps when he said his transformation was the result of a process that had been building for some time he meant that the state of "self disgust" that Yochelson and Samenow say is a necessary condition for radical change (36) had started developing in Paris once the temporary legal problems had been solved. In addition, though, his resolve to come back and face the consequences of his 1968 activity was also the beginning of a phase of change, a decision to stop, as he put it in his article in the *New York Times,* fighting old battles. Cleaver was ripe for change when he got to San Diego; the God Squad got to him after a few others had softened him. These people were not cynical and suspicious, as his old associates on the Left had been ever since Willenson's article appeared in *Newsweek* in early 1975; they offered him a new life, complete with career and money to start it out. And speaking to groups is something he had always been able to do, requiring no training or education he did not already have. It offered that alternative life-style which *The Criminal Personality* had insisted had to replace the criminal one; it demanded responsibility and morality, and it provided enough income to cut down on the temptation to "liberate" money and other articles.

Cleaver's "decision for Christ," as Billy Graham would have called it, was at least as sincere, then, as an alcoholic's decision to join Alcoholics Anonymous or an obese person's resolve to join a weight-loss and exercise program. It was his only chance to "save his life." A person with as little interest in introspection as he has always had would be unlikely to be overscrupulous about the sincerity of his feelings for Jesus. Those feelings in Cleaver were probably as strong as they are among thousands of people who attend church as a matter of habit but whose beliefs are never subjected to public scrutiny.

Such an explanation allows for Cleaver's lack of intensity in his public speaking and for his occasional verbal slips, as well as his continued devotion to his "Cleavers." He simply did not understand how solid, middle-class, Christian, "Silent Majority" people think; he still had all the wrong responses. These people do not say things like "the bitch needed her ass kicked," and they think the penis *should* be "corralled," as he had put it.

Cleaver's commitment always seemed shallow to all but the most determined and naive of observers precisely because he, unlike most converts, stood to profit from being "born again." Other convicts who have attempted to refashion their lives just as dramatically have not been mocked, at least not by the majority of noncriminal citizens, because they have refrained from taking their new needs on tour or naming whole incorporated crusades after themselves. Cleaver was sincere in his desire for change but was also fatally desirous of the spotlight. He had become addicted to interviews and speaking engagements in 1968, and never overcame his need for excitement and the feeling of power he got from being the center of attention. In part, his depression in Paris probably stemmed from his sudden anonymity as much as from his unpromising future. Thus, when Cleaver converted, he did it in public; when he was baptized, it was at a Los Angeles hotel in a swimming pool once used by Esther Williams; when he went to work, he was still, one might say, in show business.

Even those who are rehabilitated by professionals can relapse, and many do. It is not surprising, therefore, that after several years, two failed careers (one in preaching and one in politics; a third if we count fashion design), and a broken marriage, Cleaver began to use drugs and was later arrested and convicted for burglary. In fact, if Yochelson and Samenow are correct in assuming "once a criminal, always a criminal," such a return to criminal activity would be more or less expected, under the circumstances. In Cleaver's case, if his transformation was less than total he still has had a very long "nonarrestable phase," one he owes to having embraced a religiopolitical stance that represented the antithesis of his black revolutionary position, to which he will undoubtedly never return. He can look back to the past, even with nostalgia, through the doorways of his memorabilia, but he will never return to that old self again.

The Latest Cleaver

At the end of the eighties, connecting doors to the past started closing for Cleaver. Old Yippie acquaintance Abbie Hoffman, who had also had his troubles with cocaine, committed suicide on 12 April with a combination of alcohol and 150 capsules of phenobarbitol.[26] Huey Newton, with a long history of drug and alcohol abuse behind him, was found dead of multiple gunshot wounds in the streets of Oakland at dawn on 22 August ("Huey Newton . . . Found Shot to Death," *New York Times,* 23 August 1989, 1). The self-confessed killer, a drug dealer named Tyrone Robinson, appeared to be a member of the prison-based gang the Black Guerrilla Family, whom Cleaver himself had feared in 1975 ("Drug Dealer Admits Shooting Newton," *New York Times,* 27 August 1989, 13). The killer claimed that Newton had demanded cocaine of him and threatened him with a gun.

Bobby Seale, who has also rejected his past radicalism, now works as a community liaison person at Temple University in Philadelphia, where he has been affiliated with the office of the Dean of the College of Arts and Sciences. He no longer writes books like *Seize the Time* and *A Lonely Rage* (his autobiography); his latest production is a cookbook called *Barbeque'n with Bobby* (1989). He has plans to release an accompanying videotape starring himself. Since his hopes for a film career collapsed some years ago, Seale's plans for fame rest on tape rentals. "I'd like to be to barbecuing what Jane Fonda is to exercise," he says. "If she can sell 750,000 copies of her exercise videotapes, I don't see why I can't sell 200,000 or 300,000 copies of my barbecue videotape" (Bob Greene, "Bobby Seale Fired Up over Barbecuing," *Detroit Free Press,* 30 July 1987, 10). In 1988, Seale attended the National Rib Cookoff in Cleveland with more than charcoal grilling in mind: he was charged with theft and passing bad checks there ("After Revolution Failed," *Detroit Free Press,* 23 August 1989, 16A).

One of Cleaver's complaints concerns the fact that Seale and Fonda, after pasts as radical as his own, have been permitted "to blend into the mainstream," whereas he has been greeted with sneers. He says that the press and the public have refused to permit him to change, have regarded all growth on his part with cynicism. He declares, "I have a very good track record of being ahead of other people in understanding certain truths and taking political positions far in advance of the crowd and turn out to be vindicated by subsequent experience. Yet, when I take these experiences [*sic*], I have been attacked for taking them" ("Whatever," *Ebony*, 68). While it is true that Cleaver has encountered more difficulty with acceptance, it is also true that Seale and Fonda simply moved from radical righteousness to commonplace entrepreneurship, dropping controversial issues altogether. Cleaver, on the other hand, moved from left-wing radical advocacy to right-wing radical earnestness with a noticeable accompanying drop in intensity; that particular form of entrepreneurship has always been met with derision. The rejection he claims is the result of his changing is actually caused by a perception that he reversed himself only for the public and that he is actually no more committed to right-wing causes than Fonda and Seale are. Worse, if he *is* committed to such causes, then he seems like a turncoat indeed, one who was never a worthy leftist but only an impressionable fool and a grandstander. It is not at all certain, either, that he would have gained more sympathy if people saw his conversion as an attempt to redeem his character rather than his soul.

Cleaver told Gordon Parks in 1988 that "economic exploitation and suppression are worse than ever" (32). He wanted Dellums out of office and Jackson arrested, both for what he considered un-American activities, but he looks back with pride at what the Panthers did. They "played a very positive role at a decisive moment toward the liberation of Black people in America," he has said ("Whatever," *Ebony*, 68). Those who agree with him that the Panthers helped to articulate black grievances and to galvanize white youth usually have a positive opinion of Ron Dellums and Jesse Jackson as political figures with analogous roles 20 years later. Cleaver's attempt to hold both sets of opinions, even as he decorates his Berkeley duplex with mementos of both his incarnations, cuts him off from many people, and perhaps most of all from himself. His current inability to write, his "disintegration," as his ex-wife has called it (telephone interview, October 1988), may stem from his confusion of the things he believes in with the things it is safe for him to believe in. He wants to be committed to something, and he always has; he cannot be contented with noninvolvement, apathy, and perhaps anonymity in the 1990s any more than he could have been back in 1966, and without that commitment and activity it appears that he has little to say. Before his latest arrests he commented, "For the first time in my life I'm completely free," and insisted that he was content "right here on College Avenue in Berkeley. It's the best cell I've ever had" (Morrison and Morrison, 325). Imprisonment, if only as a metaphor, is still the norm for Cleaver; if he could again see writing as his way out, as it was in 1966, he could yet emerge in the nineties as a spokesman for our time.

At the moment, though, he is unpopular and even irrelevant. When Huey Newton was killed, the *San Francisco Examiner* did a "Where Are They Now?" report on several ex-Panthers, including Cleaver, the next day (23 August 1989, A13), and never referred to him again. Seale, on the other hand, was featured on the front page when Newton's funeral was reported several days later ("Seale's Farewell to Newton," *San Francisco Examiner*, 29 August 1989, 1). Whereas Cleaver was not even reported to have attended the funeral, Seale was headlined as the major eulogist. Speaking in front of the more than 4,000 people who attended the service at Oakland's Allen Temple Baptist Church, "Seale drew thunderous applause from the audience when he raised both fists and uttered the words that had inspired a revolution: 'Power to the people' " (1).

It is understandable that Cleaver would still be unwelcome among Panthers and their sympathizers. What is more surprising is that he seems to be almost forgotten. When in spring 1989 *Time* magazine did a retrospective special issue on 1968, Cleaver was omitted completely. One photograph of a group of unidentified Panthers does appear in the "Race" section and is entitled "Toward an Angry New Consciousness"; Huey Newton and Bobby Seale are mentioned as the party founders; "Panther leader Stokely Carmichael" is quoted twice. There is no reference to *Soul on Ice* or its author. Even Cleaver's short-lived fame was taken away, and radical history rewritten by reporters too young to have memories of 1968. And in a PBS "Eyes on the Prize II" segment featuring the Panthers, Cleaver received brief mention as "the spokesman" for the party and was shown briefly in an old black-and-white clip but was not interviewed in color in 1989, as were Newton, Seale, and Elaine Brown. No reference was made to *Soul on Ice* or to Cleaver's having been one of those wounded when Bobby Hutton was killed (although the Hutton shooting was mentioned), and none to Cleaver's candidacy or exile. Kathleen appeared momentarily in a clip showing a "Free Huey" rally but was not identified.

Cleaver remains optimistic in spite of everything. In 1988 he told *Ebony* that he "still wants to be a politician and even aspires to someday make a run for the U.S. presidency" ("Whatever," 68). As unlikely as it may be that one of the splinter parties would nominate him, Cleaver is ready for whatever may come. "In this heart of mine," he says, "hope always springs eternal" (68).

Appendix: October 1966 Black Panther Party Platform and Program

What We Want, What We Believe*

1. We want freedom. We want power to determine the destiny of our Black Community.
We believe that black people will not be free until we are able to determine our destiny.

2. We want full employment for our people.
We believe that the federal government is responsible and obligated to give every man employment or a guaranteed income. We believe that if the white American businessmen will not give full employment, then the means of production should be taken from the businessmen and placed in the community so that the people of the community can organize and employ all of its people and give a high standard of living.

3. We want an end to the robbery by the CAPITALIST of our Black Community.
We believe that this racist government has robbed us and now we are demanding the overdue debt of forty acres and two mules. Forty acres and two mules was promised 100 years ago as restitution for slave labor and mass murder of black people. We will accept the payment in currency which will be distributed to our many communities. The Germans are now aiding the Jews in Israel for the genocide of the Jewish people. The Germans murdered six million Jews. The American racist has taken part in the slaughter of over fifty million black people; therefore, we feel that this is a modest demand that we make.

4. We want decent housing, fit for shelter of human beings.
We believe that if the white landlords will not give decent housing to our black community, then the housing and the land should be made

*Originally published in the *Black Panther,* Excerpted from *To Die for the People: The Writings of Huey P. Newton.* ©1972 by Stronghold Productions. Reprinted by permission of Random House, Inc.

into cooperatives so that our community, with government aid, can build and make decent housing for its people.

5. **We want education for our people that exposes the true nature of this decadent American society.** We want education that teaches us our true history and our role in the present-day society.

We believe in an educational system that will give to our people a knowledge of self. If a man does not have knowledge of himself and his position in society and the world, then he has little chance to relate to anything else.

6. **We want all black men to be exempt from military service.**

We believe that Black people should not be forced to fight in the military service to defend a racist government that does not protect us. We will not fight and kill other people of color in the world who, like black people, are being victimized by the white racist government of America. We will protect ourselves from the force and violence of the racist police and the racist military, by whatever means necessary.

7. **We want an immediate end to POLICE BRUTALITY and MURDER of black people.**

We believe we can end police brutality in our black community by organizing black self-defense groups that are dedicated to defending our black community from racist police oppression and brutality. The Second Amendment to the Constitution of the United States gives a right to bear arms. We therefore believe that all black people should arm themselves for self-defense.

8. **We want freedom for all black men held in federal, state, county and city prisons and jails.**

We believe that all black people should be released from the many jails and prisons because they have not received a fair and impartial trial.

9. **We want all black people when brought to trial to be tried in court by a jury of their peer group or people from their black communities, as defined by the Constitution of the United States.**

We believe that the courts should follow the United States Constitution so that black people will receive fair trials. The 14th Amendment of the U.S. Constitution gives a man a right to be tried by his peer group. A peer is a person from a similar economic, social, religious, geographical, environmental, historical and racial background. To do this the court will be forced to select a jury from the black community from which the black defendant came. We have been, and are being tried by all-white juries that have no understanding of the "average reasoning man" of the black community.

10. **We want land, bread, housing, education, clothing, justice and peace. And as our major political objective, a United Nations-supervised plebiscite to be held throughout the black colony in which only black colonial subjects will be allowed to participate, for the purpose of determining the will of black people as to their national destiny.**

When, in the course of human events, it becomes necessary for one people to dissolve the political bands which have connected them with another, and to assume, among the powers of the earth, the separate and equal station to which the laws of nature and nature's God entitle them, a decent respect to the opinions of mankind requires that they should declare the causes which impel them to the separation.

We hold these truths to be self-evident, that all men are created equal; that they are endowed by their Creator with certain unalienable rights; that among these are life, liberty, and the pursuit of happiness. **That, to secure these rights, governments are instituted among men, deriving their just powers from the consent of the governed; that, whenever any form of government becomes destructive of these ends, it is the right of the people to alter or to abolish it, and to institute a new government, laying its foundation on such principles, and organizing its powers in such form, as to them shall seem most likely to effect their safety and happiness.** Prudence, indeed, will dictate that governments long established should not be changed for light and transient causes; and, accordingly, all experience hath shown, that mankind are more disposed to suffer, while evils are sufferable, than to right themselves by abolishing the forms to which they are accustomed. **But, when a long train of abuses and unsurpations [*sic*], pursuing invariably the same object, evinces a design to reduce them under absolute despotism, it is their right, it is their duty, to throw off such government, and to provide new guards for their future security.**

Notes and References

Chapter One

1. *Soul on Fire* (Waco, Tex.: Word Books, 1978), 35; hereafter cited in the text as *Fire*.
2. *The Black Moochie*, part 1, *Ramparts*, October 1969, 21. Part 2 was published in *Ramparts* in November 1969. Hereafter cited in the text as 1 or 2.
3. John A. Oliver, *Eldridge Cleaver Reborn* (Plainfield, N.J.: Logos, 1977), 85.
4. *Soul on Ice* (New York: McGraw-Hill, 1968), 30; hereafter cited in the text as *Ice*.
5. "The Flashlight," in *Prize Stories 1971: The O. Henry Awards*, ed. William Abrahams (Garden City, N.Y: Doubleday, 1971), 228.

Chapter Two

1. William H. Grier, M.D., and Price M. Cobbs, M.D., *Black Rage* (New York: Basic Books, 1968), 73; hereafter cited in the text.
2. Don A. Schanche, *The Panther Paradox* (New York: David McKay, 1970), 66; hereafter cited in the text as *Paradox*.
3. Sinclair Lewis, *Babbitt* (New York: Harcourt Brace, 1922), 188.
4. James Baldwin, *Nobody Knows My Name* (New York: Dial Press, 1961).
5. Norman Mailer, *Advertisements for Myself* (New York: Putnam, 1966).
6. Jervis Anderson, "Race, Rage, and Eldridge Cleaver," *Commentary*, December 1968, 67.
7. Julian Mayfield, "New Mainstream," *Nation*, 13 May 1968, 639.
8. James Cunningham, "The Case of the Severed Lifeline," *Negro Digest*, October 1969, 27.
9. Jack Kerouac, *On the Road* (New York: Viking Press, 1958), 180.
10. Frantz Fanon, *The Wretched of the Earth* (1963; reprint, New York: Grove Press, 1968), 144.
11. William F. Buckley, "Eldridge Cleaver, Come Home," *National Review*, 24 December 1976, 1423.
12. Robert Coles, "Black Anger," *Atlantic*, June 1968, 106.
13. Richard Gilman, "White Standards and Negro Writing," *New Republic*, 9 March 1968, 26.
14. Richard Gilman, "Black Writing and White Criticism," in Gilman, *Confusion of Realms* (New York: Random House, 1969), 16.

15. Harvey Swados, "Old Con, Black Panther, Brilliant Writer and Quintessential American," *New York Times Magazine,* 7 September 1969, 150; hereafter cited in the text.

16. Martin Luther King, Jr., *Where Do We Go from Here: Chaos or Community?* (New York: Harper & Row, 1967), 121–22.

17. Raymond Schroth, "Cleage and Cleaver," *America,* 1 February 1969, 142.

18. Stanley Pacion, "Soul Still on Ice? The Talents and Troubles of Eldridge Cleaver," *Dissent,* July–August 1969, 316.

Chapter Three

1. Bobby Seale, *Seize the Time* (New York: Random House, 1970), 133; hereafter cited in the text as *Seize.*

2. In "The Courage to Kill: Meeting the Panthers" (*Eldridge Cleaver: Post-Prison Writings and Speeches*), Cleaver speaks of commemorating "the fourth anniversary of the assassination of Malcolm X," an error that has subsequently been picked up by at least one other writer.

3. *Eldridge Cleaver: Post-Prison Writings and Speeeches,* ed. Robert Scheer (New York: Random House, 1969), 29; hereafter cited in the text as *Post.*

4. Bobby Seale, "Selections from the Biography of Huey P. Newton," *Ramparts,* 17 November 1968, 10; hereafter cited in the text as "Selections."

5. Introduction to "The Genius of Huey P. Newton: Minister of Defense of the Black Panther Party" (pamphlet, Oakland, Calif.: Black Panther Party, [1970]), 2; hereafter cited in the text as "Genius."

6. Earl Anthony, *Picking Up the Gun* (New York: Doubleday, 1970), 48; hereafter cited in the text.

7. Robert F. Williams, *Negroes with Guns* (Chicago: Third World Press, 1962, 1973), 63; hereafter cited in the text.

8. Che Guevara, *On Guerrilla Warfare* (New York: Praeger, 1961), 7; hereafter cited in the text.

9. LeRoi Jones (Amiri Baraka), *Home* (New York: Morrow, 1962), 208–9; hereafter cited in the text.

10. Nat Hentoff, *Call the Keeper* (New York: Viking Press, 1966), 72–73; hereafter cited in the text as *Call.*

11. James Forman, *The Making of Black Revolutionaries* (New York: Macmillan, 1972), 459; hereafter cited in the text.

12. "Revolution in the White Mother Country and National Liberation in the Black Colony," *North American Review,* July–August, 1968, 13; hereafter cited in the text as "Revolution."

13. Reginald Major, *A Panther Is a Black Cat* (New York: Morrow, 1971), 94.

14. "Ministry of Information Black Paper" (Oakland: Black Panther Party for Self-Defense, [1968]), [4].

Chapter Four

1. Lowell Bergman and David Weir, "Revolution on Ice," *Rolling Stone,* 9 September 1976, 45; hereafter cited in the text.
2. George Otis, *Eldridge Cleaver: Ice and Fire!* (Vans Nuys, Calif.: Bible Voice, 1977), 33; hereafter cited in the text.
3. Gene Marine, *The Black Panthers* (New York: Signet—New American Library, 1969), 139.
4. "The Fire Now: Field Nigger Power Takes Over the Black Movement," *Commonweal,* 14 June 1968, 375.
5. "Cleaver and Berrigan," *Commonweal,* 14 June 1968, 373.
6. Tom Hayden, *Reunion* (New York: Random House, 1988), 382; hereafter cited in the text.
7. Don A. Schanche, "Burn the Mother Down," *Saturday Evening Post,* 16 November 1968, 31.
8. *The Extent of Subversion in Campus Disorders,* part 3. (Washington, D.C: U.S Government Printing Office, 1969), 244.
9. "Professor on Ice," *Time,* 27 September 1968, 19.
10. "Berkeley at Bay Again," *Newsweek,* 21 October 1982, 92.
11. John R. Coyne, Jr., "The Cleaver Compromise," *National Review,* 5 November 1968, 1115.
12. John A. Williams, *The Man Who Cried I Am* (Boston: Little, Brown, 1967), 310; hereafter cited in the text.
13. Huey P. Newton, *To Die for the People* (New York: Random House, 1972), 7; hereafter cited in the text as *Die.*
14. "A Word to Students," in *The University and Revolution,* ed. Gary R. Weaver and James H. Weaver (Englewood Cliffs, N.J.: Prentice-Hall, 1969), 153; hereafter cited in the text as "A Word."
15. H. E. Weinstein, "Conversation with Cleaver," *Nation,* 20 January 1969, 74; hereafter cited in the text.
16. Don A. Schanche, "Panthers against the Wall," *Atlantic,* May 1970, 59; hereafter cited in the text as "Against Wall."
17. In his 1975 *Rolling Stone* interview, Cleaver incorrectly gave the year as 1969.

Chapter Five

1. Joyce Nower, "Cleaver's Vision of America and the New White Radical: A Legacy of Malcolm X," *Black American Literature Forum* 4 (March 1970): 19.
2. Louis Heath, *Off the Pigs!* (Metuchen, N.J.: Scarecrow Press, 1976), 119–20; hereafter cited in the text.
3. Skip (Henry Louis) Gates, "Cuban Experience: Eldridge Cleaver on Ice," *Transition* 49 (1975): 32; hereafter cited in the text.

4. Lee Lockwood, *Conversation with Eldridge Cleaver* (New York: McGraw-Hill, 1970), 17; hereafter cited in the text.

5. Curtice Taylor, "Eldridge Cleaver: The *Rolling Stone* Interview," *Rolling Stone,* 11 September 1975, 40; hereafter cited in the text.

6. Angela Davis, *Angela Davis: An Autobiography* (New York: Random House, 1974), 210; hereafter cited in the text.

7. "Fidel Castro's African Gambit," *Newsweek,* 3 May 1976, 13; hereafter cited in the text as "Castro's African Gambit."

8. Sanche de Gramont, "Our Other Man in Algiers," *New York Times Magazine,* 1 November 1970, 30; hereafter cited in the text.

9. Gail Sheehy, *Panthermania* (New York: Harper & Row, 1971), xii–xiv.

10. Edward Jay Epstein, "The Panthers and the Police: A Pattern of Genocide?" *New Yorker,* 13 February 1971, 52; hereafter cited in the text.

11. Joan Morrison and Robert K. Morrison, *From Camelot to Kent State: The Sixties Experience in the Words of Those Who Lived It* (New York: Times Books, 1987), 323; hereafter cited in the text.

12. "Three Notes from Exile," *Ramparts,* September 1969, 29+; hereafter cited in the text as "Notes."

13. Daniel H. Watts, "The Carmichael/Cleaver Debate," *Liberator,* September 1969, 5.

14. Stefan Aust, "An Interview from Exile," *Black Panther,* 11 October 1969, 11; hereafter cited in the text.

15. "Soul on the Lam," *Newsweek,* 9 December 1968, 31.

16. "Cleaver in Exile," *Time,* 24 October 1969, 27.

17. Introduction to *Do It! Scenarios of the Revolution,* by Jerry Rubin (New York: Simon & Schuster, 1970), 11; hereafter cited in the text as *Do It.*

18. Gordon Parks, "Eldridge Cleaver in Algiers: A Visit With Papa Rage," *Life,* 6 February 1970, 20; hereafter cited in the text.

19. Tom Wolfe, *Radical Chic* (New York: Farrar, Straus & Giroux, 1970), 36; hereafter cited in the text.

20. John McGrath, "John McGrath Interviews Eldridge Cleaver," *Black Panther,* 11 April 1970, 11; hereafter cited in the text.

21. James A. Michener, *Kent State* (New York: Random House, 1971), 7.

22. "On the Ideology of the Black Panther Party" (pamphlet, San Francisco: Black Panther Party, 1970).

23. "On Lumpen Ideology," *Black Scholar* 3 (November–December 1972): 8; hereafter cited in the text as "Lumpen."

24. Norman Hill, ed., *The Black Panther Menace: America's Neo-Nazis* (New York: Popular Library, 1971), 137–38.

25. Peter Goldman, "The Panthers: Their Decline—and Fall?" *Newsweek,* 22 March 1971, 27.

26. John Sinclair, "Long Live the Black Panther Party," in *Guitar Army* (New York: Douglas Book, 1972), 332.

27. John Sinclair, "The Lessons of July 23," in *Guitar Army*, 349; hereafter cited in the text as "Lessons."

28. Bobby Seale, *"The Black Scholar* Interviews Bobby Seale," *Black Scholar* 3 (September 1972): 14; hereafter cited in the text.

29. James M. Stephens, "Inside Report on Transformed Black Panthers," *Jet*, 11 May 1972, 25.

30. Cordell Thompson, "Mrs. Eldridge Cleaver Returns to U. S. to Give State of the Revolution Message," *Jet*, 2 December 1971, 24; hereafter cited in the text.

31. "Revolution in the Congo" (pamphlet, London: Stage 1, 1971), 16.

32. Tony Thomas, "Black Nationalism and Confused Marxists," *Black Scholar* 3 (September 1972): 47 (hereafter cited in the text), and Eldridge Cleaver, "Culture and Revolution: Their Synthesis in Africa," *Black Scholar* 2 (October 1971): 35.

33. "Mrs. Cleaver Returns to U.S.," *Jet*, 4 November 1971, 54.

34. Julia Wright Herve, *"The Black Scholar* Interviews Kathleen Cleaver," *Black Scholar* 2 (December 1971): 59; hereafter cited in the text.

35. "Panthers on Ice," *Time*, 4 September 1972, 32; hereafter cited in the text.

36. Skip (Henry Louis) Gates, "Eldridge Cleaver on Ice: Algeria and After," *Ch'Indaba* 2 (1976): 53.

37. "Cleaver on Zionism," *Win*, 19 February 1976, 19, and "Racism and Arabs," *Dissent* 2 (1976): 224.

38. John A. Oliver, *Eldridge Cleaver Reborn* (Plainfield, N.J: Logos International, 1977), 202; hereafter cited in the text.

39. T. D. Allman, "The Rebirth of Eldridge Cleaver," *New York Times Magazine*, 16 January 1977, 31; hereafter cited in the text.

Chapter Six

1. "Lumpen," 3.

2. Clarence J. Munford, "The Fallacy of Lumpen Ideology," *Black Scholar* 4 (July–August 1973): 50; hereafter cited in the text.

3. "The Crisis of the Black Bourgeoisie," *Black Scholar* 4 (January 1973): 9; hereafter cited in the text as "Crisis."

4. Lee Lockwood, *"Playboy* Interview: Huey Newton," *Playboy*, May 1973, 84; hereafter cited in the text.

5. Ross K. Baker, "Putting Down the Gun: Panthers Outgrow Their Rhetoric," *Nation*, 16 July 1973, 49; hereafter cited in the text.

6. Peter Collier, "Looking Backward: Memories of the Sixties Left," in *Political Passages*, ed. John Bunzel (New York: Free Press, 1988), 171; hereafter cited in the text.

7. Laile E. Bartlett, "The Education of Eldridge Cleaver," *Reader's Digest*, September 1976, 70; hereafter cited in the text.

8. Kim Willenson and Jane Friedman, "Old Panther with a New Purr," *Newsweek*, 17 March 1975, 40; hereafter cited in the text.

9. Elaine Douglass, "Conversion of Eldridge Cleaver," *Encore*, 2 February 1976, 15; hereafter cited in the text.

10. Jerome McFadden, "Eldridge Cleaver's Last Interview before Prison," *Sepia*, February 1976, 70; hereafter cited in the text.

11. *Jet*, 29 May 1975, 12.

12. Nikki Giovanni, "Leave It to Cleaver," *Encore*, 19 May 1975, 26; hereafter cited in the text.

13. *Report of the National Advisory Commission on Civil Disorders* (New York: New York Times Co., 1968), 52, 56.

14. William F. Buckley, "Looking for a Home," *National Review*, 5 December 1975, 1338.

15. Jacqueline Simon, "Interview with Eldridge Cleaver," *Punto de Contacto/Point of Contact* 1 (1975): 34; hereafter cited in the text.

16. *Rolling Stone*, October 1975, 65.

17. Margaret Montagno, "Home, Sweet Home," *Newsweek*, 1 December 1975, 42; hereafter cited in the text.

18. Ida Lewis, "What's the Big Deal?" *Encore*, 22 December 1975, 5.

19. "Racism and the Arabs," *Dissent*, 2 (Spring 1976): 224; hereafter cited in the text as "Racism."

20. *Supplementary Detailed Staff Reports on Intelligence Activities and the Rights of Americans* 3 (Washington, D.C: U.S. Government Printing Office, 1976), 206.

21. Buckley, "Eldridge Cleaver, Come Home," 1423.

22. Walter Rauschenbusch, *The Social Principles of Jesus* (London: International Committee of YMCA's, 1916), 31–46; hereafter cited in the text.

23. Paul Jacobs, "The Return of the Native," *Mother Jones*, August 1976, 6.

Chapter Seven

1. Charles Colson, *Born Again* (Lincoln, Va: Chosen Books, 1976), 189.

2. Randy Frame, "Whatever Happened to Eldridge Cleaver?" *Christianity Today*, 20 April 1984, 38; hereafter cited in the text.

3. Pat Boone, *Pray to Win: God Wants You to Succeed* (New York: Putnam, 1980), 79; hereafter cited in the text.

4. Mary Mace Spradling, ed. *In Black and White* (Detroit, Mich.: Gale Research, 1980), 192.

5. Eileen Keerdoja and Pamela Abramson, "Once a Panther, Now a Crusader," *Newsweek*, 13 August 1979, 12.

6. James S. Tinney, "Views of a Regenerate Radical," *Christianity Today*, 8 June 1977, 14; hereafter cited in the text.

7. Bill Bright, "Have You Heard of the Four Spiritual Laws?" (booklet,

San Bernardino, Calif.: Campus Crusade, 1965), 2–8 passim; hereafter cited in the text.

8. "The Party's Over," *Newsweek*, 5 September 1977, 29; hereafter cited in the text.

9. Jeffrey S. Goldsmith, "A Soul's Struggle," *Christian Century*, May 1979, 594.

10. Barbara Nauer, review of *Soul on Fire*, by Eldridge Cleaver, *America*, 2 June 1979, 458; hereafter cited in the text.

11. Richard Gilman, review of *Soul on Fire*, by Eldridge Cleaver, *New Republic*, 20 January 1979, 29; hereafter cited in the text.

12. Manning Marable, "Political Profiles: Eldridge Cleaver and Paul Robeson," *Alternatives* 2 (Winter 1980): 78.

13. Malcolm X, *The Autobiography of Malcolm X* (New York: Grove Press, 1965), 164–67, passim.

14. Zina Klapper, "Cleaver's a Sperm Lover," *Mother Jones*, September–October 1980, 8; hereafter cited in the text.

15. "Cleaver Reveals Why He Didn't Surrender in His Sexy Suit," *Jet*, 18 November 1976, 29.

16. "Cleaver Designs Pants 'for Men Only'," *Jet*, 21 September 1978, 23.

17. John Maust, "Cleaver: Gazing at a Different Moon," *Christianity Today*, 7 December 1979, 50; hereafter cited in the text.

18. Lynne Baranski and Richard Lemon, "Black Panthers No More: Eldridge Cleaver and Kathleen Cleaver Now Lionize the U.S. System," *People*, 22 March 1982, 84; hereafter cited in the text.

19. "Still a Brother: Eldridge Cleaver's Overture to Huey Newton," *Black Male/Female Relationships* 2 (Winter 1981): 43; hereafter cited in the text as "Brother."

20. "Whatever Happened to Eldridge Cleaver?" *Ebony*, March 1988, 67; hereafter cited in the text.

21. Kathleen Cleaver, "How TV Wrecked the Black Panthers," *Channels*, November–December 1982, 98; hereafter cited in the text as "TV."

22. "Open Letter to Jesse Jackson," *National Review*, 10 February 1984, 33; hereafter cited in the text as "Letter to Jackson."

23. Dan Goodgame, "California's Crazy Primary," *Time*, 12 May 1986, 3.

24. Gordon Parks, "What Became of the Prophets of Rage?" *Life*, 6 February 1988, 32; hereafter cited in the text.

25. Samuel Yochelson and Stanton E. Samenow, *The Criminal Personality*, vol. 1 (New York: J. Aronson, 1976), 36; hereafter cited in the text.

26. Paul Krassner, "Abbie," *Nation*, 8 May 1989, 617.

Selected Bibliography

Except for interviews, all newspaper sources are cited parenthetically in the text.

PRIMARY WORKS

Books

Eldridge Cleaver: Post-Prison Writings and Speeches. Edited by Robert Scheer. New York: Random House, 1969.
Soul on Fire. Waco, Tex.: Word Books, 1978.
Soul on Ice. New York: McGraw-Hill, 1968.

Imaginative Writing

The Black Moochie. Part 1. *Ramparts,* October 1969, 21+.
The Black Moochie. Part 2. *Ramparts,* November 1969, 8+.
"The Flashlight." *Playboy,* December 1969, 120+. Reprinted in *Prize Stories 1971: The O. Henry Awards.* Edited by William Abrahams, 226–260. New York: Doubleday, 1971.

Pamphlets

Introduction to "The Genius of Huey P. Newton: Minister of Defense of the Black Panther Party." Oakland, Calif.: Black Panther Party, [1970]. Pamphlet.
"Ministry of Information Black Paper." Oakland, Calif: Black Panther Party for Self-Defense, [1968]. Pamphlet.
"On the Ideology of the Black Panther Party." [San Francisco: Black Panther Party, 1970.] Pamphlet.
"Revolution in the Congo." London: Stage 1, 1971. Pamphlet.

Articles

"The Crisis of the Black Bourgeoisie." *Black Scholar* 5 (January 1973): 2–11.
"Culture and Revolution: Their Synthesis in Africa." *Black Scholar* 3 (October 1971): 32–39.
"Education and Revolution." *Black Scholar* 1 (November 1969): 44–52.

"Eldridge Cleaver." In *From Camelot to Kent State: The Sixties Experience in the Words of Those Who Lived It,* edited by Joan Morrison and Robert K. Morrison. New York: Times Books, 1987.
"Fidel Castro's African Gambit." *Newsweek,* 3 May 1976, 13.
"The Fire Now: Field Nigger Power Takes Over the Black Movement." *Commonweal,* 14 June 1968, 375–77.
Introduction to *Do It: Scenarios of the Revolution* by Jerry Rubin. New York: Simon & Schuster, 1970.
"On Lumpen Ideology." *Black Scholar* 4 (November–December 1972): 3+.
"Open Letter to Jesse Jackson." *National Review,* 10 February 1984, 33.
"Racism and the Arabs." *Dissent* 2 (Spring 1976): 224.
"Revolution in the White Mother Country and National Liberation in the Black Colony." *North American Review,* July 1968, 13–15.
"Still a Brother: Eldridge Cleaver's Overture to Huey P. Newton." *Black Male/ Female Relationships* 2 (Winter 1981): 43–45.
"Three Notes from Exile." *Ramparts,* September 1969, 29–35.
"A Word to Students." In *The University and Revolution,* edited by Gary R. Weaver and James H. Weaver. Englewood Cliffs, N. J.: Prentice-Hall, 1969.

Television Appearances

Firing Line. NET, 28 January 1977.
Meet the Press. NBC-TV, 29 August 1976.

SECONDARY WORKS

Interviews with Cleaver

Allman, T. D. "The Rebirth of Eldridge Cleaver." *New York Times Magazine,* 16 January 1977, 10+. The major mainstream journalistic assessment of Cleaver after his return from exile: balanced, but ultimately negative.
Aust, Stefan. "An Interview with Eldridge Cleaver." *Black Panther,* 11 October 1969, 11–12. An interview in exile stating the need for open war.
Bartlett, Laile E. "The Education of Eldridge Cleaver." *Reader's Digest,* September 1976, 65–72. A postexile interview in which Cleaver claims that he has read Walter Rauschenbusch.
"Cleaver Speaks." *New York Times Magazine,* 1 November 1970, 31+. An inset section of de Gramont's piece about the opening of the new headquarters for the international section of the Panthers in Algiers.
Fruchtman, Rob, and Carole Blue. "Eldridge Cleaver: Inside Speaking Out." *Berkeley Barb,* 30 July 1976, 7.

Gates, Henry Louis (Skip). "Cuban Experience: Eldridge Cleaver on Ice." *Transition* 49 (1975): 32–44. Part 1 of a two-part interview.

———. "Eldridge Cleaver on Ice: Algeria and After." *Ch' Indaba* 2 (1976): 50–57. Part 2 of a two-part interview. An extensive and honest interview in which Cleaver tells what seems to be the truth about his adventures in Cuba and Algeria; none of this material appears in *Soul on Fire.*

Hentoff, Nat. "*Playboy* Interview: Eldridge Cleaver." *Playboy,* December 1968, 89+. Reprinted in *Eldridge Cleaver: Post-Prison Writings and Speeches,* 163–211. A good distillation of Cleaver's point of view in late 1968, when he was highly militant and admittedly paranoid. Here he alludes to the supposed plan of the government to round up black leaders and their white sympathizers in the event of a national emergency and send them to the camps used for the Japanese in World War II.

Lockwood, Lee. *Conversation with Eldridge Cleaver.* New York: McGraw-Hill, 1970. A book-length interview with Cleaver in Algiers offering little of substance not found in the Hentoff interview but developing all ideas at greater length, such as "Yankee Doodle Socialism."

McFadden, Jerome. "Eldridge Cleaver's Last Interview before Prison." *Sepia,* February 1976, 68–72.

Parks, Gordon. "Eldridge Cleaver in Algiers: A Visit with Papa Rage." *Life,* 6 February 1970, 20–28. A short update on Cleaver in exile.

Schanche, Don A. "Burn the Mother Down." *Saturday Evening Post,* 16 November 1968, 30+.

Schaeffer, Robert. "Wrapping Himself in the Flag." *East Bay {Oakland} Voice,* July 1976, 1+. One of several negative leftist interviews with the new Cleaver.

Simon, Jacqueline. "Interview with Eldridge Cleaver." *Punto de Contacto/Point of Contact* 1 (1975): 34–56. The last interview before Cleaver's announcement of his return to the United States.

Taylor, Curtice. "Eldridge Cleaver: The *Rolling Stone* Interview." *Rolling Stone,* 11 September 1975, 40+. Conducted in Paris while Cleaver was still in exile, this interview presents his dramatically altered political ideas.

Tinney, James S. "Views of a Regenerate Radical." *Christianity Today,* 8 June 1977, 14–15. A rare Cleaver interview with a black Christian after his rebirth.

Weinstein, H. E., ed. "Conversation with Cleaver." *Nation,* 20 January 1969, 74–77. The last interview before Cleaver went into exile.

Writing about Cleaver

Anderson, Jervis. "Race, Rage, and Eldridge Cleaver." *Commentary,* December 1968, 63–69. A review article on *Soul on Ice.*

Anthony, Earl. *Picking Up the Gun.* New York: Doubleday, 1970. An account of the Panther experience by an ex-Panther.

Baker, Ross K. "Putting Down the Gun: Panthers Outgrow Their Rhetoric." *Nation*, 16 July 1973, 47–51. A pro-Newton assessment of the Newton–Cleaver split.

Baranski, Lynne, and Richard Lemon. "Black Panthers No More, Eldridge Cleaver and Kathleen Cleaver Now Lionize the U.S. System." *People*, 22 March 1982, 82–84.

Bergman, Lowell, and David Weir. "Revolution on Ice." *Rolling Stone*, 9 September 1976, 41–49. An illustrated journalistic discussion of the FBI role in creating the Newton–Cleaver split in 1971, as revealed in Senate hearings.

"Berkeley at Bay Again." *Newsweek*, 21 October 1982, 92.

Boone, Pat. *Pray to Win: God Wants You to Succeed*. New York: G. P. Putnam's Sons, 1980. An evangelistic book that includes an account of the Boone–Cleaver dinner.

Buckley, William F., Jr. "Cleaver for President." *National Review*, 3 December 1968, 1237.

———. "Eldridge Cleaver, Come Home." *National Review*, 24 December 1976, 1423.

———. "Looking for a Home." *National Review*, 5 December 1975, 1338.

Cleaver, Kathleen. "How TV Wrecked the Black Panthers." *Channels*, November–December 1982, 98.

"Cleaver and Berrigan." *Commonweal*, 14 June 1968, 372–73. An assessment by the editors of two articles in the same issue; the editors support both radicals but with varying levels of enthusiasm.

"Cleaver in Cuba." *Time*, 30 May 1969, 27. The revelation of Cleaver's whereabouts that was originally leaked to a Reuters correspondent.

"Cleaver on Zionism." *Win*, 19 February 1976, 19. Essentially the same as Cleaver's "Racism and Arabs" article for *Dissent*, asserting that Arabs are antiblack and that the Jews are also among their victims.

Cloud, Stanley. "Cleaver in Exile." *Time*, 24 October 1969, 27. A brief article resulting from Cloud's having spotted Cleaver in the Moscow airport on Cleaver's return from North Korea.

Coles, Robert. "Black Anger." *Atlantic*, June 1968, 106. A review article on *Soul on Ice*.

Collier, Peter. "Looking Backward: Memories of the Sixties Left." In *Political Passages*, edited by John Bunzel, 162–86. New York: Free Press, 1988.

"Convincing Case for a Pardon." *Christianity Today*, 18 February 1977, 36.

Coyne, John R., Jr. "The Cleaver Compromise." *National Review*, 5 November 1968, 1115+.

Cunningham, James. "The Case of the Severed Lifeline." *Negro Digest*, October 1969, 23–28.

Douglass, Elaine. "Conversion of Eldridge Cleaver." *Encore*, 2 February 1976, 8–15.

"Eldridge Cleaver Designs Pants 'for Men Only.' " *Jet,* 22 September 1978, 22–24.

Ellison, Katherine. "Moonies Join Fight for 'Free World.' " *In These Times,* 26 January 1983, 2.

Epstein, Edward Jay. "The Panthers and the Police: A Pattern of Genocide?" *New Yorker,* 13 February 1971, 45[+]. An examination of the Panther claim that police killed 28 Panthers.

Fager, Chuck. "Born Again Media." *In These Times,* 15 February 1978, 24[+].

Foner, Phillip. *The Black Panthers Speak.* Philadelphia and New York: Lippincott, 1970. Excerpts from Cleaver, Seale, Newton, and others.

Forman, James. *The Making of Black Revolutionaries.* New York: Macmillan, 1972. Forman's own account of the early years.

Frame, Randy. "Whatever Happened to Eldridge Cleaver?" *Christianity Today,* 20 April 1984, 38–39.

Gilman, Richard. "Black Writing and White Criticism." In *Confusion of Realms* by Richard Gilman, 13–21. New York: Random House, 1969.

———. Review of *Soul on Fire. New Republic,* 20 January 1979, 29[+].

———. "White Standards and Negro Writing." *New Republic,* 9 March 1968. 25[+]. Reprinted as "White Standards and Black Writing" in *Confusion of Realms,* 3–12. The first of these reviews, "White Standards and Negro Writing," touched off a controversy over Gilman's claim that the personal writings of blacks were outside the pale of literature as judged by white standards.

Giovanni, Nikki. "Leave It to Cleaver." *Encore,* 19 May 1975, 26.

Goldberg, Art. "Changing Times Changed Cleaver." *In These Times,* 13 April 1977, 20.

Goldman, Peter. "The Panthers: Their Decline—and Fall?" *Newsweek,* 22 March 1971, 26–28.

Goldsmith, Jeffrey S. "A Soul's Struggle" (review of *Soul on Fire). Christian Century,* May 1979, 594.

Goodgame, Dan. "California's Crazy Primary." *Time,* 12 May 1986, 34.

de Gramont, Sanche. "Our Other Man in Algiers." *New York Times Magazine,* 1 November 1970, 30[+]. A visit with the leader of the international section of the Black Panther party upon the opening of the new headquarters in Algiers.

Heath, Louis. *The Black Panther Leaders Speak.* Metuchen, N. J.: Scarecrow Press, 1976.

———. *Off the Pigs!* Metuchen, N. J.: Scarecrow Press, 1976. Both of Heath's books are anthologies of writings either by the leaders of the party or by assorted authors, as appearing in the party paper, *Black Panther.*

Herve, Julia Wright. "*The Black Scholar* Interviews Kathleen Cleaver." *Black Scholar* 3 (December 1971): 54–59.

Hill, Norman, ed. *The Black Panther Menace: America's Neo-Nazis.* New York:

Popular Library, 1971. A text that attempts to prove the Panthers' authoritarianism fascist in origin.

Jacobs, Paul. "The Return of the Native." *Mother Jones,* August 1976, 5.

Keerdoja, Eileen, and Pamela Abramson. "Once a Panther, Now a Crusader." *Newsweek,* 13 August 1979, 12.

Klapper, Zina. "Cleaver's a Sperm Lover." *Mother Jones,* September 1980, 8.

Lewis, Ida. "Getting Ready for Eldridge Cleaver's New Revolutionary Tales." *Encore,* 22 September 1975, 3.

————. "What's the Big Deal?" *Encore,* 22 December 1975, 5. These two editorials set the tone for leftist skepticism about Cleaver at the time of his return from exile.

Major, Reginald. *A Panther is a Black Cat.* New York: Morrow, 1971.

Marable, Manning. "Political Profiles: Eldridge Cleaver and Paul Robeson." *Alternatives* 2 (Winter 1980): 77.

Marine, Gene. *The Black Panthers.* New York: Signet-New American Library, 1969. The first study of the Panthers, this book presents their point of view and especially their side of the April 1968 shoot-out in which Bobby Hutton was killed and Cleaver injured and stripped of parole.

Maust, John. "Cleaver: Gazing at a Different Moon." *Christianity Today,* 7 December 1979, 49–50.

Mayfield, Julian. "New Mainstream." *Nation,* 13 May 1968, 638+.

Milstein, Tom. *A Perspective on the Panthers: A Commentary Report.* New York: Commentary, 1970.

Montagno, Margaret. "Home, Sweet Home." *Newsweek,* 1 December 1975, 42.

Munford, Clarence J. "The Fallacy of Lumpen Ideology." *Black Scholar* 5 (July–August 1973): 47–51.

Nauer, Barbara. Review of *Soul on Fire. America.* 2 June 1979, 458.

"The *New York Times.*" In "Shaping the Seventies." *Esquire* special issue, December 1969, 201–8. A satiric issue "dated" 3 November 1976 that speaks of Cleaver as the president of Columbia University.

Nower, Joyce. "Cleaver's Vision of America and the New White Radical: A Legacy of Malcolm X." *Negro American Literature Forum* (now *Black American Literature Forum*) 4 (March 1970): 12–21.

Oliver, John A. *Eldridge Cleaver Reborn.* Plainfield, N.J.: Logos, 1977. A book promoting Cleaver as a born-again Christian.

Otis, George. *Eldridge Cleaver: Ice and Fire!* Van Nuys, Calif.: Bible Voice, 1977. A book by a TV evangelist presenting Cleaver as a sincere convert.

Pacion, Stanley. "Soul Still on Ice? The Talents and Troubles of Eldridge Cleaver." *Dissent,* July–August 1969, 310–16.

"Panthers on Ice." *Time,* 4 September 1972, 32–33.

Parks, Gordon. "What Became of the Prophets of Rage?" In "The Dream Then and Now." *Life* special issue, Spring 1988, 32. A brief assessment of the fates of several of the "old" radicals of the sixties.

"The Party's Over." *Newsweek*, 5 September 1977, 29.

Poinsett, Alex. "Where Are the Revolutionaries?" *Ebony*, February 1976, 84[+].

"Professor on Ice." *Time*, 27 September 1968, 19–20.

Rauber, Paul. "Cleaver Chases Dellums' Seat." *In These Times*, 22 February 1984, 2.

Ritter, Bill. "Cleaver and Colson Praise the Lord." *In These Times*, 13 April 1977, 24.

Schanche, Don A. "Panthers against the Wall." *Atlantic*, May 1970, 55–61.

———. *The Panther Paradox: A Liberal's Dilemma*. New York: David McKay Co., 1970. A major study of the Panthers, and especially of Cleaver, by a liberal who was attracted to the Panthers but ultimately repelled by Cleaver's fanaticism and the apparent Panther drive to self-destruction.

Schroth, Raymond A. "Cleage and Cleaver." *America*, 1 February 1969, 142.

Sheehy, Gail. *Panthermania*. New York: Harper & Row, 1971. An account of what went on in New Haven following the murder of Alex Rackley in 1969.

Simms, Gregory. "Cleaver Reveals Why He Didn't Surrender in His Sexy Suit." *Jet*, 18 November 1976, 29.

"Soul on the Lam." *Newsweek*, 9 December 1968, 31.

Stephens, James M., Jr. "Inside Report on Transformed Black Panthers." *Jet*, 11 May 1972, 23–30.

Swados, Harvey, "Old Con, Black Panther, Brilliant Writer and Quintessential American." *New York Times Magazine*, 7 September 1969, 38[+].

Swaim, Lawrence. "Eldridge Cleaver." *North American Review*, July 1968, 18–21.

Thomas, Tony. "Black Nationalism and Confused Marxists." *Black Scholar* 4 (September 1972): 47–52.

Thompson, Cordell. "Changed Cleaver Returns to U.S." *Jet*, 4 December 1975, 12–13.

———. "Mrs. Eldridge Cleaver Returns to U.S. to Give State of Revolution Message." *Jet*, 2 December 1971, 20[+].

U. S. Congress. Senate Committee on the Judiciary. Subcommittee to Investigate the Administration of the Internal Security Act and Other Internal Security Laws. *Extent of Subversion in Campus Disorders*. Testimony of John F. McCormick and William E. Grogan. 91st Cong., 1st sess., 1969. Part 3.

U. S. Congress. Senate Select Committee to Study Governmental Operations with Respect to Intelligence Activities. *Supplementary Detailed Staff Reports on Intelligence Activities and the Rights of Americans*. 94th Cong., 2d sess., 1976. Book 3. S. Rept. 94–755.

U. S. Congress. Senate Committee on the Judiciary. Subcommittee to Investigate the Administration of the Internal Security Act and other Internal

Security Laws. Hearing on *Trotskyite Terrorist International*. 94th Cong., 1st sess., 1975.

Warnken, William P., Jr. "Eldridge Cleaver: From Savior to Saved." *Minority Voices* 1 (1977): 49–61.

Watts, Daniel H. "The Carmichael/Cleaver Debate." *Liberator,* September 1969, 3+.

"Whatever Happened to . . . Eldridge Cleaver?" *Ebony,* March 1988, 66–68.

Willenson, Kim, and Jane Friedman. "Old Panther with a New Purr." *Newsweek,* 17 March 1975, 40.

"A Word from the Peace and Freedom Candidate." *Newsweek,* 16 September 1968, 30.

Index

The Author

Kathleen Rout attended LeMoyne College in Syracuse as an undergraduate and Stanford University as a graduate student. She has been on the faculty at Michigan State University since 1967. Her doctoral dissertation was on Flannery O'Connor's increasing social consciousness as shown through a comparison of O'Connor's first and second short story collections. For 20 years, Rout has taught a three-quarter sequence called "Minorities in America" that focuses on the literary and historical records of immigrants and other minority groups in North America. Her interest in Eldridge Cleaver and the Panthers stems from her youthful radical sympathies.

The Editor

Frank Day is a professor of English at Clemson University. He is the author of *Sir William Empson: An Annotated Bibliography* and *Arthur Koestler: A Guide to Research*. He was a Fulbright Lecturer in American Literature in Romania (1980–81) and in Bangladesh (1986–87).